Lake Baikal

BARGU

CHORCHA

KAULI

Karakorum

Shang-tu

UIGHURISTAN   Barkol

Kara-khoja   Kamul   Khan-balik

DESERT   Ho-kien-fu

Lop   OF

nd   LOP   Sa-chau   CATHAY   Hwai-ngan-chau

hotan   Chorchan   Su-chau

Pem   TANGUT   Yang-chau   Su-chau

Ho-chung-fu

Si-ngan-fu   Kinsai

Siang-yang-fu   Kien-ning-fu

TIBET   Ch'eng-tu-fu

MANZI   Zaiton

Yachi

KARA-JANG

CHINA

BENGAL   SEA

MIEN   HAI-NAN

LESSER

Pegu   INDIA   CHAMBA

tupalli

Thomas

Andaman Is.

Condore Is.

Nicobar Is.

THE TRAVELS OF

marco polo

TRANSLATED AND INTRODUCED
BY RONALD LATHAM

ABARIS BOOKS INC. • NEW YORK

This edition is based on the one published by the
Folio Society, London with their kind permission
The text of this edition is used by
kind permission of Penguin Books Ltd
This translation © Ronald Latham 1958
Lettering by Lacey Everett
Endpapers and text maps by K. C. Jordan FRGS

COPYRIGHT © 1982 Abaris Books, Inc., New York
Printed in the United States of America
ISBN 0-89835-058-1

contents

Introduction   7

Prologue [1-19]   21

The Middle East [20-43]   33

The Road to Cathay [44-75]   59

Kubilai Khan [76-105]   95

From Peking to Bengal [106-131]   140

From Peking to Amoy [132-158]   167

From China to India [159-174]   210

India [175-189]   227

The Arabian Sea [190-199]   259

Northern Regions and Tartar Wars [200-234]   275

Epilogue   303

Genealogical Table of Mongol Imperial House   304-5

Index   307

Maps   40, 77

The numbers in brackets are those of the corresponding chapters in Professor Benedetto's edition.

illustrations

The Polos embark at Venice   frontispiece
The Capture of Baghdad   35
The Assassins' Paradise   69
The Battle between Prester John and Chinghiz Khan   104
The Great Khan holds a Banquet   134
The Great Khan goes Hunting   172
A Traveller arrives at Si-ngan-fu   205
The Siege of Siang-yang-fu   240
The Port of Zaiton   274
Fishing for Pearls   291

The Miniatures reproduced are taken from the Bodleian
Library MS Bodley 264. Transparencies of these exist on the
Library's film 161c.

Introduction

THE BOOK MOST FAMILIAR TO ENGLISH READERS AS *The Travels of Marco Polo* was called in the prologue that introduced it to the reading public at the end of the thirteenth century a 'Description of the World'. It was in fact a description of a surprisingly large part of the world—from the Polar Sea to Java, from Zanzibar to Japan—and a surprisingly large part of it from first-hand observation. The claim put forward in the Prologue, that its author had travelled more extensively than any man since the Creation, is a plain statement of fact, so far at least as it relates to anyone who has left a record of his travels. And to western Christendom the world he revealed was almost wholly unknown. Some stretches of the trail he blazed were trodden by no other European foot for over 600 years—not, perhaps, till the opening of the Burma Road during the last war. And the task of putting it on the map, in the most literal sense, is not yet complete.

Polo owed his opportunity to the sudden rise of the Mongol or Tartar empire, which for the first time brought Europe and the Far East into direct contact. In the twelfth century the Mongol tribes and their associates had entered into one of those phases of disruption and anarchy that are the opportunity of the military adventurer. And in the year 1206 a great confederacy of these nomad peoples gathered at their traditional holy place in the plain of Karakorum and elected as their ruler or *khan* an enterprising Mongol chief who took the name of Chinghiz (Turkish *Jenghiz*). Under his rule they conquered within twelve years the northern region of China, known at that time as *Cathay* after the *Khitai*, a tribe with Mongol affinities who had previously established an independent state there. Then, as Marco Polo puts it (p. 38), 'they made up their minds to conquer the whole world'. Within two generations, starting from scratch, they had succeeded in conquering virtually the whole land-mass of Eurasia, excluding only the four peninsulas of Indo-China (in part), India, Arabia, and western Europe. The eastern part of this stupendous empire, unequalled in extent before or since, remained under the direct rule of the Great Khan, the successor of Chinghiz. The rest was parcelled out into three main lordships under subordinate khans representing junior branches of the family: the lordship of the West, corresponding roughly to European Russia; the lordship of the Levant, as Polo calls it, stretching from eastern Persia to the Mediterranean; and the Central Asian lordship of Turkestan.

A year before the accession of Chinghiz, in the so-called Fourth Crusade, the imperial city of Constantinople had been seized by a band of 'Frankish' (West European) adventurers led by Baldwin of Flanders, with the moral support of the Papacy and the material support of the merchant princes of Venice, who were rewarded with the lion's share in the trade of the Levant. So it was nothing out of the ordinary that in the year 1260 two enterprising Venetian merchants, the brothers Niccolò and Maffeo Polo, set out from Constantinople on a voyage to the Crimean port of Sudak, where there already existed a Venetian colony, including (as we know from his will) a third brother, Marco the Elder. The train of adventures that led them to the court of the Great Khan Kubilai at Peking, then back to Europe on a special mission to the Pope, and then out once more to Peking, is related in the Prologue to this book. Though there is no independent evidence for this narrative, it fits in well enough with the history of Europe at the time (including the long-drawn-out papal election of 1268–71) and, at least in broad outline, with the history of China. Kubilai, as the Chinese historians describe him, was a very different character from his half-savage predecessors. He had absorbed many of the best elements of Chinese culture, including something of the humanitarian spirit of Buddhism, while retaining much of the simplicity and vigour of the nomad. In the courtyard of his palace at Khanbalik (Peking) he sowed seeds of prairie grass to remind him of the freer world from which he had come. And he directed the complex machine of Chinese administration with an energy and a breadth of vision which no Chinese emperor had displayed for centuries. It is wholly in keeping with his character that he should have given a courteous welcome to the two visitors from the Far West, listened attentively to all they had to tell, and eventually dispatched them on a mission to the Pope with a special invitation to send him 'a hundred men learned in the Christian religion, well versed in the seven arts', and able to demonstrate the superiority of their own beliefs (p. 24). His motives in this, as in all his dealings with the Polos, like those of the Polos themselves, may be variously assessed. Did he ever seriously contemplate conversion to the Christian faith? Was he actuated mainly by the same disinterested curiosity that made him send to Madagascar, 5,000 miles away, for information about the fabulous

Introduction

rukh? Or was he paving the way for some more practical objective—closer trade relations with the West, an alliance against the Moslems, or even a new career of conquest at the expense of western Christendom?

Whatever its ultimate aims, the mission achieved only a very limited success. In the end the Polos had to perform it alone, accompanied only by Niccolò's son Marco, a lad of seventeen. Instead of a new chapter in the relations between East and West, we are left, it seems, with an interlude in the fortunes of one family which, but for a happy conjunction of events, might have gone unchronicled.

For the next twenty years the Polos appear to have remained in the East; but how they spent their time there we do not know. Very few incidents are mentioned in this book; and while some of these can be corroborated to some extent, others seem highly questionable. The part assigned to the Polo family in the siege of Siang-yang-fu (pp. 174–5) is not easy to reconcile with Chinese sources, which, while confirming that foreign engineers were engaged, make it clear that the event occurred in 1273, when according to our narrative the Polos were still on their way back to China. It is scarcely possible that Marco was ever governor in the strict sense of Yang-chau (p. 173), since the names and nationalities of the governors are on record. It is now known that the Po-Lo, 'assessor of the Privy Council', who figures in Chinese records, can have had no connexion with the Venetian family. On the other hand, while we may question whether Marco ever held a personal appointment as the Emperor's special envoy and reporter (p. 28), it can scarcely be doubted that he enjoyed facilities for extensive travel in the Mongol empire. It is generally agreed that his outward route from Palestine to Peking is broadly indicated by the sequence of places mentioned in Chapters 1 and 2, though these include a few cities lying off the direct route (e.g. Baghdad, Samarkand, Karakorum) which he probably did not visit, at any rate on this occasion. The course of his later travels is largely conjectural; but his descriptions point to at least one journey southwest from Peking perhaps as far as Burma (Chapter 4) and another southwards (Chapter 5). And there is no reason to doubt the statement (pp. 29, 203) that he was sent on a mission to India.

It is commonly assumed not only that the travels of the Polos during these twenty years were confined to the Far East but that they were cut off from all intercourse with the West. But this is not certain. There had been an opening for European craftsmen even at

9

the court of the barbarous Mongu; the tolerant and cultured Kubilai must surely have been a far more generous patron. Even if the Polos were really the first 'Latins' he ever saw (p. 23), it does not follow that they were the last. From the meagre reports of friar Odoric of Pordenone, who visited China soon after 1320, and Giovanni di Monte Corvino, appointed first Catholic archbishop of Peking in 1307, it is clear that western Christianity was making some headway in the Far East, and with it must have gone at least a trickle of western commerce. Odoric indeed declares that there were many people in Venice who had visited Kinsai (i.e. Hang-chau); and in the *Merchant's Handbook* of Pegolotti (1340) it is calmly stated that the road from the Black Sea to Cathay is now 'perfectly safe, whether by day or by night'. Such evidence hints at developments in which the Polos were well placed for playing a prominent part. But the evidence remains deplorably scanty, and the developments in the long run proved abortive. With the disintegration of the Mongol empire, the revival of Islam, and the resurgence of Chinese nationalism under the Ming Dynasty (from 1368), the ancient barrier between East and West was rebuilt; and later generations of Europeans, finding no way through it, devoted much of their energy to the search for a way round it.

The return of the Polos in 1292 by the long sea route through the Malay Straits, escorting a bride for Arghun, khan of the Levant, is described in some detail (pp. 29–31). Here Marco's narrative touches on events well attested in Chinese and Persian history and can be shown to be substantially correct. A recently discovered Chinese document even confirms the names he gives to the leaders of the expedition. But again, for the distinguished role assigned to the Polos in this romantic episode we have only Marco's own word. With the arrival of the travellers at Venice in 1295 the narrative closes. Some additional facts or fables, derived from oral tradition, are supplied by Giambattista Ramusio in the preface to his printed edition of Marco's book (dated 1553). Ramusio tells the story of their home-coming in the best Arabian Nights manner: at first the wanderers' families, who had long believed them dead, failed to recognize these strange beings 'with a *je ne sais quoi* of the Tartar about them'; then, seeing them clad in coarse and shabby attire, they were contemptuous as well as resentful. But the story ends happily with a splendid banquet at which the travellers rip open the seams of the offending garments and let fall a shower of rubies, diamonds, and emeralds.

Introduction

In 1298, according to the Prologue (p. 21), Marco was a prisoner of war at Genoa. Ramusio says that he had been captured at the battle of Curzola (6 September 1298), when serving as 'gentleman commander' of a Venetian galley. But this again appears to be hearsay, if not mere conjecture. He was probably released under the terms of a peace treaty signed on 25 May 1299. At any rate, the captivity involved a period of enforced leisure, during which the restless wanderer had little to do but talk, and it is not surprising that his traveller's tales aroused the interest of his fellow prisoners. Among these was one Rustichello of Pisa, a romance-writer of some repute, who was interested in a more professional way. He had at one time enjoyed the patronage of Prince Edward of England, afterwards Edward I, and it is believed that he had travelled in his suite to Palestine. He may even have met the Polos there twenty-five years before, and must at least have known of their romantic mission. Now he was quick to perceive in Marco's narratives a new theme for his art, as picturesque as 'the matter of Britain' or 'the matter of Troy' or the legendary exploits of Alexander the Great—a theme that made up in novelty what it unfortunately lacked in love interest. Marco in his turn evidently co-operated by sending to Venice for his notes. And from this partnership of the merchant adventurer with the observant eye and retentive memory and the professional romancer with the all-too-fluent pen emerged one of the world's most remarkable books.

Rustichello's share in the joint venture has probably been underrated. Professor L. F. Benedetto, who produced the first critical edition of the Polo manuscripts in 1928, has clearly demonstrated, by comparison with his other writings, that Rustichello was responsible for the leisurely, conversational style of the oldest manuscript, written in the traditional French of the romance-writer but with many Italianisms, and marked by continual recapitulations and personal adjurations to the reader—a seeming-artless style that reveals in fact the art of the story-teller in an age when stories were few and time was plentiful. He has also shown not only that the opening invocation to 'emperors and kings, dukes and marquises', etc. (p. 21) occurs verbatim in an Arthurian romance by Rustichello but that whole passages of narrative have been lifted with the minimum of adaptation from the same source. Thus the dramatic account of the welcome accorded to the Polos on their second visit to Kubilai and the commendation of the young Marco (p. 27) is closely modelled on Rustichello's previous description of the arrival of Tristan at King

Arthur's court at Camelot—a description which already owed much to earlier writers and was of course in the central stream of romantic tradition. With this clue to guide us we can safely see the hand of Rustichello in the conventional battle-pieces that largely fill the last chapter of the present work, with their monotonous harangues and their insistence on all the punctilio of 'Frankish' chivalry. It is tempting to go further. The sequence of the topographical survey is rather awkwardly broken by a series of digressions in which well-known legends of the Middle East—the miracle of the mountain (pp. 40–43), the tale of the Magi (pp. 44–46), the pretended paradise of Alamut (pp. 54–57)—are related in the conventional romantic manner. Is it not possible that these stories, which could probably have been picked up by any visitor to the Holy Land, were inserted by Rustichello as a sop to his public, and that their attribution to Marco is a mere literary device? There are other features of the book that are as likely to be due to Rustichello as to Marco, such as the tendency to glamorize the status of the Polos at the Tartar court, particularly their relation to the princesses entrusted to their care (p. 131), the vein of facetiousness that often accompanies references to sexual customs (pp. 70, 144, 147), and the eagerness to acclaim every exotic novelty as a 'marvel' (pp. 202, 255, etc.). It is likely that without the aid of Rustichello Marco would never have written a best-seller. Conceivably he might have produced something not much more readable than Pegolotti's *Handbook*. More probably he would never have written a book at all.

As to Marco's own personality, apart from this book there are perhaps only two bits of evidence that throw any light on it at all. One is his will, dated 9 January 1323/4—a businesslike, unsentimental document by which he left the bulk of his possessions to be divided equally among his three daughters. The one human touch is the manumission of his Tartar slave Peter. The bequests of specified sums suggest a substantial but by no means colossal fortune. The second fact is his nickname of 'Million' (*Il Milione*), which appears in an official document of 1305; if this is really a tribute to his gift of 'talking big', it may well have been inspired by his book rather than by his conversation. He remains in fact a somewhat colourless personality, especially if we admit the possibility that such gleams of colour as appear in his book may be due to the refractive medium of the chronicler.

His travels are proof in themselves of enterprise, resource, and dogged endurance, and there can be no doubt that he travelled with his wits about him and his eyes open. Primarily they were the eyes of a practical traveller and a merchant, quick to notice the available sources of food and water along the route, the means of transport, and the obstacles interposed by nature or by man, and no less quick to observe the marketable products of every district, whether natural or manufactured, and the channels through which flowed the interlacing streams of export and import. Despite the ever-present risks of shipwreck (pp. 51, 263), piracy (pp. 247–9), brigandage (pp. 47, 49, 145), extortion (pp. 51, 201, 263), and wild beasts (pp. 143, 161), this was a world of highly organized commerce. And to Western merchants, who had hitherto known little more of it than its terminal points on the Mediterranean and the Black Sea, this inside information promised to be as useful as it was fascinating. The trade-routes followed by the Polos were mainly such as would quickly swallow the profits except on goods of very high value in proportion to their bulk. Hence in part that emphasis, to which the book owes much of its appeal, on precious gems and spices and gorgeous fabrics of silk and cloth of gold, as against the more humdrum commodities that formed the staple of medieval, as of modern, commerce. But we need not doubt that the cataloguing of these costly rarities gave pleasure to the author, as it has done to generations of readers.

From this practical standpoint, Marco judged town and countryside alike in terms of productivity: a 'fine' town is a thriving one, a 'fine' province a fertile one, and little use is made of more discriminating epithets. The descriptions of architecture (pp. 88, 103, 158) and artefacts (pp. 48, 248) suggest a taste for efficiency, sound workmanship, costly materials, and bright colours rather than artistic sensibility. But there are hints of a feeling for natural scenery unusual in that age: the descriptions of the Pamirs (p. 61) and the Gobi (p. 67) reveal rather more than a recognition of the healthiness of the hill air and the desolation of the desert. The judgements passed on men and states show something of the same mercantile approach. The languages of medieval Europe had no word to express the concept 'civilization'; but Marco comes near to conveying the notion by his use of the word *domesce* (pp. 137, 147, 246); and he has a clear enough appreciation of its blessings. His 'good' men are hard-working, law-abiding folk who live by trade and industry *si come bone jens doient faire* (p. 250); his 'bad' men are the indolent or unruly, the stuff that brigands and corsairs are made of. It is by a more chivalric standard, however, that he (or Rustichello) praises the prowess of the Tartar warriors (p. 80) or blames the climate of Lesser Armenia for the degeneracy of its inhabitants (p. 33). His reference to the stinginess of the Kashgaris (p. 64) strikes a note of personal experience.

He is true to his age in classifying the people he encounters primarily on the basis of religion rather than of culture or colour.* He does not, however, go much beyond the rudimentary classification into Christians, Jews, Saracens, and idolaters. While well aware that Nestorians, Jacobites, and Armenians are 'imperfect' Christians, he betrays no interest in doctrinal differences. Of the Jews, considering the part they played in international trade, he has surprisingly little to say. For Moslems, whom he persists in describing as 'worshippers of Mahomet', he has the traditional Christian hostility (pp. 40, 43, 111, 260), embittered perhaps by commercial rivalry. It is in his attitude to 'idolaters', primarily Buddhists and Hindus, that he displays most clearly that tolerant attitude that we might expect from one who was in such a literal sense a man of the world. He admires the austerity of their holy men, even comparing the Buddha to a Christian saint (pp. 91, 237, 241), and acknowledges the efficacy of their humanitarian doctrines (p. 132), though it cannot be said that he shows any insight into their philosophy of life.†

In the field of natural history, Marco's curiosity and powers of observation served him well. His descriptions of exotic plants, beasts, and especially birds are usually far more accurate and recognizable than those to be found in contemporary herbals and bestiaries. He was evidently a keen sportsman and shared that enthusiasm for falconry which was prevalent in his day among the aristocracies of Christendom, Islam, and the Far East alike. His curiosity, however, scarcely extended into the field of human history. Apart from echoes of Christian tradition and allusions to the Alexander legend, both of which may well be due to Rustichello, the horizon of his book barely extends beyond the rise of his Mongol patrons less than a century before. His accounts of the dynastic succession of the Khans (pp. 78, 286) and their mutual relationships are full of inaccuracies (see Genealogical Table pp. 296–7). Even his narratives of contemporary campaigns (pp. 158, 170, 207–8) are a disconcerting blend of

---

* He has no colour prejudice. He may think the Africans ugly (p. 257), but he does not regard them as an inferior race.

† His statement of the *yogis'* case for nudism, however (p. 238), shows some power of appreciating an unfamiliar point of view.

fact and fable; and he gives little indication of the use of documentary sources (but cf. pp. 180, 183, 193).

His distorted picture of earlier events is partly due to the role he assigns to 'Prester John'. It is possible that the original of this legendary priest-king was one of the Christian rulers of Abyssinia, whose successors were certainly identified with him in the fifteenth century. But in Polo's time his realm was generally believed to be somewhere in the Far East. As early as 1148 a disastrous defeat suffered by the Saracens in Turkestan was attributed to this mysterious champion of Christendom, though the actual victor was not in fact a Christian at all. Not long after this an unknown genius, possibly a Greek, had concocted a 'Letter of Prester John', purporting to be addressed to the two Christian Emperors and the Pope, which dwelt encouragingly on his power and benevolence towards the West and alluringly on the oriental splendour of his court. Thanks to this Letter, which soon became a best-seller, every European traveller in the East was on the look-out for Prester John, 'of whose great empire all the world speaks' (p. 75). Some place clearly had to be found for him in Marco's narrative. He was actually identified with a Nestorian ruler of the Turkish Kerait clan named Togrul, known to the Chinese as Wang Khan, who played a prominent part in the early career of Chinghiz, at first as an ally, later as an enemy. His story is here romanticized in the Rustichello manner, and he is said to have passed on the title to a certain George, who is known from other sources as a Christian prince subject to Kubilai.

In his geographical descriptions Marco Polo is scarcely ever influenced by those preconceptions about the shape and features of the earth that bedevil most medieval geographers, Christian, Moslem, and Chinese. A more learned writer might have avoided Polo's gaffe about travelling farther north than the Pole Star (p. 84); but he would probably have been misled into more damaging errors. As a rule, Polo is content to plot the position and extent of countries, towns, and natural features according to a rough-and-ready framework of directions and distances that makes no exaggerated claims to precision. His favourite unit of distance, the 'day's journey',* is obviously a highly elastic quantity, but no doubt sufficiently precise in its context for the traveller on a recognized caravan route. When he is reproducing hearsay evidence, as to the size of Java for instance

---

* The distances represented by this unit suggest that Polo normally travelled at a pretty leisurely pace, not that of a courier on urgent public business.

(p. 212) or the trend of the Arabian coast (p. 265), he is naturally liable to serious error. But his own observations, with due allowance for copyists' slips, are mostly pretty accurate. It would not be easy to translate them into a map, though they were certainly used by some cartographers in the fourteenth century; but they contained the essential data for a fairly reliable itinerary. We know that he fired the imagination of Columbus, who treasured a well-thumbed manuscript of his work and scribbled notes in the margin; but the Venetian cannot be held responsible for that fortunate underestimate of the size of the earth which encouraged the aspiring Genoese to seek for Cathay across the Atlantic.

It is when we turn to the wider field of 'geography' as the term is commonly used today, with an emphasis on 'human geography', that Polo's outstanding excellence is most clearly perceived. Instead of the picturesque fables★ that liven the pages of 'Sir John Mandeville' and of many more authentic travellers, he gives us no less picturesque facts, and facts in great abundance. In no previous Western writer since Strabo, thirteen centuries before, and in none again for at least another two centuries, do we find anything remotely comparable with Polo's panorama of the nations. Persians, Turks, Tartars, Chinese, Tibetans, Indians, and a score of others defile before us, not indeed revealed in their inner thoughts and feelings, but faithfully portrayed in all such particulars as might meet the eye of an observant traveller, from the oddities of their physical features or dress to the multiplicity of strange customs by which they regulated their lives from the cradle to the grave. Faced with this superb *tableau vivant*, the most captious critic cannot but agree with Marco's own view, as modestly expressed in the Prologue (p. 21): 'It would be a great pity if he did not have a written record made of all the things that he had seen and heard by true report, so that those who have not seen them and do not know them may learn them from this book.'

The present translation is intended to provide a straightforward and readable version, related as closely as possible to modern knowledge but making no claim to meet the requirements of the specialist. It is based on the oldest French manuscript (F), which is believed to represent an abridged copy of Rustichello's own words, with the addition of material from other sources that probably derive

★ The occasional fables of this sort in which Polo indulges—men with tails (p. 217) and dogs' faces (p. 219), the Male and Female Islands (p. 252), the Valley of Diamonds (p. 232), and the *rukh* (p. 257)—are not vouched for by him personally.

ultimately from the unabridged original—mainly Ramusio's Italian edition (R) and a Latin MS. (Z) which seems to be an abridgement of a lost Latin MS. used by Ramusio. The division into 234 short sections, with lengthy and not always very appropriate rubrics, has been replaced by a grouping into nine chapters plus Prologue, and repetitions, apostrophizations, and connecting formulae have been freely omitted. But the translator has tried, so far as this can be done without undue violence to modern idiom, to convey some impression of the style of the original, in particular the contrast between the bald and businesslike quality of Polo's topographical notes and the self-conscious artistry of those romantic interludes that betray most clearly the hand of Rustichello.

In order to reduce footnotes to a minimum, the identification of persons, places, and local products, where possible, has generally been effected in the text itself or in the index. The spelling of personal names is intended as a rough-and-ready (and not too unpronounce-able) compromise between the manuscript tradition and the claims of oriental scholarship.* For place-names, where an exact modern equivalent can be found, manuscript forms have been modernized in reason. In other cases, in which identification is at best doubtful, I have selected a plausible manuscript form and, if need be, Anglicized it (*Changan* for *Ciangan*, *Vuju* for *Vugiu* or *Vugui*).† If the reader finds, as he assuredly will, that the sign-posts I have endeavoured to provide are in many places defective and in others positively mis-leading, he must bear in mind that the Polo trail, for all the labour that has been expended on it, is still a pioneer trail and haunted, like the Desert of Lop, by beckoning spirits that sometimes tempt the wariest traveller to stray from the path.

* Marco probably knew both Mongol and Turkish, which are related (Altaic) languages, and it is not always clear which form he was trying to reproduce. He also seems to have had some knowledge of Persian; but it is doubtful which was the fourth language he claims to have mastered (p. 27). It can scarcely have been Chinese.

† In the case of Chinese place-names, modern spellings are normally distinguished by the use of hyphens to separate the syllables.

the travels of
marco polo

prologue

EMPERORS AND KINGS, DUKES AND MARQUISES, COUNTS, knights, and townsfolk, and all people who wish to know the various races of men and the peculiarities of the various regions of the world, take this book and have it read to you. Here you will find all the great wonders and curiosities of Greater Armenia and Persia, of the Tartars and of India, and of many other territories. Our book will relate them to you plainly in due order, as they were related by Messer Marco Polo, a wise and noble citizen of Venice, who has seen them with his own eyes. There is also much here that he has not seen but has heard from men of credit and veracity. We will set down things seen as seen, things heard as heard, so that our book may be an accurate record, free from any sort of fabrication. And all who read the book or hear it may do so with full confidence, because it contains nothing but the truth. For I would have you know that from the time when our Lord God formed Adam our first parent with His hands down to this day there has been no man, Christian or Pagan, Tartar or Indian, or of any race whatsoever, who has known or explored so many of the various parts of the world and of its great wonders as this same Messer Marco Polo. For this reason he made up his mind that it would be a great pity if he did not have a written record made of all the things he had seen and had heard by true report, so that others who have not seen and do not know them may learn them from this book.

Let me tell you, then, that to gain this knowledge he stayed in these various countries and territories fully twenty-six years. Afterwards, in the year of the Nativity of Our Lord Jesus Christ 1298, while he was in prison in Genoa, wishing to occupy his leisure as well as to afford entertainment to readers, he caused all these things to be recorded by Messer Rustichello of Pisa, who was in the same prison. But what he told was only what little he was able to remember.

In the year of Our Lord 1260, when Baldwin was Emperor of Constantinople and Messer Ponte governed the city in the name of the Doge of Venice, Messer Niccolò Polo, the father of Marco, and Messer Maffeo, who was Niccolò's brother, were in that city, having come there from Venice with their merchandise. They were men of good family, remarkable for their wisdom and foresight. After talking things over, they decided that they would go across the Black Sea in the hope of a profitable venture. So they bought many jewels of great beauty and price and set out from Constantinople by ship and went to Sudak.

After staying there for a while, they resolved to go farther afield. Let me tell you about it. They left Sudak and went on their way and rode without encountering any adventure worthy of note till they came to the court of Barka Khan, lord of a great part of Tartary, who at that time was living at Bolgara and Sarai. Barka received Messer Niccolò and Messer Maffeo with great honour and was very glad they had come. The two brothers gave him all the jewels they had brought; and Barka took them willingly and was exceedingly pleased with them, and gave them goods of fully twice the value in return. These he allowed them to sell in many places, and they were sold very profitably.

When they had stayed a year in Barka's land, war broke out between him and Hulagu, the Khan of the Levantine Tartars. They marched out against each other with all their forces and joined battle with great loss of life on both sides; but in the end the victory fell to Hulagu. On account of this battle and war, no one could travel about the country without the risk of arrest. At least, this was so in the direction from which the brothers had come; in the other direction they could travel freely. Thereupon they said to each other: 'Since we cannot return to Constantinople with our wares, let us go on towards the east. Then we can come back by a roundabout route.' So they left Barka and went to a city called Ucaca, which was the limit of the territory of the Western Khan. And from there they crossed the river Tigris * and journeyed for seventeen days through a desert, where they found no towns or villages but only Tartars with their tents, living off their beasts.

When they had crossed this desert, they came to a large and splendid city called Bukhara. The province also was called Bukhara, and its ruler's name was Barak. It was the finest city in all Persia. When the brothers came here, they could neither go on nor turn back. So here they stayed for three years.

While they were staying here, there came an envoy from Hulagu, the lord of the Levant, on his way to the Great Khan of all the

* Actually the Volga.

Tartars, whose name was Kubilai. He lived at the ends of the earth in an east-north-easterly direction. When the envoy saw Messer Niccolò and Messer Maffeo, he was greatly surprised, because no Latin had ever been seen in that country. On learning that they were merchants, he said to them: 'Sirs, if you will trust me, I can offer you an opportunity of great profit and great honour.' The two brothers said they would trust him willingly in any matter that lay within their power. The envoy replied: 'Sirs, I assure you that the Great Khan of the Tartars has never seen any Latin and is exceedingly desirous to meet one. Therefore, if you will accompany me to him, I assure you that he will be very glad to see you and will treat you with great honour and great bounty. And you will be able to travel with me in safety without let or hindrance.'

When they heard this, they were greatly pleased and said they would willingly accompany him. They set out with the envoy and travelled for a year towards the north and north-east before they arrived. On their way they encountered great wonders and a variety of things, which I will not recount to you because Messer Marco, the son of Messer Niccolò, who saw all these things also, will tell you of them in plain terms further on in the book.

When Messer Niccolò and Messer Maffeo arrived at the court of the Great Khan, he received them honourably and welcomed them with lavish hospitality and was altogether delighted that they had come. He asked them many questions: first about the Emperors, the government of their dominions, and the maintenance of justice; then about kings, princes, and other nobles. Next he asked about the Lord Pope and all the practices of the Roman Church and the customs of the Latins. And Messer Niccolò and Messer Maffeo told him all the truth about each matter in due order, well and wisely, like the wise men they were, and with a good understanding of the Tartar language.

When the Great Khan, whose name was Kubilai, who was lord of all the Tartars in the world and of all the provinces and kingdoms and regions of this vast part of the earth, had heard all about the Latins, as the two brothers had well and plainly declared it, he was exceedingly pleased. He made up his mind to send emissaries to the Pope, and asked the two brothers to go on this mission with one of his barons. They answered that they would carry out all his commands, as the commands of their liege lord. Then the Great Khan summoned to his presence one of his barons, who was named

Kogatal, and told him that he wished him to go with the brothers to the Pope. Kogatal answered: 'Sire, I am your man and ready to do all that you command to the utmost of my power.' Thereupon the Great Khan had letters written in the Turkish language to send to the Pope and entrusted them to the two brothers and to his baron and instructed them what they should say on his behalf to the Pope. You must know that the purport of his letters and his mission was this: he sent word to the Pope that he should send up to a hundred men learned in the Christian religion, well versed in the seven arts, and skilled to argue and demonstrate plainly to idolaters and those of other persuasions that their religion is utterly mistaken and that all the idols which they keep in their houses and worship are things of the Devil—men able to show by clear reasoning that the Christian religion is better than theirs. Furthermore the Great Khan directed the brothers to bring oil from the lamp that burns above the sepulchre of God in Jerusalem. Such then was the purport of their mission.

The Great Khan also gave the brothers and his baron a tablet of gold, on which it was written that the three emissaries, wherever they went, should be given all the lodging they might need and horses and men to escort them from one land to another. And when Messer Niccolò and Messer Maffeo and the other emissary were well equipped with everything they needed, they took leave of the Great and Mighty Khan, mounted their horses and took to the road.

When they had ridden a certain distance, the Tartar baron who accompanied the brothers fell ill, so that he could not continue the journey but remained at a city. Seeing that he was ill, the two brothers left him and went on their way. And I assure you that they were served and obeyed everywhere they went in whatever they chose to command. What more need I say? They rode on day after day till at last they came to Ayas. And I assure you that they were hard put to it to make the journey in three years. This was because they could not ride all the time, but were delayed by stress of weather, by snow and by swollen rivers.

From Ayas they went on to Acre, which they reached in the month of April, in the year of the Incarnation 1269. There they learnt that the Lord Pope, whose name was Clement, was dead. They went accordingly to a learned clerk, who was legate of the church of Rome for the whole kingdom of Egypt, a man of great authority named Tedaldo of Piacenza, and told him of the mission on which the Great Khan of the Tartars had sent them to the Pope. When the legate had heard what they had to say, he was filled with wonder, and it seemed to him that this affair was greatly to the profit and honour of Christendom. He said to them: 'Sirs, you see that the Pope is dead. Therefore your only wise course is to wait in patience until such time as there is a Pope. When there is a Pope, then you may fulfil your mission.' The two brothers, who saw clearly that the legate was speaking the truth, declared that pending the election of a Pope they would go to Venice to see their families. So they left Acre and went to Negropont, whence they took ship and sailed to Venice. There Messer Niccolò learnt that his wife was dead, and there was left to him a son of fifteen, whose name was Marco. This was the Marco of whom this book speaks. So Messer Niccolò and Messer Maffeo stayed at Venice about two years, waiting till there should be a Pope.

When they had waited all this time and saw that no Pope was being made, they decided that if they waited longer it might be too late for them to return to the Great Khan. So they set out from Venice, taking with them Marco the son of Niccolò. They went straight to Acre, where they met the legate of whom I spoke before. They discussed the affair with him at length and asked his leave to go to Jerusalem to get the oil from the lamp at Christ's sepulchre which the Great Khan had requested. This being granted, they went from Acre to Jerusalem and got the oil. Then, returning to the legate at Jerusalem, they said to him: 'Sir, since we see that there is no Pope, we wish to go back to the Great Khan, because we have delayed too long.' And the lord legate, who was one of the greatest lords of all the church of Rome, said to them: 'Since you wish to go, so be it.' He composed letters and a message to be sent to the Great Khan, testifying that Messer Niccolò and Messer Maffeo had come to fulfil their mission but, because there was no Pope, had been unable to do so.

Having received the legate's letters, the brothers set out from Acre and began their return journey to the Great Khan. They had scarcely got as far as Ayas, when it happened that the legate himself was elected to the Apostolic See and took the name of Pope Gregory of Piacenza. They were delighted at the news; and it was not long before an envoy came to Ayas from the legate who had been elected Pope, directing Messer Niccolò and Messer Maffeo, if they were not already gone, to turn back to him. At this they were overjoyed and said that they would do so gladly. What more need be said? The king of Armenia fitted out a galley for the two brothers and dispatched them to the legate with all honour.

Having reached Acre, they went to the lord Pope and made him a humble obeisance. He received them with honour and gave them his blessing, entertaining them with good cheer. Then he gave them two Dominican Friars, who were assuredly the wisest in all that province. One was named Brother Nicholas of Vicenza, the other Brother William of Tripoli. To the friars he gave privileges conveying plenary authority to ordain priests and bishops and grant absolution as fully as he could himself. He entrusted them with letters in which, among other things, he asked that the Great Khan's brother Abaka, lord of the Levantine Tartars, might give aid and favour to Christians so that they could visit his dominions by sea. He also sent the Great Khan many gifts, fine vessels of crystal and other things, and charged them with the message he wished to send to him. When Messer Niccolò and Messer Maffeo and the friars had received these things, they besought his blessing and then set out, all four of them, and with them Marco, the son of Messer Niccolò. When they had got as far as Ayas, it happened that Bundukdari, the sultan of Egypt, came into Armenia with a great host and wrought great havoc in the country, and the emissaries went in peril of their lives. When the friars saw this, they were scared at the prospect of going farther. Eventually they declared that they would not go. So they gave Messer Niccolò and Messer Maffeo all the privileges and letters they had received and took leave of them and departed with the Grand Master of the Templars.

So Messer Niccolò and Messer Maffeo and Marco, the son of Niccolò, set out on their journey and rode on, winter and summer, till they came to the Great Khan, who was then at a city called Kemenfu, a large city and a wealthy one. What they saw on the way will not be mentioned here, because we will recount it to you later in our book, all in due order. Here you need only know that they were hard put to it to complete the journey in three and a half years, because of snow and rain and flooded rivers and because they could not ride in winter as well as in summer. And I assure you for a fact that, when the Great Khan knew that Messer Niccolò and Messer Maffeo were coming, he sent his couriers fully forty days' journey to meet them, and they were well served and attended in everything.

Prologue

What more shall I say? When Messer Niccolò and Messer Maffeo and Marco arrived at this great city, they went to the chief palace, where they found the Great Khan and a very great company of barons. They knelt before him and made obeisance with the utmost humility. The Great Khan bade them rise and received them honourably and entertained them with good cheer. He asked many questions about their condition and how they had fared after their departure. The brothers assured him that they had indeed fared well, since they found him well and flourishing. Then they presented the privileges and letters which the Pope had sent, with which he was greatly pleased, and handed over the holy oil, which he received with joy and prized very highly. When the Great Khan saw Marco, who was a young stripling, he asked who he was. 'Sire,' said Messer Niccolò, 'he is my son and your liege man.' 'He is heartily welcome,' said the Khan. What need to make a long story of it? Be assured that great indeed were the mirth and merry-making with which the Great Khan and all his court welcomed the arrival of these emissaries. And they were well served and attended in everything. They stayed at court and had a place of honour above the other barons.

It came about that Marco, the son of Messer Niccolò, acquired a remarkable knowledge of the customs of the Tartars and of their languages and letters. I assure you for a fact that before he had been very long at the Great Khan's court he had mastered four languages with their modes of writing.* He was wise and far-sighted above the ordinary, and the Great Khan was very well disposed to him because of the exceptional merit and worth that he detected in him. Observing his wisdom, the Khan sent him as his emissary to a country named Kara-jang, which it took him a good six months to reach. The lad fulfilled his mission well and wisely. He had seen and heard more than once, when emissaries whom the Khan had dispatched to various parts of the world returned to him and rendered an account of the mission on which they had been sent but could give no other report of the countries they had visited, how their master would call them dolts and dunces, and declare that he would rather hear reports of these strange countries, and of their customs and usages, than the business on which he had sent them. When Marco went on his mission, being well aware of this, he paid close attention to all the novelties and curiosities that came his way, so that he might retail them to the Great Khan. On his return he presented himself before the Khan

* See note on p. 17.

27

and first gave a full account of the business on which he had been sent—he had accomplished it very well. Then he went on to recount all the remarkable things he had seen on the way, so well and shrewdly that the Khan, and all those who heard him, were amazed and said to one another: 'If this youth lives to manhood, he cannot fail to prove himself a man of sound judgement and true worth.' What more need I say? From this time onwards the young fellow was called Messer Marco Polo; and so he will be called henceforth in this book. And with good reason, for he was a man of experience and discretion.

What need to make a long story of it? You may take it for a fact that Messer Marco stayed with the Great Khan fully seventeen years; and in all this time he never ceased to travel on special missions. For the Great Khan, seeing that Messer Marco brought him such news from every country and conducted so successfully all the business on which he was sent, used, to entrust him with all the most interesting and distant missions. He continued to conduct his business with great success and to bring back word of many novelties and curiosities. And the Great Khan was so well satisfied with his conduct of affairs that he held him in high esteem and showed him such favour and kept him so near his own person that the other lords were moved to envy. This, then, is how it came about that Messer Marco observed more of the peculiarities of this part of the world than any other man, because he travelled more widely in these outlandish regions than any man who was ever born, and also because he gave his mind more intently to observing them.

When Messer Niccolò and Messer Maffeo and Messer Marco had stayed all this time with the Great Khan, they began to say among themselves that they would like to return to their own country. Time and again they asked the Khan to give them leave to depart, but he was so fond of them and so much enjoyed their company that nothing would induce him to give them leave.

Now at this time it happened that Queen Bulagan died. She was the wife of Arghun, lord of the Levant, and stipulated in her will that no lady should sit on her throne or be wife to Arghun who was not of her lineage. Thereupon Arghun took three of his lords whose names were as follows, the first Ulatai, the second Abushka, the third Koja. And he sent them to the Great Khan with a magnificent retinue, to ask him to send back a lady of the lineage of Bulagan, his late queen. When these three lords had come to the Great Khan, they told him the object of their journey. The Great Khan gave them honourable welcome, with merry-making and good cheer. Then he sent for a lady named Kokachin, of great beauty and charm, who was of the lineage of Queen Bulagan and seventeen years old. He told the three lords that this was the lady they had come for, and they professed themselves well satisfied. So everything was got ready and a train of attendants was arrayed to escort this new bride with all due pomp to King Arghun. Then the envoys, after taking grateful leave of the Great Khan, set out on horseback and travelled for eight months on the same road by which they had come. On the way they found that, because of a war that had recently broken out between certain kings of the Tartars, the roads were barred. Being unable to go ahead, they were obliged against their will to turn back to the court of the Great Khan, to whom they related everything that had happened to them.

At this juncture, Messer Marco had just returned from India by a voyage over strange seas and had much to report of his travels. And the three lords, who had seen Messer Niccolò and Messer Maffeo and Messer Marco, resolved among themselves that they would like these experienced Latins to make the journey with them by sea. They went to the Great Khan and begged him as a favour to dispatch them by sea and to let the three Latins accompany them. The Great Khan, who was very fond of the three, as I have told you, granted this favour with some reluctance and gave leave to the three Latins to travel with the three lords and the lady.

When the Great Khan saw that Messer Niccolò and Messer Maffeo and Messer Marco were on the point of departure, he ordered all three to be brought into his presence and gave them two tablets proclaiming that they might travel freely throughout his dominions and that wherever they went they should receive provisions for themselves and their attendants. He entrusted them with a message for the Pope and the kings of France and Spain, and the other kings of Christendom. Then he fitted out a fleet of fourteen ships, each of which had four masts and often carried as many as twelve sails. I could give you more particulars, but as this would be a lengthy matter I will not go into it at this point. Of these ships, at least four or five carried crews of 250 to 260 seamen.

When the ships were ready, the three lords and the lady and Messer Niccolò and Messer Maffeo and Messer Marco took leave of the

Great Khan and embarked on the ships with a very large company; and the Khan supplied them with provisions for two years. What more shall I say? They put to sea and sailed fully three months till they came to an island, lying towards the south, named Java.* This island is remarkable for many curiosities, of which I will tell you in this book. Then they left the island, and I assure you that they sailed over the Indian Ocean fully eighteen months before reaching their destination. And they observed many remarkable things, which will also be described in this book.

Now let me tell you the simple truth. When they embarked, they numbered fully 600 souls, not counting the seamen. Of this number every one died on the voyage, except only eighteen. Of the three envoys only Koja survived; of the 100 women in the party only one died.

On their arrival in Arghun's country they found that he himself was dead, and that his brother Kaikhatu was governing the kingdom. To him accordingly they delivered the messages entrusted to them, and referred the question of what should be done with the princess. He sent back word that they should give her to Arghun's young son Ghazan. At this time Ghazan was in the region of the Dry Tree on the borders of Persia with 60,000 troops, guarding certain passes to prevent certain hostile nations from invading and ravaging the country. And so they did. After which Messer Niccolò and Messer Maffeo and Messer Marco returned to Kaikhatu, because that was the direction in which their road lay. And there they stayed for nine months. Then they took leave of Kaikhatu and set out on their way. And you should know that he gave them, as emissaries of the Great Khan, four tablets of gold, each a cubit in length and five fingers in width and weighing three or four marks. Two bore the sign of the gerfalcon, one of the lion, and one was plain. In these tablets it was written that in reverence to the Everlasting God the name of the Great Khan should be honoured and praised throughout the length of years, and everyone who disobeyed his commands would be put to death and his goods confiscated. It was written further that these three emissaries should be honoured and served throughout his dominions like his own person, and that they should be furnished with horses and provisions and escort of every sort. And so indeed they were. Throughout his dominions they were supplied with horses and provisions and everything needful, and that in great

* Evidently 'Lesser Java', i.e. Sumatra. See below, p. 213 n.

30

plenty. I assure you for a fact that on many occasions they were given 200 horsemen, sometimes more, sometimes less, according to the number needed to escort them and ensure their safe passage from one district to another. And this was a necessary precaution, because Kaikhatu was not a lawful ruler and the inhabitants might have molested them, as they would not have done had they been subject to a lord to whom they owed allegiance.*

Let me tell you one thing more, which is worth recording to the credit of these three emissaries. For you may take it for a fact that Messer Maffeo and Messer Niccolò and Messer Marco really did enjoy such a position of dignity as I shall describe. The Great Khan reposed such confidence in them and was so favourably inclined to them that he entrusted to their care not only the princess Kokachin but also the daughter of the king of Manzi, so that they might escort them both to Arghun, khan of all the Levant. And so they did. I have already told you how they brought them by sea, and with how large a company and what provision. Let me now tell you that these two great ladies were in the care of the three emissaries. The three watched over them and guarded them as if they had been their own daughters. And the ladies, who were very young and beautiful, looked upon them as their fathers and obeyed them no less. And I assure you in all truth that queen Kokachin, who is now married to Ghazan the present ruler, was so deeply attached to the three men, both she and her husband Ghazan, that there is nothing she would not have done for them as readily as for her own father. For you must know that, when the three left her to go back to their own country, she wept for grief at their going.

So much then for this matter, which is greatly to their credit, since they were entrusted with two ladies of such quality to conduct to their lords from such a distant land. Now we shall drop this theme and continue our narrative. What more shall I say? When the three emissaries had left Kaikhatu, they set out on the journey and rode by daily stages till they reached Trebizond. From Trebizond they sailed to Constantinople, thence to Negropont, and from Negropont to Venice. This was in the year of the Incarnation of Christ 1295.

And, now that I have given you all the substance of the prologue, as you have heard, I will begin the book.

* R adds that any prospect of returning to Kubilai was ruled out by the news of his death. This did in fact occur early in 1294; but Kubilai is referred to throughout the book as if he were still alive. Cf. pp. 93, 207 etc. For Kaikhatu, see p. 280.

the middle east

LET ME BEGIN WITH ARMENIA. THE TRUTH IS THAT THERE ARE actually two Armenias, a Greater and a Lesser. The lord of Lesser Armenia is a king who maintains good and just government in his country under the suzerainty of the Tartars. It is a land of many villages and towns, amply stocked with the means of life. It also affords good sport with all sorts of wild game, both beast and fowl. The climate, however, is far from healthy; it is, in fact, extremely enervating. Hence, the nobility of the country, who used to be men of valour and stalwart soldiers, are now craven and mean-spirited and excel in nothing except drinking.

On the sea coast lies the town of Ayas, a busy emporium. For you must know that all the spices and cloths from the interior are brought to this town, and all other goods of high value; and merchants of Venice and Genoa and everywhere else come here and buy them. And merchants and others who wish to penetrate the interior all make this town the starting-point of their journey.

Lesser Armenia is bounded on the south by the Promised Land, now in the hands of the Saracens; on the north by the western district of Turkey, known as Karaman; on the north-east and east by eastern Turkey, with the towns of Kaisarieh and Sivas and many others, all subject to the Tartars; and on the west by the sea that is crossed by ships sailing to Christendom.

In Turkey there are three races of men. The Turcomans themselves, who worship Mahomet and keep his law, are a primitive people, speaking a barbarous language. They roam over the mountains and the plains, wherever they know that there is good pasturage, because they live off their flocks. They have clothing made of skins, and dwellings of felt or of skins. The country breeds good Turcoman horses and good mules of excellent quality.

The other races are the Armenians and the Greeks, who live inter-mingled among the Turcomans in villages and towns and make their living by commerce and crafts, besides agriculture. They weave the choicest and most beautiful carpets in the world. They also weave silk fabrics of crimson and other colours, of great beauty and richness,

c

33

and many other kinds of cloth. Their most celebrated cities are Konya, Kaisarieh, and Sivas; there are also many other cities and towns which I will not enumerate, because the list would run to a wearisome length. They are subject to the Tartar Khan of the Levant, who appoints governors to rule them.

Let us now leave this province and turn to Greater Armenia.

This is a very large province. Near the entrance to it stands a city called Erzincan, in which is made the best buckram in the world and countless other crafts are practised. Here are the finest baths of spring water to be found anywhere on earth. The inhabitants are Armenians and vassals of the Tartars. There are many towns and cities, of which the most splendid is Erzincan, which is the seat of an archbishop. The other chief cities are Erzerum and Ercis. And on the route from Trebizond to Tabriz is a fortress called Bayburt, where there is a large silver mine.

I can tell you that in summer all the armies of the Tartars of the Levant are stationed in this province, because it has the best summer pasturage for beasts. So the Tartars spend the summer here with their beasts; but they do not winter here, because of the intense cold of the snow, which falls in these regions in prodigious quantities, so that the beasts could not survive it. So the Tartars depart with the onset of winter and withdraw to a warmer region, where they find plenty of grass and good pasturage for their beasts.

In the heart of Greater Armenia is a very high mountain, shaped like a cube, on which Noah's ark is said to have rested, whence it is called the Mountain of Noah's Ark. It is so broad and long that it takes more than two days to go round it. On the summit the snow lies so deep all the year round that no one can ever climb it; this snow never entirely melts, but new snow is for ever falling on the old, so that the level rises. But on the lower slopes, thanks to the moisture that flows down from the melting snow, the herbage is so lush and luxuriant that in summer all the beasts from near and far resort here to batten on it and yet the supply never fails. This flow of moisture also has the effect of making the hillsides very boggy.

This province is bounded on the south-east by the kingdom of Mosul and on the north by Georgia, both of which I will describe to you later. Near the Georgian border there is a spring from which gushes a stream of oil, in such abundance that a hundred ships★ may

★ Z says: '1,000 camels'. The reference is doubtless to Baku on the Caspian.

poient mlt graut quantite despicerie et de plles
et dras dor et desoie. Encore y a une autre manie
re de gens qui habitent es montaignes de cele co
tree, qui sapelent. Caro qui sont cristien et sara
zin mlt mauuaise gent qui robent voleuti
ers les marcheans. Or laisons de mansul. Si
parlerons de baudas la graut cite. Ci dit le re
my. chapitre de la graut cite de baudas comment
ele fu prise.

Baudas est une cite mlt graut
la ou estoit le calipe de touz les
sarrazins du monde aussi come
a romme est li sieges des papes
des cristiens et parmi la cite court un mlt
graut flu et parce flun puet on aler en lamer
dynde. Si a bien. xviii. iournees de baudas. Si
que mlt graut quantite de marcheans vont
et viennent auec leur marcheandise, et arriuet
en une cite qui a non cisy, et diluec entrent en
lamer dynde. Encore sia sur le flun entre baudas
et cisy une graut cite qui a non bosra et tout
environ la cite par le bois naissent les meilleurs
dates du monde. En baudas laboureut de mai
tes facons de dras de soie aor, si sont nasich et nac
et quermesis, et de maius autres dras de mlt
bele facon, baudas est la plus noble cite et la gra
gnour qui soit en toutes ces parties. Il fu voirs
que ales. M.CC.lv. aus de crist le seignour
des tartars dulenaut que na laton auoit non.
An fu frere augraut Caam qui ore endroit reg
ne assaubla. i. graut ost et vint seur baudas et
la prist a force. Et ce fu bieu graut chose que ceste

baudas auoit plus de ceut hommes a cheual sauz
les hommes apie. Et quant il ot ce fet il trouua
au caliphe une tour toute plaine dor et dargent
et dautre tresor que ce fu la plus graut quantite
ensamble que mul home veist onques en mllieu.
Quant il vit cel graut tresor ensamble si en ot
mlt graut merueille. Si manda pour le caliphe.
Et le fist venir druant lui. Et li dist Caliphe
or medi. pour quoi tu auoies amasse si graut tr
sor. que en deuoies tu faire. Ne sauoies tu que ie
estoie ton auemi. Et que ie venoie seur toi a tout
si graut ost. pour toi descheriter. pour quoi ne pres
tu ton auoir et leusses come as sauldoiers et aus
chrs et aus gens darmes. Pour toi deffendre
et taute. Le Caliphe ne sot que respondre et ne
parla neus. Si li dist le seignour. Or caliphes
puis que ie voi que tu amastaut le tresor. Si le
te vul douner amengier. Si come le tien meismes
Si le fist prendre et mettre et dedruz la tour autres
et commanda que nule chose ne li fust donnee.
amengier ne aloire. Or le dist Caliphe or mang
ue taut de toutrfor come tu vondras puis q
il te plaisoit taut. Car ia mais ne mangeras
autre chose que de cest tresor, si demoura laieus
iiii. iours et morut come chetif. Et pour ce
eust miex valu au caliphe que il eust donne et de
parti son tresor aus hommes darmes qui li eus
sent deffendu et sa terre et ses gens que estre pris
et desheritez et mort si come il fu. Et puis sa
auaut ni ot mul Caliphe, ueu baudas ue eu autre
lieu. Or vous vul couter une mlt graut miracle
qui auint en baudas que dieu fist pour les cristiens.
Ci dit le xrv. chapitre de la graut miracle qui
a vint a baudas de la montaigne.

Il fu voirs que entre baudas et mansul auint
que. i. caliphe qui estoit a baudas au tas
qui corroit sgil. CC. lxv. de crist. qui haoit
les cristiens. Car iour et nuit il pensoit coment
il peust faire retourner sarrazins contre les cris
tiens de sa terre, ou se non faire les morir. Et de
ce se couseillot tous iours a un tres prestres de sa loy.
Car touz ensamble leur voloient aussi mout
graut mal. Et ce est chose veritable que touz les
sarrazins du monde vuelent touz iours mout
graut mal. aus cristiens du monde. Or auint q
le dist Caliphe auec ses sages troiuereut un tel pour

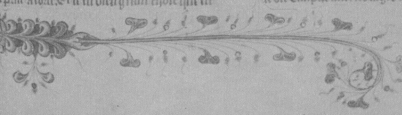

load there at once. This oil is not good to eat; but it is good for burning and as a salve for men and camels affected with itch or scab. Men come from a long distance to fetch this oil, and in all the neighbourhood no other oil is burnt but this.

In Georgia there is a king who always bears the name of David Malik, that is to say King David. He is subject to the Tartars. In former times all the kings of this province were born with the sign of an eagle on their right shoulder. The Georgians are a handsome race of doughty warriors, good archers and good fighters on the battlefield. They are Christians and observe the rule of the Greek church. They wear their hair cropped in clerical fashion.

This is the province through which Alexander could not pass when he wanted to go to the west, because the way is narrow and dangerous. On one side is the sea, on the other are high mountains and forests impassable on horseback. This narrow pass between the mountains and the sea runs for more than four leagues, so that a few men could hold it against all comers. This is why Alexander could not pass. And I should let you know that Alexander had a tower and fortress built here, so that the natives could not sally out to attack him. This was called the Iron Gates. It is the place where the *Alexander Book* relates that he shut in the Tartars between two mountains. In fact they were not Tartars, but people called Comanians and various other races besides, because there were no Tartars at that time.

The province has villages and towns in plenty. Silk is produced here in abundance, and the silken fabrics and cloth of gold woven here are the finest ever seen. There are also the best goshawks in the world. There are ample supplies of everything, and commerce and industry flourish. The whole country is full of high mountains and narrow passes which are easily defensible, so that I can assure you that the Tartars have never been able to achieve complete dominion over it. Among these mountains are woods in which the only trees are box-trees.

There is a monastery here called St Leonard's, notable for the following miraculous occurrence. You must know that there is a great lake formed of water that issues from a mountain just beside the church of St Leonard. And in this water no fish is found, big or little, at any season of the year, except that they begin to appear on the first day of Lent and continue every day throughout Lent till

Holy Saturday, that is, the eve of Easter. During all this period there are fish in plenty; but at every other season there is not one to be found.

This country looks out over two seas. To the north lies the Black Sea, to the east that called the sea of Baku or of Ghel or Ghelan, which is some 2,800 miles in circumference and is strictly speaking a lake, because it is completely surrounded by mountains and land and has no connexion with the main sea—which lies in fact twelve days' journey away. It contains many inhabited islands, with fine cities built on them. The inhabitants are refugees from the power of the Great Tartar, when he rode as a conqueror through the kingdom or province of Persia, whose cities and districts then had a system of government by the commonalty; they sought refuge in these islands and among the mountains, in the hope of finding safety there. This sea is well stocked with fish, especially sturgeon, salmon, and other big fish. Many rivers run into it, including the Euphrates.* In recent years Genoese merchants have taken to launching ships on this sea and sailing on it. This is the source of the silk called *ghilan*.

In this province is a fine city of great size named Tiflis, surrounded by subordinate towns and townships. The inhabitants are Christians (that is, Armenians and Georgians) besides a few Saracens and Jews, but not many. Silk and many other fabrics are woven here. The inhabitants live by their industry and are subject to the Great Khan of the Tartars.

You must know that we mention only the two or three principal cities of each province. There are many others which it would be tedious to enumerate, unless they are remarkable for some special curiosity. But some that we have omitted, which are situated in the places above mentioned, will be dealt with more fully below.

So much for what lies north of Armenia. Let us now turn to the lands lying south and east of it.

Mosul is a large kingdom inhabited by the following different nations. First, there are those called Arabs, who worship Mahomet. Then there are people who observe the law of Christ, but not according to the ordinances of the Roman Church, for they are at fault in several points. They are called Nestorians and Jacobites. They have a

* Presumably the Araxes. Z adds the Tigris and Gihon, two others of the four rivers that flowed out of Paradise (Genesis ii, 11–14). Polo applies the name Gihon to the Oxus (p. 267).

patriarch, whom they call Catholicus.* This patriarch makes archbishops and bishops and abbots and prelates of every degree and
sends them out everywhere, into India and Cathay and Baghdad, just
like the Roman Pope. You must understand that all the Christians
you will meet in the countries I am describing are Nestorians and
Jacobites.

Here are made all the cloths of silk and gold called *mosulin*.† And
from this kingdom hail the great merchants, also called Mosulin,
who export vast quantities of spices and other precious wares.

In the mountains of this kingdom live the people called Kurds;
some of them are Nestorian and Jacobite Christians, others are
Saracens who worship Mahomet. They are lusty fighters and lawless
men, very fond of robbing merchants.

Next to this province is one named Mus and Mardin, which produces abundance of cotton. Its industries include the manufacture of
buckram. The inhabitants are craftsmen and traders and are subject to
the king of the Tartars.

Let us now leave Mosul and turn to Baghdad.

In Baghdad, which is a very large city, the Caliph of all the Saracens
in the world has his seat, just as the head of all the Christians in the
world has his seat at Rome. Through the midst of the city flows a
very large river, by which travellers may go to the Indian Sea. By
this route merchants come and go with their merchandise. You
should know that from Baghdad to the sea is a journey of fully
eighteen days. Merchants travelling to India follow this river to a
city called Kais, where they enter the Indian Sea. On the river between
Baghdad and Kais there is a large city named Basra; and in groves all
round Basra grow the best dates in the world.

It is in Baghdad that most of the pearls are pierced that are imported from India into Christendom. Here too are woven many
fabrics of cloth of gold and silk, known as *nasich* and *nakh* and
cramoisy, very richly decorated with beasts and birds. It is a great
centre for the study of the law of Mahomet and of necromancy,
natural science, astronomy, geomancy, and physiognomy. It is the
largest and most splendid city in all these parts.

To the Caliph of Baghdad belonged the greatest treasure of gold

---

* The Jacobite patriarch had his seat near Mosul, the Nestorian at Baghdad; cf. below
p. 254.
† i.e. muslin, though evidently not in the modern sense.

and silver and precious stones that ever belonged to any man. Let me tell you about it. It happened in the year of Our Lord 1255* that the Great Khan of the Tartars, whose name was Hulagu, assembled a huge army and came against Baghdad. Hulagu was one of four brothers, lords of the Tartars, of whom the eldest was named Mongu. These brothers, after conquering Cathay and other adjoining countries, were not content with what they had won, but made up their minds to conquer the whole world. So they divided it into four quarters: one was to go eastwards on a career of conquest, one south-wards, and the others towards the other two quarters. The portion that fell by lot to Hulagu was the south. He set out first of all and started manfully to conquer these southern provinces till he came to Baghdad. Knowing the great strength of the city, due to the immense numbers of its occupants, he resolved to capture it by a ruse rather than by force. Having about 100,000 cavalry, without counting in-fantry, he wished to give the Caliph and his followers in the city the impression that they were only a few. So, before drawing near, he posted part of his force in hiding on one side and another part on the other side among the woods. With the rest he charged full tilt up to the gates. The Caliph, seeing this force was a small one, did not take much account of it. Putting his trust only in the banner of Mahomet, he planned to destroy it utterly and sallied out headlong with his following. Seeing this, Hulagu made a pretence of flight and so lured him back past the woods and thickets where his troops lay in ambush. Here he trapped his pursuers and crushed them. So the Caliph was captured together with the city. After his capture a tower was dis-covered, filled with gold. When Hulagu saw this he was amazed and ordered the Caliph to be brought before him. 'Caliph,' said he, 'why have you heaped up all this treasure? What did you mean to do with it? Did you not know that I was your enemy and was coming against you with all this host to despoil you? Knowing this, why did you not take your treasure and give it to knights and hired soldiers to defend you and your city?' The Caliph made no answer, because he did not know what to say. Then Hulagu said: 'Caliph, since I see that you love treasure so dearly, I will give you your own to eat.' Next he ordered that the Caliph should be taken and put in the treasure tower and that nothing should be given him to eat or to drink. 'Now, Caliph,' he said, 'eat your fill of treasure, since you are so fond of it; for you will get nothing else.' After that he left him in the tower,

* Actually 1258.

where at the end of four days he died. So it would have been better indeed for the Caliph if he had given away his treasure to defend his land and his people rather than died with all his people and bereft of everything. And since then there has been no other Caliph.

Before we go on to Tabriz, there is much else I might have told you about happenings and customs in Baghdad; but, as this would run to a tedious length, I have cut short my account. Instead, I will tell you of a great miracle, as you will hear.

The miracle which I will relate to you took place between Baghdad and Mosul. In the year of the Incarnation of Christ 1225 * there lived a Caliph at Baghdad who was very ill-disposed towards the Christians. Day and night he was for ever thinking how he could convert all the Christians in his country into Saracens or, failing that, have them all put to death. And on this problem he continually sought the advice of his men of religion and his counsellors. For they all joined with him in wishing ill to the Christians; indeed, it is a fact that all the Saracens in the world are agreed in wishing ill to all the Christians in the world. Now it happened that the Caliph and his advisers hit upon the following text. They found it written in one of the Gospels that, if there were a Christian who had faith as great as a grain of mustard seed, then by praying to the Lord his God he could make two mountains join together. When they found this, they were overjoyed: here, they declared, was a pretext for converting the Christians into Saracens or else putting them all to death. Thereupon the Caliph sent for all the Christians, Nestorian and Jacobite, that were in his country, who amounted to a very great number. When they had come before him, he showed them this passage and had it read to them. After they had read it, he asked them if it was true. They replied that it was most certainly true. 'Then do you affirm,' said the Caliph, 'that a Christian whose faith is as great as a grain of mustard seed is able by praying to his God to make two mountains join together?' 'Certainly we do,' said the Christians. 'Then,' said the Caliph, 'I will set you a test. Among so many Christians, there must surely be one who has a little faith. Therefore I tell you this: either you will move this mountain, which you see there,' and he pointed to a mountain not far away, 'or I will make you all die an evil death. For, if you do not make it move, you will show that you have no faith. So you will all be put to death; or else you will be converted to the good law that Mahomet our

* So Z. F has '1275', which cannot be reconciled with the preceding chapter.

41

prophet has given us, and will have true faith and be saved. To do this I will allow you ten days' grace. And if at the end of that time you have not done it, I will have you all put to death.' After that the Caliph spoke no more and gave the Christians leave to depart.

When the Christians heard the Caliph's words, they were greatly perturbed and very much afraid of death. All the same, they had good hope that their Creator would deliver them from this great peril. A council was held of all the learned Christians who were their prelates; for they had bishops and archbishops and priests in plenty. But they could see no way out of it but to pray to the Lord their God that He of His pity and mercy would send them guidance and deliver them from such a cruel death as the Caliph would inflict upon them if they did not do as he commanded. What more shall I say? You may be sure that the Christians spent day and night in prayer, and earnestly besought the Saviour, God of heaven and earth, that He of His pity would deliver them from the great peril that they were in.

In this solemn prayer and supplication the Christians continued eight days and eight nights, male and female, great and small. While they were thus occupied, it happened that an angel came in a vision bringing a message from God to a certain bishop, who was a man of very holy life. 'O bishop,' he said, 'go now to such-and-such a shoe-maker, a man with one eye, and tell him to pray that the mountain may move; and the mountain will move forthwith.'

Now, as to this shoe-maker, I will tell you what sort of man he was and what life he led. You may be well assured that he was a man of great probity and chastity. He fasted much and committed no sin. Every day he went to Church and to Mass. Every day he gave away some of his daily bread for God's sake. He was a man of such virtuous character and such holy life that you could find none better, near or far. I will tell you of one thing he did that will convince you that he was a good man of good faith and good life. He had often heard the lesson read from the Holy Gospel that if thine eye offend thee thou shouldst pluck it out of thy head or blind it, so that it may not cause thee to sin. It happened that one day a beautiful woman came to the house of this shoe-maker to buy shoes. He wished to see her leg and foot, so as to see which shoes would fit her. So he asked her to show her leg and foot, and she promptly did so. And without doubt she had a beautiful leg and a beautiful foot, so that you could not ask for greater beauty. And when the master of the shop, who was as virtuous a man as I have described him, saw this woman's leg and foot, he was forthwith tempted, because his eyes looked on them with pleasure. He let the woman go and would not sell her the shoes. When the woman had gone, the master said to himself: 'Ah, false traitor that you are, what are you thinking of? Surely I will take heavy vengeance on these eyes of mine which offend me so.' There and then he took a little awl and made it very sharp and thrust it into the midst of one of his eyes in such a way that he burst the eye inside his head, so that he never saw with it again. So he was certainly a very holy and virtuous man. And now to return to our story.

Now you may be sure that when this apparition had come several times to the bishop, bidding him send for the shoe-maker so that he by his prayer might make the mountain move, the bishop gave a full account of it to his fellow Christians. And they were all in favour of summoning the shoe-maker to come before them. And so they did. When he had come, they told him that they wished him to pray God to move the mountain. At first he declared that he was not such a good man that the Lord God would do so great a thing in answer to his prayer. But the Christians begged him and coaxed him. And what need of more words? They begged him to such purpose that he promised to do as they wished and make this prayer to his Creator.

When the last of their days of grace had come, the Christians rose early in the morning, male and female, great and small, and went to church and chanted the Holy Mass. After they had chanted and performed all the service of our Lord God, they set out all together towards the plain at the foot of this mountain, carrying the Cross of the Saviour before them. When the whole company, who numbered fully 100,000 souls, had come to this plain, they stationed themselves before the Cross of the Lord. The Caliph was there, with such a great multitude of Saracens that it was a marvel to behold; they had come to kill the Christians, because they did not in the least believe that the mountain would move. And all the Christians, great and small alike, were filled with fear and doubt; but all the same they had good hope in their Creator. And when all these people, Christians and Saracens, were in this plain, then the shoe-maker fell on his knees before the Cross and lifted his hands to heaven and besought his Saviour that the mountain might move and that such a multitude of Christians as were there assembled might not be put to a cruel death. When he had finished his prayer, he cried: 'In the name of the Father, the Son, and the Holy Ghost, I command thee, mountain, by the virtue of the Holy Ghost, to depart thence.' He had barely ceased speaking when the mountain began to crumble and to move. When the Caliph and the Saracens saw this, they were dumbfounded, and many of them turned Christian. The Caliph himself became a Christian, but in secret; for when he died, a cross was found round his neck. For this reason the Saracens did not bury him among the tombs of the other Caliphs, but put him in another place.

Now you have heard just how the miracle happened. Out of reverence to the shoe-maker and the grace vouchsafed to him, the anniversary of this miracle has been celebrated ever since by the Christians, both Nestorian and Jacobite, who regularly observe a solemn fast on the eve of the day. But in general, since Armenians, Nestorians, and Jacobites differ in certain points of doctrine, they repudiate and abhor one another.

Tabriz is a large city in a province called Iraq, which has many cities and towns. Since Tabriz is the most splendid city in the province, I will tell you about it.

The people of Tabriz live by trade and industry; for cloth of gold and silk is woven here in great quantity and of great value. The city is so favourably situated that it is a market for merchandise from India and Baghdad, from Mosul and Hormuz, and from many other places; and many Latin merchants come here to buy the merchandise imported from foreign lands. It is also a market for precious stones, which are found here in great abundance. It is a city where good profits are made by travelling merchants. The inhabitants are a mixed lot and good for very little. There are Armenians and Nestorians, Jacobites and Georgians, and Persians; and there are also worshippers of Mahomet, who are the natives of the city and are called Tabrizis. The city is entirely surrounded by attractive orchards, full of excellent fruit. The Saracens of Tabriz are wicked and treacherous. The law which their prophet Mahomet has given them lays down that any harm they may do to one who does not accept their law, and any appropriation of his goods, is no sin at all. And if they suffer death or injury at the hands of Christians, they are accounted martyrs. For this reason they would be great wrong-doers, if it were not for the government. And all the other Saracens in the world act on the same principle. When they are on the point of death, up comes their priest and asks whether they believe that Mahomet was the true messenger of God; if they answer 'Yes', then he tells them that they are saved. That is why they are converting the

Tartars and many other nations to their law, because they are allowed great licence to sin and according to their law no sin is forbidden.

Within the confines of Tabriz is a monastery named in honour of the Venerable St Barsamo. Here there is an abbot with many monks who wear a habit in the style of Carmelites. These monks, so as not to give themselves up to idleness, are continually weaving woollen girdles, which they afterwards lay on the altar of St Barsamo when they celebrate Mass. When they go through the province begging (like the friars of the order of the Holy Ghost), they give some of them to their friends and to noblemen, because they are efficacious in relieving the body of pain; and for this reason everyone devoutly wishes to have one.

Now let us leave Tabriz and turn to Persia, a very great province and at one time a very splendid and powerful one, but now ravaged and devastated by the Tartars.

In Persia is the city called Saveh, from which the three Magi set out when they came to worship Jesus Christ. Here, too, they lie buried in three sepulchres of great size and beauty. Above each sepulchre is a square building with a domed roof of very fine work-manship. The one is just beside the other. Their bodies are still whole, and they have hair and beards. One was named Beltasar, the second Gaspar, and the third Melchior. Messer Marco asked several of the inhabitants who these Magi were; but no one could tell him anything except that they were three kings who were buried there in days gone by. But at last he learnt what I will tell you.

Three days farther on, he found a town called Kala Atashparastan, that is to say Town of the Fire-worshippers. And that is no more than the truth; for the men of this town do worship fire. And I will tell you why they worship it. The inhabitants declare that in days gone by three kings of this country went to worship a new-born prophet and took with them three offerings—gold, frankincense, and myrrh —so as to discover whether this prophet was a god, or an earthly king or a healer. For they said: 'If he takes gold, he is an earthly king; if frankincense, a god; if myrrh, a healer.' When they had come to the place where the prophet was born, the youngest of the three kings went in all alone to see the child. He found that he was like himself, for he seemed to be of his own age and appearance. And he came out, full of wonder. Then in went the second, who was a man of middle age. And to him also the child seemed, as it had seemed to the other, to be of his own age and appearance. And he came out quite dumbfounded. Then in went the third, who was of riper years; and to him also it happened as it had to the other two. And he came out deep in thought. When the three kings were all together, each told the others what he had seen. And they were much amazed and resolved that they would all go in together. So in they went, all three together, and came before the child and saw him in his real likeness and of his real age; for he was only thirteen days old. Then they worshipped him and offered him the gold, the frankincense, and the myrrh. The child took all three offerings and then gave them a closed casket. And the three kings set out to return to their own country.

After they had ridden for some days, they resolved to see what the child had given them. They opened the casket and found inside it a stone. They wondered greatly what this could be. The child had given it to them to signify that they should be firm as stone in the faith that they had adopted. For, when the three kings saw that the child had taken all three offerings, they concluded that he was at once a god, and an earthly king, and a healer. And, since the child knew that the three kings believed this, he gave them the stone to signify that they should be firm and constant in their belief. The three kings, not knowing why the stone had been given to them, took it and threw it into a well. No sooner had it fallen in than there descended from heaven a burning fire, which came straight to the well into which it had been thrown. When the three kings saw this miracle, they were taken aback and repented of their throwing away the stone; for they saw clearly that its significance was great and good. They immediately took some of this fire and carried it to their country and put it in one of their churches, a very fine and splendid building. They keep it perpetually burning and worship it as a god. And every sacrifice and burnt offering which they make is roasted with this fire. If it ever happens that the fire goes out, they go round to others who hold the same faith and worship fire also and are given some of the fire that burns in their church. This they bring back to rekindle their own fire. They never rekindle it except with this fire of which I have spoken. To procure this fire, they often make a journey of ten days.

That is how it comes about that the people of this country are fire-worshippers. And I assure you that they are very numerous. All this was related to Messer Marco Polo by the inhabitants of this town; and it is all perfectly true. Let me tell you finally that one of the three Magi came from Saveh, one from Hawah, and the third from Kashan.

Now that I have told you of this matter at full length, I will go on to tell you the facts about many other cities in Persia and the customs of the inhabitants.

You must know that in Persia there are eight kingdoms, because it is a very large country. Here is a list of them by name: the first kingdom, at the entrance to the country, is called Kasvin; the second, which lies towards the south, is Kurdistan; the third, Luristan; the fourth, Shulistan; the fifth, Isfahan; the sixth, Shiraz; the seventh, Shabankara; the eighth, Tun and Kain, situated at the extremity of Persia. All these kingdoms lie south of Kasvin, except that of Tun and Kain, which adjoins the region of the Solitary Tree.

In these kingdoms there are many fine steeds, and many are exported to India for sale. As an indication of the great value of these horses, you may take it that some, indeed the great majority, are sold for fully 200 pounds of Touraine apiece. There are also the finest asses in the world, worth fully 30 marks of silver apiece. This is because they eat little, carry heavy loads, and travel long distances in a single day, enduring toil beyond the power of horses or mules. For the merchants of these parts, when they travel from one country to another, traverse vast deserts, that is to say dry, barren, sandy regions, producing no grass or fodder suitable for horses; and the wells and sources of fresh water lie so far apart that they must travel by long stages if their beasts are to have anything to drink. Since horses cannot endure this, the merchants use only these asses, because they are swift coursers and steady amblers, besides being less costly to keep. So they fetch a better price than horses. They also use camels, which likewise carry heavy loads and are cheap to maintain. The men of these kingdoms drive the horses of which I have spoken to Kais and Hormuz, two cities on the coast of the Indian Ocean. There they find traders who buy them and transport them to India, where they are sold for the high prices I have mentioned. Note that in India the climate is so hot that horses cannot be bred and are not born, or, if they are, they are monstrosities, blemished and misshapen in their limbs and quite worthless.

Among the people of these kingdoms there are many who are brutal and bloodthirsty. They are for ever slaughtering one another; and, were it not for fear of the government, that is, the Tartar lordship of the Levant, they would do great mischief to travelling merchants. The government imposes severe penalties upon them and has ordered that along all dangerous routes the inhabitants at the request of the merchants shall supply good and efficient escorts from district to district for their safe conduct on payment of two or three groats for each loaded beast according to the length of the journey. Yet, for all that the government can do, these brigands are not to be deterred from frequent depredations. Unless the merchants are well armed and equipped with bows, they slay and harry them unsparingly. And I can assure you that they all observe the law of Mahomet their prophet.

In the cities there are merchants and craftsmen in plenty, living by trade and industry. They make cloth of gold and silk of every sort. Cotton grows there in abundance. They have no lack of wheat, barley, millet, panic-grass, and every type of corn, besides wine and all kinds of fruit. Someone may object that the Saracens do not drink wine; for their law forbids it. My answer is that they gloss the text of their law thus: if wine is boiled over a fire, so that it is partly consumed and turns sweet, they are free to drink it without breach of commandment or law; for they no longer call it wine, since the change of flavour carries with it a change of name.

Among the cities of Persia is one called Yazd, a very fine and splendid city and a centre of commerce. A silken fabric called *yazdi* is manufactured here in quantity and exported profitably to many markets. The inhabitants worship Mahomet.

The traveller who leaves this city to proceed farther rides for seven days over a plain in which there are only three inhabited places where he can get shelter. Along the route there are many fine groves of date-palms, which are pleasant to ride through, and abundance of wild game, including partridges and quail, a great boon to merchants travelling that way. There are also fine wild asses. And at the end of this seven days' journey lies a kingdom called Kerman.

Kerman is a kingdom on the edge of Persia. It used to be governed by an hereditary ruler; but, since the Tartars conquered it, the lordship no longer goes by inheritance, but the Tartar suzerain grants it at his own pleasure. In this kingdom originate the stones called turquoises; they are found in great abundance in the mountains, where they are dug out of the rocks. There are also veins producing steel and *ondanique* in great plenty. The inhabitants excel in the manufacture of all the equipment of a mounted warrior—bridles, saddles, spurs, swords, bows, quivers, and every sort of armour according to local usage. The gentlewomen and their daughters are adepts with the needle, embroidering silk of all colours with beasts and birds and many other figures. They embroider the curtains of nobles and great men so well and so richly that they are a delight to the eye. And they are no less skilful at working counterpanes, cushions, and pillows.

In the mountains hereabouts are bred the best falcons in the world, and the swiftest in flight; they are red on the breast and under the tail between the thighs. And you may take my word that they fly at such incalculable speed that there is no bird that can escape from them by flight.

When the traveller leaves the city of Kerman, he rides for seven days across a plateau, finding no lack of towns and villages and homesteads. It is a pleasant and satisfying country to ride through, for it is well stocked with game and teems with partridges. After this he comes to a great escarpment, from which the road leads steadily downhill for two days through a country abounding all the way in fruits of many kinds. There used to be homesteads here; but now there is not one, but nomads live here with their grazing flocks. Between the city of Kerman and this escarpment the cold in winter is so intense that it can scarcely be warded off by any number of garments and furs.

Now let me tell you about an experiment that was made in the kingdom of Kerman. It so happens that the people of this kingdom are good, even-tempered, meek, and peaceable, and miss no chance of doing one another a service. For this reason the king once observed to the sages assembled in his presence: 'Gentlemen, here is something that puzzles me, because I cannot account for it. How is it that in the kingdoms of Persia, which are such near neighbours of ours, there are folk so unruly and contentious that they are for ever killing one another, whereas among us, who are all but one with them, there is hardly an instance of provocation or brawling?' The sages answered that this was due to a difference of soil. So the king thereupon sent to Persia, and in particular to Isfahan aforementioned, whose inhabitants outdid the rest in every sort of villainy. There, on the advice of his sages, he had seven ships loaded with earth brought to his own kingdom. This earth he ordered to be spread out like pitch over the floors of certain rooms and then covered with carpets, so that those who entered should not be dirtied by the soft surface. Then a banquet was served in these rooms, at which the guests had no sooner partaken of food than one began to round on another with opprobrious words and actions that soon led to blows. So the king agreed that the cause did indeed lie in the soil.

At the foot of the two days' descent lies a wide plain, on the verge of which stands a city called Kamadin. This was once a great city, of remarkable splendour; but now it is neither so great nor so fine, for invading Tartars have ravaged it several times. And I can assure you that in this plain it is very hot indeed.

The country that I am now describing is called Rudbar. It produces wheat and other cereals. Its fruits are dates, apples of paradise, and pistachios, besides others which do not grow in our chilly climate. Turtle-doves flock here in multitudes because of the quantities of berries which they find to eat. There is no end to their numbers. The Saracens never eat them, because they hold them in abhorrence. There are also pheasants and many other birds. In the plain there is a race of birds called francolins, which are different from the francolins of other lands. Their plumage is a mixture of black and white, and the feet and beak are red. The beasts also are different. Let me tell you first about the oxen. They are of great size and pure white like snow. Their hair is short and smooth because of the heat. Their horns are thick and stumpy and not pointed. Between their shoulders they have a round hump fully two palms in height. They are the loveliest things in the world to look at. When you want to load them, they lie down like camels; then, when they are loaded, they stand up and carry their loads very well, because they are exceedingly strong. There are also sheep as big as asses, with tails so thick and plump that they weigh a good thirty pounds. Fine, fat beasts they are, and good eating.

In this plain there are many towns and villages with earthen walls of great height and thickness to protect them against the Karaunas, bands of marauders who infest this country. They are called Karaunas, that is mongrels, because they are the off-spring of Indian mothers and Tartar fathers. These robbers, when they are bent on raiding and pillage, work an enchantment by diabolic art so that the day turns dark and no one can see more than a very short distance. This darkness they spread over an extent of seven days' journey. They know the country very well. When they have brought on the darkness, they ride side by side, sometimes as many as 10,000 of them together, sometimes more, sometimes less, so that they overspread all

D

the region they mean to rob. Nothing they find in the open country, neither man nor beast nor goods, can escape capture.When they have taken captives who cannot pay a ransom, they kill all the old, and the young they lead away and sell them as bondsmen and slaves. Their king is called Nigudar. This Nigudar went to the court of Chaghatai, a brother of the Great Khan, with fully 10,000 men of his own race and stayed with him, because Chaghatai was his uncle and a very great lord. And, while he was staying with him, Nigudar planned and perpetrated a shameful outrage, as I shall tell you. He took his 10,000 followers, a villainous band of cut-throats, and leaving his uncle Chaghatai in Greater Armenia he passed through Badakhshan and a country called Pashai and another country named Kashmir, where he lost many men and beasts because the roads were narrow and bad, and finally entered a province of India called Dilivar.* They captured a fine city, also named Dilivar, and in this city Nigudar remains as ruler, having ousted the former ruler, a great and wealthy king named Asidin Sultan. There he still remains with his followers and pays no heed to anyone. He makes war on the other Tartars who live round about his kingdom. In their marauding expeditions, which may extend to thirty or forty days' journey, they usually ride towards Rudbar. This is because in the winter all the merchants who come to do business in Hormuz, while they are awaiting the arrival of the merchants from India, send their mules and camels, which have grown thin with the long journey, to the plain of Rudbar to fatten on the rich pasturage; and here the Karaunas are on the look out to seize them.

I assure you that Messer Marco himself narrowly evaded capture by these robbers in the darkness they had made. He escaped to a town called Kamasal; but many of his companions were taken captive and sold, and some put to death. Now let us turn to other matters.

The plain of which I have been speaking extends southwards for two days' journey. At its southern rim is another downward slope, where the road drops steadily for twenty miles. It is a bad and dangerous road, being infested by robbers. When the traveller has accomplished this descent, he finds another very fine plain called the plain of Hormuz, two days' journey across, where there are fine rivers and

* Probably Lahore. According to R, which has a full but rather confused version of this story, the Karaunas learnt their black art in Malabar.

date-palms in plenty and a variety of birds, including francolins and parrots and many others quite unlike ours.

After two days' ride he reaches the Ocean. Here on the coast stands a city called Hormuz, which has an excellent harbour. Merchants come here by ship from India, bringing all sorts of spices and precious stones and pearls and cloths of silk and of gold and elephants' tusks and many other wares. In this city they sell them to others, who distribute them to various customers through the length and breadth of the world. It is a great centre of commerce, with many cities and towns subordinate to it, and the capital of the kingdom. Its king is named Ruemedan Ahmad. The climate is torrid, owing to the heat of the sun, and unhealthy. If a merchant dies here, the king confiscates all his possessions.

In this country they make date wine with the addition of various spices, and very good it is. When it is drunk by men who are not used to it, it loosens the bowels and makes a thorough purge; but after that it does them good and makes them put on flesh. The natives do not eat our sort of food, because a diet of wheaten bread and meat would make them ill. To keep well they eat dates and salt fish, that is, tunny, and also onions; and on this diet they thrive.

Their ships are very bad, and many of them founder, because they are not fastened with iron nails but stitched together with thread made of coconut husks. They soak the husk till it assumes the texture of horsehair; then they make it into threads and stitch their ships. It is not spoilt by the salt water, but lasts remarkably well. The ships have one mast, one sail, and one rudder and are not decked; when they have loaded them, they cover the cargo with skins, and on top of these they put the horses which they ship to India for sale. They have no iron for nails;* so they employ wooden pegs and stitch with thread. This makes it a risky undertaking to sail in these ships. And you can take my word that many of them sink, because the Indian Ocean is often very stormy.

The people here are black and worship Mahomet. In summer they do not stay in the cities, or they would all die of the heat; but they go out to their gardens, where there are rivers and sheets of water. Here they build arbours of hurdles, resting at one end on the bank and at the other on piles driven in below the water, and covered with foliage to fend off the sun. Even so, they would not escape, were it

---

* Z offers the alternative explanation that the local wood is hard but brittle, like earthenware, so that it cracks when a nail is driven in.

not for one thing of which I will tell you. It is a fact that several times in the summer there comes a wind from the direction of the sandy wastes that lie around this plain, a wind so overpoweringly hot that it would be deadly if it did not happen that, as soon as men are aware of its approach, they plunge neck-deep into the water and so escape from the heat. To show just how hot this wind can be, Messer Marco gives the following account of something that happened when he was in these parts. The king of Kerman, not having received the tribute due to him from the lord of Hormuz, resolved to seize his opportunity when the men of Hormuz were living outside the city in the open. He accordingly mustered 1,600 horse and 5,000 foot-soldiers and sent them across the plain of Rudbar to make a surprise attack. One day, having failed through faulty guidance to reach the place appointed for the night's halt, they bivouacked in a wood not far from Hormuz. Next morning, when they were on the point of setting out, the hot wind came down on them and stifled them all, so that not one survived to carry back the news to their lord. The men of Hormuz, hearing of this, went out to bury the corpses, so that they should not infect the air. When they gripped them by the arms to drag them to the graves, they were so parched by the tremendous heat that the arms came loose from the trunk, so that there was nothing for it but to dig the graves beside the corpses and heave them in.

In this district they sow their wheat and barley and other grains in November, and they have got in all their harvest before the end of March. And so with all their fruits: by March they are ripened and done with. After that you will find no vegetation anywhere except date-palms, which last till May. This is due to the great heat, which withers up everything.

Another feature of the ships here is that they are not caulked with pitch but anointed with a sort of fish oil.

Let me tell you next that when a man has died here, or a woman, they make a great to-do about mourning. Gentlewomen mourn their dead fully four years after death, at least once a day. They assemble with their kinsfolk and neighbours and give themselves up to loud wailing and keening and lamenting the dead. Since deaths are frequent, they are never done with mourning. There are even women among them who specialize in lamentation and are daily on hire to bewail the lost ones of other men and women.

So much for this city. We shall not touch on India at this point; for I will deal with it later at the appropriate time and place. Now I will turn back towards the north to speak of the countries in that quarter. We shall return by another route to the city of Kerman of which I have spoken, because there is no way of going to these countries except from this city. And you must understand that king Ruemedan Ahmad, whom we have just left, is a vassal of the king of Kerman.

The return journey from Hormuz to Kerman passes through a fine plain amply stocked with foodstuffs. It is blessed with natural hot baths. Partridges are plentiful and very cheap. Fruit trees and date-palms abound. The wheaten bread here is so bitter that no one can eat it unless he is accustomed to it. This is due to the bitterness of the water. The baths, of which I have spoken above, are formed from springs of very hot water; they are good for many ailments, especially affections of the skin.

Now let me start my account of the countries lying to the north. When the traveller leaves Kerman, he rides for seven days along a very uninviting road through wild and barren country. I will tell you what it is like. For three days he finds no running water, or as good as none. What water there is is brackish and green as meadow grass and so bitter that no one could bear to drink it. Drink one drop of it and you void your bowels ten times over. It is the same with the salt that is made from it: if you eat one little granule, it produces violent diarrhoea. So the men who travel this way carry water with them to drink. Animals will drink the brackish water under stress of extreme thirst, and you may take my word that it afflicts them violently with diarrhoea. And in all these three days' journey there is no habitation; it is all a desolate and arid waste. There are no beasts at all, because they could find nothing to eat.

At the end of this time the traveller arrives at a stream of fresh water which runs underground. In certain places there are caverns carved and scooped out by the action of the stream; through these it can be seen to flow, and then suddenly it plunges underground. Nevertheless, there is abundance of water, by whose banks wayfarers wearied by the hardships of the desert behind them may rest and refresh themselves with their beasts.

Then begins another stretch of four days' duration, just as desolate and arid, where the water is just as bitter and there are no trees or beasts, excepting only asses. At the end of this stretch we leave the kingdom of Kerman and reach the city of Kuh-banan.

This is a large city. Its inhabitants worship Mahomet. There is iron and steel and *ondanique* in plenty, and they make steel mirrors of large size and excellent quality. They also make *tutty*, which is a very good salve for the eyes, and *spodium*. Let me explain how they do it. They take a vein of earth that is suited for the purpose and heap it in a furnace with a blazing fire, above which is an iron grid. The fumes and vapour given off by this earth and trapped by the grid constitute *tutty*; the residue remaining in the fire is *spodium*. Now let us continue our journey.

When the traveller leaves Kuh-banan he goes for fully eight days through a desert in which there is utter drought and neither fruit nor trees and where the water is as bitter and as bad as before. He is obliged to carry with him all that he needs to eat and drink, except the water that the beasts drink very reluctantly—they may be tempted to drink by mixing flour with it. After these eight days he reaches a province called Tun and Kain, where there are cities and towns in plenty. It is situated on the northern borders of Persia. There is an immense plain here, in which stands the Solitary Tree, which the Christians call the Dry Tree. Let me describe it to you. It is of great size and girth. Its leaves are green on one side, white on the other. It produces husks like chestnut husks; but there is nothing in them. Its wood is hard and yellow like box-wood. And there are no trees near it for more than 100 miles, except in one direction where there are trees ten miles away. It is here, according to the people of the country, that the battle was fought between Alexander and Darius. The villages and towns hereabouts enjoy great abundance of good things of every sort; for the climate is admirably tempered, neither too hot nor too cold. The people all worship Mahomet. They are a good-looking race and the women in particular are of outstanding beauty.

Now let us proceed farther, and I will tell you about a country called Mulehet.

Mulehet, which means 'heretics' according to the law of the Saracens, is the country where the Sheikh of the Mountain used to live in days gone by. I will tell you his story just as I, Messer Marco, have heard it told by many people.

The Sheikh was called in their language Alaodin. He had had made in a valley between two mountains the biggest and most beautiful garden that was ever seen, planted with all the finest fruits in the world and containing the most splendid mansions and palaces that were ever seen, ornamented with gold and with likenesses of all that is beautiful on earth, and also four conduits, one flowing with wine, one with milk, one with honey, and one with water. There were fair ladies there and damsels, the loveliest in the world, unrivalled at playing every sort of instrument and at singing and dancing. And he gave his men to understand that this garden was Paradise. That is why he had made it after this pattern, because Mahomet assured the Saracens that those who go to Paradise will have beautiful women to their hearts' content to do their bidding and will find there rivers of wine and milk and honey and water. So he had had this garden made like the Paradise that Mahomet promised to the Saracens, and the Saracens of this country believed that it really was Paradise. No one ever entered the garden except those whom he wished to make Assassins. At the entrance stood a castle so strong that it need fear no man in the world, and there was no other way in except through this castle. The Sheikh kept with him at his court all the youths of the country from twelve years old to twenty, all, that is, who shaped well as men at arms. These youths knew well by hearsay that Mahomet their prophet had declared Paradise to be made in such a fashion as I have described, and so they accepted it as truth. Now mark what follows. He used to put some of these youths in this Paradise, four at a time, or ten, or twenty, according as he wished. And this is how he did it. He would give them draughts that sent them to sleep on the spot. Then he had them taken and put in the garden, where they were wakened. When they awoke and found themselves in there and saw all the things I have told you of, they believed they were really in Paradise. And the ladies and damsels stayed with them all the time, singing and making music for their delight and ministering to all their desires. So these youths had all they could wish for and asked nothing better than to remain there.

Now the Sheikh held his court with great splendour and magnificence and bore himself most nobly and convinced the simple mountain folk round about that he was a prophet; and they believed it to be the truth. And when he wanted emissaries to send on some mission of murder, he would administer the drug to as many as he pleased; and while they slept he had them carried into his palace. When these youths awoke and found themselves in the castle within the palace, they were amazed and by no means glad, for the Paradise from which they had come was not a place that they would ever willingly have left. They went forthwith to the Sheikh and humbled themselves before him, as men who believed that he was a great prophet. When he asked them whence they came, they would answer that they came from Paradise, and that this was in truth the Paradise of which Mahomet had told their ancestors; and they would tell their listeners all that they had found there. And the others who heard this and had not been there were filled with a great longing to go to this Paradise; they longed for death so that they might go there, and looked forward eagerly to the day of their going.

When the Sheikh desired the death of some great lord, he would first try an experiment to find out which of his Assassins were the best. He would send some off on a mission in the neighbourhood at no great distance with orders to kill such and such a man. They went without demur and did the bidding of their lord. Then, when they had killed the man, they returned to court—those of them that escaped, for some were caught and put to death. When they had returned to their lord and told him that they had faithfully performed their task, the Sheikh would make a great feast in their honour. And he knew very well which of them had displayed the greatest zeal, because after each he had sent others of his men as spies to report which was the most daring and the best hand at murdering. Then, in order to bring about the death of the lord or other man which he desired, he would take some of these Assassins of his and send them wherever he might wish, telling them that he was minded to dispatch them to Paradise: they were to go accordingly and kill such and such a man; if they died on their mission, they would go there all the sooner. Those who received such a command obeyed it with a right good will, more readily than anything else they might have been called on to do. Away they went and did all that they were commanded. Thus it happened that no one ever escaped when the Sheikh of the Mountain desired his death. And I can assure you that many kings and many lords paid tribute to him and cultivated his friendship for fear that he might bring about their death. This happened because at that time the nations were not united in their allegiance, but torn by conflicting loyalties and purposes.

I have told you about the Sheikh of the Mountain and his Assassins. Now let me tell you how he was overthrown and by whom. But first I will tell you something else about him that I had omitted. You must know that this Sheikh had chosen as his subordinates two other

Sheikhs, who adopted all his practices and customs. One of these he dispatched to the neighbourhood of Damascus, the other to Kurdistan. Let us now turn to the subject of his overthrow. It happened about the year of Our Lord's nativity 1262 that Hulagu, lord of the Tartars of the Levant, knowing of all the evil deeds this Sheikh was doing, made up his mind that he should be crushed. So he appointed some of his barons and sent them against this castle with a powerful force. For fully three years they besieged the castle without being able to take it. Indeed they never would have taken it so long as the besieged had anything to eat, but at the end of the three years they had no food left. So they were taken, and the Sheikh, Alaodin, was put to death with all his men. And from that time to this there have been no more of these Sheikhs and no more Assassins; but with him there came an end to all the power that had been wielded of old by the Sheikhs of the Mountain and all the evil they had done.

Let us now change the subject.

the road to cathay

WHEN THE TRAVELLER LEAVES THIS CASTLE, HE RIDES THROUGH a fine plain and a fine valley and along fine hillsides, where there is rich herbage, fine pasturage, fruit in plenty, and no lack of anything. Armies are prone to loiter here because of the abundance of supplies. This country extends for fully six days' journey and contains villages and towns whose inhabitants worship Mahomet. Sometimes the traveller encounters stretches of desert fifty or sixty miles in extent, in which there is no water to be found. Men must carry it with them; the beasts go without drinking till they have come out of the desert into the places where they find water.

After these six days he reaches a city called Shibarghan, plentifully stocked with everything needful. Here are found the best melons in the world in very great quantity, which they dry in this manner: they cut them all round in slices like strips of leather, then put them in the sun to dry, when they become sweeter than honey. And you must know that they are an article of commerce and find a ready sale through all the country round. There are also vast quantities of game, both beasts and birds. We will now leave this city and tell you of another whose name is Balkh.

Balkh is a splendid city of great size. It used to be much greater and more splendid; but the Tartars and other invaders have sacked and ravaged it. For I can tell you that there used to be many fine palaces and mansions of marble, which are still to be seen, but shattered now and in ruins. It was in this city, according to local report, that Alexander took to wife the daughter of Darius. The inhabitants worship Mahomet. And you should know that this city, which marks the limit of the Tartar lordship of the Levant, stands on the east-north-easterly frontier of Persia.

Leaving this city, we shall begin our account of another land called Talikhan. When the traveller leaves Balkh, he rides fully twelve days' journey towards the east-north-east without finding any habitation, because the people have all fled to mountain fastnesses for fear of the bandits and invaders who used to molest them. The country has water enough and game enough, and also lions. Food is not to be found in all this twelve days' journey; so those who pass this way must carry food with them for their horses as well as for themselves.

At the end of these twelve days the traveller finds a town called Talikhan, where there is a great corn-market. It stands in very fine country, and the mountains to the south of it are very large and are all made of salt. Men come from all the country round, for thirty days' journey, to fetch this salt, which is the best in the world. It is so hard that it cannot be got except with a stout iron pick. And I assure you that it is so plentiful that it would suffice for all the world to the end of time. There are also mountains abounding in almonds and pistachios, which are marketed on a big scale.

Leaving this city, the traveller proceeds for three days towards the east-north-east, finding fine country all the way, thickly peopled and rich in fruits, grain, and vines. The inhabitants worship Mahomet. They are an ill-conditioned and murderous folk. They devote a great deal of their time to tippling; for they have an excellent boiled wine, to which they are much addicted. They wear nothing on the head but a cord ten palms in length, which they wind round it. They are very good huntsmen and catch any amount of game. They wear no clothes but the skins of the beasts they catch, which they cure and make into clothing and footwear. They all know how to cure the skins of these beasts.

At the end of the three days' journey lies a city called Ishkasham, which is ruled by a count; his other cities and towns are in the mountains. Through the midst of this city flows a river of considerable size. In this district there are a lot of porcupines. When hunters set their dogs on them in hopes of a kill, the porcupines curl up and then shoot out the quills with which their backs and flanks are armed and so wound the dogs in several places.

This city is in a big province of the same name, which has a language of its own. The countryfolk, who are herdsmen, live among the mountains, where they provide themselves with fine and spacious abodes; these are caves, which are easily made because the mountains are of earth.

When he leaves this city, the traveller goes three days' journey without finding habitation or food or drink; he must take his own provisions with him, but there is enough grass for horses. After this he reaches the province of Badakhshan which I will describe to you.

Badakhshan or Balashan is a country whose inhabitants worship Mahomet and have a language of their own. It is a large kingdom, twelve days' journey in length, ruled by hereditary kings of a lineage descended from King Alexander and the daughter of Darius, the Great King of Persia. In honour of Alexander the Great, all its kings still bear the title Zulkarnein, the Saracen equivalent of our name Alexander.

In this country originate the precious stones called balass rubies, of great beauty and value. They are dug out of rocks among the mountains by tunnelling to great depths, as is done by miners working a vein of silver. They are found in one particular mountain called Sighinan. And I would have you know that they are mined only for the king and by his orders; no one else could go to the mountain and dig for these gems without incurring instant death, and it is forbidden under pain of death and forfeiture to export them out of the kingdom. The king sends them by his own men to other kings and princes and great lords, to some as tribute, to others as a token of amity; and some he barters for gold and silver. This he does so that these balass rubies may retain their present rarity and value. If he let other men mine them and export them throughout the world, there would be so many of them on the market that the price would fall and they would cease to be so precious. That is why he has imposed such a heavy penalty on anyone exporting them without authority.

And it is a fact that in this same country, in another mountain, are found the stones from which is made lapis lazuli, of the finest quality in the world. These stones originate among the mountains as a vein like the veins of other minerals. There are also mountains here in which are found veins yielding silver, copper, and lead in great abundance.

This district, and the whole country, is very cold. You should know that very good horses are bred here. They are great runners and are not shod with iron, though they are in constant use on mountain trails. There used to be horses in this country that were directly descended from Alexander's horse Bucephalus out of mares that had conceived from him and they were all born like him with a horn on the forehead. This breed was entirely in the possession of one of the king's uncles, who, because he refused to let the king have any, was put to death by him. Thereupon his wife, to avenge her husband's death, destroyed the whole breed, and so it became extinct. These mountains are also the home of saker falcons—fine birds and good fliers—and of lanner falcons. They abound in game, both beast and bird, and in wild sheep. The sheep sometimes roam in flocks of four to six hundred; and, however many of them are taken, their numbers never grow less. There is good wheat here, and barley without a husk. There is no olive oil, but oil is made of sesame and nuts.

This kingdom has many narrow passes and natural fortresses, so that the inhabitants are not afraid of any invader breaking in to molest them. Their cities and towns are built on mountain tops, or sites of great natural strength. It is a characteristic of these mountains that they are of immense height, so that for a man to climb from the bottom to the top is a full day's journey, from dawn till dusk. On the top are wide plateaux, with a lush growth of grass and trees and copious springs of the purest water, which pour down over the crags like rivers into the valley below. In these streams are found trout and other choice fish. On the mountain tops the air is so pure and so salubrious that if a man living in the cities and houses built in the adjoining valleys falls sick of a fever, whether tertian, quartan, or hectic, he has only to go up into the mountains, and a few days' rest will banish the malady and restore him to health. Messer Marco vouches for this from his own experience.* Two or three of the mountains consist largely of sulphur, and springs of sulphurous water issue from them.

The people here are good archers and keen huntsmen and most of them wear costumes of skin, because they are very short of cloth. The ladies of the nobility and gentry wear trousers, such as I will describe to you. There are some ladies who in one pair of trousers or breeches put anything up to a hundred ells of cotton cloth, folded in pleats. This is to give the impression that they have plump hips, because their menfolk delight in plumpness.

Ten days' journey south of Badakhshan is a country called Pashai. The inhabitants, who have brown skins and speak a language of their own, are idolaters. They are adepts in enchantment and diabolic arts. The men wear ear-rings and brooches of gold and silver and pearls and precious stones in profusion. They are very crafty folk and artful in their own way. The climate is very hot. The stock diet is flesh and rice.

* According to R, he was ill in these parts for a year (perhaps since his stay at Hormuz), but recovered immediately after acting on the advice to go up into the mountains.

So much for Pashai. Let us deal next with another country, distant some seven days' journey to the south-east, whose name is Kashmir.

The people of Kashmir are also idolaters, speaking a language of their own. Their knowledge of devilish enchantments is something marvellous. They make their idols speak. They change the weather by enchantment and bring on thick darkness. They accomplish such marvels by magic and craft that no one who has not seen them could believe them. I may say that they are the past masters of idolatry and it is from them that idols are derived.

From this country there is a route leading to the Indian Sea. The inhabitants are brown-skinned and thin; the women are very beautiful, with such beauty as goes with a brown skin. Their diet is flesh and rice. They enjoy a temperate climate, without extremes of heat and cold. They have cities and towns in plenty, as well as forests and deserts and fastnesses so strong that they have no fear of any foe. They maintain their independence under their own kings, who are the upholders of justice. They have hermits according to their own usage, who dwell in their hermitages, practising strict abstinence in eating and drinking and avoidance of all unchastity and taking the utmost pains to commit no sin that is contrary to their law. They are accounted very holy by their own people, and I assure you that they live to a great age; and this avoidance of sin is all exercised for love of their idols. They also have abbeys and monasteries in plenty of their own faith, where the brethren live an austere life and wear tonsures like Dominican and Franciscan friars. The men of this country do not kill animals or shed blood; but certain Saracens who live intermingled with them kill their animals to provide them with food. The coral that is exported from our country for sale is sold more here than anywhere else.

We shall now leave this district without going any farther, because that would mean entering India, which I do not wish to do at present; on our return journey we shall tell you all about India in due order. We shall therefore retrace our steps as far as the province of Badakhshan, because there is no other route by which we can proceed on our way.

When the traveller leaves Badakhshan, he goes twelve days' journey east-north-east up a river valley belonging to the brother of the lord of Badakhshan, where there are towns and homesteads in plenty, peopled by a warlike race who worship Mahomet. After these twelve days he reaches a country called Wakhan of no great size, for it is three days' journey across every way. The people, who worship Mahomet and speak a language of their own, are doughty warriors. They have no ruler except one whom they call *nona*, that is to say in our language 'count', and are subject to the lord of Badakhshan. They have wild beasts in plenty and game of all sorts for the chase.

When the traveller leaves this place, he goes three days' journey towards the north-east, through mountains all the time, climbing so high that this is said to be the highest place in the world. And when he is in this high place, he finds a plain between two mountains, with a lake from which flows a very fine river. Here is the best pasturage in the world; for a lean beast grows fat here in ten days. Wild game of every sort abounds. There are great quantities of wild sheep of huge size. Their horns grow to as much as six palms in length and are never less than three or four. From these horns the shepherds make big bowls from which they feed, and also fences to keep in their flocks. There are also innumerable wolves, which devour many of the wild rams. The horns and bones of the sheep are found in such numbers that men build cairns of them beside the tracks to serve as landmarks to travellers in the snowy season.

This plain, whose name is Pamir, extends fully twelve days' journey. In all these twelve days there is no habitation or shelter, but travellers must take their provisions with them. No birds fly here because of the height and the cold. And I assure you that, because of this great cold, fire is not so bright here nor of the same colour as elsewhere, and food does not cook well.

Now let us pursue our course towards the north-east and east. At the end of this twelve days' journey, the traveller must ride fully forty days more east-north-east, always over mountains and along hill-sides and gorges, traversing many rivers and many deserts. And in all this journey he finds no habitation or shelter, but must carry his stock of provisions. This country is called Belor. The inhabitants live very high up in the mountains. They are idolaters and utter savages, living entirely by the chase and dressed in the skins of beasts. They are out and out bad.

We shall now leave this country and tell you of the province of Kashgar, which lies towards the east-north-east.

Kashgar was once a kingdom, but now it is subject to the Great Khan. It has villages and towns in plenty. The biggest city, and the most splendid, is Kashgar. The inhabitants live by trade and industry. They have very fine orchards and vineyards and flourishing estates. Cotton grows here in plenty, besides flax and hemp. The soil is fruitful and productive of all the means of life. This country is the starting-point from which many merchants set out to market their wares all over the world. The folk here are very close-fisted and live very poorly, neither eating well nor drinking well. There are some Nestorian Christians in this country, having their own church and observing their own religion. The inhabitants have a language of their own. The province is five days' journey in extent.

And now to speak of Samarkand, a very large and splendid city lying towards the north-west. It is inhabited by Christians and Saracens. They are subject to the nephew of the Great Khan,* who is no friend of his but is often at enmity with him. Let me tell you of a great miracle that occurred in this city.

It happened not long ago that Chaghatai, who was a brother of the Great Khan and lord of this country and many others, became a Christian. When the Christians of Samarkand saw that their lord was a Christian, they were overjoyed. They built a big church in the city to the honour of St John the Baptist and called by his name. And to make the base of the column which stood in the centre of the church and supported the roof they took a very beautiful stone belonging to Saracens. After Chaghatai's death, the Saracens, who had always been very resentful about this stone that stood in the Christian church, resolved to take it by force. And this they could easily have done; for they were ten times as many as the Christians. Then some of the leading Saracens went to the church of St John and told the Christians there that they wanted this stone, which had once belonged to them. The Christians promised to give them all they wanted if they would leave the stone, because its removal would do irreparable damage to the church. The Saracens declared that they did not want gold or treasure, but would have the stone at all costs. What need of more words? The government was now in the hands of the Great Khan's nephew; and he ordered the Christians to hand over the stone to the Saracens within two days. When they received this order they were greatly perplexed and did not know what to do. And then the miracle happened. You must know that, when morning came on the day on which the stone was to be handed over, the

* I.e. Kaidu (see below, p. 267).

column that rested on the stone rose up, by the will of our Lord Jesus Christ, to a height of fully three palms and stayed there as firmly supported as if the stone had still been underneath. And from that day onwards the column has remained in this position, and there it still is. And this was, and still is, accounted one of the greatest miracles that have happened in the world.

Let us turn next to the province of Yarkand, five days' journey in extent. The inhabitants follow the law of Mahomet, and there are also some Nestorian Christians. They are subject to the Great Khan's nephew, of whom I have already spoken. It is amply stocked with the means of life, especially cotton.* But, since there is nothing here worth mentioning in our book, we shall pass on to Khotan, which lies towards the east-north-east.

Khotan is a province eight days' journey in extent, which is subject to the Great Khan. The inhabitants all worship Mahomet. It has cities and towns in plenty, of which the most splendid, and the capital of the kingdom, bears the same name as the province, Khotan. It is amply stocked with the means of life. Cotton grows here in plenty.† It has vineyards, estates, and orchards in plenty. The people live by trade and industry; they are not at all war-like.

Passing on from here we come to the province of Pem, five days' journey in extent, towards the east-north-east. Here too the inhabitants worship Mahomet and are subject to the Great Khan. It has villages and towns in plenty. The most splendid city and the capital of the province is called Pem. There are rivers here in which are found stones called jasper and chalcedony in plenty. There is no lack of the means of life. Cotton is plentiful. The inhabitants live by trade and industry.

The following custom is prevalent among them. When a woman's husband leaves her to go on a journey of more than twenty days, then, as soon as he has left, she takes another husband, and this she is fully entitled to do by local usage. And the men, wherever they go, take wives in the same way.

You should know that all the provinces I have described, from Kashgar to Pem and some way beyond, are provinces of Turkestan.

* Z adds that most of the people here have one foot much bigger than the other but can walk perfectly well. R refers in addition to the prevalence of a goitre on the throat, due to a peculiarity of the local water, and speaks simply of swollen legs, without suggesting that one is larger than the other.

† R adds flax, hemp, and corn.

E

I will tell you next of another province of Turkestan, lying east-north-east, which is called Charchan. It used to be a splendid and fruitful country, but it has been much devastated by the Tartars. The inhabitants worship Mahomet. There are villages and towns in plenty, and the chief city of the kingdom is Charchan. There are rivers producing jasper and chalcedony, which are exported for sale in Cathay and bring in a good profit; for they are plentiful and of good quality.

All this province is a tract of sand; and so is the country from Khotan to Pem and from Pem to here. There are many springs of bad and bitter water, though in some places the water is good and sweet. When it happens that an army passes through the country, if it is a hostile one, the people take flight with their wives and children and their beasts two or three days' journey into the sandy wastes to places where they know that there is water and they can live with their beasts. And I assure you that no one can tell which way they have gone, because the wind covers their tracks with sand, so that there is nothing to show where they have been, but the country looks as if it had never been traversed by man or beast. That is how they escape from their enemies. But, if it happens that a friendly army passes that way, they merely drive off their beasts, because they do not want to have them seized and eaten; for the armies never pay for what they take. And you should know that, when they harvest their corn, they store it far from any habitation, in certain caves among these wastes, for fear of the armies; and from these stores they bring home what they need month by month.

After leaving Charchan, the road runs for fully five days through sandy wastes, where the water is bad and bitter, except in a few places where it is good and sweet; and there is nothing worth noting in our book. At the end of the five days' journey towards the east-north-east, is a city which stands on the verge of the Great Desert. It is here that men take in provisions for crossing the desert. Let us move on accordingly and proceed with our narrative.

The city I have mentioned, which stands at the point where the traveller enters the Great Desert, is a big city called Lop, and the desert is called the Desert of Lop. The city is subject to the Great Khan, and the inhabitants worship Mahomet. I can tell you that travellers who intend to cross the desert rest in this town for a week to refresh themselves and their beasts. At the end of the week they stock up with a month's provisions for themselves and their beasts. Then they leave the town and enter the desert.

This desert is reported to be so long that it would take a year to go from end to end; and at the narrowest point it takes a month to cross it. It consists entirely of mountains and sand and valleys. There is nothing at all to eat. But I can tell you that after travelling a day and a night you find drinking water—not enough water to supply a large company, but enough for fifty or a hundred men with their beasts. And all the way through the desert you must go for a day and a night before you find water. And I can tell you that in three or four places you find the water bitter and brackish; but at all the other watering-places, that is, twenty-eight in all, the water is good. Beasts and birds there are none, because they find nothing to eat. But I assure you that one thing is found here, and that a very strange one, which I will relate to you.

The truth is this. When a man is riding by night through this desert and something happens to make him loiter and lose touch with his companions, by dropping asleep or for some other reason, and afterwards he wants to rejoin them, then he hears spirits talking in such a way that they seem to be his companions. Sometimes, indeed, they even hail him by name. Often these voices make him stray from the path, so that he never finds it again. And in this way many travellers have been lost and have perished. And sometimes in the night they are conscious of a noise like the clatter of a great cavalcade of riders away from the road; and, believing that these are some of their own company, they go where they hear the noise and, when day breaks, find they are victims of an illusion and in an awkward plight. And there are some who, in crossing this desert, have seen a host of men coming towards them and, suspecting that they were robbers, have taken flight; so, having left the beaten track and not knowing how to return to it, they have gone hopelessly astray. Yes, and even by daylight men hear these spirit voices, and often you fancy you are listening to the strains of many instruments, especially drums, and the clash of arms. For this reason bands of travellers make a point of keeping very close together. Before they go to sleep they set up a sign pointing in the direction in which they have to travel. And round the necks of all their beasts they fasten little bells, so that by listening to the sound they may prevent them from straying off the path.

That is how they cross the desert, with all the discomfort of which

apelons labielec. et vous dirai comment il e
fait. Il est moult grant et gros, et ses escorches
sont dune part vert, et de lautre blanche et
haut, aussi comme chastains mais il est
mut dedenz, il est iaunes comme bois et son
ce naoul arbre pres aumains de .C. aoilles.
mais que dune part ya arbres bien a .x. oub
les et iluec dient ceulz de cele contree que la sil
la saoule dalixandre et de daire les oileo et leo
chastiaus oint grant habondance de toutes
choses et dioelles. Car le pays est trop bien co
plexionez nechaut ne froit. les greus aoueret
tout mahommet il ya moult de oileo gens, et
proprement les femes sont outre mesure oelle
ellec et de ce nous partirons. et vous conte
rons dune contree qui est appele mileete la ou
le oiel de la montaigne souloit demourer a
nec les hacacis si comme vous ourez

Ci dit le .xl. chapitre du oiel de la montaigne

Mileette est une
contree ou le oiel de le montaigne sou
loit demourer anciennement. et vaut adire
mileette en francois dieu terrien. Or vous co
terons de son afaire selonc ce meismes que
mesire marc pol oi conter apluseurs homes
des contrees. li oiex estoit apelez en leur lan
gage aloaidi il auoit fait fermer en contre ij.
montaignes en une valee le plus grant iar
dinc et le plus bel qui onques fust veus plan
de touz les fruis du monde et sanoit les plus
belles maisons et palais que onques fussent
veu touz dorez et pour trais de toutes belles
choses moult bien et si auoit conduis qui
couroient de oin et tel de lait et tel dmiel et
tel dsaue et plain de dames et de damoiseles
les plus belles du monde qui sauoient souner
de touz psteumens et chantoient et dancoient
moult bien. et ce estoit .i. delit. et lor faisoit
entendant le oiel que ycel iardin estoit pa
radis. Et pour ce lauoit il fait de tel manie
re que mahommet dist que leur paradiz sera
biaus iardins et plains de conduis de oin
et de lait et de miel et dsaue. et plain de belles
femmes aus lit de chascun en tele maniere
conobn du oiel. et pource auoient il que ce soit

paradis en cel iardinc ne entroit nus fors
ceulz de qui il oouloit faire ses hacacis. il auoit
.i. chastiau aleutre de cel iardin si fort que tout
le mont ne le porroit prendre et ne port on en
tirer ou dit iardin que par iluec. il tenoit en sa
court iouenes de xij. aus de sa contree qui auoi
ent oulie de destriers homme dames et leur disoit
coment mahommet disoit que leur paradiz es
toit de la maniere que ie vous aidit. et ceulz le
creoient comme sairazin qui estoient et les
faisoit mectre dedenz cel iardin a .x. et a vj. et
a iiij. en sanble en ceste maniere. Car il leur
faisoit bouure .i. beuerage des qui se dormoient
maintenant puis les faisoit prendre et me
tre en son iardin. et la les ueilloient et se tro
uoient la. Ci dit le xlj. Chapitre. Coment
li oiex fait par fais ses hacacis

Et quant il se treuuent laiens et
se voient en si biau lieu il croie
estre en paradis uraient les da
mes et les damoiseles les soula
cent touziours alour volente si
que ces iones ont ce quil veulent. Et iamais
alour volente nenstroit de laiens, le seignour
oiel que ie vous aidit si tient sa court si noble
et si grant et fait acroire a cele simple gent q
il est encor .i. grant pphete. et aussi le croient
tout certainement. Et quant il veult enuoier
aucun de ses hacacis en aucun lieu, si li fait
donner le beurage aaucun de ceulz du iardin et
le fait porter en son palais. Et quant il est esoeil
liez si se treuue hors de son paradis en cele chastel

you have heard. Now that I have told you all about it, let us take our leave of it and speak of the provinces you find when you emerge from it.

When the traveller has ridden for these thirty days of which I have spoken across the desert, he reaches a city called Sa-chau, lying towards the east-north-east, which is subject to the Great Khan. It lies in a province called Tangut, whose inhabitants are all idolaters, except that there are some Turks who are Nestorian Christians and also some Saracens. The idolaters speak a language of their own. They do not live by trade, but on the profit of the grain which they harvest from the soil. They have many abbeys and monasteries, all full of idols of various forms to which they make sacrifices and do great honour and reverence.

You must know that all the men here who have children rear a sheep in honour of the idols; and at the new year, or on the feast of their particular idol, those who have reared the sheep bring it with their children before the idol, and both they and the children perform a solemn act of devotion. This done, they have the sheep cooked whole. Then they bring it before the idol with great reverence and leave it there till they have recited their service and their prayer to the idol to save their children; and they say that the idols eat the substance of the flesh.* When they have done this, they take the flesh that has lain before the idol and carry it home, or wherever else they may wish, and send for their kinsfolk and eat it with great reverence and great festivity. When they have eaten the flesh, they collect the bones and preserve them very carefully in a chest. The priests of the idols, however, have the head, feet, entrails and fleece and part of the flesh.

You should know also, what is true of all the idolaters in the world, that when they die their bodies are cremated. When the dead man is being carried from his house to the place where he is to be cremated, then at some point on the route his kinsfolk have erected in the middle of the road a wooden house draped with silk and cloth of gold. On arriving in front of this house, thus adorned, the cortège halts; and the mourners fling down wine and food in plenty before the dead. This they do because they say that he will be received with like honour in the next world. When he is brought to the place where he is to be cremated, his kindred provide images cut out of paper repre-

* Z adds: 'or suck up its savour'.

70

senting horses and camels and pieces of money as big as bezants;*
and all these they burn with the body. And they say that in the next
world the dead will have as many slaves and beasts and coins as the
paper images that are burnt. Lastly, let me tell you that when a body
is being taken to the pyre, all the instruments in the land go in front
of it making music. And all this is done in proportion to the rank of
the deceased and the requirements of his station.

Now let me tell you something else. When one of these idolaters
is dead, they send for their astrologer and tell him the nativity of the
deceased, that is, the month, day, and hour of his birth. Armed with
this knowledge, the astrologer makes his divination by diabolical art
and afterwards declares on what day the corpse must be cremated. In
some cases he prescribes a delay of a week before cremation, in
others of a month, in others of six months. Then the relatives
must keep the body in their house for this length of time; for they
would never think of burning it till the diviners tell them that the
time has come. While the body remains unburnt in the house, they
preserve it in this manner. They take a coffin of boards of the thickness of a palm firmly joined together and all splendidly painted, and
put the body inside, embalmed with camphor and other spices.
Then they stop the chinks in the coffin with pitch and lime, so that it
does not cause a stench in the house, and cover it with silken shrouds.
Meanwhile, so long as the body remains in the house, the relatives,
that is the inhabitants of the house, lay a table every day for the
deceased and serve food and drink for him just as if he were alive;
they set it in front of the coffin and leave it long enough to be eaten,
and say that the soul has eaten some of this food. This is how they
keep it till the day when they take it away for cremation. And here
is another thing that they do. It often happens that these diviners
tell the relatives that it is not auspicious to carry the corpse out
of the house by way of the door, on the pretext that some
star or other power is adverse to this door. Then the relatives
have the body carried out by another door or even, on occasion,
have the walls broken open and the body carried out through the
breach.

All this they do for fear of offending the spirits of the dead. And if
it happens that some member of the household meets with some
mischance or dies, the astrologers say that the spirit of the dead has
done this because he was not carried out during the ascendancy of the

* Z adds that clothing is burnt with the body.

planet under which he was born, or of one not contrary to it, or on the proper side of the house.

So much, then, for this matter. Now I will tell you of some other cities, which lie towards the north-west near the edge of this desert.

The province of Kamul, which used to be a kingdom, contains towns and villages in plenty, the chief town being also called Kamul. The province lies between two deserts, the Great Desert and a small one three days' journey in extent. The inhabitants are all idolaters and speak a language of their own. They live on the produce of the soil; for they have a superfluity of foodstuffs and beverages, which they sell to travellers who pass that way. They are a very gay folk, who give no thought to anything but making music, singing and dancing, and reading and writing according to their own usage, and taking great delight in the pleasures of the body. I give you my word that if a stranger comes to a house here to seek hospitality he receives a very warm welcome. The host bids his wife do everything that the guest wishes. Then he leaves the house and goes about his own business and stays away two or three days.* Meanwhile the guest stays with his wife in the house and does what he will with her, lying with her in one bed just as if she were his own wife; and they lead a gay life together. All the men of this city and province are thus cuckolded by their wives; but they are not the least ashamed of it. And the women are beautiful and vivacious and always ready to oblige.

Now it happened during the reign of Mongu Khan, lord of the Tartars, that he was informed of this custom that prevailed among the men of Kamul of giving their wives in adultery to outsiders. Mongu thereupon commanded them under heavy penalties to desist from this form of hospitality. When they received this command, they were greatly distressed; but for three years they reluctantly obeyed. Then they held a council and talked the matter over, and this is what they did. They took a rich gift and sent it to Mongu and entreated him to let them use their wives according to the traditions of their ancestors; for their ancestors had declared that by the pleasure they gave to guests with their wives and goods they won the favour of their idols and multiplied the yield of their crops and their tillage. When Mongu Khan heard this he said: 'Since you desire your own shame, you may have it.' So he let them have their way. And I can

* R adds that he sends in provisions to meet all the guest's needs, but expects payment.

72

assure you that since then they have always upheld this tradition and uphold it still.

Another province, also subject to the Great Khan, is Uighuristan. It is a large province containing many cities and towns. The chief city, which is called Kara Khoja, has many other cities and towns dependent on it. The people are idolaters, but they include many Christians of the Nestorian sect and some Saracens. The Christians often intermarry with the idolaters. They declare that the king who originally ruled over them was not born of human stock, but arose from a sort of tuber generated by the sap of trees, which we call *esca*; and from him all the others descended. The idolaters are very well versed in their own laws and traditions and are keen students of the liberal arts. The land produces grain and excellent wine. But in winter the cold here is more intense than is known in any other part of the world.

Another province on the edge of the desert towards the north-north-east is Ghinghintalas, sixteen days in extent, which is also subject to the Great Khan. It has cities and towns in plenty. The inhabitants consist of three groups, idolaters, Mahometans, and Nestorian Christians.

Towards the northern boundary of this province is a mountain with a rich vein of steel and *ondanique*. In this same mountain occurs a vein from which is produced salamander. You must understand that this is not a beast as is commonly asserted; but its real nature is such as I will now describe. It is a well known fact that by nature no beast or other animal can live in fire, because every animal is composed of the four elements. For lack of any certain knowledge about salamander, men spoke of it, and still do, as a beast; but this is not true. I will now tell you the real facts. First, let me explain that I had a Turkish companion named Zurficar, a man of great intelligence, who spent three years in this province, in the service of the Great Khan, engaged in the extraction of this salamander and *ondanique* and steel and other products. For the Great Khan regularly appoints governors every three years to govern this province and supervise the salamander industry. My companion told me the true facts and I have also seen them for myself. When the stuff found in this vein of which you have heard has been dug out of the mountain and crumbled into bits, the particles cohere and form fibres like wool. Accordingly, when the stuff has been extracted, it is first dried, then pounded in a large copper mortar and then washed. The residue consists of this fibre of which I have spoken and worthless earth, which is separated from it. Then this wool-like fibre is carefully spun and made into cloths. When the cloths are first made, they are far from white. But they are thrown into the fire and left there for a while; and there they turn as white as snow. And whenever one of these cloths is soiled or discoloured, it is thrown into the fire and left there for a while, and it comes out as white as snow. The account I have given you of the salamander is the truth, and all the other accounts that are put about are lies and fables. Let me tell you finally that one of these cloths is now at Rome; it was sent to the Pope by the Great Khan as a valuable gift, and for this reason the sacred napkin of our lord Jesus Christ was wrapped in it.

Let us now leave this province and turn to others lying towards the east-north-east.

When the traveller leaves the province of which I have spoken, he journeys for ten days east-north-east. And all this way there is no habitation, or none to speak of, and nothing worthy of mention in our book. At the end of the ten days he reaches a province called Su-chau, in which there are cities and towns in plenty, the chief city being also called Su-chau. The inhabitants are Christians and idolaters, subject to the Great Khan. This province, together with the two last-named, forms part of the major province of Tangut. In all the mountains of this region, rhubarb grows in great abundance; it is bought here by merchants, who export it far and wide. Travellers passing this way do not venture to go among these mountains with any beasts except those of the country, because a poisonous herb grows here, which makes beasts that feed on it lose their hoofs; but beasts born in the country recognize this herb and avoid it. The climate of this province is healthy, and the inhabitants are brown-skinned. They live by the produce of the soil and have little dealing with trade.

Let us now pass on to Kan-chau, a large and splendid city in Tangut proper and the capital of the whole province. The inhabitants are idolaters, with some Mahometans. There are also some Christians, who have three fine large churches in the city. The idolaters have many monasteries and abbeys according to their own usage. They have a vast quantity of idols; and I can assure you that some are as much as ten paces in length. Some are of wood, some of earthenware, some of stone, and they are all covered with gold and of excellent workmanship. These huge idols are recumbent, and groups of lesser ones are set round about them and seem to be doing them humble obeisance.

Since I have not told you of the customs of the idolaters, I will do so here.

First, you should know that those idolaters who live under a religious rule lead more virtuous lives than the others. They avoid lechery, but do not regard it as a major sin. Their principle of conduct is that, if a woman makes love to them, they may accept her overtures without sin; but, if they make the first advances, they account that a sin. If they find that any man has had unnatural intercourse with a woman, they condemn him to death. They distinguish lunar cycles as we distinguish the months. There is one such cycle in which for five days all the idolaters in the world kill neither beast nor bird; nor do they eat the flesh of animals killed during these days. And for these five days they live more virtuously than at other times. And some of them, that is the monks, abstain from flesh all their lives out of reverence and piety; but the laity do not observe this rule. They marry anything up to thirty wives, more or fewer according to what each man can afford. The men give their wives a marriage-portion in cattle, slaves, and money proportionate to their means. You should understand that they treat the first wife as having the highest status. Moreover, if the husband finds that one of his wives misbehaves or displeases him, he is free to put her away and do as he likes. Men marry their own cousins and also their fathers' widows. Many things that we regard as grave sins are not sins at all in their eyes; for they live like beasts.

So much, then, for that. Let us now speak of other regions towards the north, after remarking that Messer Niccolò and Messer Maffeo and Messer Marco spent a year in this city, but without any experiences worth recording. So we shall leave it and start on a journey of sixty days towards the north.

When the traveller leaves this city of Kan-chau, he rides for twelve days till he reaches a city called Etzina, which lies on the northern edge of the desert of sand. This is still in the province of Tangut. The inhabitants are idolaters. They have camels and cattle in plenty. The country breeds lanner and saker falcons, and very good ones. The people live by agriculture and stock-rearing; they are not traders.

In this city the traveller must take in a forty days' stock of provisions; for, when he leaves Etzina for the north, he has forty days' journey ahead of him across a desert without house or inn, where nobody lives except among the valleys and mountains in summer. It is a land teeming with wild life, including wild asses, and clothed with pine-woods. Forty days' ride northwards through this desert will bring you to another province; you shall hear which.

We have come now to Karakorum, a city three miles in circumference, surrounded by a strong rampart of earth, because stones are scarce here. This was the first seat of the Tartars when they came out of their country.

I will now tell you all about the Tartars and how they acquired their empire and spread throughout the world.

The fact is that the Tartars used to live farther north, in the region of Chorcha. This was a country of far-stretching plains, with no habitations in the form of cities or towns but with good pasturage, wide rivers, and no lack of water. They were a lordless people, but were actually tributary to a great lord who was called in their language Ung Khan. This was that Prester John, of whose great empire all the world speaks. The Tartars paid him a tribute of one beast in every ten. Now it happened that their population increased greatly. When Prester John saw how their numbers had grown, he realized that they might be a danger to him; so he resolved to divide them among several countries. In order to accomplish this, he sent some of his barons to their land. When the Tartars heard what Prester John meant to do with them, they were so distressed that they departed in a body and went into a desert place towards the north, where he could not trouble them. And they rebelled against his rule and withheld their tribute. And so they continued for some time.

Now it happened in the year of Christ's incarnation 1187 that the Tartars chose a king to reign over them whose name in their language was Chinghiz Khan, a man of great ability and wisdom, a gifted orator and a brilliant soldier. After his election, all the Tartars in the world, dispersed as they were among various foreign countries, came to him and acknowledged his sovereignty. And he exercised it well and honourably. What more shall I tell you? The number of Tartars who rallied round him was past belief. When Chinghiz Khan saw what a following he had, he equipped them with bows and their other customary weapons and embarked on a career of

conquest. And I assure you that they conquered no less than eight provinces.* He did not harm the inhabitants or despoil them of their goods, but led them along with him to conquer other nations. That is how he conquered the great multitude of nations of which you have heard. And those he had conquered, when they saw his good government and gracious bearing, asked nothing better than to join his following. Then, when he had amassed such a multitude of followers that they covered the face of the earth, he made up his mind to conquer a great part of the world.

First, he sent emissaries to Prester John—this was in the year of Christ's nativity 1200—telling him that he wished to marry his daughter. This request met with a very scornful reception. 'Is not Chinghiz Khan ashamed,' cried Prester John, 'to seek my daughter in marriage? Does he not know that he is my vassal and my thrall? Go back to him and tell him that I would sooner commit my daughter to the flames than give her to him as his wife. And tell him that my word to him is that I have good cause to put him to death as a traitor and recreant against his liege lord.' Then he bade the emissaries begone forthwith from his presence and never return. They thereupon departed and went their way till they came to their lord and duly told him all that Prester John had commanded, omitting nothing.

When Chinghiz Khan heard the insulting message that Prester John had sent him, his heart swelled within him to such a pitch that it came near to bursting within his breast. For I assure you that he had all the pride of lordship. After a brief silence he proclaimed, in a voice so loud that every bystander could hear, that he would on no account retain his sovereignty if the insult put upon him by Prester John did not cost its author dearer than any insult had ever yet cost any man. He would soon have occasion to learn whether Chinghiz Khan was his thrall. Thereupon he mustered all his followers and got ready the greatest armament that was ever seen or heard of. He gave Prester John fair warning to defend himself as best he could, because he was coming against him with all his forces. When Prester John knew this for a fact, he made light of it and judged it of no account; for he said that his enemies were men of no prowess. But all the same

* R adds: 'And this was quite natural; for at that time the lands and provinces in these parts were either ruled by popular government or each had its own king and lord, so that lacking mutual union they could not individually resist such a multitude.'

he inwardly resolved to do his utmost to ensure that, if Chinghiz Khan did come, he would be seized and put to an evil death. So he sent out word to summon and equip all his followers, far and wide throughout his dominions. And to such purpose did he exert himself that none has ever heard tell of a greater host. So the two armies were arrayed against each other. What need to make a long tale of it? You may take it for a fact that Chinghiz Khan, with all his followers, entered a wide and pleasant plain called Tenduc, which belonged to Prester John, and there encamped. And I assure you that they were such a multitude that their number was beyond count. There he learnt to his joy that Prester John was coming; for it was a pleasant plain and a spacious one, where a battle could be fought spaciously. So there he eagerly awaited his coming to join battle with him.

At this point the story ceases to speak of Chinghiz Khan and his men; and we shall return to Prester John and his men.

Now the story relates that, when Prester John knew that Chinghiz Khan with all his followers was coming against him, he went against him with all his own followers. On they went till they came to this plain of Tenduc and there they pitched camp at twenty miles' distance from the camp of Chinghiz Khan. And both armies rested so as to be fresh and brisk on the day of battle. So these two great hosts lay on the plain of Tenduc. Then one day Chinghiz Khan summoned to his presence astrologers, Christian and Saracen, and bade them tell him who would win the fight between him and Prester John. The astrologers looked for the truth by their art. The Saracens could not tell it; but the Christians declared it to him plainly. They set before him a wand which they split lengthwise and then put one half on one side and the other on the other, so that no one was holding it. To one half they gave the name Chinghiz Khan, to the other Prester John. Then they said to Chinghiz Khan: 'Sire, observe these wands and note that this half bears your name and the other that of Prester John. Hence, when we have performed our incantation, the one whose wand gains the upper hand will win the battle.' Chinghiz Khan professed himself most anxious to see this and bade them demonstrate it to him as soon as they could. So the Christian astrologers took the psalter and read certain psalms and performed their incantation. Thereupon the wand that bore the name of Chinghiz Khan, without anyone touching it, joined itself on to the other and came to rest above it. And this was seen by all the bystanders. When Chinghiz Khan saw it, he was overjoyed. And, finding that the Christians spoke truth, he treated them ever afterwards with great honour and esteemed them both then and thereafter as truthful men and true prophets.

Two days after this both forces armed themselves and met in stubborn combat. This was the greatest battle that was ever seen. Heavy losses were suffered on both sides; but in the end the fight was won by Chinghiz Khan. In this battle Prester John was killed. And from that day he lost his land, which Chinghiz Khan continued day after day to subdue. And you must know that after this battle Chinghiz Khan reigned a further six years and conquered many towns and many provinces.* But at the end of this time, while attacking a town named Ho-chau, he was wounded in the knee by an arrow, and of this wound he died. This was a great misfortune, since he was a brave and prudent ruler.

Now that I have told you how the Tartars chose their first ruler, namely Chinghiz Khan, and how at the outset they conquered Prester John, I will tell you of their manners and customs.

You must know that after Chinghiz Khan the next ruler was Kuyuk Khan, the third Batu Khan, the fourth Altou Khan,† the fifth Mongu Khan and the sixth Kubilai Khan, who is greater and more powerful than any of the others. For all the other five put together would not have such power as belongs to Kubilai. And here is a greater claim still, which I can confidently assert: that all the emperors of the world and all the kings of Christians and of Saracens combined would not possess such power or be able to accomplish so much as this same Kubilai, the Great Khan. And this I will clearly demonstrate to you in this book.

You should know that all the great lords who are of the lineage of Chinghiz Khan are conveyed for burial to a great mountain called Altai. When one of them dies, even if it be at a distance of a hundred days' journey from this mountain, he must be brought here for burial. And here is a remarkable fact: when the body of a Great Khan is being carried to this mountain—be it forty days' journey or more or less—all those who are encountered along the route by which the body is being conveyed are put to the sword by the attendants who

* R rounds off the romance with the statement that he duly married Prester John's daughter.

† Some MSS read *Alau* or *Ulau* (i.e. Hulagu, who, like Batu, was never Great Khan; see p. 14). Benedetto does his best for Polo by treating *Altou* as a corruption of *Oktai* (i.e. Ogodai, the second Great Khan).

are escorting it. 'Go!' they cry, 'and serve your lord in the next world.' For they truly believe that all those whom they put to death must go and serve the Khan in the next world. And they do the same thing with horses: when the Khan dies, they kill all his best horses, so that he may have them in the next world. It is a fact that, when Mongu Khan died, more than 20,000 men were put to death, having encountered his body on the way to burial.

Since we have begun to speak of the Tartars, I have much to tell you about them. They spend the winter in steppes and warm regions where there is good grazing and pasturage for their beasts. In summer they live in cool regions, among mountains and valleys, where they find water and woodland as well as pasturage. A further advantage is that in cooler regions there are no horse-flies or gad-flies or similar pests to annoy them and their beasts. They spend two or three months climbing steadily and grazing as they go, because if they confined their grazing to one spot there would not be grass enough for the multitude of their flocks.

They have circular houses made of wood and covered with felt, which they carry about with them on four-wheeled wagons wherever they go. For the framework of rods is so neatly and skilfully constructed that it is light to carry. And every time they unfold their house and set it up, the door is always facing south. They also have excellent two-wheeled carts covered with black felt, of such good design that if it rained all the time the rain would never wet anything in the cart. These are drawn by oxen and camels. And in these carts they carry their wives and children and all they need in the way of utensils.

And I assure you that the womenfolk buy and sell and do all that is needful for their husbands and households. For the men do not bother themselves about anything but hunting and warfare and falconry. They live on meat and milk and game and on Pharaoh's rats, which are abundant everywhere in the steppes. They have no objection to eating the flesh of horses and dogs and drinking mares' milk. In fact they eat flesh of any sort. Not for anything in the world would one of them touch another's wife; they are too well assured that such a deed is wrongful and disgraceful. The wives are true and loyal to their husbands and very good at their household tasks. Even if there are as many as ten or twenty of them in one household, they live together in a concord and unity beyond praise, so that you would never hear a harsh word spoken. They all devote themselves to their various tasks and the care of the children, who are held among them in common. Their mode of marriage is such that any man may take as many wives as he pleases, even up to a hundred, if he is able to support them. The husband gives a dowry to his wife's mother; the wife gives nothing to the husband. You must understand that the first wife is reckoned the best and enjoys the highest status. Because they have so many wives, they have more children than other men. They may marry their cousins; and, when a father dies, the eldest son marries his father's wives, excluding his own mother. He may also marry his brother's wife, if the brother dies. When they take a wife, they hold a great wedding celebration.

I will now tell you of their religion. They say that there is a High God, exalted and heavenly to whom they offer daily prayer with thurible and incense, but only for a sound understanding and good health. They also have a god of their own whom they call Natigai. They say that he is an earthly god and watches over their children, their beasts, and their crops. They pay him great reverence and honour; for each man has one in his house. They make this god of felt and cloth and keep him in their house; and they also make the god's wife and children. They set his wife at his left hand and his children in front. And they treat them with great reverence. When they are about to have a meal, they take a lump of fat and smear the god's mouth with it, and the mouths of his wife and children. Then they take some broth and pour it outside the door of the house. When they have done this, they say that their god and his household have had their share. After this they eat and drink. You should know that they drink mare's milk; but they subject it to a process that makes it like white wine and very good to drink, and they call it *koumiss*.

As to their costume, the rich wear cloth of gold and silk and rich aurs—sable and ermine and miniver and fox. And all their trappings are very fine and very costly. Their weapons are bows and swords and clubs; but they rely mainly on their bows, for they are excellent archers. On their backs they wear an armour of buffalo hide or some other leather which is very tough.

They are stout fighters, excelling in courage and hardihood. Let me explain how it is that they can endure more than any other men. Often enough, if need be, they will go or stay for a whole month without provisions, drinking only the milk of a mare and eating wild game of their own taking. Their horses, meanwhile, support themselves by grazing, so that there is no need to carry barley or straw. They are very obedient to their masters. In case of need they will stay all night on horseback under arms, while their mount goes on steadily cropping the grass. They are of all men in the world the best able to endure exertion and hardship and the least costly to maintain and therefore the best adapted for conquering territory and overthrowing kingdoms.

Now the plan on which their armies are marshalled is this. When a lord of the Tartars goes out to war with a following of 100,000 horsemen, he has them organized as follows. He has one captain in command of every ten, one of every hundred, one of every thousand and one of every ten-thousand, so that he never needs to consult with more than ten men. In the same way each commander of ten-thousand or a thousand or a hundred consults only with his ten immediate subordinates, and each man is answerable to his own chief. When the supreme commander wishes to send someone on some operation, he orders the commander of ten-thousand to give him a thousand men; the latter orders the captain of a thousand to contribute his share. So the order is passed down, each commander being required to furnish his quota towards the thousand. At each stage it is promptly received and executed. For they are all obedient to the word of command more than any other people in the world. You should know that the unit of 100,000 is called a *tuk*, that of 10,000 a *tomaun*, and there are corresponding terms for the thousands, the hundreds, and the tens.

When an army sets out on some operation, whether it be in the plains or in the mountains, 200 men are sent two days' ride in advance as scouts, and as many to the rear and on the flanks; that is four scouting parties in all. And this they do so that the army cannot be attacked without warning.

When they are going on a long expedition, they carry no baggage with them. They each carry two leather flasks to hold the milk they drink and a small pot for cooking meat.* They also carry a small tent to shelter them from the rain. In case of need, they will ride a good ten days' journey without provisions and without making a fire, living only on the blood of their horses; for every rider pierces a vein of his horse and drinks the blood. They also have their dried milk, which is solid like paste; and this is how they dry it. First they bring

---

* According to R, the total number of horses and mares amounts to eighteen for each man, to allow for frequent changes of mount.

F

the milk to the boil. At the appropriate moment they skim off the cream that floats on the surface and put it in another vessel to be made into butter, because so long as it remained the milk could not be dried. Then they stand the milk in the sun and leave it to dry. When they are going on an expedition, they take about ten pounds of this milk; and every morning they take out about half a pound of it and put it in a small leather flask, shaped like a gourd, with as much water as they please. Then, while they ride, the milk in the flask dissolves into a fluid, which they drink. And this is their breakfast.

When they join battle with their enemies, these are the tactics by which they prevail. They are never ashamed to have recourse to flight. They manoeuvre freely, shooting at the enemy, now from this quarter, now from that. They have trained their horses so well that they wheel this way or that as quickly as a dog would do. When they are pursued and take to flight, they fight as well and as effectively as when they are face to face with the enemy. When they are fleeing at top speed, they twist round with their bows and let fly their arrows to such good purpose that they kill the horses of the enemy and the riders too. When the enemy thinks he has routed and crushed them, then he is lost; for he finds his horses killed and not a few of his men. As soon as the Tartars decide that they have killed enough of the pursuing horses and horsemen, they wheel round and attack and acquit themselves so well and so courageously that they gain a complete victory. By these tactics they have already won many battles and conquered many nations.

All that I have told you concerns the usages and customs of the genuine Tartars. But nowadays their stock has degenerated. Those who live in Cathay have adopted the manners and customs of the idolaters and abandoned their own faith, while those who live in the Levant have adopted the manners of the Saracens.

Let me tell you next of the Tartar fashion of maintaining justice. For a petty theft, not amounting to a capital offence, the culprit receives seven strokes of the rod, or seventeen or twenty-seven or thirty-seven or forty-seven, ascending thus by tens to 107 in proportion to the magnitude of his crime. And many die of this flogging. If the offender has stolen a horse or otherwise incurred the death penalty, he is chopped in two by the sword. If, however, he can afford to pay, and is prepared to pay nine times the value of what he has stolen, he escapes other punishment.

All the great lords, and other owners of flocks and herds, including horses, mares, camels, oxen, cows, and other large beasts, have them branded with their own mark. Then they turn them loose to graze on the plains and hillsides with no herdsman to guard them. If the herds intermingle, each beast is duly returned to the owner whose mark it bears. Their sheep and rams are entrusted to the care of shepherds. All their beasts are of great size and fat and exceedingly fine.

Here is another strange custom which I had forgotten to describe. You may take it for a fact that, when there are two men of whom one has had a male child who has died at the age of four, or what you will, and the other has had a female child who has also died, they arrange a marriage between them. They give the dead girl to the dead boy as a wife and draw up a deed of matrimony. Then they burn this deed, and declare that the smoke that rises into the air goes to their children in the other world and that they get wind of it and regard themselves as husband and wife. They hold a great wedding feast and scatter some of the food here and there and declare that that too goes to their children in the other world. And here is something else that they do. They draw pictures on paper of men in the guise of slaves, and of horses, clothes, coins, and furniture and then burn them; and they declare that all these become the possessions of their children in the next world. When they have done this, they consider themselves to be kinsfolk and uphold their kinship just as firmly as if the children were alive.

Now I have given you an unvarnished account of the usages and customs of the Tartars. Not that I have told you of the lofty state of the Great Khan, the Great Lord of all the Tartars, or of his high imperial court. I will tell you all about them in this book in due time and place. For they are truly wonderful things to set down in writing. Meanwhile, let us resume the thread of our discourse in the great plain where we were when we began to talk about the doings of the Tartars.

If the traveller leaves Karakorum and Altai, where, as I have told you, the Tartars bury their dead, and journeys towards the north, he traverses a country called the plain of Bargu, which extends for forty days' journey. The inhabitants, who are called Mekrit, are a savage race. Their livelihood depends on beasts, mostly reindeer, which they even use for riding. They resemble the Tartars in their customs and are subject to the Great Khan. They have neither corn nor wine. In summer they have plenty of game for hunting, both beasts and birds; but in winter neither beast nor bird lives there because of the great cold. The birds especially congregate during the moulting season in summer round the numerous lakes, meres, and marshes; and when they have shed all their old plumage, so that they cannot fly, the hunters take as many as they want. They also live on fish.

At the end of forty days, the traveller reaches the Ocean. Here there are mountains where peregrine falcons build their nests. You must understand that there are neither men nor women here, nor beasts nor birds, except a species of bird called *bargherlac* on which the falcons prey. They are of the size of partridges and have feet like parrots and tails like swallows. They are strong fliers. When the Great Khan wants eyasses of the peregrine falcon, he sends for them all the way to this district. The islands in this ocean breed gerfalcons. I assure you that this region is so far north that the Pole Star is left behind towards the south. The gerfalcons of which I have spoken are so abundant here that the Great Khan has as many of them as he wants. So you must not suppose that those who export them from Christendom to the Tartars send them to the Great Khan; they actually export them to the Khan of the Levant, to Arghun or whoever it may be.

Such are the plain facts about the northern provinces as far as the Ocean. We shall now return to the provinces along the route to the Great Khan, starting from Kan-chau, about which I have already written.

When the traveller leaves Kan-chau, he journeys eastward for five days through a country haunted by spirits, whom he often hears talking in the night, till he reaches a kingdom called Erguiul. This is subject to the Great Khan and forms part of the great province of Tangut, which comprises many kingdoms. The inhabitants include Nestorian Christians, idolaters, and Mahometans. There are cities in plenty, of which the capital is called Erguiul. And from this city the road leads south-eastwards towards the countries of Cathay.

Along this road lies a city called Sinju, which is also the name of the province. This has towns and cities in plenty and is likewise a part of Tangut and subject to the Great Khan. The inhabitants are idolaters and Mahometans, with some Christians. There are many wild cattle here, as big as elephants and very handsome in appearance; for they are covered with long hair, except on the back, and are white and black in colour. The length of their hair is fully three palms.⋆ They are so handsome that they are a wonder to behold. There are also plenty of these cattle in domestication; for many wild ones have been captured and their numbers increased by breeding. They are used as beasts of burden and in the plough; and I assure you that they get through twice as much ploughing as other cattle and have twice the strength.

This country produces the best and finest musk in the world; and this is how it is obtained. You must know that it comes from a small animal about the size of a gazelle, with thick hair like that of a deer, the feet and tail of a gazelle, no horns, but four slender teeth, two above and two below, about the length of three fingers, two growing upwards and two down. It is a very handsome creature. When it has been caught, there is found next to the navel right under the belly, between the skin and the flesh, a little sac of blood. This is cut away, skin and all, and taken out; and this blood is the musk, which gives off such a powerful perfume.† And you may take it that in this country it is available in great abundance and of the excellent quality to which I have referred.

The inhabitants live by trade and industry and have no lack of corn. The extent of the province is twenty-five days' journey. There are pheasants here twice as large as those of our country; for they are as big as peacocks, or very little less. Some of them have tails fully ten palms in length, others of nine or eight, or at least seven. There are other pheasants of the same size as ours. There are also other birds of many sorts with very fine plumage and very gaily coloured.

The people here are idolaters. They are fat and have small noses and black hair. They are beardless, except for a few strong hairs on the chin. The women have no hair on any part of the body except the head. They are very fair-complexioned with delicate flesh and all their limbs admirably proportioned. The men are much addicted to sexual indulgence and take several wives, since neither law nor custom forbids. They are free to take as many as they wish and as they can afford to keep. If there is a beautiful woman of lowly birth and

⋆ R adds that the hair of these cattle (which are evidently yaks) is finer and whiter than silk and that Marco brought back a sample to Venice, which excited the wonder of all who beheld it.

† R adds that the musk is generated and obtained at the full moon (cf. p. 144) and afterwards dried in the sun; that the flesh of the animals (i.e. musk-deer) is very good to eat; and that Marco brought back the dried head and feet of one of them to Venice.

some baron or other magnate takes her to wife because of her beauty, he gives her mother a large sum of money, as much as is agreed upon between them.

Let us now continue our journey towards the East.

When the traveller leaves Erguiul and journeys eastwards for eight days, he reaches another province of Tangut called Egrigaia, where there are cities and towns in plenty. The chief city is called Kalachan. The inhabitants are idolaters, but there are three churches of Nestorian Christians. They are subject to the Great Khan. In this city the finest camlets in the world are made of camel hair. Camlets are also made of white wool; these are white camlets, and they are produced in great abundance and of excellent quality. They are exported by merchants far and wide to many countries, including Cathay.

Let us now proceed to another province farther east, called Tenduc, where we shall enter the dominion of Prester John.

Tenduc is a province containing many towns and villages. The chief city is named Tenduc. The people are subject to the Great Khan, for so also are the descendants of Prester John. The province is ruled by a king of the lineage of Prester John, who is a Christian and a priest and also bears the title 'Prester John'. His personal name is George. He holds the land as a vassal of the Great Khan—not all the land that was held by Prester John, but a part of it. I may tell you that the Great Khans have always given one of their daughters or kinswomen to reigning princes of the lineage of Prester John.

This province produces lapis lazuli in plenty and of good quality, besides excellent camlets of camel hair. The inhabitants live by stock-rearing and agriculture. There is also a certain amount of commerce and industry. The rulers, as I have said, are Christians; but there are also many idolaters and Mahometans. There is also a class of men called *Argon*, that is to say 'half-breeds', who are born of a blend of the two stocks native to Tenduc, the idolaters and the Mahometans. They are a handsome race, more so than the other natives, besides being more intelligent and more businesslike.

It is in this province that Prester John had his chief residence when he was lord of the Tartars and of all these neighbouring provinces and kingdoms; and it is here that his descendants still live. King George, of whom I have already spoken, is the sixth ruler in descent from Prester John. This is the place which we call in our language

Gog and Magog; the natives call it Ung and Mungul. Each of these two provinces was inhabited by a separate race: in Ung lived the Gog, in Mungul the Tartars.

When the traveller rides through this province* for seven days towards the east in the direction of Cathay, he finds many cities and towns inhabited by Mahometans, idolaters, and Nestorian Christians. They live by commerce and industry, weaving the cloths of gold called *nasich* and *nakh* and silk of various types. Just as we have woollen cloths of many different types, so have they of cloth of gold and silk. They are subject to the Great Khan.

There is a city here called Sindachu where crafts of many kinds are practised and accoutrements are made for the use of armies. In the mountains of this province there is a place called Ydifu in which there is a very rich silver mine producing great quantities of silver. There is also plenty of wild game, both beasts and birds.

If we leave this province and city and go on our way for three days, we shall find a city called Chagan-nor,† where there is a large palace belonging to the Great Khan. He enjoys staying in this palace because there are lakes and rivers here in plenty, well stocked with swans. There are also fine plains, teeming with cranes, pheasants and partridges, and many other sorts of wild fowl; and that is a further attraction for the Great Khan, who is a keen sportsman and takes great delight in hawking for birds with falcons and gerfalcons. There are five sorts of crane, which I will describe to you. One is entirely black, like a raven, and very large. The second is pure white. Its wings are beautiful, with all the plumage studded with round eyes like those of a peacock but of the colour of burnished gold. It has a scarlet and black head and a black and white neck and is larger than any of the others. The third species is like the cranes we know. The fourth is small, with long plumes by its ears, scarlet and black in colour and very beautiful. The fifth is a very large bird, quite grey with shapely head coloured scarlet and black.

Beyond this city lies a valley in which the Great Khan keeps flocks of *cators*, which we call 'great partridges', in such quantities that they are a sight to behold. In order to feed them, he regularly has crops sown on the slopes in summer, consisting of millet and panic and other favourite foods of such fowl, and allows no one to reap them,

* It would seem that Polo is here speaking of another province, east of Tenduc.
† R adds, quite correctly, that this is equivalent (in Turkish) to 'White Pool'.

so that they may eat their fill. And many guards are set to watch these birds, to prevent anyone from taking them. And in winter their keepers scatter millet for them; and they are so used to this feeding that, if a man flings some of the grain on the ground, he has only to whistle and, wherever they may be, they flock to him. And the Great Khan has had many huts built, in which they spend the night. So, when he visits this country, he has a plentiful supply of these fowl, as many as he wants. And in winter, when they are nice and plump, since he does not stay there himself at this season because of the intense cold, he has camel-loads of them brought to him, wherever he may be.

When the traveller leaves this city and journeys north-north-east for three days, he comes to a city called Shang-tu, which was built by the Great Khan now reigning, whose name is Kubilai. In this city Kubilai Khan built a huge palace of marble and other ornamental stones. Its halls and chambers are all gilded, and the whole building is marvellously embellished and richly adorned. At one end it extends into the middle of the city; at the other it abuts on the city wall. At this end another wall, running out from the city wall in the direction opposite to the palace, encloses and encircles fully sixteen miles of park-land well watered with springs and streams and diversified with lawns. Into this park there is no entry except by way of the palace. Here the Great Khan keeps game animals of all sorts, such as hart, stag, and roebuck, to provide food for the gerfalcons and other falcons which he has here in mew. The gerfalcons alone amount to more than 200. Once a week he comes in person to inspect them in the mew. Often, too, he enters the park with a leopard on the crupper of his horse; when he feels inclined, he lets it go and thus catches a hart or stag or roebuck to give to the gerfalcons that he keeps in mew. And this he does for recreation and sport.

In the midst of this enclosed park, where there is a beautiful grove, the Great Khan has built another large palace, constructed entirely of canes, but with the interior all gilt and decorated with beasts and birds of very skilful workmanship. It is reared on gilt and varnished pillars, on each of which stands a dragon, entwining the pillar with his tail and supporting the roof on his outstretched limbs. The roof is also made of canes, so well varnished that it is quite waterproof. Let me explain how it is constructed. You must know that these canes are more than three palms in girth and from ten to fifteen paces long.

They are sliced down through the middle from one knot to the next, thus making two shingles. These shingles are thick and long enough not only for roofing but for every sort of construction. The palace, then, is built entirely of such canes. As a protection against the wind each shingle is fastened with nails. And the Great Khan has had it so designed that it can be moved whenever he fancies; for it is held in place by more than 200 cords of silk.

The Great Khan stays at Shang-tu for three months in the year, June, July, and August, to escape from the heat and for the sake of the recreation it affords. During these three months he keeps the palace of canes erected; for the rest of the year it is dismantled. And he has had it so constructed that he can erect or dismantle it at pleasure.

When it comes to the 28th day of August, the Great Khan takes his leave of this city and of this palace. Every year he leaves on this precise day; and I will tell you why. The fact is that he has a stud of snow-white stallions and snow-white mares, without a speck of any other colour. Their numbers are such that the mares alone amount to more than 10,000. The milk of these mares may not be drunk by anyone who is not of the imperial lineage, that is to say of the lineage of the Great Khan. To this rule there is one exception; the milk may be drunk by a race of men called Horiat, by virtue of a special privilege granted to them by Chinghiz Khan because of a victory that they won with him in the old days. When these white steeds are grazing, such reverence is shown to them that if a great lord were going that way he could not pass through their midst, but would either wait till they had passed or go on until he had passed them. The astrologers and idolaters have told the Great Khan that he must make a libation of the milk of these mares every year on the 28th of August, flinging it into the air and on the earth, so that the spirits may have their share to drink. They must have this, it is said, in order that they may guard all his possessions, men and women, beasts, birds, crops, and everything besides.

For this purpose the Great Khan leaves this palace and goes elsewhere. But, before we follow him, let me tell you of a strange thing which I had forgotten. You must know that, when the Great Khan was staying in his palace and the weather was rainy or cloudy, he had wise astrologers and enchanters who by their skill and their enchantments would dispel all the clouds and the bad weather from above the palace so that, while bad weather continued all around, the weather above the palace was fine. The wise men who do this are called Tibetans and Kashmiris; these are two races of men who practise idolatry. They know more of diabolic arts and enchantments than any other men. They do what they do by the arts of the Devil; but they make others believe that they do it by great holiness and by the work of God. For this reason they go about filthy and begrimed, with no regard for their own decency or for the persons who behold them; they keep the dirt on their faces, never wash or comb, but always remain in a state of squalor. These men have a peculiar custom, of which I will tell you. When a man is condemned to die and is put to death by the authorities, they take the body and cook and eat it. But, if anyone dies a natural death, they would never think of eating him.

Here is another remarkable fact about these enchanters, or *Bakhshi** as they are called. I assure you that, when the Great Khan is seated in his high hall at his table, which is raised more than eight cubits above the floor, and the cups are on the floor of the hall, a good ten paces distant from the table, and are full of wine and milk and other pleasant drinks, these *Bakhshi* contrive by their enchantment and their art that the full cups rise up of their own accord from the floor on which they have been standing and come to the Great Khan without anyone touching them. And this they do in the sight of 10,000 men. What I have told you is the plain truth without a word of falsehood. And those who are skilled in necromancy will confirm that it is perfectly feasible.

Here is a further fact about these *Bakhshi*. When the feast-days of their idols come round, they go to the Great Khan and say: 'Sire, the feast of such-and-such of our idols is approaching.' And they mention the name of some idol, whichever they may choose, and then continue: 'You are aware, Sire, that it is the practice of this idol to cause bad weather and damage to our property and to cattle and crops unless it receives oblations and holocausts. We accordingly beseech you, Sire, that we may be given so many black-faced sheep, so much incense, so much aloes wood, so much of this and so much of that, so that we may offer great worship and sacrifice to our idols in order that they may save us, our bodies, cattle, and crops.' This they say to the barons who surround the Great Khan and to those

* R explains that this term denotes a special religious order, like the Dominican or Franciscan Friars.

who hold authority under him. And these repeat their words to the Great Khan, so that the *Bakhshi* have everything they ask for in order to celebrate the feast of their idol. Thereupon they proceed to perform their rites with much chanting and festivity. For they regale their idols with fragrant incense from these sweet spices; and they cook the meat and set it before them and sprinkle some of the gravy here and there, declaring that the idols are taking as much of it as they want. That is how they do honour to their idols on their feast-days.

You may take it for a fact that all the idols have their own feasts on the days assigned to them, just as our saints have. They have huge monasteries and abbeys, of such a size that I assure you that some resemble small cities inhabited by more than 2,000 monks according to their usage, who are better dressed than other men. They wear their heads and chins clean-shaven. They make the most magnificent feasts for their idols with the most magnificent hymns and illuminations that were ever seen.

A further point about these *Bakhshi* is that among their other privileges they are entitled according to their order to take wives. And so they do, and rear children in plenty.

Besides these there is another order of devotees who are called *Sien-seng*. They are men of extreme abstinence according to their own observances, and lead a life of great austerity which I will describe to you. The plain truth is that all their lives long they eat nothing but bran, that is to say the husk left over from wheat flour. For they take wheaten grain and put it in hot water and leave it there a little while till all the kernel or marrow is separated from the husk; then they eat the bran that has been washed in this way, without anything to give it a flavour. They fast many times in the year, besides eating absolutely nothing but this bran of which I have told you. They have huge idols, and many of them, and sometimes they worship fire. The other devotees declare that those who live this life of abstinence are heretics, as it were Patarins, because they do not worship their idols in the same manner as the rest. There is one great difference between the two orders of devotees; those who observe the stricter rule would not take a wife for anything in the world. They also have their heads and chins shaven. They wear black and blue robes of sackcloth; if they should happen to wear silk, it is still of the same colours. They sleep on mats of wicker-work. Altogether they lead the most austere lives of any men in the world.

Their idols are all female, that is to say they all bear the names of women.

So much, then, for that. I will now tell you the truly amazing facts about the greatest lord of the Lords of all the Tartars, the right noble Great Khan whose name is Kubilai.

kubilai khan

I HAVE COME TO THE POINT IN OUR BOOK AT WHICH I WILL tell you of the great achievements of the Great Khan now reigning. The title Khan means in our language 'Great Lord of Lords'. And certainly he has every right to this title; for everyone should know that this Great Khan is the mightiest man, whether in respect of subjects or of territory or of treasure, who is in the world today or who ever has been, from Adam our first parent down to the present moment. And I will make it quite clear to you in our book that this is the plain truth, so that everyone will be convinced that he is indeed the greatest lord the world has ever known. Here, then, is my proof.

First, you should know that he is undoubtedly descended in the direct imperial line from Chinghiz Khan; for only one of that lineage may be Lord of all the Tartars. He is sixth in succession of the Great Khans of all the Tartars, having received the lordship and begun his reign in the year of Christ's nativity 1256. He won the lordship by his own valour and prowess and good sense; his kinsfolk and brothers tried to debar him from it, but by his great prowess he won it. And you must know that it was properly his by right. From the beginning of his reign down to the present year 1298 is a period of forty-two years. His age today may well be as much as eighty-five years. Before he became Khan, he used to go out regularly on military expeditions and he showed himself a valiant soldier and a good commander. But thereafter he went out only once; that was in 1286, and I will tell you how it came about.

The fact is that a certain man named Nayan, who was Kubilai's uncle, found himself while still a youth the lord and ruler of many lands and provinces, so that he could easily raise a force of 400,000 horsemen. Like his ancestors before him, he was subject to the Great Khan. But, seeing that he was a young man of thirty with so many men at his command, he resolved that he would be subject no longer but to the best of his ability would despoil his overlord of the suzerainty. This Nayan, then, sent envoys to Kaidu, who was a great and powerful lord and nephew to the Great Khan, but had rebelled against him and was his bitter enemy. He proposed that Kaidu should attack the Great

Khan from one quarter while he himself advanced against him from the opposite one, so as to despoil him of land and lordship. Kaidu welcomed the proposal and promised to have his forces fully arrayed by the date fixed and to march against the Great Khan. And this he was well able to do; for he could put 100,000 horsemen in the field. What need of more words? These two barons, Nayan and Kaidu, made their preparations and mustered a great array of horse and foot to attack the Great Khan.

When the Great Khan got word of this plot, he was not unduly perturbed; but like a wise man of approved valour he began to marshal his own forces, declaring that he would never wear his crown or hold his land if he did not bring these two false traitors to an evil end. He completed his preparations in twenty-two days, so secretly that no one knew anything about them except those of his own Council. He had assembled 360,000 cavalry and 100,000 infantry. The reason why he confined himself to this number was that these were drawn from the troops in his own immediate neighbourhood. His other armies, which were twelve in all and totalled an immense number of men, were so far away on campaigns of conquest in many parts that he could not have got them together at the right time and place. If he had assembled all his forces he would have had as many horsemen as he could possibly desire and their numbers would have been past all reckoning or belief. The 360,000 men whom he actually levied were his falconers and other members of his personal bodyguard.*

If he had summoned the armies which he keeps continually on guard over the provinces of Cathay, this would inevitably have consumed thirty or forty days. Moreover, the levy would have become common knowledge and Kaidu and Nayan would have joined forces and occupied strong and advantageous positions. But Kubilai intended by means of speed, the companion of victory, to forestall Nayan's preparations and catch him alone, because he could more easily defeat him alone than in conjunction with his ally.

This is a convenient place to record a few facts about the armies of the Great Khan. You should know that in all the provinces of Cathay and Manzi and in all the rest of his dominions there are many disaffected and disloyal subjects who, if they had the chance, would rebel

---

* The two following paragraphs occur only in R, which also adds that the troops levied were drawn from within a radius of ten days' journey from Khan-balik and that Kubilai set guards on the passes to prevent the news from reaching Nayan and Kaidu.

against their lord. Accordingly, in every province where there are big cities and a large population he is obliged to maintain armies. These are stationed in the open country four or five miles from the cities, which are not allowed to have gates or walls so as to bar the ingress of anyone who chooses to enter. These armies the Great Khan changes every two years, and so likewise the captains who command them. And with this bridle to restrain them the people stay quiet, and cannot cause any disturbance or insurrection. Besides the pay which the Great Khan gives them regularly from the revenues of the provinces, these armies live on the immense herds of cattle that are assigned to them and on the milk which they send into the towns to sell in return for necessary provisions. They are stationed at various points, thirty, forty, or sixty days' journey apart.

When the Great Khan had mustered the mere handful of men of which I have spoken, he consulted his astrologers to learn whether he would defeat his enemies and bring his affairs to a happy issue.* They assured him that he would deal with his enemies as he pleased. Thereupon he set out with all his forces and went on until after twenty days they came to a great plain where Nayan lay with all his forces, who were not less than 400,000 horsemen. They arrived early in the morning and caught the enemy completely unawares; the Great Khan had had all the roads so carefully watched that no one could come or go without being intercepted, and had thus ensured that the enemy had no suspicion of their approach. Indeed, when they arrived Nayan was in his tent, dallying in bed with his wife, to whom he was greatly attached.

What more shall I say? When the day of battle dawned, the Great Khan suddenly appeared on a mound that rose from the plain where Nayan's forces were bivouacked. They were quite at their ease, like men who had not the faintest suspicion that anyone was approaching with hostile intent. Indeed they felt so secure that they had posted no sentries round their camp and sent out no patrols to van or rear. And suddenly there was the Great Khan on the hill I have mentioned. He stood on the top of a wooden tower, full of crossbowmen and archers, which was carried by four elephants wearing stout leather armour draped with cloths of silk and gold. Above his head flew his banner with the emblem of the sun and moon, so high that it could be clearly seen on every side. His troops were marshalled in thirty

* R explains that the astrologers performed their divinations before the whole army, and that this was a stock device of the Great Khans to encourage their troops.

squadrons of 10,000 mounted archers each, grouped in three divisions; and those on the left and right he flung out so that they encircled Nayan's camp in a moment. In front of every squadron of horse were 500 foot-soldiers with short pikes and swords. They were so trained that, whenever the cavalry purposed a retreat, they would jump on the horses' cruppers and flee with them; then, when the retreat was halted, they would dismount and slaughter the enemies' horses with their pikes. Such, then, was the formation in which the Great Khan's forces were drawn up round Nayan's camp in readiness for the battle.

When Nayan and his men saw the troops of the Great Khan surrounding their camp, they were utterly taken aback. They rushed to arms, arrayed themselves in haste, and formed their ranks in due order.

When both parties were lined up in battle array, so that nothing remained but to come to blows, then might be heard a tumult of many instruments, the shrilling of fifes and the sound of men singing at the pitch of their voices. For the usage of the Tartars is such that when they are confronting the foe and marshalled for the fray they do not join battle till the drums begin to beat—that is the drums of the commander. While they wait for the beat of the drums, all the Tartar host sound their instruments and join in song. That is why the noise of instruments and of singing was so loud on both sides alike.

When all the troops were in readiness on both sides, then the drums of the Great Khan began to beat. After that there was no more delay; but the two armies fell upon each other with bow and sword and club, and a few with lances. The foot-soldiers had cross-bows also and other weapons in plenty. What more shall I say? This was the start of a bitter and bloody battle. Now you might see arrows flying like pelting rain, for the whole air was full of them. Now you might see horsemen and horses tumbling dead upon the ground. So loud was the shouting and the clash of arms that you could not have heard the thunder of heaven. You must know that Nayan was a baptized Christian and in this battle he had the cross of Christ on his standard.*

What need to make a long story of it? Enough that this was the most hazardous fight and the most fiercely contested that ever was seen. Never in our time were so many men engaged on one battle-

* R adds that, though he had been secretly baptized, he had not hitherto acted as a Christian; and that his army included countless Christians, who were all killed.

field, especially so many horsemen. So many died on either side that it was a marvel to behold. The battle raged from daybreak till noon, and for a long time its issue hung in the balance; Nayan's followers were so devoted to him, for he was an open-handed master, that they were ready to die rather than turn their backs. But in the end the victory fell to the Great Khan. When Nayan and his men saw that they could hold out no longer, they took to flight. But this availed them nothing; for Nayan was taken prisoner, and all his barons and his men surrendered to the Great Khan.

When the Great Khan learnt that Nayan was a prisoner, he commanded that he should be put to death. And this was how it was done. He was wrapped up tightly in a carpet and then dragged about so violently, this way and that, that he died. Their object in choosing this mode of death was so that the blood of the imperial lineage might not be spilt upon the earth, and that sun and air might not witness it.

After this victory, all Nayan's men and barons did homage to the Great Khan and swore fealty to him. They were men of four different provinces named Chorcha, Kauli, Barskol, and Sikin-tinju.

After the Great Khan had won this victory, the various races of men who were there—Saracens, idolaters, and Jews, and many others who do not believe in God—made mock of the cross which Nayan had borne on his banner. They jeered at the Christians who were there: 'See how the cross of your God has helped Nayan, who was a Christian!' So unrestrained was their mockery and their jeering that it came to the ears of the Great Khan. Thereupon he rebuked those who mocked at the cross in his presence. Then he summoned many Christians who were there and began to comfort them. 'If the cross of your God has not helped Nayan,' he said, 'it was for a very good reason. Because it is good, it ought not to lend its aid except in a good and righteous cause. Nayan was a traitor who broke faith with his liege lord. Hence the fate that has befallen him was a vindication of the right. And the cross of your God did well in not helping against the right.' The Christians answered: 'Most mighty lord, what you say is quite true. The cross would not lend itself to wrong-doing and disloyalty like that of Nayan, who was a traitor to his liege lord. He has received what he well deserved.' Such were the words that passed between the Great Khan and the Christians about the cross that Nayan had borne on his standard.

After this victory over Nayan, the Great Khan returned to his

G

capital of Khan-balik. And there he stayed, amid great rejoicing and merry-making.

As for that other rebellious baron, the prince whose name was Kaidu, when he heard of Nayan's defeat and death he was greatly perturbed and abandoned his campaign, for fear lest he might meet the same fate.

It was in the month of November that Kubilai returned to Khan-balik. And there he stayed till February and March, the season of our Easter. Learning that this was one of our principal feasts, he sent for all the Christians and desired them to bring him the book containing the four Gospels. After treating the book to repeated applications of incense with great ceremony, he kissed it devoutly and desired all his barons and lords there present to do the same. This usage he regularly observes on the principal feasts of the Christians, such as Easter and Christmas. And he does likewise on the principal feasts of the Saracens, Jews, and idolaters. Being asked why he did so, he replied: 'There are four prophets who are worshipped and to whom all the world does reverence. The Christians say that their God was Jesus Christ, the Saracens Mahomet, the Jews Moses, and the idolaters Sakyamuni Burkhan, who was the first to be represented as God in the form of an idol. And I do honour and reverence to all four, so that I may be sure of doing it to him who is greatest in heaven and truest; and to him I pray for aid.' But on the Great Khan's own showing he regards as truest and best the faith of the Christians, because he declares that it commands nothing that is not full of all goodness and holiness. He will not on any account allow the Christians to carry the cross before them, and this because on it suffered and died such a great man as Christ.

Someone may well ask why, since he regards the Christian faith as the best, he does not embrace it and become a Christian. The reason may be gathered from what he said to Messer Niccolò and Messer Maffeo when he sent them as emissaries to the Pope. They used from time to time to raise this matter with him; but he would reply: 'On what grounds do you desire me to become a Christian? You see that the Christians who live in these parts are so ignorant that they accomplish nothing and are powerless. And you see that these idolaters do whatever they will; and when I sit at table the cups in the middle of the hall come to me full of wine or other beverages without anyone touching them, and I drink from them. They banish bad weather in any direction they choose and perform many marvels. And, as you know, their idols speak and give them such predictions as they ask. But, if I am converted to the faith of Christ and become a Christian, then my barons and others who do not embrace the faith of Christ will say to me: "What has induced you to undergo baptism and adopt the faith of Christ? What virtues or what miracles have you seen to his credit?" For these idolaters declare that what they do they do by their holiness and by virtue of their idols. Then I should not know what to answer, which would be a grave error in their eyes. And these idolaters, who by their arts and sciences achieve such great results, could easily compass my death. But do you go to your Pope and ask him on my behalf to send me a hundred men learned in your religion, who in the face of these idolaters will have the knowledge to condemn their performances and tell them that they too can do such things but will not, because they are done by diabolic art and evil spirits, and will show their mastery by making the idolaters powerless to perform these marvels in their presence. On the day when we see this, I too will condemn them and their religion. Then I will be baptized, and all my barons and magnates will do likewise, and their subjects in turn will undergo baptism. So there will be more Christians here than there are in your part of the world.' And if, as was said at the beginning, men had really been sent by the Pope with the ability to preach our faith to the Great Khan, then assuredly he would have become a Christian. For it is known for a fact that he was most desirous to be converted.

You have heard how on this one campaign Kubilai led his army out to battle. On all his other enterprises or campaigns he used to send his sons or barons; but on this occasion he would have no one in command but himself, so serious and so culpable did he consider the rebellion of this baron. Let us now leave this subject and return to a recital of the great achievements of the Great Khan.

We have told you of his lineage and his age. We shall now relate how he dealt with those barons who acquitted themselves well in the battle and how with those who showed themselves cowards and poltroons.* Of the former, he promoted those who were commanders of 100 men to the command of 1,000, and commanders of 1,000 to the command of 10,000; and he gave them lavish gifts of

* R adds that the Khan has twelve wise barons, charged with observing and reporting on the military operations of the captains and soldiers.

silver plate and tablets of authority, each according to his rank. For a commander of 100 has a tablet of silver; a commander of 1,000 a tablet of gold, or rather of silver gilt; and a commander of 10,000 a tablet of gold with a lion's head. The tablets of command over 100 or 1,000 weigh 120 *saggi* apiece;* those with a lion's head weigh 220. On all these tablets is written a command in these words: 'By the might of the Great God and the great grace he has given to our Emperor, blessed be the name of the Khan, and death and destruction to all who do not obey him.' Let me add that all who have these tablets also have warrants setting forth in writing all the powers vested in them by their office.

As for the commander of 100,000, or the generalissimo of a great army, he has a tablet of gold weighing 300 *saggi*, with an inscription such as I have mentioned; and at the foot of the tablet is portrayed the lion, and above it is an image of the sun and moon. In addition he has warrants of high command and great authority. And whenever he goes riding he must carry an umbrella over his head in token of his exalted rank; and when he sits he must sit on a silver chair. To these dignitaries the Great Khan also gives a tablet with the sign of the gerfalcon; these tablets are given to the very great barons so that they may exercise full powers equivalent to his own. When one of them wishes to send a courier or other emissary, he is authorized to requisition a king's horses if he wishes; and when I say a king's horses, this naturally implies the horses of any other man.

Let me tell you next of the personal appearance of the Great Lord of Lords whose name is Kubilai Khan. He is a man of good stature, neither short nor tall but of moderate height. His limbs are well fleshed out and modelled in due proportion. His complexion is fair and ruddy like a rose, the eyes black and handsome, the nose shapely and set squarely in place.

He has four consorts who are all accounted his lawful wives; and his eldest son by any of these four has a rightful claim to be emperor on the death of the present Khan. They are called empresses, each by her own name. Each of these ladies holds her own court. None of them has less than 300 ladies in waiting, all of great beauty and charm. They have many eunuchs and many other men and women in attendance, so that each one of these ladies has in her court 10,000 persons. When he wishes to lie with one of his four wives, he invites her to his chamber; or sometimes he goes to his wife's chamber.

* The Venetian *saggio* weighed about ⅙ oz.

He also has many concubines, about whom I will tell you. There is a province inhabited by Tartars who are called Kungurat, which is also the name of their city. They are a very good-looking race with fair complexions. Every two years or so, according to his pleasure, the Great Khan sends emissaries to this province to select for him out of the most beautiful maidens, according to the standard of beauty which he lays down for them, some four or five hundred, more or less as he may decide. This is how the selection is made. When the emissaries arrive, they summon to their presence all the maidens of the province. And there valuers are deputed for the task. After inspecting and surveying every girl, feature by feature, her hair, her face, her eyebrows, her mouth, her lips, and every other feature, to see whether they are well-formed and in harmony with her person, the valuers award to some a score of sixteen marks, to others seventeen, eighteen, or twenty, or more or less according to the degree of their beauty. And, if the Great Khan has ordered them to bring him all who score twenty marks, or perhaps twenty-one, according to the number ordered, these are duly brought. When they have come to his presence, he has them assessed a second time by other valuers, and then the thirty or forty with the highest score are selected for his chamber. These are first allotted, one by one, to the barons' wives, who are instructed to observe them carefully at night in their chambers, to make sure that they are virgins and not blemished or defective in any member, that they sleep sweetly without snoring, and that their breath is sweet and they give out no unpleasant odour. Then those who are approved are divided into groups of six, who serve the Khan for three days and three nights at a time in his chamber and his bed, ministering to all his needs. And he uses them according to his pleasure. After three days and nights, in come the next six damsels. And so they continue in rotation throughout the year. While some of the group are in attendance in their lord's chamber, the others are waiting in an ante-chamber hard by. If he is in need of anything from outside, such as food or drink, the damsels inside the chamber pass word to those outside, who immediately get it ready. In this way the Khan is served by no one except these damsels. As for the other damsels, who are rated at a lower score, they remain with the Khan's other women in the palace, where they are instructed in needlework, glove-making, and other elegant accomplishments. When some nobleman is looking for a wife, the Great Khan gives him one of these damsels with a great dowry. And in this way he marries them all off honourably.

loin fist il tous iours grant honnour et les tenoit
pour honme de verite et tout iour puis.
Ci dit le lxviii. chapitre de la bataille de chingis
Can et de prestre iehan qui fu occis.

Pres ces .iiii. iours quant les os
se furent bien reposez si sarmerent
ambdeus les parties et se combati
rent ensamble durement et fu la
graignour bataille qui onques
fust une et fu moult grant occison dune part
et dautre. mais au derrain vainqui la bataille.
Chingis Can et fu en cele bataille occis prestre
iehan. Et de ce iour en avant par toute sa terre
que chingis can, la conquestoit tous les iours
et vous di que puis cele bataille regna chingis
Can vi. ans, et ala tous iours conquestant mai
ntes provinces et maintes citez et mainte chastel
mais au chief de vi. ans a la assoir .i. chastel que
len nommoit. Takais et si vne fu feru dune sa
ette en genouil si que il mourut dont. Dont ce fu
grant damages pource que il estoit preudomme
et sage. Des vous ai devise comment li tartar oret
premierement seignour Chingis Can. Et co
ment il vainqui premierement prestre iehan. la
vous conterons qui regna apres et de lor coustu
mes et de lor usances. Ci dit le lxix. chapitre
qui regna apres Chingis Can et de leur
usages et tout coustumes.
Vraiement que apres chingis can que
li lor sires fu regna Curchecan. le tiers baras saui
le quart alton can. le quint mogu can. le sixt
est cublay can qui est le plus grant, et le plus...

saut des autres .v. qui furent devant lui. Car
se tout li autre .v. fussent en samble nauroient
il tant de povoir comme celui .i. Encore vous di
plus que se tout li crestien du monde empereurs
et roys fussent tout ensamble et li sarrazin ua
roient pour auoir a lui. ne tant ne pourroient faire co
me celui Cublay le grant Can porroit lequel
est seignour de tous les tartars du monde. Et
de ceuls de levant et de ceuls de ponent sont tous
sont si homme et sougiet a lui. Et si ougrant po
oir vous moutrerai en cest liure apertement. Et sa
chiez que tout li grant Can. Et tout cil qui sont
descendu de lor primer seignour Chingis can la se
pueut en seuelir a vne grant montaigne qui est a
pele Altaij, et la ou li sires muert il est aporte
en seuelir en la dite montaigne auec les autres.
Car sil estoit C. iournees loins seroit il aportes la
aporte pour enseuelir, et si vous dirai vne grant
merueille que quant il portent le cois pour ense
uelir tous ceuls quil encontrent en la voie sont mis
a la mort par ceuls qui le cois conduient et dient
allez seruir nostre seigneur en lautre siecle. Car
il cuident devoir que tous ceuls quil occient doient
seruir lour seignour en lautre mond, et ce meisme
font il des cheuaus. Et quant li sires muert
il occient tout le meillour quel il ait a ce que il ait
en lautre siecle si comme il croient. Et si vous di
que quant mogu Can mourut plus de xx. mil
en furent occis en la voie, si comme ie vous ai de
en estoient en contre. Or de puis que nous a
nous en commence aparler des tartars si vous
en dirai maintes choses. les tartars demourent
les ce espains a eschaus liens ou il fa heritag
ges a pastures pour lor bestes et hiuer demou
rent es plus liens eschautaignes a eschaulas
ou il truiuent herbes et boscages. il ont mai
sons de verges a les couuertures de cordes a les
portent auec eulx. la ou il uncques vont. Car il
lient les verges si ordreement que illes porent
monter legierement et toutes fois que il centrre
lor maisons la porte est toute fois par deuers
midi. il ont charetes couuertes de feutre non sibie
que pour mille pluie ne puet passer et le tout
mont aus cheuaus a aus chomeus et sur ces
charetes portent leur femmes et leur enfans.

You may be inclined to ask: 'Do not the men of this province regard it as a grievance that the Great Khan robs them of their daughters?' Most certainly not. They esteem it a great favour and distinction; and those who have beautiful daughters are delighted that he should deign to accept them. They reason thus: 'If my daughter is born under a good planet and happy auspices, the Khan will be better able to satisfy her than I; he will marry her to a noble husband, which is more than my means would permit of.' And if she does not behave well or it does not turn out well for her, then the father says: 'This has happened to her because her planet was not propitious.'

You should know further that by his four wives the Great Khan has twenty-two male children. The eldest was called Chinghiz, for love of the good Chinghiz Khan.* He was to have succeeded his father as Great Khan and lord of the whole empire. But it happened that he died, leaving a son named Temur; this Temur is now destined to be Great Khan and lord, because he is the son of the eldest son of the Great Khan. I can assure you that this Temur is a man of wisdom and prowess, as he has already proved many times on the field of battle.

By his mistresses the Great Khan has a further twenty-five sons, all good men and brave soldiers. And each of them is a great baron.

Of his sons by his four wives, seven are kings of great provinces and kingdoms. They all exercise their authority well, lacking neither prudence nor prowess. And for this there is good reason, for I give you my word that their father the Great Khan is the wisest man and the ablest in all respects, the best ruler of subjects and of empire and the man of the highest character of all that have ever been in the whole history of the Tartars.

You must know that for three months in the year, December, January, and February, the Great Khan lives in the capital city of Cathay, whose name is Khan-balik. In this city he has his great palace, which I will now describe to you.†

The palace is completely surrounded by a square wall, each side

---

* The name of Kubilai's son was actually Chinkim. R adds that he had been confirmed in his seigniory during his father's lifetime. His son Temur succeeded Kubilai in 1294.
† R gives a somewhat fuller description of the palace, of which some particulars have been incorporated in the translation. He mentions a third (outermost) wall, a square with each side eight miles in length, surrounded by a ditch; it has a gate in the middle of each side, through which enter the crowds who throng there, after which comes a space of a mile where the troops are stationed. This may refer to the city wall.

being a mile in length so that the whole circuit is four miles. It is a very thick wall and fully ten paces in height. It is all white-washed and battlemented. At each corner of this wall stands a large palace of great beauty and splendour, in which the Great Khan keeps his military stores. In the middle of each side is another palace resembling the corner palaces, so that round the whole circuit of the walls there are eight palaces, all serving as arsenals. Each is reserved for a particular type of munition. Thus, one contains saddles, bridles, stirrups, and other items of a horse's harness. In another are bows, bow-strings, quivers, arrows, and other requisites of archery. In a third are cuirasses, corselets, and other armour of boiled leather. And so with the rest.

In the southern front of this wall there are five gates. There is one great gate in the middle, which is never opened except when the Great Khan is leaving or entering. Next to this, one on either side, are two small gates, by which everyone else enters. There are also two more large gates, one near each corner, which are likewise used by other people.

Within this outer wall is another wall, somewhat greater in length than in breadth. In this also there are eight palaces, just like the others, and used in the same way to house military stores. It also has five gates in its southern front, corresponding to those in the outer wall. In each of the other sides it has one gate only; and so has the outer wall.

Within this wall is the Great Khan's palace, which I will now describe to you. It is the largest that was ever seen.* It has no upper floor, but the basement on which it stands is raised ten palms above the level of the surrounding earth; and all round it there runs a marble wall level with the basement, two paces in thickness. The foundation of the palace lies within this wall, so that as much of the wall as projects beyond it forms a sort of terrace, on which men can walk right round and inspect the outside of the palace. At the outer edge of this wall is a fine gallery with columns, where men can meet and talk. At each face of the palace is a great marble staircase, ascending from ground level to the top of this marble wall, which affords an entry into the palace.

The palace itself has a very high roof. Inside, the walls of the halls and chambers are all covered with gold and silver and decorated with

* R adds that it abuts on the inner curtain wall to the north, leaving an empty space to the south where the barons and soldiers parade.

pictures of dragons and birds and horsemen and various breeds of beasts and scenes of battle. The ceiling is similarly adorned, so that there is nothing to be seen anywhere but gold and pictures. The hall is so vast and so wide that a meal might well be served there for more than 6,000 men. The number of chambers is quite bewildering. The whole building is at once so immense and so well constructed that no man in the world, granted that he had the power to effect it, could imagine any improvement in design or execution. The roof is all ablaze with scarlet and green and blue and yellow and all the colours that are, so brilliantly varnished that it glitters like crystal and the sparkle of it can be seen from far away. And this roof is so strong and so stoutly built as to last for many a long year.

In the rear part of the palace are extensive apartments, both chambers and halls, in which are kept the private possessions of the Khan. Here is stored his treasure: gold, and silver, precious stones and pearls, and his gold and silver vessels. And here too are his ladies and his concubines. In these apartments everything is arranged for his comfort and convenience, and outsiders are not admitted.

Between the inner and the outer walls, of which I have told you, are stretches of park-land with stately trees. The grass grows here in abundance, because all the paths are paved and built up fully two cubits above the level of the ground, so that no mud forms on them and no rain-water collects in puddles, but the moisture trickles over the lawns, enriching the soil and promoting a lush growth of herbage. In these parks there is a great variety of game, such as white harts, musk-deer, roebuck, stags, squirrels, and many other beautiful animals. All the area within the walls is full of these graceful creatures, except the paths that people walk on.

In the north-western corner of the grounds is a pit of great size and depth, very neatly made, from which the earth was removed to build the mound of which I shall speak. The pit is filled with water by a fair-sized stream so as to form a sort of pond where the animals come to drink. The stream flows out through an aqueduct near the mound and fills another similar pit between the Great Khan's palace and that of Chinghiz his son, from which the earth was dug for the same purpose. These pits or ponds contain a great variety of fish. For the Great Khan has had them stocked with many different species, so that, whenever he feels inclined, he may have his pick. At the farther end of the pond there is an outlet for the stream, through which it flows away. It is so contrived that at the entrance and the outlet there are gratings of iron and copper to stop the fish from escaping. There are also swans and other water-fowl. It is possible to pass from one palace to the other by way of a bridge over this stream.

On the northern side of the palace, at the distance of a bow-shot but still within the walls, the Great Khan has had made an earthwork, that is to say a mound fully 100 paces in height and over a mile in circumference. This mound is covered with a dense growth of trees, all evergreens that never shed their leaves. And I assure you that whenever the Great Khan hears tell of a particularly fine tree he has it pulled up, roots and all and with a quantity of earth, and transported to this mound by elephants. No matter how big the tree may be, he is not deterred from transplanting it. In this way he has assembled here the finest trees in the world. In addition, he has had the mound covered with lapis lazuli, which is intensely green, so that trees and rock alike are as green as green can be and there is no other colour to be seen. For this reason it is called the Green Mound. On top of this mound, in the middle of the summit, he has a large and handsome palace, and this too is entirely green. And I give you my word that mound and trees and palace form a vision of such beauty that it gladdens the hearts of all beholders. It was for the sake of this entrancing view that the Great Khan had them constructed, as well as for the refreshment and recreation they might afford him.

Let me tell you also that beside this palace the Great Khan has had another one built, just like his own and no whit inferior. This is built to be occupied by his son when he shall succeed him as ruler. That is why it is built in the same style and on the same scale as the Great Khan's own, which I have described above, and with walls of equal size. This is the residence of Temur the son of Chinghiz, of whom I have already spoken, who is destined to be Khan; and he observes the same ceremony and usages as the Great Khan, because he has been chosen to rule after the Great Khan's death. The bull and seal of empire are his already, though so long as the Great Khan is alive he does not enjoy them so absolutely.

Now that I have told you about these palaces, I will go on to tell you of the great town of Taidu in which they are situated, and why and how it came to be built.

On the banks of a great river in the province of Cathay there stood an ancient city of great size and splendour which was named Khanbalik, that is to say in our language 'the Lord's City'. Now the Great

Khan discovered through his astrologers that this city would rebel
and put up a stubborn resistance against the Empire. For this reason
he had this new city built next to the old one, with only the river
between. And he removed the inhabitants of the old city and settled
them in the new one, which is called Taidu, leaving only those whom
he did not suspect of any rebellious designs; for the new city was not
big enough to house all those who lived in the old.

Taidu is built in the form of a square with all its sides of equal
length and a total circumference of twenty-four miles. It is enclosed
by earthen ramparts, twenty paces high and ten paces thick at the
base; the sides slope inwards from base to summit, so that at the top
the width is only about three paces. They are all battlemented and
white-washed. They have twelve gates, each surmounted by a fine,
large palace. So on each of the four sides there are three gates and
five palaces, because there is an additional palace at each corner. In
these palaces there are immense halls, which house the weapons of
the city guards.

I assure you that the streets are so broad and straight that from the
top of the wall above one gate you can see along the whole length of
the road to the gate opposite. The city is full of fine mansions, inns,
and dwelling-houses. All the way down the sides of every main street
there are booths and shops of every sort. All the building sites
throughout the city are square and measured by the rule; and on every
site stand large and spacious mansions with ample courtyards and
gardens. These sites are allotted to heads of households, so that one
belongs to such-and-such a person, representing such-and-such a
family, the next to a representative of another family, and so all the
way along. Every site or block is surrounded by good public roads;
and in this way the whole interior of the city is laid out in squares
like a chess-board with such masterly precision that no description
can do justice to it.

In this city there is such a multitude of houses and of people, both
within the walls and without, that no one could count their number.
Actually there are more people outside the walls in the suburbs than
in the city itself. There is a suburb outside every gate, such that each
one touches the neighbouring suburbs on either side. They extend in
length for three or four miles. And in every suburb or ward, at about
a mile's distance from the city, there are many fine hostels which
provide lodging for merchants coming from different parts: a particular hostel is assigned to every nation, as we might say one for the

Lombards, another for the Germans, another for the French. Merchants and others come here on business in great numbers, both because it is the Khan's residence and because it affords a profitable market. And the suburbs have as fine houses and mansions as the city, except of course for the Khan's palace.

You must know that no one who dies is buried in the city. If an idolater dies there, his body is taken to the place of cremation, which lies outside all the suburbs. And so with the others also; when they die they are taken right outside the suburbs for burial. Similarly, no act of violence* is performed inside the city, but only outside the suburbs.

Let me tell you also that no sinful woman dares live within the city, unless it be in secret—no woman of the world, that is, who prostitutes her body for money. But they all live in the suburbs, and there are so many of them that no one could believe it. For I assure you that there are fully 20,000 of them, all serving the needs of men for money. They have a captain general, and there are chiefs of hundreds and of thousands responsible to the captain. This is because, whenever ambassadors come to the Great Khan on his business and are maintained at his expense, which is done on a lavish scale, the captain is called upon to provide one of these women every night for the ambassador and one for each of his attendants. They are changed every night and receive no payment; for this is the tax they pay to the Great Khan. From the number of these prostitutes you may infer the number of traders and other visitors who are daily coming and going here about their business.

You may take it for a fact that more precious and costly wares are imported into Khan-balik than into any other city in the world. Let me give you particulars. All the treasures that come from India—precious stones, pearls, and other rarities—are brought here. So too are the choicest and costliest products of Cathay itself and every other province. This is on account of the Great Khan himself, who lives here, and of the lords and ladies and the enormous multitude of hotel-keepers and other residents and of visitors who attend the courts held here by the Khan. That is why the volume and value of the imports and of the internal trade exceed those of any other city in the world. It is a fact that every day more than 1,000 cart-loads of silk enter the city; for much cloth of gold and silk is woven here. Furthermore, Khan-balik is surrounded by more than 200 other cities, near and far,

* Possibly a reference to public execution.

from which traders come to it to sell and to buy. So it is not surprising that it is the centre of such a traffic as I have described.

In the centre of the city, stands a huge palace in which is a great bell; in the evening this peals three times as a signal that no one may go about the town. Once this bell has sounded the due number of peals, no one ventures abroad in the city except in case of childbirth or illness; and those who are called out by such emergencies are obliged to carry lights. Every night there are guards riding about the city in troops of thirty or forty, to discover whether anyone is going about at an abnormal hour, that is after the third peal of the bell. If anyone is found, he is promptly arrested and clapped into prison. Next morning he is examined by the officials appointed for the purpose, and if he is found guilty of any offence, he is punished according to its gravity with a proportionate number of strokes of a rod, which sometimes cause death. They employ this mode of punishment in order to avoid bloodshed, because their Bakhshi, that is, the adepts in astrology, declare that it is wrong to shed human blood.

It is ordered that every gateway must be guarded by 1,000 men. You must not suppose that this guard is maintained out of mistrust of the inhabitants. It is there, in fact, partly as a mark of respect to the Great Khan who lives in the city, partly as a check upon evil-doers—although, because of the prophecy of his astrologers, the Khan does harbour certain suspicions of the people of Cathay.

Let me now tell you how on one occasion the Cathayans in the city actually did plan to revolt. It is an established practice, as will be explained below, that twelve men are appointed with full powers of disposal over territories and public offices at their own discretion. Among these was a Saracen called Ahmad, a man of great energy and ability, who surpassed all the rest in his authority and influence over the Great Khan. The Emperor was so fond of him that he gave him a completely free hand. It seems, as was learnt after his death, that this Ahmad used to bewitch the Emperor by his black arts to such purpose that he won a ready hearing and acceptance for everything he said; and so he was free to do whatever he chose. He used to make all appointments to office and punish all delinquents. Whenever he wished to cause the death of anyone whom he hated, whether justly or unjustly, he would go to the Emperor and say to him: 'So-and-so deserves to die, because he has offended your Majesty in such-and-such a way.' Then the Emperor would say: 'Do as you think best.' And Ahmad would thereupon put him to death. Therefore, seeing the complete liberty he enjoyed and the absolute faith reposed in him by the Emperor, men did not venture to thwart him in anything. There was no one so great or of such authority as not to fear him. If anyone was accused by him to the Emperor of a capital offence and wished to plead his cause, he had no chance to rebut the charge or state his own case, because he could count on no support—everyone was too much afraid of going against Ahmad. In this way he caused the death of many innocent people.

Furthermore, there was not a pretty woman who took his fancy but he would have his will with her, taking her as a wife if she was not already married or otherwise enforcing her submission. Whenever he learnt that someone had a good-looking daughter, he would send his ruffians to the girl's father, and they would say: 'What is your ambition? Well then, how about this daughter of yours? Give her to the Bailo (for Ahmad was called by the title of Bailo or Lord-Lieutenant) and we will see that he gives you such-and-such a post or office for three years.' So the man would give him his daughter. Then Ahmad would say to the Khan: 'Such-and-such a post is vacant, or will fall vacant on such-and-such a date. So-and-so is the right man for the job.' To which the Khan would answer: 'Do as you think best.' And Ahmad would promptly install him. By this means, playing partly on men's ambition for office, partly on their fears, Ahmad got possession of all the best-looking women as his wives and his concubines. He also had sons, some twenty-five of them, whom he installed in the highest offices. Some of them, under cover of their father's name, used to practise adultery in their father's fashion and commit many other crimes and abominations. Ahmad had also accumulated an immense fortune, because everyone who aspired to any post or office used to send him a handsome present.

Ahmad exercised this authority as governor for twenty-two years. At length the people of the country, that is the Cathayans, seeing that there was no end to the iniquities and abominations that he perpetrated beyond all measure at the expense of their womenfolk as well as their own persons, reached the point where they could endure it no longer. They made up their minds to assassinate him and revolt against the government of the city. Among their number was a Cathayan named Ch'ien-hu, a commander of 1,000, whose mother, daughter, and wife had all been ravished by Ahmad. Ch'ien-hu, moved by fierce indignation, plotted the destruction of the governor with another Cathayan named Wan-hu, a commander of 10,000.★ They planned to do the deed when the Great Khan had completed his three months' sojourn at Khan-balik and had left for the city of Shang-tu, where he would likewise spend three months, and his son Chinghiz had also set out for his accustomed residences. At such times Ahmad was left to keep guard over the city: when the need arose, he would send word to the Great Khan at Shang-tu and the Khan would send back word of his wishes. The two plotters decided to impart their plot to the leading Cathayans of the country, and by common consent they made it known in many other cities to their own friends. The scheme was to take effect on the appointed day in the following manner. At the sight of a signal fire, all the conspirators were immediately to put to death any man wearing a beard and to pass on the signal to other cities by means of beacons that they should do the same. The reason for killing the bearded men was that the Cathayans are naturally beardless, whereas the Tartars, Saracens, and Christians wear beards. You must understand that all the Cathayans hated the government of the Great Khan, because he set over them Tartar rulers, mostly Saracens, and they could not endure it, since it made them feel that they were no more than slaves. Moreover the Great Khan had no legal title to rule the province of Cathay, having acquired it by force. So, putting no trust in the people, he committed the government of the country to Tartars, Saracens, and Christians who were attached to his household and personally loyal to him and not natives of Cathay.

Then Wan-hu and Ch'ien-hu, on the appointed date, entered the palace by night. And Wan-hu seated himself on the throne and had many lights lit in front of him. And he sent a courier to Ahmad, who lived in the old city, announcing that Chinghiz, the Khan's son, had just arrived that very night and summoned the Bailo to wait upon him without delay. When Ahmad heard this, he went immediately, greatly puzzled and not a little alarmed. On his way in through the city gate he met a Tartar named Kogatai, who was in command of the 12,000 men who kept constant watch and ward over the city. 'Where are you going at this late hour?' asked Kogatai. 'To Chinghiz, who has just arrived.' 'How is it possible,' asked Kogatai, 'that he can have arrived so secretly that I have heard nothing of it?' And he followed him with a detachment of his guard. Now the conspirators

★ The titles *Ch'ien-hu* and *Wan-hu* (*Chenchu* and *Vanchu* in R) mean respectively commander of 1,000 and of 10,000.

had said among themselves: 'If only we can kill Ahmad, we have nothing to fear from anything else.' The moment Ahmad entered the palace and saw it such a blaze of lights, he knelt before Wan-hu, mistaking him for Chinghiz; and Ch'ien-hu, who was there armed with a sword, cut off his head.

When Kogatai, who had stopped at the entrance to the palace, saw this, he shouted 'Treason!' And there and then he aimed an arrow at Wan-hu, who was seated on the throne, and shot him dead. Then, calling on his followers, he seized Ch'ien-hu. And he issued a proclamation throughout the city that anyone found out of doors would be killed on the spot. The Cathayans, seeing that the Tartars had discovered their plot and that they were left without a head, one of their leaders being killed and the other captured, stayed quietly in their homes and hence could give no sign to the other cities to carry out their plan of rebellion. Kogatai promptly sent couriers to the Great Khan with a full account of everything that had happened, and received in reply an order to conduct a thorough investigation and punish the guilty according to their deserts. When morning came, Kogatai examined all the Cathayans, and put to death many whom he found to be ring-leaders in the conspiracy. And the same thing was done in the other cities, when it came out that they were involved in the crime.

When the Great Khan had returned to Khan-balik, he wanted to know the cause of this occurrence. He then learnt the truth about the abominable outrages committed, as already related, by the execrable Ahmad and his sons. He found out that Ahmad himself and seven of his sons—for they were not all wicked—had taken innumerable ladies to be their wives, not to speak of those whom they had possessed by force. Then he caused all the treasure that Ahmad had amassed in the Old City to be brought into the New City; and put it with his own treasure; and it was found to be beyond all reckoning. He ordered Ahmad's body to be taken from the grave and flung in the street to be torn to pieces by dogs. And those of his sons who had followed the example of his evil deeds he caused to be flayed alive. And when he called to mind the accursed doctrine of the Saracens, by which every sin is accounted a lawful act even to the killing of any man who is not of their creed, so that because of it the execrable Ahmad and his sons were not conscious of committing any sin, he utterly contemned it and held it in abomination. He summoned the Saracens to his presence and expressly forbade them to do many things which their law commanded. In particular he commanded them to take their wives according to the law of the Tartars and not to cut the throats of animals, as they used to do, in order to eat their flesh, but to slit their bellies. And at the time when all this happened, Messer Marco was in this place.

As for the Great Khan's guard of 12,000 men, you must know that they are called *Keshikten*, which is as much as to say 'knights and liegemen of the lord'. He employs them not out of fear of any man but in token of his sovereignty. These 12,000 horsemen have four captains, one over every 3,000. Each 3,000 in turn reside in the Khan's palace for three days and three nights and eat and drink there, and at the end of that time another 3,000 take their place, and so they continue throughout the year. By day indeed the other 9,000 do not leave the palace, unless it happens that one of them goes off on the Khan's affairs or on some urgent private business and then only if it is legitimate and he has his captain's leave. If he is faced with something really serious, such as the impending death of a father or brother or other near relative, or the threat of some heavy loss which would not permit of his immediate return, then he must get leave from the Khan. But at night the 9,000 are free to go home.

When the Great Khan is holding court, the seating at banquets is arranged as follows. He himself sits at a much higher table than the rest at the northern end of the hall, so that he faces south. His principal wife sits next to him on the left. On the right, at a somewhat lower level, sit his sons in order of age, Chinghiz the eldest being placed rather higher than the rest, and his grandsons and his kinsmen of the imperial lineage. They are so placed that their heads are on a level with the Great Khan's feet. Next to them are seated the other noblemen at other tables lower down again. And the ladies are seated on the same plan. All the wives of the Khan's sons and grandsons and kinsmen are seated on his left at a lower level, and next to them the wives of his nobles and knights lower down still. And they all know their appointed place in the lord's plan. The tables are so arranged that the Great Khan can see everything, and there are a great many of them. But you must not imagine that all the guests sit at table; for most of the knights and nobles in the hall take their meal seated on carpets for want of tables. Outside the hall the guests at the banquet number more than 40,000. For they include many visitors with costly gifts, men who come from strange countries bringing strange things, and some who have held high office and aspire to further advancement. Such are the guests who attend on such occasions, when the Great Khan is holding court or celebrating a wedding.

In the midst of the hall where the Great Khan has his table is a very fine piece of furniture of great size and splendour in the form of a square chest, each side being three paces in length, elaborately carved with figures of animals finely wrought in gold. The inside is hollow and contains a huge golden vessel in the form of a pitcher with the capacity of a butt, which is filled with wine. In each corner of the chest is a vessel with the capacity of a firkin, one filled with mares' milk, one with camels' milk, and the others with other beverages. On the chest stand all the Khan's vessels in which drink is served to him. From it the wine or other precious beverage is drawn off to fill huge stoups of gold, each containing enough to satisfy eight or ten men. One of these is set between every two men seated at table. Each of the two has a gold cup with a handle, which he fills from the stoup. And for every pair of ladies one stoup and two cups are provided in the same way. You must understand that these stoups and the rest are of great value. I can assure you that the Great Khan has such a store of vessels of gold and silver that no one who did not see it with his own eyes could well believe it. And the waiters who serve his food and drink are certain of his barons. They have their mouths and noses swathed in fine napkins of silk and gold, so that the food and drink are not contaminated by their breath or effluence.

Certain barons are also appointed to look after new-comers unfamiliar with court etiquette and show them to their allotted and appropriate seats. These barons are continually passing to and fro through the hall, asking the guests if they lack anything. And if there are any who want wine or milk or anything else, they have it promptly brought to them by the waiters. At all the entrances of the hall, or wherever else the Great Khan may be, stand two men of gigantic stature, one on either side, with staves in their hands. This is because it is not permissible for anyone to touch the threshold of the door, but all who enter must step over it. If anyone should happen to touch it by accident, the guardians take his clothes from him and he must pay a fine to redeem them. Or if they do not take his clothes, they administer the appointed number of blows. But if they are new-comers who do not know of the rule, certain barons are assigned to introduce them and warn them of the rule. This is done because

H

touching the threshold is looked upon as a bad omen. In leaving the hall, since some of the guests are overcome with drinking so that they could not possibly exercise due care, no such rule is enjoined.

There are many instruments in the hall, of every sort, and when the Great Khan is about to drink they all strike up. As soon as the cup-bearer has handed him the cup, he retires three paces and kneels down; and all the barons and all the people present go down on their knees and make a show of great humility. Then the Great Khan drinks. And every time he drinks the same performance is repeated. Of the food I say nothing, because everyone will readily believe that there is no lack of it. Let me add that there is no baron or knight at the banquet but brings his wife to dine with the other ladies. When they have fed and the tables are removed, a great troupe of jugglers and acrobats and other entertainers comes into the hall and performs remarkable feats of various kinds. And they all afford great amusement and entertainment in the Khan's presence, and the guests show their enjoyment by peals of laughter. When all is over, the guests take their leave and return each to his own lodging or house.

You must know that all the Tartars celebrate their birthdays as festivals. The Great Khan was born on the twenty-eighth day of the lunar cycle in the month of September. And on this day he holds the greatest feast of the year, excepting only the new year festival of which I will tell you later. On his birthday he dons a magnificent robe of beaten gold. And fully 12,000 barons and knights robe themselves with him in a similar colour and style—not so costly as his, but still of the same colour and style, in cloth of silk and gold, and all with gold belts. These robes are given to them by the Great Khan. And I assure you that the value of some of these robes, reckoning the precious stones and pearls with which they are often adorned, amounts to 10,000 golden bezants. Of such there are not a few. And you must know that the Great Khan gives rich robes to these 12,000 barons and knights thirteen times a year, so that they are all dressed in robes like his own and of great value. You can see for yourselves that this is no light matter, and that there is no other prince in the world besides himself who could bear such an expense.

On this royal birthday all the Tartars in the world, all the provinces and regions where men hold land and lordship under the Great Khan, give him costly presents proportionate to the giver and in accordance with prescribed order. And rich gifts are also brought to him by many others, petitioners for high office—which is awarded to applicants according to merit by twelve barons appointed for the purpose. And on this day all the idolaters and all the Christians and all the Saracens and all the races of men offer solemn prayers to their idols and their gods, with singing of hymns and lighting of lamps and burning of incense, that they may save their lord and give him long life and joy and health. So this day is passed in merry-making and birthday festivities. Now that I have fully described them, let us turn to another great feast which is celebrated at the new year and is called the White Feast.

The new year begins with them in February, and this is how it is observed by the Great Khan and all his subjects. According to custom they all array themselves in white, both male and female, so far as their means allow. And this they do because they regard white costume as auspicious and benign, and they don it at the new year so that throughout the year they may enjoy prosperity and happiness. On this day all the rulers, and all the provinces and regions and realms where men hold land or lordship under his sway, bring him costly gifts of gold and silver and pearls and precious stones and abundance of fine white cloth, so that throughout the year their lord may have no lack of treasure and may live in joy and gladness. Let me tell you also that the barons and knights and all the people make gifts to one another of white things. And they greet one another gaily and cheerfully saying, very much as we do: 'May this year be a lucky one for you and bring you success in all you undertake.' And this they do so that throughout the year all may go well with them and all their enterprises prosper.

I can also assure you for a fact that on this day the Great Khan receives gifts of more than 100,000 white horses, of great beauty and price.* And on this day also there is a procession of his elephants, fully 5,000 in number, all draped in fine cloths embroidered with beasts and birds. Each one bears on its back two strong-boxes of great beauty and price filled with the Khan's plate and with costly apparel for this white-robed court. With them come innumerable camels also draped with cloths and laden with provisions for the feast. They all defile in front of the Great Khan and it is the most splendid sight that ever was seen.

* R adds that the horses, if not pure white, are mainly white; that white horses are very plentiful in these parts, and that whatever a province presents to the Khan, whether it be horses, pieces of gold or cloth, or anything else, the number given must amount to nine times nine.

On the morning of this feast, before the tables are set up, all the kings and all the dukes, marquises and counts, barons, knights, astrologers, physicians, falconers, and many other officials and rulers of men and lands and armies appear before the Khan in the great hall. And those who do not achieve this assemble outside the palace in a spot where the Khan can readily inspect them. Let me tell you in what order they are stationed. In front are his sons and grandsons and those of his imperial lineage. Next come the kings, then the dukes and then all the other ranks, one behind another, in due order. And when they are all seated, each in his proper station, up stands a great dignitary and proclaims in a loud voice: 'Bow down and worship!' No sooner has he said this than they bow down, then and there, and touch the ground with their foreheads, and address a prayer to the lord and worship him as if he were a god. Then the dignitary proclaims: 'God save our lord and long preserve him in gladness and joy!' And one and all reply: 'God do so!' Once again the dignitary proclaims: 'God increase and multiply his empire from good to better and keep all his subjects in untroubled peace and good will and in all his lands grant universal prosperity!' And one and all reply: 'God do so!' In this manner they worship him four times. Then they go to an altar, adorned with great splendour, on which is a scarlet tablet bearing the name of the Great Khan, and also a splendidly wrought censer. They cense this tablet and the altar with great reverence.* Then they return, each to his place. When they have all done this, then the precious gifts of which I have spoken are presented. After this, when the Great Khan has viewed all the gifts, the tables are laid and the guests take their places in due order as I have already related—the Khan alone at his high table with his first wife, and the others each in his degree, and their ladies on the empress's side of the hall, just as I have described it to you before. When they have fed, the performers come in and entertain the court as before. Finally they return, everyone to his own lodging or home.

Next let me tell you that the Great Khan has ordained thirteen feasts, one for each of the thirteen lunar months, which are attended by the 12,000 barons called *Keshikten*, that is to say the henchmen most closely attached to the Khan. To each of these he has given thirteen robes, every one of a different colour. They are splendidly adorned with pearls and gems and other ornaments and are of im-

* In R's version it is the dignitary only who applies the incense, while the others do reverence.

mense value. He has also given to each of the 12,000 a gold belt of great beauty and price, and shoes of fine leather (called *canaut* or *borgal*) cunningly embroidered with silver thread, which are likewise beautiful and costly. All their attire is so gorgeous and so stately that when they are fully robed any one of them might pass for a king. One of these robes is appointed to be worn at each of the thirteen feasts.* The Great Khan himself has thirteen similar robes—similar, that is, in colour, but more splendid and costly and more richly adorned; and he always dresses in the same colour as his barons.

The cost of these robes, to the number of 156,000 in all, amounts to a quantity of treasure that is almost past computation, to say nothing of the belts and shoes, which also cost a goodly sum. And all this the Khan does for the embellishment or enhancement of his feasts.

Let me conclude with one more fact, a very remarkable one well worthy of mention in our book. You must know that a great lion is led into the Great Khan's presence; and as soon as it sees him it flings itself down prostrate before him with every appearance of deep humility and seems to acknowledge him as lord. There it stays without a chain, and is indeed a thing to marvel at.

We will turn next to the Great Khan's hunting parties.

You may take it for a fact that during the three months which the Great Khan spends in the city of Khan-balik, that is, December, January, and February, he has ordered that within a distance of sixty days' journey from where he is staying everybody must devote himself to hunting and hawking. The order goes out to every governor of men or lands to send all such large beasts as wild boars, harts, stags, roebucks, bears, and the like, or at any rate the greater part of them. So every governor gathers round him all the huntsmen of the district, and together they go wherever these beasts are to be found, beating their coverts in turn and killing some of them with their hounds but most with their arrows. That is how they hunt them. And those beasts that they wish to send to the Great Khan they first disembowel and then load on carts and so dispatch. This applies to all those within thirty days' journey, and their combined bag is enormous. Those distant from thirty to sixty days do not send the flesh—the journey is too long for that—but send the hides duly dressed and tanned, so that the Khan may use them in the manufacture of necessary equipment for his armies.

* R adds that each robe lasts for ten years, more or less.

You must know also that the Great Khan has a plentiful supply of leopards skilled in hunting game and of lynxes trained in the chase and past masters of their craft. He has a number of lions of immense size, bigger than those of Egypt; they have very handsome, richly coloured fur, with longitudinal stripes of black, orange, and white. They are trained to hunt wild boars and bulls, bears, wild asses, stags, roebuck, and other game. A grand sight it is to see the stately creatures that fall a prey to these lions. When the lions are led out to the chase, they are carried on carts in cages, each with a little dog for company. They are caged because otherwise they would be too ferocious and too eager in their pursuit of game, so that there would be no holding them. They must always be led upwind; for if their prey caught wind of the smell they would not wait, but would be off in a flash. He has also a great many eagles trained to take wolves and foxes and fallow-deer and roe-deer, and these too bring in game in plenty. Those that are trained to take wolves are of immense size and power, for there is never a wolf so big that he escapes capture by one of these eagles.

Now that you have heard what I have to tell on this subject, I will tell you of the numbers and excellence of the Great Khan's hounds. You must know that among his barons there are two brothers in blood who are named Bayan and Mingan. They bear the title *kuyukchi*, that is to say, keepers of the mastiffs. Each of them has 10,000 subordinates, who all wear livery of one colour; and the other 10,000 all wear another colour. The two colours are scarlet and blue. Whenever they accompany the Great Khan in the chase, they wear these liveries. Among either 10,000 there are 2,000 of whom each one leads a mastiff, or maybe two or more, so that the total number is immense. When the Great Khan goes hunting, one of the two brothers with his 10,000 men and fully 5,000 hounds goes with him on one side and the other with his 10,000 and his hounds goes on the other. The two bands keep pace with each other exactly, so that the whole line extends in length over a day's journey. And not a wild beast do they find but falls a prey. What a sight it is to see the hunt and the performance of the hounds and the hunters! For you must picture that, while the Great Khan rides out hawking with his barons across the open country, then packs of these hounds are to be seen advancing on either side, hunting bears and stags and other beasts, so that it is truly a fine sight to see. These two brothers are bound by covenant to provide the Great Khan's court every day, beginning in

October and continuing to the end of March, with a thousand head of game, including both beasts and birds, except quails, and also fish to the best of their ability, reckoning as the equivalent of one head as much fish as would make a square meal for three persons.

When the Khan has spent the three months of December, January, and February in the city of which I have spoken, he sets off in March and travels southward to within two days' journey of the Ocean. He is accompanied by fully 10,000 falconers and takes with him fully 5,000 gerfalcons and peregrine falcons and sakers in great abundance, besides a quantity of goshawks for hawking along the riversides. You must not imagine that he keeps all this company with him in one place. In fact he distributes them here and there, in groups of a hundred or two hundred or more. Then they engage in fowling, and most of the fowl they take are brought to the Great Khan. And I would have you know that when he goes hawking with his gerfalcons and other hawks, he has fully 10,000 men in parties of two who are called *toscaor*, which signifies in our language 'watchmen'. These men are posted here and there in couples, so as to occupy a wide enough area. Each has a call and a hood, so that they can call in the hawks and hold them. And when the Khan orders the hawks to be cast, there is no need for the casters to go after them, because the men of whom I have spoken, dispersed here and there, keep such careful watch that wherever a hawk may go they are always on the spot and if one is in need of help they are prompt to render it.

All the Great Khan's hawks and those of the other barons have a little tablet of silver attached to their feet on which is written the name of the owner and also that of the keeper. By this means the bird is recognized as soon as it is taken, and is returned to the owner. If the finder does not know whose it is, he takes it to a baron who is called *bularguchi*, which is as much as to say 'keeper of lost property'. For, I would have you know that, if anyone finds a horse or a sword or a hawk or anything else and cannot discover the owner, it is immediately brought to this baron, and he takes charge of it. If the finder does not hand it over forthwith, he is reckoned a thief. And the losers apply to this baron, and if he has received their property he promptly returns it. He always has his official residence, with its flag flying, at the highest point in the whole camp, so as to be readily seen by those who have lost anything. By this means nothing can be lost without being found and returned.

When the Great Khan goes on the journey of which I have told you towards the Ocean, the expedition is marked by many fine displays of huntsmanship and falconry. Indeed, there is no sport in the world to compare with it. He always rides on the back of four elephants,* in a very handsome shelter of wood, covered inside with cloth of beaten gold and outside with lion skins. Here he always keeps twelve gerfalcons of the best he possesses and is attended by several barons to entertain him and keep him company. When he is travelling in this shelter on the elephants, and other barons who are riding in his train call out, 'Sire, there are cranes passing,' and he orders the roof of the shelter to be thrown open and so sees the cranes, he bids his attendants fetch such gerfalcons as he may choose and lets them fly. And often, the gerfalcons take the cranes in full view while the Great Khan remains all the while on his couch. And this affords him great sport and recreation. Meanwhile the other barons and knights ride all round him. And you may rest assured that there never was, and I do not believe there ever will be, any man who can enjoy such sport and recreation in this world as he does, or has such facilities for doing so.

When he has travelled so far that he arrives at a place called Cachar Modun, then he finds his pavilions ready pitched there and those of his sons and his barons and his mistresses to the number of more than 10,000; and very fine they are, and very costly. Let me tell you how his pavilion is made. First, the tent in which he holds his court is big enough to accommodate fully a thousand knights. This tent has its entrance towards the south and serves as a hall for the barons and other retainers. Adjoining this is another tent which faces west and is occupied by the Khan himself. It is to this tent that he summons anyone with whom he wishes to converse. At the back of the great hall is a large and handsome chamber in which he sleeps. There are also other chambers and other tents; but they do not adjoin the great tent. Let me tell you how these two halls and the chamber are constructed. Each hall has columns of spicewood very skilfully carved. On the outside they are all covered with lion-skins of great beauty, striped with black and white and orange. They are so well designed that neither wind nor rain can harm them or do any mischief. Inside they are all of ermine and sable, which are the two finest and richest and costliest furs there are. The truth is that a superfine sable fur big

---

* R adds that when he is hawking he confines himself to two elephants or even one, so as to pass more easily through narrow defiles, and that he adopts this mode of transport because he suffers from gout.

enough for a man's cloak is worth up to 2,000 golden bezants, while an ordinary one is worth 1,000. The Tartars call it 'the king of furs'. The sable is about the size of a marten. With these two sorts of skin the two great halls are lined, pieced together with such artistry that it is a truly amazing spectacle. And the chamber where the Khan sleeps, which adjoins the two halls, is also of lion-skins without and ermine and sable within, magnificent in workmanship and design. The cords that hold up the halls and chamber are all of silk. So precious indeed and so costly are these three tents that no petty king could afford them.

Round these three tents are pitched all the other tents, also well designed and appointed. The Khan's mistresses too have splendid pavilions. And for the gerfalcons and falcons and other birds and beasts there are tents in vast numbers. What need of more words? You may take it for a fact that the number of people in this camp almost passes belief. You might well fancy that the Khan was here in residence in his finest city. For it is thronged with multitudes from all parts. His whole household staff is here with him, besides physicians and astrologers and falconers and other officials in great numbers, and everything is as well ordered as in his capital.

In this place he stays till spring, which in these parts falls about our Easter Day. Throughout his stay he never ceases to go hawking by lake or stream, and he makes an ample catch of cranes and swans and other birds. And his followers who are dispersed about the neighbourhood send in lavish contributions of game and fowl. All this time he enjoys the finest sport and recreation in the world, so that no one in the world who has not seen it could ever believe it; so far do his magnificence and his state and his pleasures surpass my description.

Let me tell you one thing more. No merchant or artisan or peasant dare keep any falcon or bird of prey or any hound for the chase within twenty days' journey of the Great Khan's residence; but in every other province and region of his dominions they are free to hunt and do as they please with hawks and hounds.* And you must understand, furthermore, that throughout his empire no king or baron or any other person dares to take or hunt hare or hart, buck or stag, or

* Probably there is an omission here, so that 'they' does not refer to these commoners. According to R these three classes are forbidden to hunt or hawk anywhere in the Khan's dominions. Barons and knights are normally permitted; but within a certain distance of the Khan's residence, ranging from five to fifteen days' journey, they must be enrolled under the captain of falconers or possess a special privilege.

any other such beast between the months of March and October, so that they may increase and multiply. And anyone who contravenes this rule is made to repent it bitterly, because it is the Khan's own enactment. And I assure you that his commandment is so strictly obeyed that hares and bucks and other beasts I have mentioned often come right up to a man, and he does not touch them or do them any harm.

After spending his time here in this fashion till about Easter Day, the Great Khan sets out with all his retainers and returns direct to the city of Khan-balik by the same route by which he came, hunting and hawking all the way and enjoying good sport.

It is in this city of Khan-balik that the Great Khan has his mint; and it is so organized that you might well say that he has mastered the art of alchemy. I will demonstrate this to you here and now.

You must know that he has money made for him by the following process, out of the bark of trees—to be precise, from mulberry trees (the same whose leaves furnish food for silk-worms). The fine bast between the bark and the wood of the tree is stripped off. Then it is crumbled and pounded and flattened out with the aid of glue into sheets like sheets of cotton paper, which are all black. When made, they are cut up into rectangles of various sizes, longer than they are broad. The smallest is worth half a small tornesel; the next an entire such tornesel; the next half a silver groat; the next an entire silver groat, equal in value to a silver groat of Venice; and there are others equivalent to two, five, and ten groats and one, three, and as many as ten gold bezants. And all these papers are sealed with the seal of the Great Khan. The procedure of issue is as formal and as authoritative as if they were made of pure gold or silver. On each piece of money several specially appointed officials write their names, each setting his own stamp. When it is completed in due form, the chief of the officials deputed by the Khan dips in cinnabar the seal or bull assigned to him and stamps it on the top of the piece of money so that the shape of the seal in vermilion remains impressed upon it. And then the money is authentic. And if anyone were to forge it, he would suffer the extreme penalty.*

Of this money the Khan has such a quantity made that with it he

---

* The preceding five sentences and a few minor details included in this section are found only in R. This account of Chinese paper money, apart from its general economic misconceptions, raises several technical questions that are still unresolved.

could buy all the treasure in the world. With this currency he orders all payments to be made throughout every province and kingdom and region of his empire. And no one dares refuse it on pain of losing his life. And I assure you that all the peoples and populations who are subject to his rule are perfectly willing to accept these papers in payment, since wherever they go they pay in the same currency, whether for goods or for pearls or precious stones or gold or silver. With these pieces of paper they can buy anything and pay for anything. And I can tell you that the papers that reckon as ten bezants do not weigh one.

Several times a year parties of traders arrive with pearls and precious stones and gold and silver and other valuables, such as cloth of gold and silk, and surrender them all to the Great Khan. The Khan then summons twelve experts, who are chosen for the task and have special knowledge of it, and bids them examine the wares that the traders have brought and pay for them what they judge to be their true value. The twelve experts duly examine the wares and pay the value in the paper currency of which I have spoken. The traders accept it willingly, because they can spend it afterwards on the various goods they buy throughout the Great Khan's dominions.* And I give you my word that the wares brought in at different times during the year amount up to a value of fully 400,000 bezants, and they are all paid for in this paper currency.

Let me tell you further that several times a year a fiat goes forth through the towns that all those who have gems and pearls and gold and silver must bring them to the Great Khan's mint. This they do, and in such abundance that it is past all reckoning; and they are all paid in paper money. By this means the Great Khan acquires all the gold and silver and pearls and precious stones of all his territories.

Here is another fact well worth relating. When these papers have been so long in circulation that they are growing torn and frayed, they are brought to the mint and changed for new and fresh ones at a discount of 3 per cent. And here again is an admirable practice that well deserves mention in our book: if a man wants to buy gold or silver to make his service of plate or his belts or other finery, he goes to the Khan's mint with some of these papers and gives them in

* R adds that the traders are allowed a profit on the exchange, and if they come from regions where the paper money is not current, they invest it in other goods that have a value in their own countries.

payment for the gold and silver which he buys from the mint-master. And all the Khan's armies are paid with this sort of money.

I have now told you how it comes about that the Great Khan must have, as indeed he has, more treasure than anyone else in the world. I may go further and affirm that all the world's great potentates put together have not such riches as belong to the Great Khan alone.

Let me tell you next of the magnates who exercise authority from Khan-balik.

You must know that the Great Khan, as already mentioned, has appointed twelve great and powerful barons to supervise all decisions concerning the movement of the armies, changes in the high command, and dispatch of troops to one theatre or another in greater or less force, as need may require, according to the importance of the war. In addition it rests with them to sort out the staunch and fearless fighters from the faint-hearted, promoting the former and degrading those who prove incompetent or cowardly. And if anyone is captain of a thousand and has disgraced himself in any action, these barons decide that he has shown himself unworthy of his office and debase him to the rank of captain of a hundred. But if he has conducted himself creditably and with distinction, so that they judge him fit for a higher command, they advance him to a captaincy of ten thousand. In every case, however, they act with the knowledge of the Great Khan. When they propose to degrade anyone, they say to the Khan, 'So-and-so is unworthy of such-and-such an office,' to which he replies, 'Let him be degraded to a lower rank'; and so it is done. If they have it in mind to promote anyone in acknowledgement of his merits, they say, 'Such-and-such a captain of a thousand is fit and worthy to be captain of ten thousand'; then the Khan confirms the appointment and gives him the appropriate tablet, as previously described, and immediately orders him to be given presents of great value, so as to encourage the others to make the most of their abilities. This council of twelve barons is called *Thai*, that is to say 'Supreme Court', because there is no higher authority except the Great Khan himself.

Besides these there are twelve other barons to whom the Khan has committed authority over all the affairs of the thirty-four provinces. And this is how they are organized. Let me tell you first that they live in a palace in the town of Khan-balik, a palace of great size and beauty with many halls and residential quarters. For every province there is a judge and a staff of clerks, who all live in this palace, each in his own private residence. And the judge and his staff administer all the affairs of the province to which they are assigned, subject to the will and authority of the twelve barons. It rests with these barons to choose the governors of all the provinces. And when they have chosen men whom they consider competent and suitable, they recommend them to the Great Khan, who confirms their appointment and confers the appropriate tablet. They also supervise the collection of taxes and revenues together with their administration and expenditure and all else that concerns the imperial government throughout these provinces, except purely military matters. This Council goes by the name of *Shieng*, and the palace in which it is housed is also called *Shieng*.

Both the Thai and the Shieng are supreme courts, having no authority above them except the Great Khan himself, and enjoying the power to confer benefits on whom they will. The Thai, however, that is to say the military court, is esteemed more highly and carries greater dignity than any other office.

I do not propose to enumerate the provinces at this stage, as I shall be giving a full account of them later in the book. Let us turn now to the system of post-horses by which the Great Khan sends his dispatches.

You must know that the city of Khan-balik is a centre from which many roads radiate to many provinces, one to each, and every road bears the name of the province to which it runs. The whole system is admirably contrived. When one of the Great Khan's messengers sets out along any of these roads, he has only to go twenty-five miles and there he finds a posting station, which in their language is called *yamb* and in our language may be rendered 'horse post'. At every post the messengers find a spacious and palatial hostelry for their lodging. These hostelries have splendid beds with rich coverlets of silk and all that befits an emissary of high rank. If a king came here, he would be well lodged. Here the messengers find no less than 400 horses, stationed here by the Great Khan's orders and always kept in readiness for his messengers when they are sent on any mission. And you must understand that posts such as these, at distances of twenty-five or thirty miles, are to be found along all the main highways leading to the provinces of which I have spoken. And at each of these posts the messengers find three or four hundred horses in readiness awaiting their command, and palatial lodgings such as I have described. And this holds good throughout all the provinces and kingdoms of the Great Khan's empire.

When the messengers are travelling through out-of-the-way country, where there are no homesteads or habitations, they find that the Great Khan has had posts established even in these wilds, with the same palatial accommodation and the same supply of horses and accoutrements. But here the stages are longer; for the posts are thirty-five miles apart and in some cases over forty miles.*

By this means the Great Khan's messengers travel throughout his dominions and have lodgings and horses fully accoutred for every stage. And this is surely the highest privilege and the greatest resource ever enjoyed by any man on earth, king or emperor or what you will. For you may be well assured that more than 200,000 horses are stabled at these posts for the special use of these messengers. Moreover, the posts themselves number more than 10,000, all furnished on the same lavish scale. The whole organization is so stupendous and so costly that it baffles speech and writing.†

If anyone is puzzled to understand how there can be enough people to execute such tasks, and what is the source of their livelihood, my answer is this. All the idolaters, and likewise the Saracens, take six, eight or ten wives apiece, as many as they can afford to keep, and beget innumerable children. Hence there will be many men with more than thirty sons of their own, who all follow them under arms. This follows from the plurality of wives. With us, on the other hand, a man has only one wife, and if she should prove barren he will end his days with her and beget no children. Hence our population is less than theirs. As to the means of life, they have no shortage, because they mostly use rice, panic, or millet, especially the Tartars and the people of Cathay and Manzi, and these three cereals in their countries yield an increase of a hundredfold on each sowing. These peoples do not use bread, but simply boil these three sorts of grain with milk or flesh and then eat them. Wheat in their country does not yield such an increase; but such of it as they harvest they eat only in the form of noodles or other pasty foods. Among them no land is left idle that might be cultivated. Their beasts increase and multiply without end.

* R adds that the Khan sends people to live at these places and till the soil and serve the posts, so that they grow into good-sized villages.
† There is evidently some confusion about the foregoing figures.

When they are on military service, there is not one of them who does not lead with him six, eight, or more horses for his own use. So it is not difficult to understand why the population in these parts is so enormous and the means of life so plentiful.

Now let me tell you another thing which I forgot to mention—one that is very germane to the matter in hand. The fact is that between one post and the next, at distances of three miles apart, there are stations which may contain as many as forty buildings occupied by unmounted couriers, who also play a part in the Great Khan's postal service. I will tell you how. They wear large belts, set all round with bells, so that when they run they are audible at a great distance. They always run at full speed and never for more than three miles. And at the next station three miles away, where the noise they make gives due notice of their approach, another courier is waiting in readiness. As soon as the first man arrives, the new one takes what he is carrying and also a little note given to him by the clerk, and starts to run. After he has run for three miles, the performance is repeated. And I can assure you that by means of this service of unmounted couriers, the Great Khan receives news over a ten days' journey in a day and a night. For it takes these runners no more than a day and a night to cover a ten days' journey, or two days and two nights for a twenty days' journey. So in ten days they can transmit news over a journey of a hundred days. And in the fruit season it often happens that by this means fruit gathered in the morning in the city of Khan-balik is delivered on the evening of the next day to the Great Khan in the city of Shang-tu, ten days' journey away.

At each of these three-mile stations there is appointed a clerk who notes the day and hour of the arrival of every courier and the departure of his successor; and this practice is in force at every station. And there are also inspectors charged with the duty of going round every month and examining all these stations, in order to detect any couriers who have been remiss and punish them. From these couriers, and from the staff at the stations, the Great Khan exacts no tax, and he makes generous provision for their maintenance.

As for the horses of which I have spoken, which are kept in such numbers at the posts to carry the imperial messengers, I will tell you exactly how the Great Khan has established them. First he inquires, 'Which is the nearest city to such-and-such a post?'; then, 'How many horses can it maintain for the messengers?' Then the civic authorities investigate by means of experts how many horses can be maintained in the neighbouring post by the city and how many by the local towns and villages, and they apportion them according to the resources available. The cities act in concert, taking into consideration that between one post and the next there is sometimes another city, which makes its contribution with the rest. They provide for the horses out of the taxes due to the Great Khan: thus, if a man is assessed for taxation at a sum that would maintain a horse and a half, he is ordered to make corresponding provision at the neighbouring post. But you must understand that the cities do not maintain 400 horses continuously at each post. Actually they keep 200 for a month, to sustain the burdens of the post, while the other 200 are fattening. At the end of the month the fattened horses are transferred to the post while the others take their turn at grass. So they alternate perpetually.

If it happens at any point that there is some river or lake over which the couriers and mounted messengers must pass, the neighbouring cities keep three or four ferry-boats continually in readiness for this purpose. And if there is a desert to cross of many days' journey in extent, in which no permanent habitation can be established, the city next to the desert is obliged to furnish horses to the Khan's envoys to see them across, together with provisions for their escort. But to such cities the Khan affords special aid. And in out-of-the-way posts the horses are maintained partly by the Khan himself, partly by the nearest cities, towns, and villages.

When the need arises for the Great Khan to receive immediate tidings by mounted messenger, as of the rebellion of a subject country or of one of his barons or any matter that may concern him deeply, I assure you that the messengers ride 200 miles in a day, sometimes even 250. Let me explain how it is done. When a messenger wishes to travel at this speed and cover so many miles in a day, he carries a tablet with a sign of the gerfalcon as a token that he wishes to ride post haste. If there are two of them, they set out from the place where they are on two good horses, strongly built and swift runners. They tighten their belts and swathe their heads and off they go with all the speed they can muster, till they reach the next post-house twenty-five miles away. As they draw near they sound a sort of horn which is audible at a great distance, so that horses may be got ready for them. On arrival they find two fresh horses, ready harnessed, fully rested, and in good running form. They mount there and then, without a moment's breathing-space, and are no sooner mounted than off they go again, taking the last ounce out of their horses and not pausing till they reach the next post, where they find two more horses harnessed as before. Then up and off again. And so it goes on till evening. That is how these messengers manage to cover 250 miles a day with news for the Great Khan. Indeed, in extreme urgency, they can achieve 300 miles. In such cases they ride all night long; and if there is no moon the men of the post run in front of them with torches as far as the next post. But they cannot ride as fast by night as by day, because they are delayed by the slower pace of the runners. Messengers who can endure the fatigue of such a ride as this are very highly prized.

Now let me tell you something of the bounties that the Great Khan confers upon his subjects. For all his thoughts are directed towards helping the people who are subject to him, so that they may live and labour and increase their wealth. You may take it for a fact that he sends emissaries and inspectors throughout all his dominions and kingdoms and provinces to learn whether any of his people have suffered a failure of their crops either through weather or through locusts or other pests. And if he finds that any have lost their harvest, he exempts them for that year from their tribute and even gives them some of his own grain to sow and to eat—a magnificent act of royal bounty. This he does in the summer. And in winter he does likewise in the matter of cattle. If he finds any man whose cattle have been killed by an outbreak of plague, he gives him some of his own, derived from the tithes of other provinces, and to help him further he relieves him of tribute for the year.

Again, if it should happen that lightning strikes any flock of sheep or herd of other beasts, whether the herd belong to one person or more and no matter how big it may be, the Great Khan will not take tithe of it for three years. And similarly if it chances to strike a ship laden with merchandise, he will not have any due or share of the cargo, because he accounts it an ill omen when lightning strikes any man's possessions. He reasons: 'God must have been angry with this man, since He launched a thunderbolt at him.' Therefore he does not wish that such possessions, struck by the wrath of God, should find their way into his treasury.

Here is another benefit that he confers.

Along the main highways frequented by his messengers and by merchants and other folk, he has ordered trees to be planted on both

I

sides, two paces distant from one another. They are so large that they can be seen from a long way off. And he has done this so that any wayfarer may recognize the roads and not lose his way. For you will find these wayside trees in the heart of the wilderness; and a great boon they are to travellers and traders. They extend throughout every province and every kingdom. Where the roads traverse sandy deserts or rocky mountain ranges, so that it is not possible to plant trees, he has other land-marks set up in the form of cairns or pillars to indicate the track. He has certain officials whose duty it is to ensure that these are always kept in order. Besides the reasons already mentioned, he is all the more willing to have these trees planted because his soothsayers and astrologers declare that he who causes trees to be planted lives long.

You must know that most of the inhabitants of the province of Cathay drink a wine such as I will describe to you. They make a drink of rice and an assortment of excellent spices, prepared in such a way that it is better to drink than any other wine. It is beautifully clear and it intoxicates more speedily than any other wine, because it is very heating.

Let me tell you next of stones that burn like logs. It is a fact that throughout the province of Cathay there is a sort of black stone, which is dug out of veins in the hillsides and burns like logs. These stones keep a fire going better than wood. I assure you that, if you put them on the fire in the evening and see that they are well alight, they will continue to burn all night, so that you will find them still glowing in the morning.* They do not give off flames, except a little when they are first kindled, just as charcoal does, and once they have caught fire they give out great heat. And you must know that these stones are burnt throughout the province of Cathay. It is true that they also have plenty of firewood. But the population is so enormous and there are so many bath-houses and baths continually being heated, that the wood could not possibly suffice, since there is no one who does not go to a bath-house at least three times a week and take a bath, and in winter every day, if he can manage it. And every man of rank or means has his own bathroom in his house, where he takes a bath. So it is clear that there could never be enough wood to maintain such a conflagration. So these stones, being very plentiful and very cheap, effect a great saving of wood.

* It is surprising that a Venetian should regard coal as a curiosity at a time when Londoners were already complaining of the smog caused by 'sea coal' from the Tyne.

To return to the provision of grain, you may take it for a fact that the Great Khan, when he sees that the harvests are plentiful and corn is cheap, accumulates vast quantities of it and stores it in huge granaries, where it is so carefully preserved that it remains unspoilt for three or four years. So he builds up a stock of every sort of grain—wheat, barley, millet, rice, panic, and others—in great abundance. Then, when it happens that some crops fail and there is a dearth of grain, he draws on these stocks. If the price is running at a bezant for a measure of wheat, for instance, he supplies four measures for the same sum. And he releases enough for all, so that everyone has plenty of corn to meet his needs. In this way he sees to it that none of his subjects need ever go short. And this he does throughout all parts of his empire.

Let me now tell you how the Great Khan bestows charity on the poor people of Khan-balik. When he learns that some family of honest and respectable people have been impoverished by some misfortune or disabled from working by illness, so that they have no means of earning their daily bread, he sees to it that such families (which may consist of six to ten persons or more) are given enough to cover their expenses for the whole year. These families, at the time appointed, go to the officials whose task it is to superintend the Great Khan's expenditure and who live in a palatial building assigned to their office. And each one produces a certificate of the sum paid to him for his subsistence the year before, and provision is made for them at the same rate this year. This provision includes clothing inasmuch as the Great Khan receives a tithe of all the wool, silk, and hemp used for cloth-making. He has these materials woven into cloth in a specially appointed building in which they are stored. Since all the crafts are under obligation to devote one day a week to working on his behalf, he has this cloth made up into garments, which he gives to the poor families in accordance with their needs for winter and for summer wear. He also provides clothing for his armies by having woollen cloth woven in every city as a contribution towards the payment of its tithe.

You must understand that the Tartars according to their ancient customs, before they became familiar with the doctrines of the idolaters, never used to give any alms. Indeed, when a poor man came to them, they would drive him off with maledictions, saying: 'Go with God's curse upon you! If he had loved you as he loves me, he would have blessed you with prosperity!' But since the sages of the idolaters, in particular the Bakhshi of whom I have spoken above, preached to the Great Khan that it was a good work to provide for the poor and that their idols would be greatly pleased by it, he was induced to make such provision as I have described. No one who cares to go to his court in quest of bread is ever turned away empty-handed. Everyone receives a portion. And not a day passes but twenty or thirty thousand bowls of rice, millet, and panic are doled out and given away by the officials appointed. And this goes on all the year round. For this amazing and stupendous munificence which the Great Khan exercises towards the poor, all the people hold him in such esteem that they revere him as a god.

There are also in the city of Khan-balik, including Christians, Saracens, and Cathayans, about 5,000 astrologers and soothsayers, for whom the Great Khan makes yearly provision of food and clothing as he does for the poor. These regularly practise their art in the city. They have a sort of almanack in which are written the movements of the planets through the constellations, hour by hour and minute by minute, throughout the year. Every year these astrologers, Christian, Saracen, and Cathayan, each sect on its own account, examine in this almanack the course and disposition of the whole year and of each particular moon. For they search out and discover what sort of conditions each moon of the year will produce in accordance with the natural course and disposition of the planets and constellations and their special influences: in such-and-such a month there will be thunder-storms, in another earthquakes, in another lightning and heavy rain, in yet another deadly outbreaks of pestilence and wars and civil dissensions. And so month by month in accordance with their findings. And they will declare that so it should happen in harmony with the natural and orderly sequence of things, but God may send more or less. So they will make many little booklets in which they will set down everything that is due to happen in the course of the year, moon by moon. These booklets are called *tacuim* and are sold at a groat apiece to anyone who cares to buy, so that he may know what will happen throughout the year. And those who prove to be the most accurate in their predictions will be reckoned the most accomplished masters of their art and will gain the greatest honour.

If anyone proposes to embark on some important enterprise or to travel somewhere on a trading venture or on other business, or has in mind some other project whose outcome he would like to know, he will consult the astrologers, telling them the year, month, hour, and minute of his nativity. This he is able to do, because in accordance with their custom everyone is taught from birth what he must say about his nativity, and parents are careful to note the particulars in a book. They divide the years into cycles of twelve, each with its own sign: the first bears the sign of the lion, the second of the ox, the third of the dragon, the fourth of the dog, and so on up to twelve. So, when a man is asked when he was born, he answers 'in a year of the lion, on such-and-such a day or night, hour, and minute of such-and-such a moon', according as the time and the year-sign may have been. When they have completed the cycle of twelve years, they begin again at the first sign and repeat the series, always in the same order. So, when anyone asks an astrologer or soothsayer how his proposed venture will turn out and tells him the hour and minute of his nativity and the sign of the year, then the soothsayer, having ascertained under which constellation and which planet he was born, will predict in due sequence all that is to happen to him on his travels and what fortune, good or bad, will attend his undertaking. Likewise, the inquirer may be warned, if he is a merchant, that the planet then in the ascendant will be hostile to his venture, so that he should await the ascendancy of one more favourable; or that the constellation directly facing the gate by which he is planning to leave the city will be adverse to the one under which he was born, so that he should leave by another gate or wait till the constellation has moved past; or that in such a place and on such a date he will encounter robbers, in another he will be assailed by rain and storm, in another his horse will break a leg, here his trafficking will involve him in loss, there it will bring in a profit. So the soothsayer will foretell the vicissitudes of his journey, propitious or disastrous, according to the sequence of favourable or unfavourable constellations.

As I have already said, the people of Cathay are all idolaters. Every man has in his house an image hanging on his chamber wall which represents the High God of Heaven, or at least a tablet on which the name of God is written. And every day they cense this with a thurible and worship it with uplifted hands, gnashing their teeth three times and praying that the god will give them a long and happy life, good health, and a sound understanding. From him they ask nothing else. But down below on the ground they have another image representing Natigai, the god of earthly things, who guides the course of all

nagreau grant sire. Et quant le grant sire doit boire
tous les instrumens tout il y a graut quautite de
toutes manieres commencent a souner. Et quit
il neut la coupe en sa main tous les barons, et
tous ceulx qui la sont sage noullent, et sont sig
ue de grant humilite. Et aboit soit le grant sire
et toutes les fois que il boit sait on ainsi comme
ie vous ay dit des viandes ne vous conterai ane
pur ce que chascun soit euore que il en y a de grit
habondauce de toutes manieres. Et sachies que
nul baron ne cheualier qui la meueuent, il couu
eut que sa faue soit ainsi aduueur auec les an
tres daues. Et quant co ont mierige, et les table
sont ostees si leuent en la sale deuant le seignor et
deuant tous les autres grant quite de iougleurs.
et de tresteurs et de plusieur autres manieres de gui
seureurs, et tut sont grant soulaz et grant feste
deuaut lui, et deuaut tous. si que chascun en rist de
la ioie, et du soulas qui y est. Et quaut tout ce
est fait, si se departent les gens, e ua chascun a son
hostel. Ci deuise li xiij. et vj. chapitre de la grant
feste que le grant cam fait chascun an de sa nati

R sachies que les tartars sont
chascuu au feste de leur natiui
te, et le grant Cam saue le
xxviij. de la lune du mois de
septembre, si quen celui iour
fait la greigneur feste de tout lau, fors celle que
il fait au chief de lau si comme ie vous conterai
apres ceste. Ci sachies que le ior de sa natiuite que
le grant cam des meilleurs draps a or fait que

il fait et bien xij. barons se bestent auec lui et celle
mesme couleur, et tout semblable ala neture
du grant sire. mais non pas que il soient si chi
er. mais dune couleur, + tous sont draps dor
et encore a chascun de ceulx vcha i. sanctuaire
dor eu leur bestemens que le seigneur leur donne.
Et si vous di que il y a de telz de ces bestemens
qui ont tant de perles et de pierres deffus qui va
leut plus de x. besaus dor, et de ces bestemens y a
plusieurs. Et sachies que le grant cam xiij. fois
lan leur donne, a ces iiij. barons et chiualiers.
et ces bestemens comme ie vous ay dit, et tous
se uest auec eulx dune couleur. si que chascuue
fois est deuse lune couleur de lante, et a ce pouez
veoir que ce est moult grant chose. Car il neft
nul seigneur qui le peust faire ne maintenir
fors que lui tant seulement. Et le ior de la
sainte natiuite tous les tartars du monde li
sont chascun grans pesens de son pouoir, qui sont
couuenable et qui est ordene. Encore y vueut
maint autre gent chascun a tout grant pesens
pour demander graces du seigneur. Et le grit
sire a esleu xij. barons qui sont seur de fait adou
ner a chascun ce quil leur semble quil appertient.
Encore en cestui iour tous les y dolastres, et tous
les sarrazins, et tous les cristiens, et toutes les
autres geuracions sont oraisons, et grus congre
gacions, et grans prieurs chascun a leur dieu
auec grans chas et graut humiliur en graus euaz
que il leur faue leur seigneur, et li couuient longue
vie et ioie + saute. et en telle maniere comme ie
vous ay couue dure en cestui iour la ioie, + la feste
de sa natiuite. Or vuis lairons de ce, que bien
vous en auons conte. Et vous conterous dune
autre grant feste que il fait le chief de leur au q
est appelle la blanche feste. Ci dit li iiij. et vij.
chapitre de la grant feste que le grant fait cam
il est uoir que il font leur au chief de leur au q
chief de lau. le mois de feurier. et le grant sire.
Et tout cil qui sout souspoit Alui. bien souffruue
stelle feste comme ie vous conterai. Il est ysau
ce que le grant Cam auec tous les soubgis. se
bestent tout de robe blanche. si que en celui iour
hommes et faues, petit + grant sont tous vef
tu de blanc. + ce sont pour ce que il leur semble

that is born on earth. They make him with a wife and children and worship him in the same way, with incense and gnashing of teeth and uplifted hands; and to him they pray for good weather and harvests and children and the like.

They surpass other nations in the excellence of their manners and their knowledge of many subjects, since they devote much time to their study and to the acquisition of knowledge. They speak in an agreeable and orderly manner, greet one another courteously with bright and cheerful faces, are dignified in their demeanour, cleanly at table, and so forth. But they have no regard for the welfare of their souls, caring only for the nurture of their bodies and for their own happiness. Concerning the soul, they believe indeed that it is immortal, but in this fashion. They hold that as soon as a man is dead he enters into another body; and according as he has conducted himself well or ill in life, he passes from good to better or from bad to worse. That is to say, if he is a man of humble rank and has behaved well and virtuously in life, he will be reborn after death from a gentlewoman and will be a gentleman, and thereafter from the womb of a noblewoman and will become a nobleman; and so he follows an ever upward path culminating in assumption into the Deity. But, if he is a man of good birth and has behaved badly, he will be reborn as the son of a peasant; from a peasant's life he will pass to a dog's and so continually downwards.

They treat their father and mother with profound respect. If it should happen that a child does anything to displease his parents or fails to remember them in their need, there is a department of state whose sole function it is to impose severe penalties on those who are found guilty of such ingratitude.

Perpetrators of various crimes who are caught and put in prison, if they have not been set free* at the time appointed by the Great Khan for the release of prisoners, which recurs every three years, are then let out; but they are branded on the jaw, so that they may be recognized.

The present Khan prohibited all the gambling and cheating that used to be more prevalent among them than anywhere else in the world. To cure them of the habit he would say: 'I have acquired you by force of arms and all that you possess is mine. So, if you gamble, you are gambling with my property.' He did not, however, make this a pretext to take anything from them.

* This word (*spacciati* in R) may possibly mean 'dispatched by strangling'.

Kubilai Khan

I will not omit to tell you about the behaviour of the Khan's people and noblemen when they come into the presence. First, all those who are within half a mile from the Great Khan, wherever he may be, show their reverence for his majesty by conducting themselves deferentially, peaceably, and quietly so that no hubbub or uproar may be heard, nor the voice of anyone shouting or talking loudly. Next, every baron or nobleman continually carries with him a little vessel of pleasing design into which he spits so long as he is in the hall, so that no one may make so bold as to spit on the floor; and when he has spat he covers it up and keeps it. Likewise they have handsome slippers of white leather, which they carry about with them. When they have come to court, if they are about to enter the hall at the Lord's invitation, they put on these white slippers and hand their others to the attendant, so as not to dirty the beautiful and elaborate carpets of silk, wrought in gold and other colours.

from peking to bengal

LET US NOW LEAVE THE CITY OF KHAN-BALIK AND TRAVEL into Cathay, so that you may learn something of its grandeurs and its treasures.

You must understand that Messer Marco himself was sent by the Great Khan as an emissary towards the west, on a journey of fully four months from Khan-balik. So we will tell you what he saw on the way, going and coming.

After leaving the city and covering a distance of ten miles, the traveller reaches a large river called Pulisanghin, which flows into the Ocean and carries many merchants and much merchandise. This river is crossed by a magnificent stone bridge. There is not a bridge in the world to compare with it, and I will tell you why. It is fully 300 paces in length and eight in width, so that ten horsemen can easily ride across it abreast. It has twenty-four arches and twenty-four piers in the water and it is built entirely of grey marble, finely worked and firmly set. On the upward slope the roadway narrows a little; but along the top it runs as even as if it were drawn with a ruler. On either side of the bridge is a wall of marble slabs and columns, constructed as follows. At the top of the slope there stands a lofty column resting on a marble tortoise. At the foot of the column is a marble lion and on top of the column another of great beauty and size and fine workmanship. One and a half paces distant from this column stands another of the same pattern, with two lions. The space between one column and the next is filled with slabs of grey marble, variously engraved and inset into the columns, to prevent passers-by from falling into the water. And so it continues the whole way across, so that the whole structure is a sight to see. The downward slope is like the upward one.

After crossing this bridge, the traveller proceeds for thirty miles towards the west, finding splendid inns and vineyards and fertile fields all the way, till he reaches a large and handsome city called Cho-chau. Here there are many abbeys of the idolaters. It is a commercial and industrial city, producing fabrics of silk and gold and fine sendal and well supplied with hostelries for travellers.

A mile beyond this city the road forks, one branch going westward through Cathay, the other south-eastward towards the great province of Manzi. The westward road extends for ten days' journey through Cathay to T'ai-yuan-fu. And all the way it runs through a country of splendid cities and fine towns, with thriving trades and industries, and through well-tilled fields and vineyards. Otherwise there is nothing remarkable.* The people of this district are all quite civilized, because of the frequency of cities, the constant traffic on the roads and passage of goods from one city to another, and the fairs held in every city. At the end of five out of the ten days' journey there is a city said to be of greater size and splendour than the rest, which bears the name of Ak-balik. This marks the boundary in this direction of the Khan's hunting grounds, within which no one dares to go hunting except the Khan and his household and those who are registered under the Chief Falconer. But beyond this limit a man may hunt provided he is of noble birth. In this particular district, however, the Great Khan hardly ever went hunting, so that the wild animals increased and multiplied to such an extent, especially the hares, that they were a menace to the crops of the whole province. When word of this was passed to the Khan, he came here with all his court and the animals taken were past all reckoning.

At the end of the ten days' journey the traveller reaches the kingdom of T'ai-yuan-fu of which the capital is the city also called T'ai-yuan-fu, at which we have now arrived. It is a large and prosperous city, a great centre of trade and industry, which supplies great quantities of the equipment needed for the Great Khan's armies. It has many fine vineyards, producing wine in great abundance. Wine is produced nowhere else in the province except in this district, and from here it is exported throughout the whole province. There is also a plentiful supply of silk, since mulberry trees and silkworms abound.

From T'ai-yuan-fu, seven days' ride towards the west through pleasant country full of thriving towns and villages, where the roads are thronged with merchants plying a profitable trade, will bring you to P'ing-yang-fu, another large and wealthy industrial city much frequented by traders. Here too a great deal of silk is produced.

Two days' journey to the west of P'ing-yang-fu there stands a fine

* R adds that wine from here is exported into Cathay (i.e. presumably into other parts of Cathay) because none is produced there; also that there are many mulberry trees whose leaves supply the inhabitants with silk. There seems to be some confusion with the passage in the following paragraph where F states that wine is produced nowhere else in the province 'of Taianfu' (probably an error for 'Cathay').

castle named Caichu, which was built once upon a time by a king who was called the Golden King. In this castle there is a very fine palace containing a vast hall adorned with admirably painted portraits of all the kings who ruled over this province in former times— a splendid sight to see. This was all the work of the kings who reigned in this kingdom.

The Golden King was a great and powerful lord. During his residence here he had no one in attendance on his person except fair young damsels, of whom he kept a great multitude in his court. When he travelled about the grounds of his castle for recreation in a chariot, he was drawn by these damsels—easily enough because of its slight build. And they ministered in every way to his comfort and pleasure. He exercised his power royally and conducted himself nobly and justly. A good story is told of his dealings with Prester John, which I will tell you as it is related by the folk of this country.

The truth is, as they recount it, that there was war between the two kings. The Golden King was subject to that Ung Khan who, as I have already told you, called himself Prester John, but through arrogance and presumption he rebelled against his suzerain. Such was the strength of his position that Prester John could not get the better of him or do him any harm, which made him exceedingly angry. Now there were seven henchmen of Prester John who declared that they would bring the Golden King to him alive. And Prester John assured them that he would be very glad of this and they would deserve well of him if they accomplished it. So the seven took their leave of him and set out with a goodly company of esquires and went to the Golden King and told him that they had come from a far country to enter his service. The king assured them that they were very welcome and that he would treat them honourably and according to their desires.

So the seven henchmen of Prester John entered into the service of the Golden King. After about two years they had won his high regard by their good service. What need of more words? The king trusted them as whole-heartedly as if all seven had been his own sons, and whenever he went out hunting he was glad of their company. Now hear what these wicked henchmen did, and you will realize that no one can guard himself against treachery and disloyalty. It happened one day that the Golden King went out for his sport with only a handful of followers, and among them were these seven traitors. When they had crossed a river about a mile distant from the palace of which I have spoken, and left their companions on the farther bank, the seven henchmen, seeing that the king had no one to protect him, resolved to carry out the purpose for which they had come. So they laid hand to hilt and told him that either he must come with them or they would put him to death. When the king saw this, he asked in sheer amazement: 'What is the meaning of this, my young friends? Where is it you would have me go?' 'You shall come,' they replied, 'to our lord and master, Prester John.'

At this the king was bitterly mortified and came near to dying with chagrin. 'Have mercy, my young friends!' said he. 'Have I not done you honour enough under my roof, that you should wish to betray me into the hands of my enemies? Assuredly, if you do this, you will be guilty of great wrong and great disloyalty.' They answered that so it must needs be, and led him forthwith to Prester John. When Prester John saw him, he was overjoyed, and told him that he had earned an ill welcome. The Golden King found no words to speak and made no answer. Thereupon Prester John ordered him to be taken out and set to look after beasts. So the Golden King was sent to be a cow-herd. And this task was imposed upon him by Prester John as a token of contempt in order to humiliate him and show that he was nothing. And for two years he lived in great hardship under strict surveillance, so that he might not run away.

When he had herded beasts for two years, he was summoned to appear before Prester John, who dressed him in rich robes and treated him honourably. Then Prester John said to him: 'Sir king, now do you perceive that you are not the man to presume to make war against me?' 'Assuredly, Sire,' replied the king, 'I know well, and have always known, that there is no man who can stand against you.' 'Since you have admitted so much,' said Prester John, 'I ask no more of you. Henceforth I will do you service and honour.' Thereupon he gave the Golden King a horse and harness and a splendid retinue and let him go. And the king returned to his own kingdom and from that time onward remained a faithful friend and vassal of his overlord.

Let us now turn to other matters.

On leaving this castle and riding westward for twenty miles, the traveller reaches a river called Kara-moran, which is too big to be crossed by a bridge; for it is very wide and very deep. It flows out into the Ocean. On its banks stand many cities and towns, much frequented by traders plying a brisk trade. The country bordering on this river produces ginger and silk in great abundance and a limitless quantity of stout canes, some measuring a foot round and some a foot and a half, which supply many needs of the inhabitants. The multitude of birds is truly marvellous. Three pheasants can be bought here for one Venetian groat—that is to say one *asper*, which is worth scarcely more.

Two days' journey to the west of this river lies a splendid city called Ho-chung-fu. The inhabitants, like all the people of Cathay, are idolaters. It is a thriving centre of trade and industry, including the manufacture of cloth of gold and silken fabrics of every sort. The neighbourhood produces silk in plenty, besides ginger, galingale, spikenard, and many other spices that never find their way to our part of the world. As this city offers nothing specially remarkable, we shall pass on.

After leaving Ho-chung-fu the traveller rides westward for eight days, through a country full of towns and thriving commercial and industrial cities and fruitful gardens and fields. I must add that it is also full of mulberry trees, whose leaves are the food of the silkworms. The inhabitants are all idolaters. There is no lack of wild game, both beasts and birds of many sorts. At the end of the eight days he reaches the great and splendid city of Si-ngan-fu, the capital of the kingdom of Si-ngan-fu, which was once a noble realm, renowned for its riches and power. Many good and valiant kings have reigned over it. The present ruler is a son of the Great Khan, whose name is Mangalai. For his father gave him the kingship and crowned him king.

Si-ngan-fu is a busy centre of trade and industry, producing great quantities of silk. The chief manufactures are cloth of gold, silken fabrics, and all sorts of military accoutrements. There is ample provision for man's every bodily need to ensure a life of plenty at a low cost. The town lies to the west, and the people are idolaters.

Outside the town stands King Mangalai's palace, whose beauty I will describe to you. It lies in a great plain, well watered with rivers, lakes, pools, and springs. It is surrounded by a stout and lofty wall about five miles in circuit, crowned with battlements and strongly built. Within the wall is a park stocked with wild animals and birds. In the middle stands the palace, of such size and beauty that it could not be bettered. It has many fine halls and chambers all decorated with pictures in beaten gold with the finest azure and a superabundance of marble. Mangalai rules his kingdom well, maintaining just and upright government, and is well loved by his subjects. His troops are stationed round the palace and enjoy good sport in the chase.

After a journey of three days towards the west from this palace, through a fertile plain full of towns and villages whose inhabitants live by trade and industry and produce quantities of silk, the traveller comes to the high mountains and deep valleys that form the province of Han-chung. On the mountains and in the valleys alike there are cities and towns. The people are idolaters and live on the fruits of fields and woods and of the chase. For you must know that there are extensive forests, harbouring many wild animals, such as lions, bears, and lynxes, harts, stags, roebuck, and other game in plenty, of which the countryfolk take great numbers and from which they derive great profit. Through this sort of country the journey continues for twenty days, that is to say through mountains and valleys and forests, with towns and villages all the way and good hostelries, where travellers are accommodated in comfort.

At the end of these twenty days among the mountains, the traveller comes out into a province called Ak-balik Manzi, which is all plain. There are cities and towns in plenty, lying towards the west. The people are idolaters, living by trade and industry. And I can assure you that this province produces such a vast quantity of ginger that it is exported throughout the whole of the major province of Cathay, to the great profit of the natives. They have wheat and rice and other grain in great abundance and very cheap, and the whole country is amply provided with every commodity. The capital is named Ak-balik Manzi, that is to say 'the white city on the borders of Manzi'. This plain, with its smiling fields, towns, and villages, extends for two days' journey. After this the traveller enters a country of great mountains and valleys and forests, through which he makes his way for twenty days towards the west, passing towns and villages in plenty. The people are idolaters, living on the fruits of the earth, on wild game and domestic animals. There are lions, bears, and lynxes, harts, stags, and roebuck, besides great numbers of the little deer that produce musk.

At the end of these twenty days the traveller reaches a plain and a province still lying on the borders of Manzi which bears the name of Ch'êng-tu-fu. The capital, which is also called Ch'êng-tu-fu, was once a great and splendid city, the seat of powerful and wealthy kings. The whole city is fully twenty miles in circuit; but it is now split up in the following manner. The fact is that the king of this province, when he came to die, left three sons and accordingly divided the city into three parts. Each of these parts is encircled by its own wall, but all three are enclosed within the wall of the main city. And I assure you that each of the king's three sons was a king and possessed wide domains and had no lack of treasure to spend; for their father had been very powerful and rich. But the Great Khan conquered this kingdom and disinherited the three kings and took the kingship for himself.

Through this city there run several large rivers of fresh water, in which quantities of fish are caught. These rivers come down from distant mountains and flow round the city and through it in various parts. They range in width from half-a-mile down to 150 paces, some more, some less, and are very deep. On leaving the city the rivers reunite into one immense river which is henceforth called Kiang-sui, and this continues its course for a journey of eighty to a hundred days till it flows out into the Ocean, of which I shall have more to say later. On its banks are innumerable cities and towns, and the amount of shipping it carries and the bulk of merchandise that merchants transport by it, upstream and down, is so inconceivable that no one in the world who had not seen it with his own eyes could possibly credit it. Its width is such that it is more like a sea than a river.

The branch-streams within the city are crossed by stone bridges of great size and beauty. They are eight paces in width, and in length up to half-a-mile according to the width of the stream. Along the bridges on either side are fine columns of marble that support the roof; for all the bridges are covered with handsome wooden roofs richly decorated and painted in red. The roofing is of tiles. All along the bridges on either side are rows of booths devoted to the practice of various forms of trade and craft. They are wooden structures, erected every morning and taken down at night. Here too are the Great Khan's toll-gatherers, who collect the customs payable to him from goods sold on the bridge. The revenue* received from this source amounts to fully 1,000 gold bezants. The inhabitants of the city are all idolaters.

On leaving Ch'êng-tu-fu the traveller rides for five days through plain and valley, passing villages and hamlets in plenty. The people here live on the yield of the earth. The country is infested with lions, bears, and other wild beasts. There is some local industry, in the

* Some MSS say 'the daily revenue'.

weaving of fine sendal and other fabrics. This country is part of Ch'êng-tu-fu province. But at the end of the five days the route enters another province whose name is Tibet.*

The province of Tibet is terribly devastated, for it was ravaged in a campaign by Mongu Khan. There are many towns and villages and hamlets lying ruined and desolate.

This country produces canes of immense size and girth; indeed I can assure you that they grow to about three palms in circumference and a good fifteen paces in length, the distance from one knot to the next amounting to fully three palms. Merchants and other travellers who are passing through this country at night use these canes as fuel because, when they are alight, they make such a popping and banging that lions and bears and other beasts of prey are scared away in terror and dare not on any account come near the fire. So fires of this sort are made by travellers to protect their own animals from the savage predators with which the country is infested. Let me tell you —for it is well worth telling—how it happened that the crackling of these canes is so loud and terrifying and what effect it produces. You must understand that the canes are taken when quite green and thrown on a fire made of a substantial pile of logs. When they have lain for some time on a fire of this size, they begin to warp and to burst, and then they make such a bang that it can be heard at nights fully ten miles away. Anyone who is not accustomed to the noise is startled out of his wits by it; it is such a terrifying sound to hear. I assure you that horses that have never heard it before are so scared when they hear it that they snap their halters and all the cords that tether them and take to their heels. Many travellers have experienced this. So, when they have horses that are known never to have heard this noise, they bandage their eyes and shackle all the feet with iron fetlocks. Then, when they hear the crackling of the canes, however hard they try to bolt, they cannot do it. And by this means travellers keep safe at nights; both they and their beasts, from the lions and ounces and other dangerous beasts that abound in these parts.

This desolate country, infested by dangerous wild beasts, extends for twenty days' journey, without shelter or food except perhaps every third or fourth day, when the traveller may find some habitation where he can renew his stock of provisions. Then he reaches a

* Polo's account of 'Tebet' applies primarily to districts now included in the provinces of Sze-ch'wan and Yun-nan to the east of the present Tibetan frontier.

region with villages and hamlets in plenty and a few towns perched on precipitous crags. Here there prevails a marriage custom of which I will tell you. It is such that no man would ever on any account take a virgin to wife. For they say that a woman is worthless unless she has had knowledge of many men. They argue that she must have displeased the gods, because if she enjoyed the favour of their idols then men would desire her and consort with her. So they deal with their womenfolk in this way. When it happens that men from a foreign land are passing through this country and have pitched their tents and made a camp, the matrons from neighbouring villages and hamlets bring their daughters to these camps, to the number of twenty or forty, and beg the travellers to take them and lie with them. So these choose the girls who please them best, and the others return home disconsolate. So long as they remain, the visitors are free to take their pleasure with the women and use them as they will, but they are not allowed to carry them off anywhere else. When the men have worked their will and are ready to be gone, then it is the custom for every man to give to the woman with whom he has lain some trinket or token so that she can show, when she comes to marry, that she has had a lover. In this way custom requires every girl to wear more than a score of such tokens hung round her neck to show that she has had lovers in plenty and plenty of men have lain with her. And she who has most tokens and can show that she has had most lovers and that most men have lain with her is the most highly esteemed and the most acceptable as a wife; for they say that she is the most favoured by the gods. And when they have taken a wife in this way they prize her highly; and they account it a grave offence for any man to touch another's wife, and they all strictly abstain from such an act. So much, then, for this marriage custom, which fully merits a description. Obviously the country is a fine one to visit for a lad from sixteen to twenty-four.

The natives are idolaters and out-and-out bad. They deem it no sin to rob and maltreat and are the greatest rogues and the greatest robbers in the world. They live by the chase and by their herds and the fruits of the earth. The country abounds with animals that produce musk, which in their language are called *gudderi*. They are so plentiful that you can smell musk everywhere. I have already explained that a sac in the form of a tumour and filled with blood grows next to the beast's navel, and this blood is musk. But I must add that once in every moon the sac becomes overcharged with blood and discharges its contents. So it happens, since these animals are very plentiful here, that they discharge their musk in many places, so that the whole country is pervaded with the scent. The rascally natives have many excellent dogs, who catch great numbers of these animals; so they have no lack of musk.

The natives have no coinage and do not use the Khan's paper currency; but for money they use salt. They are very poorly clad, in skins, canvas, and buckram. They speak a language of their own and call themselves 'Tibet'.

This province of Tibet is of immense size and lies on the confines of Manzi and many other provinces. The natives are idolaters and notorious brigands. The province is so huge that it contains eight kingdoms and a great many cities and towns. In many places there are rivers and lakes and mountains, in which gold-dust is found in great quantity. There is also great abundance of cinnamon. In this province coral fetches a high price, for it is hung round the necks of women and of idols with great joy.* The province produces plenty of camlets and other cloths of gold, silk, and fustian, and many sorts of spice that were never seen in our country. Here are to be found the most skilful enchanters and the best astrologers according to their usage that exist in any of the regions hereabouts. Among other wonders they bring on tempests and thunder-storms when they wish and stop them at any time. They perform the most potent enchantments and the greatest marvels to hear and to behold by diabolic arts, which it is better not to relate in our book, or men might marvel overmuch. Their customs are disagreeable. They have mastiffs as big as donkeys, very good at pulling down game, including wild cattle, which are plentiful there and of great size and ferocity. They also have a great variety of other hunting dogs, besides excellent lanner and saker falcons, good fliers and apt for hawking. Before leaving Tibet, of which we have now given a full account, let me make it clear that it belongs to the Great Khan, as do all the other kingdoms and provinces and regions described in this book, except only the provinces mentioned at the beginning of our book which belong to the son of Arghun, as I have told you. So you may understand from this, without further indication, that with this exception the provinces described in this book are all subject to the Great Khan.

* Or, more probably, 'in the form of great beads' (*zoje*), the reading of Z, which also mentions amber.

K

We will tell you next of the province of Kaindu, which lies toward the west.* It has only one king.† The people are idolaters and subject to the Great Khan. It has cities and towns in plenty. The chief city, also called Kaindu, lies near the entrance to the province. There is also a lake‡ in which are found many pearls—pure white but not round, being rather knobbly as though four, five, six, or more were joined together. The Great Khan will not let anyone take them; for if all the pearls that were found there were taken out, so many would be taken that they would be cheap and lose their value. So the Great Khan, when he has a mind, has pearls taken from it for his own use only; but no one else may take them on pain of death. There is also a mountain there in which is found a sort of stone called turquoise. These are very fine gems and very plentiful. But the Great Khan does not allow them to be taken except at his bidding.

Let me tell you that in this province there prevails a usage concerning women such as I will describe to you. A man does not think it an outrage if a stranger or some other man makes free with his wife or daughter or sister or any woman he may have in his house. But it is taken as a favour when anyone lies with them. For they say that by this act their gods and idols are propitiated, so as to enrich them with temporal blessings in great abundance. And for that reason they deal with their wives in the following open-handed fashion. You must know that when a man of this country sees that a stranger is coming to his house to lodge, or that he is entering his house without intending to lodge, he immediately walks out, telling his wife to let the stranger have his will without reservation. Then he goes his way to his fields or vineyards and does not return so long as the stranger remains in his house. And I assure you that he often stays three days and lies in bed with this wittol's wife. And as a sign that he is in the house he hangs out his cap or some other token. This is an indication that he is within. And the wretched wittol, so long as he sees this sign in his house, does not return. This usage prevails throughout the province. The Great Khan has forbidden it; but they continue to observe it nonetheless, since, as they are all addicted to it, there is no one to accuse another. There are some residents in the

* R notes that the word 'west' is to be understood in a strictly relative sense. In fact Kaindu, which appears to be Ning-yuen in the Kien-ch'ang valley (Sze-ch'wan province), lies more south than west of Ch'êng-tu-fu.
† Z and R add that its king has now been replaced by governors appointed by the Great Khan.
‡ R: 'a great salt lake'.

villages and homesteads perched on crags by the wayside who have beautiful wives and offer them freely to passing traders. And the traders give the women a piece of some fine cloth, perhaps a yard or so, or some other trinket of trifling value. Having taken his pleasure for a while, the trader mounts his horse and rides away. Then the husband and wife call after him in mockery: 'Hi, you there—you that are riding off! Show us what you are taking with you that is ours! Let us see, ne'er-do-well, what profit you have made! Look at what you have left to us—what you have thrown away and forgotten.' And he flourishes the cloth they have gained from him. 'We have got this of yours, you poor fool, and you have nothing to show for it!' So they mock at him. And so they continue to act.

Let me tell you next about their money. They have gold in bars and weigh it out by *saggi*; and it is valued according to its weight. But they have no coined money bearing a stamp. For small change they do as follows. They have salt water from which they make salt by boiling it in pans. When they have boiled it for an hour, they let it solidify in moulds, forming blocks of the size of a twopenny loaf, flat below and rounded on top. When the blocks are ready, they are laid on heated stones beside the fire to dry and harden. On these blocks they set the Great Khan's stamp. And currency of this sort is made only by his agents. Eighty of these blocks are worth a *saggio* of gold. But traders come with these blocks to the people who live among the mountains in wild and out-of-the-way places and receive a *saggio* of gold for sixty, fifty, or forty blocks, according as the place is more isolated and cut off from cities and civilized people. Here the natives cannot dispose of their gold and other wares, such as musk, for want of purchasers. So they sell their gold cheap, because they find it in rivers and lakes as you have heard. These traders travel all over the highlands of Tibet, where the salt money is also current. They make an immense profit, because these people use this salt in food as well as for buying the necessities of life; but in the cities they almost invariably use fragments of the blocks for food and spend the unbroken blocks.

There are vast numbers here of the beasts that produce musk, and hunters catch them and take great quantities of the musk. There are plenty of good fish, which are caught in the same lake that produces the pearls. There are also lions, lynxes, bears, stags, and roebuck in plenty, and birds of every sort abound. There is no grape wine, but wine is made of wheat and rice with many spices, and a very good drink it is. The province is also a great source of cloves, which grow on a little tree with leaves like laurel but slightly longer and narrower, and little white flowers like clove-pinks. There is also ginger in abundance and cinnamon, not to speak of spices that never come to our country.

When the traveller leaves the city of Kaindu, he rides for ten days through a country not lacking in towns and villages, and well stocked with game, both bird and beast. The people have the same manners and customs as those I have described. At the end of these ten days he reaches a great river called Brius, which is the farther boundary of the province of Kaindu. In it are found great quantities of gold dust. The district is also rich in cinnamon. This river runs into the Ocean.

On the farther side of the river Brius lies Kara-jang, a province of such size that it contains no less than seven kingdoms.* It lies towards the west, and the inhabitants are idolaters and subject to the Great Khan. Its king is his son, whose name is Essen-Temur, a very great king and rich and powerful. He rules his land well and justly; for he is a wise and upright man.

After leaving the river, the traveller continues westwards for five days, through a country with numerous cities and towns which breeds excellent horses. The people live by rearing animals and tilling the soil. They speak a language of their own, which is very difficult to understand. At the end of the five days he reaches the capital of the kingdom,† which is called Yachi, a large and splendid city. Here there are traders and craftsmen in plenty. The inhabitants are of several sorts: there are some who worship Mahomet, some idolaters, and a few Nestorian Christians. Both wheat and rice are plentiful; but wheat bread is not eaten because in this province it is unwholesome. The natives eat rice, and also make it into a drink with spices, which is very fine and clear and makes a man drunk like wine. For money they use white cowries, i.e. the sea-shells that are used to make necklaces for dogs: 80 cowries are equivalent to 1 *saggio* of silver, which is worth 2 Venetian groats, and 8 *saggi* of fine silver may be taken to equal 1 of fine gold. They also have brine wells, from which

* Kara-jang is the Turkish name for what is now the Chinese province of Yün-nan. The Brius is the Kin-sha-kiang ('Gold Dust River'), one of the sources of the Yang-tze-kiang.

† Presumably the first of the seven kingdoms—there may be an omission here. Yachi is Yün-nan-fu or Kun-ming on the Burma Road.

they make salt that is used for food by all the inhabitants of the country. And I assure you that the king derives great profit from this salt. The men here do not mind if one touches another's wife, so long as it is with her consent.

Before leaving this kingdom let me tell you something which I had forgotten. There is a lake here, some 100 miles in circumference, in which there is a vast quantity of fish, the best in the world. They are of great size and of all kinds. The natives eat flesh raw—poultry, mutton, beef, and buffalo meat. The poorer sort go to the shambles and take the raw liver as soon as it is drawn from the beasts; then they chop it small, put it in garlic sauce and eat it there and then. And they do likewise with every other kind of flesh. The gentry also eat their meat raw; but they have it minced very small, put it in garlic sauce flavoured with spices and then eat it as readily as we eat cooked meat.

On leaving Yachi and continuing westwards for ten days, the traveller reaches the kingdom of Kara-jang, the capital of which is also called Kara-jang. The people are idolaters and subject to the Great Khan. The king is Hukaji, a son of the Great Khan. In this province gold dust is found in the rivers, and gold in bigger nuggets in the lakes and mountains. They have so much of it that they give a *saggio* of gold for six of silver. Here too the cowries of which I have spoken are used for money. They are not found in this province, but come here from India.

In this province live huge snakes and serpents* of such a size that no one could help being amazed even to hear of them. They are loathsome creatures to behold. Let me tell you just how big they are. You may take it for a fact that there are some of them ten paces in length that are as thick as a stout cask: for their girth runs to about ten palms. These are the biggest. They have two squat legs in front near the head, which have no feet but simply three claws, two small and one bigger, like the claws of a falcon or a lion. They have enormous heads and eyes so bulging that they are bigger than loaves. Their mouth is big enough to swallow a man at one gulp. Their teeth are huge. All in all, the monsters are of such inordinate bulk and ferocity that there is neither man nor beast but goes in fear of them. There are also smaller ones, not exceeding eight paces in length, or six or it may be five.

Let me tell you now how these monsters are trapped. You must know that by day they remain underground because of the great

* Evidently crocodiles.

153

heat; at nightfall they sally out to hunt and feed and seize whatever prey they can come by. They go down to drink at streams and lakes and springs. They are so bulky and heavy and of such a girth that when they pass through sand on their nightly search for food or drink they scoop out a furrow through the sand that looks as if a butt full of wine had been rolled that way. Now the hunters who set out to catch them lay traps at various places in the trails that show which way the snakes are accustomed to go down the banks into the water. These are made by embedding in the earth a stout wooden stake, to which is fixed a sharp steel tip like a razor-blade or lance-head, projecting about a palm's breadth beyond the stake and slanting in the direction from which the serpents approach. This is covered with sand, so that nothing of the stake is visible. Traps of this sort are laid in great numbers. When the snake, or rather the serpent, comes down the trail to drink, he runs full-tilt into the steel, so that it pierces his chest and rips his belly right to the navel and he dies on the spot. The hunter knows that the serpent is dead by the cry of the birds, and then he ventures to approach his prey. Otherwise he dare not draw near.

When hunters have trapped a serpent by this means, they draw out the gall from the belly and sell it for a high price, for you must know that it makes a potent medicine. If a man is bitten by a mad dog, he is given a drop of it to drink—the weight of a halfpenny—and he is cured forthwith. And when a woman is in labour and cries aloud with the pangs of travail, she is given a drop of the serpent's gall and as soon as she has drunk it she is delivered of her child forthwith. Its third use is when someone is afflicted by any sort of growth: he puts a drop of this gall on it and is cured in a day or two. For these reasons the gall of this serpent is highly prized in these provinces. The flesh also commands a good price, because it is very good to eat and is esteemed as a delicacy.

Another thing about these serpents: they go to the dens where lions and bears and other beasts of prey have their cubs and gobble them up—parent as well as young—if they can get at them.

Let me tell you further that this province produces a sturdy breed of horses, which are exported when young for sale in India. And you must know that it is the custom to remove two or three joints of the tail-bone, so that the horse cannot flick the rider with its tail or swish it when galloping; for it is reckoned unsightly for a horse to gallop with swishing tail. The horsemen here ride with long stirrups after the French fashion*—long, that is, in contrast to the short stirrups favoured by the Tartars and most other races who go in for archery, since they use their stirrups for standing upright when they shoot.

For armour they wear cuirasses of buffalo hide. They carry lances and shields. They also use cross-bows, with all the quarrels dipped in poison. All the natives, women as well as men, especially those who are bent on evil courses, carry poison about with them. If it should chance that anyone is caught after committing a crime for which he is liable to suffer torture, rather than face the penalty of the scourge, he puts the poison in his mouth and swallows it, so as to die as quickly as possible. But, since the authorities are well aware of this trick, they always have some dog's dung handy, so that if a prisoner swallows poison for this purpose he is immediately made to swallow the dung and so vomit up the poison. Such is the remedy they have found for this practice, and it is a well-tried one. Another practice of theirs, before they were conquered by the Great Khan, was this. If it happened that a gentleman of quality, with a fine figure, or a 'good shadow', came to lodge in the house of a native of this province, they would murder him in the night, by poison or other means, so that he died. You must not suppose that they did this in order to rob him; they did it rather because they believed that his 'good shadow' and the good grace with which he was blessed and his intelligence and soul would remain in the house. In this way many met their deaths before the conquest. Since then—that is, during the last thirty-five years or so—they have abandoned this evil practice for fear of the Great Khan, who has strictly forbidden it.

After leaving Kara-jang, the traveller continues westwards for five days till he reaches a province called Zar-dandan. Its chief city is called Vochan. The people here are idolaters and subject to the Great Khan. They have all their teeth of gold—that is to say, every tooth is covered with gold. They make a cast in gold of the shape of their teeth, and with this they cover both their lower and their upper teeth. It is only the men that do this, not the women. The men also make a sort of stripe or circlet round their arms and legs with black dots. These are produced by means of five needles tied together, with which they prick the flesh till they draw blood, whereupon they rub in a black ink that produces an indelible stain. And they

* R: 'as we Frenchmen do', where 'Frenchmen' is presumably equivalent to 'Franks', i.e. West Europeans or 'Latins'.

reckon it a distinction and an ornament to have such a stripe of black dots. The men are all gentlemen, according to their notions. They have no occupation but warfare, the chase, and falconry. All the work is done by the women, and by the other men whom they have taken captive and keep as slaves.

When a woman has given birth to a child, she washes and swaddles him. Then her husband goes to bed and takes the baby with him and lies in bed for forty days without leaving it except for necessary purposes. And all his friends and kinsmen come to see him and cheer him up and amuse him. This they do because they say that his wife has had her share of trouble in carrying the infant in her womb, so they do not want her to endure more during this period of forty days. And the wife is no sooner delivered of her child than she rises from bed and does all the work of the house and waits upon her lord in bed.

The natives here eat all sorts of meat, both cooked and raw. They eat rice with meat and other foods according to local custom. They drink a wine made of rice and flavoured with spices, which is very good. Their money is of gold, and the cowries are also current. And I assure you that they give one *saggio* of gold in exchange for five of silver. This is because they have no silver-mines within five months' journey. So traders come here with loads of silver and change it in this country, giving five *saggi* of silver for one gold. And from this exchange the traders reap a handsome profit.

These people have no idols or church; but they worship the head of the house, saying: 'From him we have our being'. They have no letters or writing. And this is not surprising; for their homes are in very out-of-the-way places among huge forests and lofty mountains which no one may visit in summer at any price, because the air in summer is so unwholesome and pestilent that it is death to any foreigner. When they have dealings with one another, they take a bit of wood, either square or round, and split it in two, keeping half each. But first they make notches in it—two or three or as many as they require. When the time comes for payment, then the one who owes money, or whatever it may be, demands the other one's half of the stick.

I must tell you that in all the provinces I have been describing— Kara-jang, Vochan, and Yachi—there are no physicians. When someone falls ill, he sends for the magicians—that is, the conjurers of devils and guardians of idols. When these magicians have arrived and the patient has told them his symptoms, they begin forthwith to play on their instruments and leap and dance till one of their number falls prostrate on the earth or the paved floor and froths at the mouth and lies like one dead. This is because the devil has entered into his body. And in this state he remains. When his fellow magicians, who are present in force, see that one of their company has collapsed in the way I have described, they begin to speak to him and ask with what malady the patient is afflicted. To which the reply comes: 'Such-and-such a spirit has touched him, because he has incurred his displeasure.' Then the magicians cry to him: 'We beseech thee, pardon him and in requital for restoration of his blood take whatsoever thou wilt.' When they have uttered many words and many prayers, the spirit who has entered into the prostrate magician makes answer. If the patient is due to die, the answer runs thus: 'This sick man has done such grievous wrong to such-and-such a spirit and is such a sinful man that the spirit will not pardon him for anything in the world.' Such is the answer given when death is imminent. If the patient is due to recover, then the spirit lodged in the magician's body utters a different answer: 'The sick man has sinned greatly, but he will be forgiven. If he wishes to recover, let two or three sheep be taken.' Then further instructions are added: ten drinks or more are to be prepared, of good quality and high price; the sheep are to have black heads, or are otherwise particularized; a sacrifice is to be offered to such-and-such an idol or spirit, attended by so many magicians or women, of those who have charge of the spirits and idols; and a great festival is to be held in honour of the chosen idol or spirit. When the response has been delivered, the patient's friends immediately act upon the instructions given. They take sheep corresponding to the particulars specified and prepare drinks of the prescribed quality and number. They slaughter the sheep and sprinkle the blood in the places prescribed, as a sacrifice in honour of the spirit named. Then they have the sheep cooked in the sick man's house and invite the requisite number of the magicians and the women. When these have all come and the sheep and drinks are got ready, then they begin to make music and dance and chant their praises of the spirits. They pour out a libation of the mutton broth and the drink. They have wood of aloes and incense, with which they go to and fro censing the place. And they make a great show of lights. And when they have done this for a while, then one of them falls down and the others ask whether the patient is forgiven and is due to recover. This time the answer is that he is not yet forgiven, but that certain things must still be done and then forgiveness will be granted. The instructions are promptly obeyed. Finally the spirit answers: 'Since the sacrifice and all else that is required has been performed, he is forgiven and will soon recover.' When this answer has been received, after the libations have been duly poured and the lights lit and the incense burned, they say that the spirit is now fully propitiated. Thereupon the magicians and the women—who are still possessed by these spirits—eat the sheep and drink the beverages provided, with great mirth and revelry. Then they return each to his house. And after all is done, the patient recovers forthwith. These ceremonies are not performed for all and sundry, but two or three times a month for some person of wealth and consequence. The same practice is observed throughout Cathay and Manzi and by almost all the idolaters owing to their lack of physicians.*

You must know that I had forgotten a very fine battle that was fought in the kingdom of Vochan, one that is well worthy of mention in this book. So I will now tell you how it came about and what was the manner of it.

The truth is that in the year 1272 the Great Khan sent a large force into the kingdom of Vochan and Kara-jang so as to safeguard it against a threatened attack. He had not yet established one of his family there, as he did later when he gave the kingship to Essentemur, the son of his late son. Now it so happened that the king of Mien and Bengal, a very powerful monarch in lands and riches and subjects, who was still independent of the Great Khan, though no long time was to elapse before he was conquered by him and lost the two kingdoms I have named—this king of Mien and Bengal, when he learnt that the Khan's army was stationed at Vochan, decided that his proper course was to march against them with such a multitude of men that he would make an end of them all, so that the Great Khan would never feel inclined to send another army there. Thereupon he assembled an immense host, of which I will give you particulars. You may take it for a fact that he had 2,000 large

* The last two sentences are taken from R, which also adds an explanation scarcely consistent with the text and probably derived from some pious commentator: if by the providence of God the patient recovers, the idol receives the credit; if not, the authors of the sacrifice are taxed with defrauding the idol by tasting some of the food before offering it; so the devil beguiles the blindness of the idolaters.

elephants. On each of these was erected a wooden castle of great strength and admirably adapted for warfare. Each of these castles was manned by at least twelve fighting-men, and some by sixteen or more. In addition he had fully 40,000 men, mainly cavalry but including some infantry. The whole force was equipped in a style befitting such a powerful and mighty ruler. It was an army fit to do great deeds. What more need I say? The king, when he had mustered this formidable host, lost no time in setting out in person with all his following against the Great Khan's army that was stationed at Vochan. They advanced without meeting any adventure worthy of mention till they had come within three days' march of the Tartar army. And here he pitched camp to rest and refresh his men.

When the commander of the Tartar army knew for a fact that this king was coming against him with such a multitude, he could not but be perturbed, since his own force amounted to no more than 12,000 cavalry. But there can be no doubt that he was a man of great prowess and an able commander. His name was Nasr-uddin. He disposed his troops with great skill and put them in good heart, doing all that in him lay to defend the country and his men. Why make a long story of it? Suffice it that all the Tartars, to the number of 12,000 horsemen, came into the plain of Vochan and there awaited the attack of their enemies. And this move was dictated by prudent resolve and wise generalship. For you must know that on the edge of the plain lay a wide and densely wooded forest.

Now let us for the moment leave the Tartars awaiting their enemies in this plain and turn for a short while to speak of their enemies. You must know that the king of Mien, after halting for a space with all his host, set out once more and proceeded on his way till he came to the plain of Vochan, where the Tartars were waiting in battle array. When they had come into the plain within a mile of the enemy, he marshalled his elephants with the castles and the men on their backs well armed for the fray. He posted his cavalry and his infantry with skill and prudence, like the prudent king he was. And when he had disposed and marshalled his whole array, he launched an attack with all his forces upon the foe.

When the Tartars saw them coming, they gave no sign of dismay, but showed themselves resolute and doughty warriors. For you may be well assured that they swung into action all together in an orderly and disciplined advance against the enemy. But, when they were at close quarters and nothing remained but to begin the battle, then the horses of the Tartars, catching sight of the elephants, were seized with such terror that their riders could no longer urge them forward against the foe, but they continued to turn tail. And the king with his troops and his elephants continued to advance.

When the Tartars saw this, they were hard put to it and at a loss what to do; for they saw clearly that if they could not induce their horses to face the foe they were utterly undone. But they dealt with their plight very shrewdly, as I will tell you. When they saw that their horses were so panic-stricken, they dismounted, every man of them, led their mounts into the wood and tethered them to the trees. Then they grasped their bows, fitted their arrows to the string, and let fly at the elephants. They loosed upon them such a shower of arrows that it was truly marvellous, and the elephants were grievously wounded. Meanwhile the king's men discharged volley upon volley against the Tartars in a fierce assault. But the Tartars, who were far stouter combatants than their foemen, defended themselves stubbornly. What need of more words? Be well assured that, when most of the elephants were as sorely wounded as I have told you, they turned in flight towards the king's men in such a turmoil that it seemed as if all the world were tumbling to bits. They did not stop till they had reached the woods and then they plunged in and smashed their castles and wrecked and ruined everything. This way and that they hurtled through the woods, goaded to frenzy by their terror. When the Tartars saw this, they did not lose a moment, but sprang to horse and charged down upon the king and his men. They began their attack with arrows; and a deadly onslaught it was, for the king and his men put up a stubborn defence. When all their arrows were shot away, they set hand to their swords and clubs and laid about them lustily, dealing mighty blows. Then you might have seen many a shrewd stroke of sword and club given and received, riders and steeds laid low, hands and arms hewn off, and heads severed from their trunks. Many there were who fell to earth dead or wounded to death. So loud was the tumult and the uproar that the thunder of heaven would have gone unheard. Bloody and bitter was the fighting on every side. But never doubt that the Tartars had the better of it. It was an ill hour for the king and his men when that day's fighting began: so many of them lost their lives in the fray. When the battle had lasted till midday and beyond, then the king and his men were in such straits and so many of them slain that they could endure no longer. For it was borne in upon them that if they made any longer stay they would all be dead. So they stayed no longer, but took to flight as best they could. When the Tartars saw that they had turned to flight, they gave chase with a will, smiting and slaying so grievously that it was pitiful to behold. After a while they abandoned the pursuit and went into the woods to capture some of the elephants. They tried to block their paths by felling tall trees so that they could not pass. But all their efforts availed them nothing. It was some of the king's men, who had been taken captive themselves, that effected the capture; for elephants have greater intelligence than any other animal that exists. By this means they caught more than two hundred of them. And from this day forward the Khan began to have elephants in plenty.

Such then was the course of this battle.*

When the traveller leaves the province of Zar-dandan, of which I have told you above, he embarks on a long descent. You may take it for a fact that the way leads steadily downhill for fully two days and a half. The only thing worth noting on this stretch of the road is a great market-place, where all the people of the country come to market on the appointed days, that is three days a week. They change gold for silver, giving one *saggio* for five. Merchants come here from a great distance to change their silver for the local gold; and I assure you that they make a handsome profit. As for the natives who bring the gold, no one can go to their dwelling-places to do them harm; they dwell in such impregnable and inaccessible spots. Indeed no one knows where their homes are, because no one goes there but themselves.

At the end of this descent the traveller finds himself in a province lying towards the south on the confines of India, the name of which is Mien. He then proceeds for fifteen days through very inaccessible places and through vast jungles teeming with elephants, unicorns, and other wild beasts. Men and habitations there are none. So we will say good-bye to the jungles and relate a story for you to hear.

* R, which has an even more long-winded account of the battle than the foregoing, appends a passage attributing the Tartar victory to the inadequacy of their opponents' defensive armour and the poor strategy that allowed the cavalry to take refuge in the woods instead of encircling them in the open. Chinese sources, which confirm Polo's narrative in the main, fix the date as 1277 rather than 1272. The kingdom or province of Mien is Burma. The city of Mien is probably Tagaung on the Irrawaddy. The countries east of Burma—Kaugigu, Aniu, Toloman, and Kuiju (Cuigiu, etc.)—cannot be identified with confidence.

You must know that at the end of this fifteen days' journey lies a city called Mien of great size and splendour, which is the capital of the kingdom. The inhabitants are idolaters and speak a language of their own. They are subject to the Great Khan. And in this city is a very remarkable object of which I will now tell you.

There once lived in this city a rich and powerful king. When this king came to die, he commanded that above his tomb or monument there should be erected two towers, one of gold and one of silver, such as I will describe. One tower was built of fine stones and then covered with gold, a full finger's breadth in thickness, so completely that it appeared as if made of gold only. It was fully ten paces high and of a width appropriate to its height. In form it was circular, and round the whole circuit were set little gilded bells which tinkled every time the wind blew through them. The other tower was of silver and was built on the same plan as the golden one and of the same size and structure.* This structure was designed as a token of the king's greatness and for the sake of his soul. And I assure you that the towers were the fairest to be seen in all the world and were of incalculable value.

Let me tell you next how this province was conquered by the Great Khan. The truth is that at his court there were great numbers of jugglers and acrobats. The Khan told them that he wished them to go and conquer the province of Mien and that he would give them a leader and supporting troops. The jugglers willingly accepted the charge and set out on their way with the leader and troops provided. What need of more words? Suffice it that these jugglers with their helpers conquered this province of Mien. After the conquest, when they came to this splendid city and found these two beautiful and costly towers, they were amazed. They sent word to where the Khan was staying to tell him of these towers and of their beauty and worth, and offered, if he so desired, to demolish them and send him the gold and silver. But the Khan, who knew that the king had had them built for the welfare of his soul, and so that he might be remembered after his death, declared that he did not wish them to be demolished but would have them remain in the state in which the king had established them. And this was not surprising, because I can assure you that a Tartar† never touches the property of the dead.

* R adds that the tomb itself was partly covered with gold and silver plate.
† Z says 'the great Tartar', and adds that this applies also to things struck by lightning or pestilence through the divine judgement, and that no tribute was levied from such

In this province there are plenty of elephants and wild oxen of great size and beauty, besides harts, stags, and roebuck and all sorts of other animals in great abundance.

Let us now pass on to talk of another province, whose name is Bengal. This also lies towards the south on the confines of India. In the year 1290, when I, Marco, was at the court of the Great Khan, it had not yet been conquered; but the Khan's armies were already there and engaged in the conquest. This province has a king and a language of its own. The people are grossly idolatrous. The province contains many eunuchs and supplies them to the nobles and lords of the surrounding territories. The oxen here are as high as elephants, though not so stout. The people live on meat, milk, and rice. They have cotton in plenty. They are great traders, exporting spikenard, galingale, ginger, sugar, and many other precious spices. The Indians come here and buy the eunuchs of whom I have spoken, who are very plentiful here because any prisoners that are taken are immediately castrated and afterwards sold as slaves. So merchants buy many eunuchs in this province and also many slave girls and then export them for sale in many other countries. Since this province contains nothing else worthy of mention, we will pass on to another lying towards the east, which is called Kaugigu.

Kaugigu has its own king. The people are idolaters and speak a language of their own. They have submitted to the Great Khan and pay him a yearly tribute. The king is so lecherous that I assure you that he has fully 300 wives. Whenever any woman in the country excels in beauty, he takes her to wife. This province is rich in gold. It also abounds in precious spices of many sorts; but they are very far from the sea and for this reason are of little value as merchandise and are sold very cheap. There are plenty of elephants and animals of many other kinds and no lack of game. The people live on meat, milk, and rice. They have no grape wine, but make an excellent wine of rice and spices. All the people alike, male and female, have their flesh decorated in the following fashion. They have their flesh covered all over with pictures of lions and dragons and birds and other objects, made with needles in such a way that they are

things. Chinese and Burmese sources agree that this conquest took place in 1284. As there is no other evidence for a Mongol conquest of Bengal, it is possible that Polo's 'Bangala' is a confusion of Bengal and Pegu.

indelible. They make these on their faces, their necks, their bellies, their hands, their legs, and every part of their bodies. And this they do as a mark of gentility: the more elaborately anyone is decorated, the greater and the handsomer he is considered. First of all a man will have such images as he may desire sketched out in black all over his body. This done, he will be tied hand and foot, and two or more persons will hold him. Then the master craftsman will take five needles, four of them fastened together in a square and the fifth in the centre, and with these he will work all over his body, pricking out the images previously sketched. As soon as the pricks are made, ink is applied to them, and then the figure as sketched appears in the pricks. During the process the victim suffers what might well pass for the pains of Purgatory. Many even die during the operation through loss of blood.

To the east of Kaugigu lies the province of Aniu. The inhabitants are subject to the Great Khan. They are idolaters and speak a language of their own. They live by stock-rearing and agriculture. The ladies wear gold and silver bangles of great value on their legs and arms. The men also wear the like, but of better quality and higher cost. They have plenty of good horses and sell great numbers to the Indians, who drive a brisk trade in them. They also have buffaloes, oxen, and cows in great number, because the country is well suited to them and the pasturage excellent. The province is well supplied with every sort of foodstuff. You should know that it lies fifteen days' journey beyond Kaugigu, which in its turn is thirty days beyond Bengal.

We shall now leave Aniu and proceed to another province, distant eight days' journey towards the east, which is named Toloman. Here also the people are idolaters, speak a language of their own and are subject to the Great Khan. They are a very handsome race, not fair-complexioned but brown, and are good fighting men. They have a fair number of cities and a multitude of villages situated among high mountains and fastnesses. When they die, they have their bodies cremated; and the bones which will not burn are taken and put in little caskets and then carried high up into great mountains and there suspended in vast caves in such a way that neither men nor beasts can touch them. The country is rich in gold. For small change they use cowries, such as I have already described. And gold and cowries are likewise current in all these provinces, that is, in Bengal, Kaugigu, and Aniu. There are few traders; but those there are are very rich and drive a brisk trade. The staple foods are meat, milk, and rice. There is no grape wine; but an excellent wine is made of rice and spices. As there is nothing else worthy of note in this province, we shall now pass on to another, lying towards the east, whose name is Kuiju.

Kuiju is reached by a journey of twelve days from Toloman along the course of a river,* where there are towns and villages in plenty but nothing especially noteworthy. At the end of this journey the traveller arrives at the city of Kuiju, which is very fine and splendid. The inhabitants are idolaters and subject to the Great Khan. They live by trade and industry. Let me tell you that they weave cloths of excellent quality from the bark of trees, which they wear in summer. They are a warlike race. They have no currency except the Great Khan's paper money, of which I have told you; for from now on we are in the territories where this money is current.

There are so many lions here that no one can sleep out of doors at night; for the lions would eat him forthwith. And let me tell you another thing: when men are travelling on this river and stop somewhere for the night, unless they sleep well away from the bank, a lion will come out to the boat and snatch a man from it and carry him off to devour. But men have learnt how to protect themselves—let me tell you how. Though the lions are of great size and ferocity, it is a remarkable fact that in this country there are dogs that have the hardihood to attack them. But there must be two of them; for I assure you that one man and two dogs will kill a full-grown lion in the following manner. When a man is riding along a road with a bow and arrows and two huge hounds and chances upon a full-sized lion, the hounds, which are brave and strong, no sooner catch sight of him than they run up to him most courageously, one attacking him in the rear while the other barks in front. The lion rounds upon them; but as fast as he attacks they withdraw so that he cannot touch them, till at last he goes his own way. As soon as the hounds see this, they run after him, snapping at his haunches or his tail. Then round he wheels again in a fury, but cannot get at them, because they are well able to look after themselves. What more shall I say? The lion is scared by the noisy clamour of the dogs and retires in search of a tree to lean back on while he faces them. While he retires, they keep on biting him in the rear, and he continues to wheel round this way or

* The MSS indicate that the journey was made upstream; but this is hard to reconcile with any possible route back to Ch'êng-tu-fu.

L

that. When the hunter sees this, he draws his bow and lets fly an arrow, two arrows, and more, till at length the lion falls dead. By this means they kill many; for they cannot defend themselves against a mounted man with two good hounds.

This province also produces silk in plenty and all sorts of merchandise in great abundance, which is distributed over a wide area by this river.

The route continues along this river for a further twelve days, through a region abounding in cities and towns. The people are idolaters and subject to the Great Khan. They use the Khan's paper money and live by commerce and industry and some are good fighting men. At the end of these twelve days the traveller finds himself back in Ch'êng-tu-fu, which has been mentioned earlier in this book. From here he rides for fully eighty days through provinces and countries in which we have been before and of which we have written above in our book, till he reaches Cho-chau, which we have already visited.

from peking to amoy

STARTING FROM CHO-CHAU, THE TRAVELLER RIDES SOUTH-wards for four days through a country full of cities and towns, where the people live by commerce and industry and are idolaters and subject to the Great Khan and use his paper money. At the end of the four days he reaches the city of Ho-kien-fu, which is in the province of Cathay. And of this we shall now tell you.

Ho-kien-fu is a great and splendid city, lying towards the south. The people are idolaters and burn their dead.* They are subject to the Great Khan and use paper money. They live by trade and industry, for they have silk in plenty. They produce cloths of gold and silk and sendal in great abundance. This city has many cities and towns subject to its dominion. Through the midst of the city flows a great river, by which quantities of merchandise are transported to Khan-balik; for they make it flow thither through many different channels and artificial waterways.

Leaving Ho-kien-fu, we travel southwards for three days and reach another city called Changlu. This is a very large city of Cathay, subject to the Great Khan and using paper money. The inhabitants are idolaters and burn the bodies of the dead. You must know that a great quantity of salt is produced here by the following process. Men take a sort of earth, which is very saline, and of this they make great mounds. Over these they pour a lot of water, so that it trickles down through it and becomes briny owing to the property of the earth. Then they collect this water by means of pipes and put it in big vats and big iron cauldrons not more than four fingers deep and boil it thoroughly. The salt thus produced is very pure and white and fine-grained. And I assure you that it is exported into many countries round about and is a great source of wealth to the inhabitants and of revenue to the Great Khan. The province also produces peaches of great size, weighing fully two small pounds apiece.†

As there is nothing else here worth noting, we shall continue

* Z and R add that there are also some Christians who have a church in the city.
† 'Changlu' is identifiable as an old name of T'sang-chau. The name 'Changli' apparently refers to T'si-nan-fu, and 'Tandinfu' to Yen-chau (formerly Tai-ting-fu); but the descriptions of the two cities seem to have been interchanged by some confusion.

southwards to another city of Cathay called Changli, also subject to the Great Khan, where the people are idolaters and use paper money. It is distant from Changlu by a five days' journey through a country thronged with towns and villages and rich in merchandise, yielding a great revenue to the Great Khan. Through the midst of Changli flows a broad river by which great quantities of silken goods and spices and other precious wares are carried upstream and downstream.

On leaving Changli and proceeding southwards for six days, the traveller passes many cities and towns of great prosperity and splendour, inhabited by idolaters who burn their dead, men subject to the Great Khan, using paper money, living by commerce and industry and enjoying great abundance of all sorts of foodstuffs. But there is nothing calling for special mention till we reach Tandinfu. This is a very large city and was once a great kingdom; but the Great Khan conquered it by force of arms. I can assure you, however, that it is still the finest city in all this region. It has wealthy merchants who maintain a thriving commerce. The abundance of silk is quite amazing. There are many delightful gardens full of excellent fruit. You must know also that Tandinfu has under its dominion eleven imperial cities, that is to say cities of outstanding splendour and prosperity; for they are all centres of active and profitable trade, producing silk past all reckoning.

Let me tell you that in the year 1272* the Great Khan had appointed one of his barons named Litan Sangon to hold this city and province with a force of 80,000 mounted men. When Litan had stayed in the province for some time with this force, as directed, he planned a monstrous act of disloyalty, as you shall hear. He consorted with all the leading men of these cities and hatched a plot with them against the Great Khan. And then with the good will of all the inhabitants of the province they rebelled against the Great Khan and refused him all obedience. When the Khan knew of this, he sent against them two of his barons named Ajul and Mongotai with fully 100,000 mounted men. What need to make a long story of it? You may take it for a fact that these two with their following fought against the rebel Litan and all the men he could muster, who amounted to some 100,000 cavalry and immense numbers of infantry. But the fortune of the day was such that Litan lost the battle

* Actually 1262, when a Chinese governor, Li-tan, headed a revolt in support of the Sung Emperor, who was then still reigning in South China.

and was killed there with many others. After his defeat and death, the king ordered an inquiry to be made into all who had been guilty of this treachery. All those who were found guilty were put to a cruel death; all the others were pardoned and suffered no harm and never afterwards failed in their loyalty.

You must know that the young ladies of the province of Cathay excel in modesty and the strict observance of decorum. They do not frisk and frolic and dance or fly into a pet. They do not keep watch at the windows gazing at passers-by or exposing themselves to their gaze. They do not offer a ready ear to improper stories. They do not gad about to parties and entertainments. If it happens that they go out to some respectable place, as for instance to the temples of their idols or to visit the houses of relatives, they walk in the company of their mothers, not glancing brazenly about them but some of them wearing pretty hoods over their heads which obstruct their upward view. On the way they always walk with their eyes cast down in front of their feet. In the presence of their elders they are respectful and never utter a needless word—indeed they do not speak at all in their presence unless addressed. In their own chambers they remain intent on their own tasks, seldom presenting themselves to the sight of fathers and brothers and the older members of the household and never listening to suitors. The same applies to young lads of good family. They never presume to speak in the presence of their elders unless addressed. What need of more words? Such is their modesty among themselves, that is to say as between members of a family and kinsmen, that two of them would never think of entering a hot or cold bath together.

When someone wishes to give his daughter in marriage or receives a request for her hand, the father will pledge his daughter to the prospective son-in-law as a virgin, and the two will draw up contracts on that basis, so that if it should be found to be otherwise the marriage would not stand. When the contracts and covenants have been duly entered into and confirmed between the parties, the intended bride is conducted to the baths for her chastity to be put to the proof. Here the mothers and kinswomen of the betrothed pair will be waiting, and certain matrons specially deputed by both parties will first test her virginity with a pigeon's egg. If the women of the bridegroom's party are not satisfied with this test, on the ground that loss of integrity may well be disguised by means of medicaments, one of these matrons, having wrapped one finger in fine white linen, will slightly bruise the *vena virginalis*, so that the linen may be slightly stained with the virginal blood. For it is a distinctive property of this blood that its stain cannot be removed from cloth by any washing. So, if the stain is washed out, that is a sign that the blood is not that of an undefiled virgin. When the test has been carried out, if the bride is found to be a virgin, the marriage is valid. If not, it is invalid and the girl's father is obliged to pay a penalty specified in the contract. You must know that, to ensure this strict preservation of virginity, the maidens always walk so daintily that they never advance one foot more than a finger's breadth beyond the other, since physical integrity is often destroyed by a wanton gait. This rule must be understood as applying to the natives of Cathay. The Tartars do not trouble about such refinements, since their daughters and wives often go riding with them, so that it is quite credible that their integrity might be somewhat affected. The people of the province of Manzi also observe this custom in common with those of Cathay.

There is another practice current in Cathay which is worthy of record. Among the idolaters there are eighty-four idols, each with its own name. They declare that the supreme god has assigned to each of these its own distinctive faculty, one concerned with the finding of lost objects, one with ensuring the fertility of the crops and tempering the weather for their growth, one with the safeguarding of flocks; and so with other activities, whether in prosperity or in adversity. And every idol is called by its own name, and of each they know and declare that such or such is its function and faculty. The idols whose function it is to find lost property take the form of two small wooden statues representing twelve-year-old children, which are adorned with handsome ornaments. In their temples an old woman is in perpetual residence as sacristan. If anyone has lost anything, either because he has been robbed or because he does not know where he left it or for some reason or other is unable to lay hands on it, he will go in person or send someone to the old woman, so that she may inquire of these idols about the missing object. She will then instruct him to offer incense to the idols, and he will duly cense them. After this she will question them about the lost object, and they will reply as the case may be. Then she will say to the loser: 'Look in such-and-such a place and you will find it.' Or, if someone has taken it, she will say: 'So-and-so has it. Tell him to give it to you. If he refuses, come back to me and I will make him restore it without fail. Otherwise I will see to it that he is wounded in his hand or foot, or falls and breaks an arm or a leg or suffers some other injury, so that he will be compelled willy nilly to restore it.' And so it turns out in practice. If anyone has stolen anything from another and, on being admonished, obstinately refuses to restore it, then, if the thief is a woman, while she is handling a knife in the kitchen or in the course of some other task, she cuts her hand or stumbles into the fire, or some such misfortune befalls her; if the thief is a man, then in like manner while he is chopping wood he cuts his foot or he breaks an arm or a leg or some other part of his body. Since people have learnt by experience that such is the fate of those who refuse to return stolen property, they are prompt to restore what they have taken. If the idols do not answer immediately, the old woman will say: 'The spirits are not here. Go away and come back at such-and-such an hour, because they will return in the meantime and I will question them.' The client will return at the prescribed hour, and the spirits meanwhile will have given their answer to the old woman. They deliver their response in a thin low voice, like a whispered hiss. Then the old woman thanks them profusely by uplifting her hands before them and gnashing her teeth three times, as though she were saying: 'Oh, what a worthy deed! How holy! How virtuous!' To a man who has lost horses she will say: 'Go to such-and-such a place and there you will find them.' Or it may be: 'Robbers found them in such-and-such a place and are leading them off by such-and-such a route. Make haste and you will find them.' And it turns out precisely as she has said. Thus it happens that nothing is ever lost that cannot be found. When the lost property is found, then men make an offering to the idols out of reverence and devotion, such as a yard or two of some costly fabric, linen or silk or cloth of gold. And by this means I, Marco, found a ring that I had lost—but not by making any offering to the idols or paying them homage.

When the traveller leaves Tandinfu, he continues southwards for three days, passing many splendid cities and towns, centres of thriving commerce and industry. The country teems with game of every sort and is well stocked with every kind of product. At the end of this time he reaches the splendid city of Sinju Matu,* a city of great size

* This is apparently T'si-ning-chau. Piju and Siju have been identified as Pei-chau and Su-t'sien. Linju remains a mystery: it may represent an older name for Sü-chau-fu.

and wealth and great commercial and industrial activity. The people are idolaters and subject to the Great Khan and use paper money. They have a river, which they turn to good account, as I shall tell you. The truth is that this river flows from the south as far as this city of Sinju Matu; and the townsmen have made it into two, one half flowing eastwards and the other westwards, so that one leads to Manzi and the other through Cathay. And I assure you that this town has so much shipping that no one who has not seen it could believe it. You must not suppose that they are big ships; but they are such as best suit a large river. And I assure you that the amount of merchandise transported to Manzi and through Cathay by this multitude of craft is simply staggering. And then, when the boats come back, they carry return cargoes. So it is indeed a marvellous sight to see the traffic going up and down this river.

On leaving Sinju Matu the traveller proceeds southwards for eight days, passing many cities and towns of great size and splendour and wealth, centres of thriving commerce and industry. The inhabitants are idolaters and burn their dead. They are subject to the Great Khan and use paper money. At the end of the eight days he reaches a city called Linju, which is also the name of the province. It is the capital of the kingdom and a very splendid and wealthy city, whose citizens are skilled in arms, though they also practise commerce and industry on a big scale. The neighbourhood abounds in game, both beast and bird, and is well supplied with foodstuffs. It produces quantities of jujubes, which are twice the size of dates and are used by the natives for making bread. It still lies on the river of which I have spoken. But here they have bigger ships for carrying merchandise of great bulk as well as value.

Let us now leave Linju and go on our way, so that I may tell you of yet other novelties.

The road continues southwards for three days, through a land of fine cities and towns. The people are like those of whom I have already told you: they are idolaters who cremate their dead, are subject to the Great Khan and use paper money. The country still abounds with the best game in the world, both beast and bird, and with provisions of every sort. At the end of these three days the traveller reaches a city called Piju of great size and splendour and a great centre of trade and industry. Silk is produced here in great abundance. This city lies at the entrance to the major province of Manzi. Here traders load their wagons with a variety of goods for transport into Manzi by way of various cities and towns. It is a city that yields a handsome revenue to the Great Khan. Since there is nothing else worth mentioning, we shall continue our journey towards the south.

From Piju the road runs southwards for two days through very fine country, rich in products of every sort and teeming with game, both beast and bird, till it reaches Siju, a large city with thriving trade and industry. The inhabitants are idolaters who cremate their dead. They use paper money and are subject to the Great Khan. The city lies in the midst of fertile plains and fields that yield abundance of wheat and other grain. But, since there is nothing else worth noting, we shall go on our way.

For three days' journey to the south of Siju the way lies through a pleasant country of fine towns and villages and well-tilled fields, abounding in game and in wheat and other cereals and inhabited by idolaters who are subject to the Great Khan and use paper money. After this the traveller comes to the great river of Kara-moran, which flows from the land of Prester John. You must know that it is a mile in width. It is very deep, so that big ships can sail on it without difficulty. It teems with big fish, and there are cities all along its banks. I am afraid to tell you how many ships there are on this river, for fear I should be called a liar. They amount to no less than 15,000, all belonging to the Great Khan and available to carry his armies to the isles of the sea; for I must tell you that the sea is a mere day's journey from this place. Each transport ship has a crew of twenty and carries about fifteen horses with the riders and provisions. There are really two cities, facing each other across the river, one named Hwai-ngan-chau and the other Kaiju. The former is a big city, the latter small.

When you cross this river, you enter the great province of Manzi; and I will now go on to tell you how this province was conquered by the Great Khan. But you must not suppose that we have dealt exhaustively with the whole province of Cathay, or indeed with the twentieth part of it. Only such cities have been described as I, Marco, passed through on my journey through the province, leaving out those on either side and the intervening regions whose enumeration would be too tedious.

The lord and master of the great province of Manzi was a certain Facfur, a mighty king and plentifully endowed with wealth and subjects and territories, so that a greater has scarcely been known in the world.* Certainly there was no richer or more powerful ruler apart from the Great Khan himself. But you must understand that he was no soldier. He took great delight in women, and was beneficent to the poor. In his province he had no horses. His subjects were not trained to battle and arms and campaigns, because this province of Manzi possesses great natural strength. All its cities are surrounded by broad and deep stretches of water, so that there is not a city but has water round it more than a bowshot in width and very deep. So I can assure you that, if the inhabitants had been practised soldiers, they would never have lost it. It was only through lack of valour and of military training that they did lose it. For there is no entry into any of the cities except by bridge.

This is how it happened. In the year of Christ's incarnation 1268, the Great Khan now reigning, that is to say Kubilai, sent here one of his barons whose name was Bayan Chincsan, which means 'Bayan Hundred-eyes'.† And I assure you that the king of Manzi had discovered by his astrology that he could not lose his kingdom except at the hands of a man who had a hundred eyes. So this man Bayan, with a great force of cavalry and infantry committed to him by the Great Khan, set out for Manzi. He had in addition a large fleet of ships to transport his troops, both horse and foot, when required. When he had come with all his forces to the entrance to Manzi, that is, to the city of Hwai-ngan-chau where we now are and of which I shall have more to say later, he ordered the inhabitants to submit to the Great Khan. They refused outright. When Bayan saw this, he advanced till he reached another city, which likewise refused to submit; so he continued to advance as before. This he did because he knew that the Great Khan was sending another large force after him. What need of more words? He went thus to five cities and could take none of them, and none would submit. But when he came to the sixth he took it by storm.‡ Then he took a second and a third, so that it happened in this way that he took twelve cities, one after the other. To cut a long story short, you may take it for a fact that Bayan, when he

* R adds: 'within the last century'. *Facfur* is the Arabic form of the Persian *Baghbur*, which represents the Chinese imperial title 'Son of Heaven'. Polo appears to confuse the Sung emperor Tu-tsong with his infant son and successor Chao-hien. The queen was Tu-tsong's mother, the dowager empress Sie-chi.

† Actually it is the name 'Bayan', not the official title '*ching-siang*' that can be interpreted 'Hundred-eyes'.

‡ R adds that he put to death all the inhabitants.

had captured all these cities, went straight to the capital of the kingdom, the city of Kinsai, where the king and queen had their residence. When the king saw Bayan with his army, he was greatly dismayed. He left the city with a large following and embarked on some thousand ships and took flight to the islands in the Ocean. The queen, who had remained in the city with a powerful force, set about defending it as best she could. Now it so happened that she asked the name of the commander and was told that he was called Bayan Hundred-eyes. When she heard the name Hundred-eyes, she called to mind the prediction of the astrologers that a man who had a hundred eyes would rob them of their kingdom. Thereupon she surrendered to Bayan. After she had surrendered, all the other cities and the whole kingdom surrendered too without further resistance. And this was a mighty conquest indeed; for in all the world there was no kingdom worth half as much as this. The wealth the king had at his disposal passes all belief. Let me tell you something of the largesse he was accustomed to bestow.

You must know that every year he paid for the rearing of fully 20,000 little children. I will tell you how. In this province the custom prevails of exposing babies at birth. This is done by poor women who have no means of rearing them. All these rejected infants were taken in charge by the king, who had a record made of the constellation and the planet under which each was born. Then he had them reared in many places and many establishments; for he had a great many nurses in his employ. And when a rich man had no son, he would go to the king and get leave to adopt any that he might choose and such as pleased him best. Moreover, when the boys and girls reached the age of marriage, he would marry them to one another and provide the couples with a livelihood. In this way, year by year, he would bring up fully 20,000 including males and females. Here is another thing that the king used to do. When he was out riding along the road and chanced to catch sight of two fine houses and between them another that was much smaller, he would inquire why this house was so small and mean in comparison with its neighbours. On learning that it belonged to a poor man who could afford no better, he would give orders to have the little house made as fine and as high as those on either side. Let me tell you further that he always maintained as his personal attendants a retinue of more than 1,000, including pages and maids in waiting. And he kept order and justice in his kingdom so effectually that there were no wrong-doers. At night the shops stood open, and nothing was ever taken from them. It was as safe to travel by night as by day. There is no telling the great wealth that there was in this kingdom.

Now that I have told you about the kingdom, I will tell you more of the queen. She was conducted to the Great Khan. And he, when he saw her, directed that she should be treated with honour and consideration, as befitted a great lady. As for the king her husband, it was his fate never to leave the isles of the Ocean; but there he died. So enough of him and his wife and of this subject. We shall turn back now to the province of Manzi and tell of all the manners and customs of the people and of their doings, all in due order, so that you may hear plainly what there is to say. We shall begin accordingly at the beginning, that is, at the city of Hwai-ngan-chau.

Hwai-ngan-chau is a very big city, of great wealth and splendour, standing at the entrance to the province of Manzi as one approaches from the north-west. The inhabitants are idolaters who burn their dead and are subject to the Great Khan. They have enormous numbers of ships; for you know, as I have told you, that the city stands on the river called Kara-moran. And I can assure you that it imports enormous quantities of merchandise, being the chief city of the kingdom in these parts. This is imported from many other cities and widely distributed by means of this river. The salt made here is exported to meet the needs of forty cities and more. So the Great Khan derives a huge revenue from this city, both from the salt and from imposts on its trade.

On leaving Hwai-ngan-chau the traveller proceeds south-eastwards for a day's journey along a causeway which lies at the entrance to Manzi. This causeway is built of very fine stones; and just beside it, on either hand, lies water—on one side mainly marshes, on the other marshes and deep water, which is navigable. There is no way into the province except along this causeway or by boat. At the end of the day's journey lies a fine large city called Pao-ying. The people here are idolaters who burn their dead. They are subject to the Great Khan, use paper money, and live by commerce and industry. They have abundance of silk and make fabrics of silk and cloth of gold of all sorts in great quantity. The means of life are very plentiful here. But there is nothing else worth noting.

On leaving Pao-ying the traveller continues south-eastwards for another day and reaches a large and splendid city called Kao-yu. Here again the people are idolaters, using paper money, subject to the Great Khan, and living by trade and industry. They are plentifully supplied with the means of life—fish without stint and game in abundance, both beast and bird. A Venetian groat of silver will buy three pheasants.

From Kao-yu the way runs south-eastwards for another day through a thriving region of villages and fields to a city called Tai-chau which is not large but amply provided with all earthly goods. The inhabitants are idolaters, using paper money, subject to the Great Khan, and living by trade and industry. They derive great profit from their thriving commerce. They have ships in plenty and no lack of game, both beast and bird.

Three days' journey from here, on the left-hand side towards the east, lies the Ocean. And at every place between here and the Ocean are produced great quantities of salt. There is a big city here called Chinju of great riches and splendour, where enough salt is made to supply the whole province. And you may take my word for it that the revenue accruing to the Great Khan from this source is so stupendous that, unless it were seen, it could scarcely be credited. The people are idolaters, using paper money and subject to the Great Khan. We shall now return to Tai-chau and continue our journey towards the southeast.

From Tai-chau a day's journey through very fine country full of towns and villages brings the traveller to a large and splendid city called Yang-chau. You must know that it is so great and powerful that its authority extends over twenty-seven cities, all large and prosperous and actively engaged in commerce. This city is the seat of one of the Great Khan's twelve barons; for it has been chosen for one of the twelve prefectures. The people are idolaters using paper money and subject to the Great Khan. Messer Marco Polo himself, who is the subject of this book, governed this city for three years.* The inhabitants live by trade and industry; for accoutrements for horses and men-at-arms are produced here in great quantities. For I give you my word that in this city and its adjoining dependencies there live a great many men-at-arms. Since there is nothing else here worthy of note, I will go on to tell you of two great provinces lying farther west which also form part of Manzi. Since there is much to tell of them, I will relate all their customs and usages.

* R adds that he held the office 'by the Great Khan's commission in place of one of the said barons'. Cf. p. 9.

The first of these, a very splendid and wealthy one, is called Ngan-king. The people are idolaters, using paper money and subject to the Great Khan. They live by trade and industry. They have silk in abundance and manufacture cloths of gold and silk fabrics of all sorts. They are amply supplied with grain and other foodstuffs; for it is a very fruitful province. They also have game in plenty. They burn their dead. There are many lions here. And there are many rich merchants, so that the province yields a heavy tribute and a big revenue to the Great Khan. But, as there is nothing else worthy of note, let us turn to the very splendid city of Siang-yang-fu, which well deserves a place in our book, because it is concerned in a matter of great consequence.

Siang-yang-fu is a great and splendid city whose authority extends over twelve others, all large and wealthy. It is an important centre of trade and industry. The people are idolaters, use paper money and burn their dead. They are subject to the Great Khan. They have silk in plenty and weave cloths of gold and silk of all sorts. Game too is plentiful. It has all that appertains to a truly noble city.

What is more, I can tell you for a fact that this city held out three years after the whole of Manzi had submitted. And all this time a great army of the Great Khan was encamped against it; but the army could occupy only one side, that is, the north, because on every other side it was protected by a large and deep lake. So the army could besiege it only on this northern side. From every other side it continued to receive provisions in plenty, which were brought over by water. And I assure you that the besiegers would never have taken it, but for a circumstance which I will now relate. You must know that when they had been engaged for three years in this siege without success, they were provoked beyond endurance. Then Messer Niccolò and Messer Maffeo and Messer Marco declared: 'We shall find you a means by which the city will be forced to surrender forthwith.' The besiegers said that nothing would please them better. All these words were spoken in the presence of the Great Khan; for envoys from the army had come to tell him how they were unable to take the city by siege and how provisions were coming in by ways that they were unable to block. The Great Khan said: 'Something must be done to ensure that this city is taken.' Thereupon the two brothers and their son Marco declared: 'Sire, we have with us in our retinue men who will make mangonels that will hurl such huge stones that the besieged will be unable to endure it but will surrender forthwith as soon as the mangonels, that is the trebuchets, have begun their hurling. The Great Khan told Messer Niccolò and his brother and his son that nothing would please him better, and directed that they should have this mangonel made as speedily as they could. Then Messer Niccolò and his brother and son, who had among their retinue a German and a Nestorian Christian who were masters of this art, bade them make two or three mangonels that hurled stones of 300 pounds. And these two made three fine mangonels.* When they were made, the Great Khan had them carried to his army who were engaged in the siege of Siang-yang-fu. As soon as the trebuchets arrived, they were set up; and they impressed the Tartars as the greatest wonder in the world. What more need I say? When the trebuchets were erected and wound up, then one of them hurled a stone into the city. The stone landed on houses, shattering and wrecking everything and making a terrific din and uproar. When the citizens saw this disaster, of which they had never seen the like, they were so bewildered and aghast that they did not know what to say or do. They held counsel together and could not hit on any scheme for escaping from these trebuchets. They came to the conclusion that unless they surrendered they were all dead men. So they made up their minds to surrender at all costs, and sent word to the commander of the army that they were willing to surrender on the same terms as the other cities of the province and submit to the suzerainty of the Great Khan. The commander was well content with these terms. He accepted their submission, and the citizens surrendered. And the credit for this achievement was due to the good offices of Messer Niccolò and Messer Maffeo and Messer Marco. And it was no small achievement. For you must know that this city and the dependent province is one of the very best in the dominions of the Great Khan and makes a great contribution to his revenues. So much, then, for this episode.

You must know that, when the traveller leaves Yang-chau and continues south-eastwards† for fifteen miles, he reaches a city called Sinju, which is of no great size but is a busy resort of ships and

* One MS (FG) adds that sixty round stones were prepared; that they were hurled a great distance; and that a demonstration before the Khan and his court won great applause. R also refers to this demonstration. It seems possible that the 'German' (*Alamainz*), who does not appear in R, was really an 'Alan', unless indeed the whole passage is to be rejected (cf. p. 9).
† Actually 'south-westwards', if Sinju is rightly identified as Iching.

merchandise. The people are idolaters and subject to the Great Khan. Their money is of paper. This city stands on the biggest river in the world, which is called Kiang. In some places it is ten miles wide, in some eight, in others six, and in length it extends to 100 days' journey.* Thanks to this river it is a city of innumerable ships, carrying quantities of goods and merchandise, and consequently a great source of revenue to the Great Khan.

I assure you that this river runs for such a distance and through so many regions and there are so many cities on its banks that truth to tell, in the amount of shipping it carries and the total volume and value of its traffic, it exceeds all the rivers of the Christians put together and their seas into the bargain. I give you my word that I have seen in this city fully 5,000 ships at once, all afloat on this river. Then you may reflect, since this city, which is not very big, has so many ships, how many there must be in the others. For I assure you that the river flows through more than sixteen provinces, and there are on its banks more than 200 cities, all having more ships than this. This excludes the cities and territories situated on rivers flowing into the main stream, which also carry much shipping. And all these ships carry goods to this city of Sinju and back again. The chief article of commerce on the river is salt, which traders load at this city and carry throughout all the regions lying on the river and also up-country away from the main stream along the tributaries, supplying all the regions through which they flow. For this reason salt is brought from a long stretch of the sea-coast into Sinju and there it is put on board ship and transported into all these regions. The same ships also carry iron. On their return journey downstream they bring into this city wood, charcoal, hemp, and many other articles on which the coastal regions are dependent. Even so, the shipping does not suffice to carry everything; a great many wares are transported on rafts. Hence this port or city provides the Great Khan with a substantial income. At many points in the river there are projecting crags and rocky islands on which are built monasteries of the idols and other habitations, and there are villages and homesteads everywhere.

The ships are decked and have only one mast, but their capacity is considerable; for I assure you that they carry from 200 to 600 tons, by the reckoning of our country. Before leaving this city, of which I have given you a full account, let me add one point that I had for-

* Z gives the length of the river (Yang-tze Kiang) as 120 days and adds that it is swollen by countless tributaries from various quarters.

gotten, which well deserves a place in our book. You must know that not all the ships have hempen ropes, except that the masts and sails are rigged with them. But I assure you that the cables by which they are towed upstream are made of cane. You must understand that these are the long stout canes of which I have spoken before, fully fifteen paces in length. They split them and bind them together into lengths of fully 300 paces, and they are stronger than if they were made of hemp. And each of these ships has eight or ten or twelve horses which tow it upstream. Let us now leave here, and we shall tell you of another city which is called Kwa-chau.

Kwa-chau is a small city lying towards the south-east on the river. Its inhabitants are idolaters, subject to the Great Khan and using paper money. Into this city are imported great quantities of corn and rice, which are exported from here as far as the great city of Khan-balik, to the Great Khan's court, by water—I do not mean by sea, but by way of rivers and lakes. You must know that the grain that comes into this city constitutes a great part of the food supply of the court. And I can tell you that it is the Great Khan who has had this water-way constructed from Kwa-chau to Khan-balik. He has made a huge canal of great width and depth from river to river and from lake to lake, and made the water flow along it so that it looks like a big river. It affords passage for very large ships. By this means it is possible to go from Manzi as far as Khan-balik. It is equally possible to go by land; for alongside the waterways there runs a causeway. So that there is a way, as you have heard, by land and water alike.

In the middle of the river opposite this city is a rocky island on which stands a monastery of the idolaters, peopled by 2,000 brethren. In this great monastery there is an immense number of idols. You must know that it is set in authority over many other idol-mona-steries, as it were an archbishopric.

Let us now leave here and cross the river, and we will tell you of a city called Chin-kiang-fu. This is a city of Manzi. The people are idolaters and subject to the Great Khan and use paper money. They live by trade and industry. They have plenty of silk and make cloth of gold and silk of many varieties. There are merchants here of wealth and consequence. There is no lack of game, both beast and bird, and abundance of grain and food-stuffs. There are two churches here of Nestorian Christians. This came about in the year 1278, and I will tell you how. The truth is that there was never a Christian church here, nor any believer in the God of the Christians, till this year 1278,

M

when the city was governed for three years in the name of the Great Khan by Mar Sergius, who was a Nestorian Christian. It was this Mar Sergius who had these two churches built. And ever since then there have been Churches here, where before there was neither Church nor Christian.

When the traveller leaves Chin-kiang-fu and proceeds south-eastwards for three days, he finds cities and towns in plenty all the way, centres of thriving trade and industry. The people are all idolaters, subject to the Great Khan and using paper money. At the end of this time he reaches the large and splendid city of Chang-chau. Here too the people are idolaters, subject to the Great Khan, using paper money, and living by trade and industry. They have silk in plenty and make cloth of gold and silken fabrics of all sorts. They are well supplied with game, both beast and bird, and with all the necessities of life; the soil here is very fertile.

I will tell you of a wicked deed that was done by the people of this city and how they paid for it dearly. The truth is that, when the province of Manzi was conquered by the Great Khan's men under the command of Bayan, it happened that Bayan sent a party of his men, who were Alans and Christians, to this city to take it. Now it so happened that these Alans forced their way into the outer city and found there such good wine that they drank themselves into a drunken stupor and lost all consciousness of good or ill. When the citizens within the inner walls of the city saw the state their captors were in and that they were like dead men, they did not lose a moment, but turned upon them there and then and killed them all that very night, so that not one escaped. When Bayan, the commander-in-chief of the army, learnt that the men of this city had slain his men so treacherously, he sent a sufficient detachment to take the city by force. And when they had taken it, I assure you that they put all the inhabitants to the sword. So it came about that the whole population of this city was massacred.

Moving on from here, we shall tell you next of a large and very splendid city called Su-chau. The people here are idolaters, subject to the Great Khan and using paper money. They live by trade and industry, have silk in great quantity and make much silken cloth for their clothing. There are merchants here of great wealth and consequence. The city is so large that it measures about forty miles in circumference. It has so many inhabitants that no one could reckon their number. I give you my word that the men of the province of

Manzi, if they were a war-like nation, would conquer all the rest of the world. But they are not war-like. I can assure you rather that they are capable merchants and skilled practitioners of every craft, and among them are wise philosophers and natural physicians with a great knowledge of nature.*

Let me tell you that in this city there are fully 6,000 stone bridges, such that one or two galleys could readily pass beneath them. In the adjacent mountains rhubarb and ginger grow in great profusion, so that one Venetian groat would buy forty pounds of fresh ginger of excellent quality. The city exercises authority over sixteen others, all large and busy centres of trade and industry. You must know that its name Su-chau signifies in our language 'Earth', and another city not far away is called 'Heaven'. These names have been bestowed upon them in recognition of their grandeur. We will tell you later of the city called 'Heaven'. Meanwhile let us leave Su-chau and go on to a city called Vuju.† This is one day's journey from Su-chau. It is a large and prosperous city, a centre of trade and industry. But, since it offers no novelties worth mentioning, we shall pass on to another city, called Vughin. This too is a large and splendid city. The people are idolaters and subject to the Great Khan and they use paper money. They are rich in silk and many other articles of commerce and are skilful traders and craftsmen. On leaving here we come to Changan, a large and wealthy city. The people are idolaters, subject to the Great Khan and using paper money. They live by trade and industry. Sendal of various kinds is made here, and game is plentiful. As there is nothing else worth mentioning, we will go on our way and I will tell you next of the splendid city of Kinsai, which is the chief city of the king of Manzi.

For three‡ days' journey from Changan the traveller passes through a fine country full of thriving towns and villages, living by commerce and industry. The people are idolaters, using paper money and subject to the Great Khan, and amply provided with all the means of life. Then he reaches the splendid city of Kinsai, whose name means 'City of Heaven'. It well merits a description, because it is without doubt the finest and most splendid city in the world. I will follow the

---

* Z adds: 'and many magicians and diviners'.
† Polo's route from Su-chau to Hang-chau (Kinsai) is uncertain, and the three cities through which it passes are all unidentified.
‡ Z reads: 'one'.

account of it sent in writing by the queen of the realm to Bayan, the conqueror of the province, when he was besieging it. This was for him to pass on to the Great Khan, so that, learning of its magnificence, he might not let it be sacked or laid waste. I will recount the contents of her letter in due order; and it is all true, as I, Marco Polo, later saw clearly with my own eyes.

First, then, it was stated that the city of Kinsai is about 100 miles in circumference, because its streets and watercourses are wide and spacious. Then there are market-places, which because of the multitudes that throng them must be very large and spacious. The lay-out of the city is as follows. On one side is a lake of fresh water, very clear. On the other is a huge river, which entering by many channels, diffused throughout the city, carries away all its filth and then flows into the lake, from which it flows out towards the Ocean. This makes the air very wholesome. And through every part of the city it is possible to travel either by land or by these streams. The streets and the watercourses alike are very wide, so that carts and boats can readily pass along them to carry provisions for the inhabitants. There are said to be 12,000 bridges, mostly of stone, though some are of wood. Those over the main channels and the chief thoroughfare are built with such lofty arches and so well designed that big ships can pass under them without a mast, and yet over them pass carts and horses; so well are the street-levels adjusted to the height. Under the other bridges smaller craft can pass. No one need be surprised that there are so many bridges. For the whole city lies in water and surrounded by water, so that many bridges are needed to let people go all over the town.

On the other side the city is confined by a moat, some forty miles long and very wide and deep, which flows out of the river. This was made by the ancient kings of the province, so as to draw off floodwater whenever the river rises above its banks. It serves also to fortify the city. And the earth dug from it was heaped on the inner side, forming a low mound that encircles the city.

There are ten principal market-places, not to speak of innumerable local ones. These are square, being half a mile each way. In front of them lies a main thoroughfare, forty paces wide, which runs straight from one end of the city to the other. It is crossed by many bridges, carefully designed to avoid sharp inclines. And every four miles there is one of these squares, with a circumference, as stated, of two miles. Correspondingly there is a very wide canal, which runs along the side of the squares opposite to the thoroughfare. On the nearer bank of this are constructed large stone buildings, in which all the merchants who come from India and elsewhere store their wares and merchandise, so that they may be near and handy to the market squares. And in each of these squares, three days in the week, there is a gathering of forty to fifty thousand people, who come to market bringing everything that could be desired to sustain life. There is always abundance of victuals, both wild game, such as roebuck, stags, harts, hares, and rabbits, and of fowls, such as partridges, pheasants, francolins, quails, hens, capons, and as many ducks and geese as can be told; for so many are reared in the lake that for a silver groat of Venice you may have a brace of geese or two brace of ducks. Then there are the shambles, where they slaughter the bigger animals, such as calves, oxen, kids, and lambs, whose flesh is eaten by the rich and the upper classes. The others, the lower orders, do not scruple to eat all sorts of unclean flesh.

Among the articles regularly on sale in these squares are all sorts of vegetables and fruits, above all huge pears, weighing 10 lb. apiece, white as dough inside and very fragrant, and peaches in season, yellow and white, which are great delicacies. Grapes and wine are not produced locally; but raisins of excellent quality are imported from other ports and so too is wine, though the inhabitants do not set much store by this, being accustomed to the wine made of rice and spices. Every day a vast quantity of fish is brought upstream from the ocean, a distance of twenty-five miles. There is also abundance of lake fish, varying in kind according to the season, which affords constant employment for fishermen who have no other occupation. Thanks to the refuse from the city, these fish are plump and tasty. Seeing the quantity on sale, you would imagine they could never be disposed of. But in a few hours the whole lot has been cleared away—so vast are the numbers of those accustomed to dainty living, to the point of eating fish and meat at one meal. All the ten squares are surrounded by high buildings, and below these are shops in which every sort of craft is practised and every sort of luxury is on sale, including spices, gems, and pearls. In some shops nothing is sold but spiced rice wine, which is being made all the time, fresh and fresh, and very cheap. There are many streets giving on to these squares. In some of these are many baths of cold water, well supplied with attendants, male and female, to look after the men and ladies who go there for a bath; for these people, from childhood upwards, are used to taking cold baths all the time, a habit which they declare to be most conducive to good health. They also maintain in these bath-houses some rooms with hot water for the benefit of foreigners who, not being accustomed to the cold, cannot readily endure it. It is their custom to wash every day, and they will not sit down to a meal without first washing.

Other streets are occupied by women of the town, whose number is such that I do not venture to state it. These are not confined to the neighbourhood of the squares—the quarter usually assigned to them —but are to be found throughout the city, attired with great magnificence, heavily perfumed, attended by many handmaids, and lodged in richly ornamented apartments. These ladies are highly proficient and accomplished in the use of endearments and caresses, with words suited and adapted to every sort of person, so that foreigners who have once enjoyed them remain utterly beside themselves and so captivated by their sweetness and charm that they can never forget them. So it comes about that, when they return home, they say they have been in 'Kinsai', that is to say in the city of Heaven, and can scarcely wait for the time when they may go back there.

In other streets are established the doctors and astrologers, who also teach reading and writing; and countless other crafts have their allotted places round the squares. Fronting on each of these squares are two palatial buildings, one at either end, in which are the offices of the magistrates appointed by the king to impose a summary settlement if any dispute arises among the traders or among the inhabitants of these quarters. It is the task of these magistrates to check every day whether the guards that are stationed on the neighbouring bridges, as will be explained below, are duly posted or have failed in their duty, and to punish any negligence at their discretion.

Along both sides of the main street, which runs, as we have said, from one end of the city to the other, are stately mansions with their gardens, and beside them the residences of artisans who work in their shops. Here at every hour of the day are crowds of people going to and fro on their own business, so that anyone seeing such a multitude would believe it a stark impossibility that food could be found to fill so many mouths. Nevertheless, every market day all these squares are thronged with a press of customers and traders bringing in supplies by cart and by boat, and the whole business is accomplished. Let me quote as an illustration the amount of pepper consumed in this city so that from this you may be able to infer the quantities of provisions—meat, wine, and groceries—that are required to meet the total consumption. According to the figures ascertained by Messer Marco from an official of the Great Khan's customs, the pepper consumed daily in the city of Kinsai for its own use amounts to 43 cart-loads, each cart-load consisting of 223 lb.

It was further stated in the report that the city was organized in twelve main guilds, one for each craft, not to speak of the many lesser ones. Each of these twelve guilds had 12,000 establishments, that is to say 12,000 workshops, each employing at least ten men and some as many as forty. I do not mean that they were all masters, but men working under the command of masters. All this work is needed because this city supplies many others of the province. As for the merchants, they are so many and so rich and handle such quantities of merchandise that no one could give a true account of the matter; it is so utterly beyond reckoning. And I assure you that the great men and their wives, and all the heads of the workshops of which I have spoken, never soil their hands with work at all, but live a life of as much refinement as if they were kings. And their wives too are most refined and angelic creatures, and so adorned with silks and jewellery that the value of their finery is past compute. It was decreed by their king, in the days of his rule, that every man must follow his father's craft: if he possessed 100,000 bezants, he could still practise no other craft than his father had done before him.* Not, of course, that he was obliged to labour at it with his own hands, but rather, as I have said above, to employ men to work at it. But this rule is by no means enforced by the Great Khan. Nowadays, if a craftsman has attained to such riches that he is able and desirous to abandon his craft, he is no longer constrained by anyone to practise it. For the Great Khan reasons thus: if a man practises a craft because he is poor and could not get a living without it, and then in process of time so prospers in his fortunes that he can lead an honourable life without the practice of his craft, why should he be compelled against his will to go on practising it? For it would seem unfitting and unjust, if the gods were generous to him, that men should oppose their will.

Let me tell you further that on the southern side of the city is a lake, some thirty miles in circuit. And all round it are stately palaces and mansions, of such workmanship that nothing better or more splendid could be devised or executed. These are the abodes of the nobles and magnates. There are also abbeys and monasteries of the idolaters in

* R's version suggests that the law of the ancient kings actually compelled men to work at their fathers' crafts, and the privilege accorded to the rich of merely employing men to work at it was a later relaxation.

very great numbers. Furthermore in the middle of the lake there are two islands, in each of which is a marvellous and magnificent palace, with so many rooms and apartments as to pass belief, and so sumptuously constructed and adorned that it seems like the palace of an emperor. When anyone wishes to celebrate a wedding or hold a party, he goes to this palace. Here their wedding-parties and feasts are held, and here they find all that is needful for such an occasion in the way of crockery, napery, and plate, and everything else, all kept in stock in the palaces for this purpose for the use of the citizenry; for it was they who had made it all. On occasion the need may arise to cater for a hundred clients at once, some ordering banquets, others wedding-feasts; and yet they will all be accommodated in different rooms and pavilions so efficiently that one does not get in the way of another. Besides this, the lake is provided with a great number of boats or barges, big and small, in which the people take pleasure-trips for the sake of recreation. These will hold ten, fifteen, twenty, or more persons, as they range from fifteen to twenty paces in length and are flat-bottomed and broad in the beam, so as to float without rocking. Anyone who likes to enjoy himself with female society or with his boon companions hires one of these barges, which are kept continually furnished with fine seats and tables and all the other requisites for a party. They are roofed over with decks on which stand men with poles which they thrust into the bottom of the lake (for it is not more than two paces in depth) and thus propel the barges where they are bidden. The deck is painted inside with various colours and designs and so is the whole barge, and all round it are windows that can be shut or opened so that the banqueters ranged along the sides can look this way and that and feast their eyes on the diversity and beauty of the scenes through which they are passing. And indeed a voyage on this lake offers more refreshment and delectation than any other experience on earth. On one side it skirts the city, so that the barge commands a distant view of all its grandeur and loveliness, its temples, palaces, monasteries, and gardens with their towering trees, running down to the water's edge. On the lake itself is the endless procession of barges thronged with pleasure-seekers. For the people of this city think of nothing else, once they have done the work of their craft or their trade, but to spend a part of the day with their womenfolk or with hired women in enjoying themselves either in these barges or in riding about the city in carriages—another pleasure in which, as I ought to mention, these people indulge in the same way as they do in boat-trips. For their minds and thoughts are intent upon nothing but bodily pleasure and the delights of society.

Here and there throughout the city there are big stone towers in which the townsfolk deposit all their valuables when a fire breaks out. You must understand that such outbreaks are very frequent, because many of the houses are made of wood. The houses in general are very solidly built and richly decorated. The inhabitants take such delight in ornaments, paintings, and elaborations that the amount spent on them is something staggering. The natives of Kinsai are men of peace, through being so cosseted and pampered by their kings, who were of the same temper. They have no skill in handling arms and do not keep any in their houses. There is prevalent among them a dislike and distaste for strife or any sort of disagreement. They pursue their trades and handicrafts with great diligence and honesty. They love one another so devotedly that a whole district might seem, from the friendly and neighbourly spirit that rules among men and women, to be a single household. This affection is not accompanied by any jealousy or suspicion of their wives, for whom they have the utmost respect. A man who ventured to address an unseemly remark to any married woman would be looked upon as a thorough blackguard. They are no less kind to foreigners who come to their city for trade. They entertain them in their houses with cordial hospitality and are generous of help and advice in the business they have to do. On the other hand, they cannot bear the sight of a soldier or of the Great Khan's guards, believing that it is through them that they have been deprived of their own natural kings and lords.

The people of Kinsai are idolaters, subject to the Great Khan and using paper money. Men as well as women are fair-skinned and good-looking. Most of them wear silk all the time, since it is produced in great abundance in all the surrounding territory, not to speak of the great quantity continually imported by traders from other provinces. They eat all sorts of flesh, including that of dogs and other brute beasts and animals of every kind which Christians would not touch for anything in the world.

Let me tell you further that each of the 12,000 bridges is guarded by ten men, five by day and five by night, who are stationed under cover. These are to protect the city from malefactors and check any attempt at rebellion. In every guardhouse there is a big wooden drum with a big gong and a clock by which they tell the hours of the night and also of the day. At the beginning of every night, when the first hour has passed, one of the guards strikes a single blow on the drum and the gong, so that the whole neighbourhood knows that it is one o'clock. At the second hour they strike two blows; and so on, hour by hour, increasing the number of strokes. They never sleep, but are always on the alert. In the morning after sunrise they strike first one hour, as they did after nightfall, and so from hour to hour. A detachment of them patrols the district to see if anyone has a light or a fire burning beyond the authorized hours. When they find an offending house, they put a mark on the door; and in the morning the owner is summoned to appear before the magistrates and, unless he can offer a legitimate excuse, he is punished. If they find anyone abroad at night after the approved hours, they arrest him, and in the morning they bring him before the magistrates. Again, if they come across some poor man by day, who is unable to work on account of illness, they have him taken to one of the hospitals, of which there are great numbers throughout the city, built by the ancient kings and lavishly endowed. And when he is cured, he is compelled to practise some trade. As soon as the guards see that fire has broken out in some house, they give warning of it by beating the drum, and the guards from other bridges come running up to extinguish it and rescue the goods of the merchants, or whoever it may be, by stowing them in the towers of which I have spoken or by loading them on barges and taking them out to the islands in the lake. For no resident in the city would venture to leave his house during the night even to go to the fire except the owners of the goods and these guards who come to help, of whom there cannot be less than one or two thousand.*

Let me tell you also that at one point in the city there stands a hill crowned by a tower inside which is a big wooden drum, which a man beats from within with a mallet, so as to be heard at a great distance. This is beaten as a danger signal in case of a conflagration or a civil disturbance.

The reason why the Great Khan has such a careful watch kept in this city and by so many guards is because it is the capital of the whole province of Manzi, a great repository of his treasure and the source of

---

* It is not clear how the foregoing paragraph (from R) is related to the following (from F). There is independent evidence both for the guardhouses and for the Drum Tower.

such immense revenue that one who hears of it can scarcely credit it. So he is at special pains to guard against rebellion here, and to this end he keeps huge forces of infantry and cavalry in the city and its environs, and especially of his leading barons and most trusted henchmen.

You may take it for a fact that all the streets of this city are paved with stone and brick. So too are all the high roads and causeways of the province of Manzi, so that it is possible to ride or to walk dry-shod through the length and breadth of the land. But since the Great Khan's couriers could not ride post-haste on horseback over paved roads, one strip of road at the side is left unpaved for their benefit. The main street, which we have already described as running from one end of the city to the other, is likewise paved with stones and bricks for a width of ten paces on either side. But the strip down the middle is filled with fine gravel, with vaulted sewers leading from it to drain off the rain water into the neighbouring canals so that it keeps permanently dry. Along this street you may see passing to and fro a continuous procession of long carriages, decked with awnings and cushions of silk, which seat six persons. These are hired by the day by gentlemen and ladies bent on taking pleasure-trips. Countless numbers of these carriages are to be seen at all hours of the day passing along the middle of this street on their way to the gardens, where they are welcomed by the garden-keepers under arbours specially designed for the purpose. Here they stay all day long enjoying a good time with their womenfolk; and then in the evening they return home in these carriages.

Let me tell you further that in this city there are fully 3,000 public baths,* to which men resort for their pleasure several times a month; for they believe in keeping their bodies very clean. I assure you that they are the finest baths and the best and biggest in the world—indeed they are big enough to accommodate a hundred men or a hundred women at once.

I would also have you know that twenty-five miles distant from this city, between north-east and east, lies the Ocean. There stands a city called Kan-p'u, at which there is a very fine port frequented by great quantities of shipping with valuable merchandise from India and elsewhere. Between the city and the port runs a big river by which ships can come as far as the city. The course of the river also extends much farther afield than this city.

* The versions disagree as to whether the baths were hot or cold.

I should add that the province of Manzi has been split up by the Great Khan into nine parts—that is to say, he has put it under the rule of nine great kings, each with a great kingdom of his own. But you must understand that these kings govern on behalf of the Great Khan, and on such terms that they render a yearly account of their several kingdoms to his agents for the revenue and everything else, and they are changed every three years like all the other officials. This city is the residence of one of these nine kings, whose rule extends over more than 140 large and wealthy cities. In the whole province of Manzi, incredible as it may seem, there are fully 1,200 cities, and each one of them has a garrison of the Khan's troops on the following scale. You may take it for a fact that no city has a garrison of less than 1,000 men, and some are manned by 10,000, some by 20,000 and some (including Kinsai) by 30,000, so that the total number is almost beyond reckoning. You must not suppose that these troops are all Tartars. The Tartars are horsemen and are stationed only near those cities that do not stand on watery sites but on firm, dry ground, where they can exercise themselves on horseback. In the cities on watery sites he stations Cathayans or such of the men of Manzi as are accustomed to arms. Out of all his subjects he has a yearly levy made of those who devote themselves to arms for enrolment in his forces, and all these are counted as his soldiers. The men who are recruited from the province of Manzi are not set to guard their own cities but are posted to others twenty days' journey away, where they stay four or five years. They then return home and others are sent in their place. This arrangement applies both to the Cathayans and to the men of Manzi. The greater part of the revenue of these cities that is paid into the Great Khan's treasury is devoted to the maintenance of these garrisons of soldiers. And if ever it happens that some city rebels—for there are times when the men in a sudden access of madness or intoxication massacre their rulers—then as soon as the news is known the neighbouring cities send a sufficient detachment of these troops to crush the erring cities; for any attempt to bring up a force from another province of Cathay would be a long operation, involving a lapse of two months.

To sum up, I can tell you in all truthfulness that the business of the province of Manzi—its riches, its revenue and the profit derived from it by the Great Khan—is on such a stupendous scale that no one who hears tell of it without seeing it for himself can possibly credit it. Indeed it is scarcely possible to set down in writing the magnificence of this province. So I will hold my peace on the subject to the extent of telling you very little further about it. I will tell you just one thing more, and then we shall pass on.

You must know that all the people of Manzi have a usage such as I will describe. The truth is that as soon as a child is born the father or the mother has a record made of the day and the minute and the hour at which he was born, and under what constellation and planet, so that everyone knows his horoscope. Whenever anyone intends to make a journey into another district or a business deal, he consults an astrologer and tells him his horoscope; and the astrologer tells him whether it is good to undertake it or not. And often they are deterred from the venture. For you must know that their astrologers are skilled in their art and in diabolic enchantment, so that many of their predictions prove true and the people repose great faith in them. When a marriage is planned, the astrologers first investigate whether the bridegroom and bride are born under concordant planets. If so, it is put into effect; if not, it is called off. Great numbers of these astrologers, or rather magicians, are to be found on every square of the city.

Let me tell you next that when some rich man dies and his body is being carried to the pyre, all the relatives, male and female, don a mourning garb of sack-cloth and escort the body on its way, to the accompaniment of musical instruments, chanting prayers to their idols. When they have reached the spot where the body is to be burnt, they halt. They are provided with horses and slaves, male and female, and camels and cloth of gold in great abundance—all made of paper! When all these have been got ready, they make a big fire and burn the body with the effigies. And they say that the dead will have all these things in the next world, alive in flesh and bone, and the money in gold, and that all the honour they do him while he is burning will be done to him correspondingly in the next world by their gods and their idols. Because of this faith they have no fear or anxiety about dying, so long as they are honoured in death with these rites, firmly believing that the like honour will be done to them in another world. So the men of Manzi are more prone than any other race to fits of passion, and very often out of sheer anger and mortification they will put an end to their own lives. For if it should happen that one of them gives another a box on the ear or tweaks his hair or in some way wrongs or slights him, and the offender is such a powerful and important personage that the other is powerless to avenge himself, then the injured party in the violence of his resentment will commit suicide by hanging himself by night at the offender's door as an insult and an expression of contempt. So, when the offender is discovered by the testimony of neighbours, they condemn him to compensate for the wrong done by honouring the victim at his funeral pyre with festal pomp—music, attendants, and all the rest of it according to their custom. His chief reason for hanging himself is just this—so that his rich and powerful enemy may honour him in death and thus ensure him similar honours in another world.

In this city also is the palace of the fugitive king, the one-time lord of Manzi, which is the most beautiful and splendid palace in the world. No words of mine could describe its superlative magnificence, but I will briefly relate some of its main features. You must know that the king's predecessors had enclosed a space of land some ten miles in circumference with lofty battlemented walls and divided it into three parts. The middle part was entered through a wide gateway flanked by pavilions of vast dimensions standing at ground level with their roofs supported by columns painted and wrought in fine gold and azure. Ahead was seen the largest and most important of these pavilions, similarly adorned with paintings and with gilded columns, and the ceiling gorgeously embellished with gold. On the inner walls were pictures of beasts and birds, knights and ladies, and scenes from the history of past kings, portrayed with consummate artistry. On every wall and every ceiling nothing met the eye but a blaze of gold and brilliant colour. Here every year, on certain days dedicated to his idols, King Facfur used to hold court and offer banquets to the chief lords and magnates and the wealthy industrialists of the city of Kinsai. At one service ample accommodation was found in all the halls of the palace, which numbered no less than twenty, for 10,000 persons. These festivities lasted for ten or twelve days on end and were a truly stupendous affair. It was a sight past all believing to behold the magnificence of the guests, robed in silk and gold and laden with precious stones, because everyone was at pains to make the greatest possible display of opulence.

Behind this chief pavilion, which faced the great gateway, was a wall with one way through, which shut off the other part of the palace. Beyond this was a large court, made in the style of a cloister with pillars supporting a portico which extended right round it. Here there were various chambers for the king and queen, adorned with the same elaborate workmanship, and all the walls likewise. Leading out of this cloister was a long covered corridor six paces wide, which ran right through to the lake at the other end. Communicating with this corridor were ten courtyards on one side and ten on the other, constructed in the form of long cloisters with surrounding colonnades. Every cloister or courtyard had fifty chambers with their gardens, and these were occupied in all by 1,000 damsels whom the king kept in his service and some of whom used to accompany him and the queen when he went out for recreation on the lake in barges canopied with silk or to visit the temples of the idols.

The other two-thirds of the enclosure were laid out in lakes filled with fish and groves and exquisite gardens, planted with every conceivable variety of fruit-tree and stocked with all sorts of animals such as roebuck, harts, stags, hares, and rabbits. Here the king would roam at pleasure with his damsels, partly in carriages, partly on horseback, and no man ever intruded. He would have the damsels hunt with hounds and give chase to the animals. When they were tired, they would withdraw to the groves which rimmed the lakes. Here they would doff their robes and run out naked and plunge into the water and set themselves to swim, some on one side, some on the other. And the king would stand and watch them with the utmost delight. And then he would return home. Sometimes he would have a meal brought to him in these groves, which were densely wooded with tall trees, and the damsels would wait upon him. Amid this perpetual dalliance he idled his time away without once hearing the name of arms. And this at last was his undoing, because through his unmanliness and self-indulgence he was deprived by the Great Khan of all his state to his utter shame and disgrace, as has been related above.

All this account was given to me by a rich merchant of Kinsai whom I encountered in the city, a man of ripe years who had been intimately acquainted with King Facfur and knew all about his life and had seen the palace in its glory. He undertook to conduct me through it. The pavilions in front, being occupied by the Great Khan's viceroy, are just as they used to be. But the chambers of the damsels have all fallen in ruin, and only vestiges of them remain. Likewise the wall that encircled the groves and gardens has fallen to the ground, and neither trees nor animals are left.

It chanced that Messer Marco found himself in this city of Kinsai when account was being rendered to the Great Khan's agents of its total revenue and population. Thus he learnt that it contained 160 *tomauns* of hearths, that is, of houses. I should explain that a *tomaun* is 10,000. So you may take it that the city contains 1,600,000 houses, including a large number of palatial mansions. There is just one church of Nestorian Christians.

Now that I have described the city I will tell you something that is well worthy of report. You must know that all the townsfolk of this city—and of all the others as well—have the following custom. Each one has written on the door of his house his own name and his wife's and those of his sons and his sons' wives and his slaves and of all the occupants of the house, and also how many horses he possesses. If it happens that one of them dies, he has the name struck out. If anyone is born there, his name is added to the list. In this way the governor of every city is kept informed about all the people who live in it. This usage prevails throughout the provinces of Manzi and Cathay.

Another good custom is this. All those who keep inns or provide lodgings for travellers write down the names of all those who lodge with them and the dates of their stay. So throughout the year the Great Khan can know who is coming and going through all his dominions. And this is a useful piece of knowledge to prudent statesmen.

Again, in the province of Manzi almost all the poor and needy sell some of their sons and daughters to the rich and noble, so that they may support themselves on the price paid for them and the children may be better fed in their new homes.

Let me tell you now of a marvel that occurred while Bayan was besieging this city. It happened, after King Facfur had taken to flight, that a multitude of the townsfolk were fleeing by boat by way of a broad, deep river that flows past one side of the city. All of a sudden, while they were actually on the river, the water completely dried up, so that Bayan, on learning the news, came to this part and compelled all the fugitives to return to the city. And a fish was found lying high and dry across the river-bed—and what a fish! For it was fully 100 paces long, but its girth was by no means proportionate to its length. Its whole body was hairy. Many people ate of it, and many of those who did so died. Messer Marco, as he relates, saw the head of this fish with his own eyes in a certain temple of the idols.

I will tell you next of the immense revenue that the Great Khan draws from this city of Kinsai and from the cities subject to its authority, which extends over one of the nine divisions of the province of Manzi. First I will tell you of the salt, since this makes the biggest contribution to the total. You may take it for a fact that the salt of this city yields an average yearly revenue of 80 *tomauns* of gold: as a *tomaun* is equivalent to 70,000 *saggi* of gold, this brings the total to 5,600,000 *saggi*, of which every *saggio* is worth more than a gold florin or ducat. This is indeed a thing to marvel at and an inordinate sum of money. The reason for it is that, since the city stands on the edge of the sea, there are many lagoons or marshes nearby in which the seawater condenses in summer, and such quantities of salt are dug out that they supply the needs of five other kingdoms of the province of Manzi.

So much for salt. Let me tell you next that this province produces more sugar than all the rest of the world put together, and this too is the source of an immense revenue. I will not give particulars for each item separately but will group the various spices* together, for they all pay a duty of $3\frac{1}{3}$ per cent. The same duty is paid on merchandise in general imported into the city by land or exported from it by land or by sea. Merchandise imported by sea pays 10 per cent. Likewise of all the yield of the flocks and the soil one-tenth is appropriated to the service of the Great Khan. A great revenue also accrues from rice wine and from charcoal and from all the twelve guilds of which I have spoken above as having 12,000 establishments each. These guilds are a great source of revenue; for they pay duty on everything. So is silk, which is produced in abundance and pays a heavy duty. But why make a long reckoning of it? Suffice it that silk pays 10 per cent, and this amounts to an immense sum of money. And there are many other articles that also pay 10 per cent. So I, Marco Polo, who have often heard the reckoning made, can assure you personally that the sum total of the revenue from all these sources, excluding salt, amounts in normal years to 210 *tomauns* of gold, equivalent to 14,700,000 gold pieces. This is surely one of the most inordinate computations that anyone has ever heard made. And it concerns the revenue of one only of the nine divisions of the province. Yet all these revenues are expended by the Great Khan on the garrisons stationed in the cities and districts and on relieving the needs of the inhabitants.

* *Especerie*, which apparently included sugar, should perhaps be translated 'groceries'.

N

Let us now leave Kinsai, of whose salient features I may claim to have described a fair share, and continue on our way.*

On leaving Kinsai, the traveller proceeds south-eastwards for a day's journey through a country full of delightful mansions, villages, and gardens and abounding in all the means of life. At the end of the day he reaches the city of Tanpiju, which I have mentioned above—a large and splendid city subordinate to Kinsai. The inhabitants are subject to the Great Khan and use paper money. They are idolaters and burn their dead in the way I have described above. They live by commerce and industry and are amply supplied with all the means of life. But, as there is nothing here worth mentioning, let us pass on.

On leaving Tanpiju, the traveller proceeds south-eastwards for three days, passing cities and towns all the way of great size and beauty and finding goods of all sorts very plentiful and very cheap. The people are idolaters subject to the Great Khan and under the government of Kinsai. There are no novelties worth mentioning. At the end of this time he reaches a big city called Vuju. The people here are idolaters subject to the Great Khan and living by trade and industry. They are still under the government of Kinsai. As there is nothing here that we wish to put in our book, we shall pass on our way.

You must know that on leaving Vuju the traveller proceeds south-eastwards for two days, passing towns and villages all the way, so that he seems to be traversing a city. The country abounds in all sorts of products. It produces the stoutest and tallest canes in all this land; for you must know that some of them grow to a girth of four palms and a height of fully fifteen paces. There is nothing else worth mentioning. At the end of the two days he reaches a fine large city called Ghiuju, subject to the Great Khan and still under the government of Kinsai. The people are idolaters, living by trade and industry. They have silk in plenty and are amply provided with the means of life. Here again there is nothing worth mentioning, so we shall go on our way.

On leaving Ghiuju the traveller proceeds south-eastwards for four

* The route from Kinsai to Zaiton presents many problems. The one fixed point is 'Quenlifu', generally accepted as Kien-ning-fu. Zaiton itself probably refers specifically to Chüan-chau, though the name seems also to have been loosely applied to the whole Amoy harbour region. The identification of the city of 'Fugiu' as Fu-chau has been questioned; the kingdom called 'Fugiu' or (?) 'Choncha' corresponds to the province of Fu-kien.

days, through a country full of cities, villages, and homesteads and amply stocked with the means of life. The people are all idolaters subject to the Great Khan and are still under the government of Kinsai. They live by trade and industry. They have no lack of game, both beast and bird. There are plenty of lions of great size and ferocity. There are no sheep in the whole of Manzi, but they have cattle and goats and pigs in plenty. As there is nothing else worth mentioning, we shall go on and talk of other matters.

At the end of the four days the traveller reaches the city of Chanshan, which is very large and fine. It stands on a hill that divides a river, so that half flows on one side of it and half on the other. It is still under the government of Kinsai and subject to the Great Khan. The people are idolaters and live by trade and industry. But there is nothing here worth mentioning; so we shall pass on.

You may take it for a fact that after leaving Chanshan the traveller proceeds for three days through very beautiful country where there are cities and towns and homesteads in plenty, inhabited mainly by traders and craftsmen. They are idolaters subject to the Great Khan and still under the government of Kinsai. They are amply provided with the means of life and have no lack of game, both beast and bird. There is nothing else worth mentioning; so we shall pass on.

After three days the traveller arrives at the city of Kuju, which is very large and fine. The people are idolaters subject to the Great Khan. This is the last city under the government of Kinsai. From now onwards Kinsai has no further say in affairs; but this is the beginning of another kingdom, that is to say, another of the nine divisions of Manzi, which is called Fu-chau.

On quitting the kingdom of Kinsai and entering that of Fu-chau the traveller journeys south-eastwards for six days through mountains and valleys, passing cities and towns and homesteads in plenty. The people are idolaters subject to the Great Khan and are all under the government of Fu-chau, with which we have now begun to deal. They live by trade and industry and are amply provided with the means of life. There is abundance of game here, both beast and bird, besides lions of great size and ferocity. Ginger and galingale are superabundant: indeed for a Venetian groat you could buy a quantity of fresh ginger equivalent to 80 lb. There is a fruit here that resembles saffron; though it is actually nothing of the sort, it is quite as good as saffron for practical purposes. Furthermore, you must know that the natives eat all sorts of brute beast. They even relish human flesh. They do not touch the flesh of those who have died a natural death; but they all eat the flesh of those who have died of a wound and consider it a delicacy. Among soldiers and men at arms the following practice prevails: they have their hair close-cropped as far back as the ears, and in the middle of their faces they paint in blue what looks like the blade of a sword. They all march on foot except their captain. They carry lances and swords and are the most blood-thirsty lot in the world. For I assure you that they go about every day killing men and drink the blood and then devour the whole body. This is their daily occupation—to go about killing men in order to drink their blood and then devour their flesh.

To turn to another subject, you must know that after travelling three of the six days mentioned above the traveller reaches the city of Kien-ning-fu, a very large and splendid city subject to the Great Khan. This city has three bridges, the finest and best in the world. They are more than a mile long and fully nine paces wide, and are all built of stone with columns of marble. They are so magnificent and so marvellous that it would cost a vast sum to build any one of them. The people here live by trade and industry. They have no lack of ginger and galingale or of silk. So much cotton cloth is woven here of dyed yarn that it supplies the whole province of Manzi. The women here are very good-looking. There is one curiosity worthy of note: I assure you that there are hens here that have no feathers but have hair like cats and are pure black. They lay as many eggs as the hens of our country and are very good to eat. As there is nothing else worth mentioning, we shall pass on.

During the remaining three days the way lies through many cities and towns crowded with merchants plying their trade and with craftsmen. The people are idolaters subject to the Great Khan and have silk in plenty and no lack of game. The lions, of great strength and ferocity, are a danger to wayfarers. Towards the end of the three days, with fifteen miles still to go, the traveller reaches a city called Unken, in which is produced a vast quantity of sugar. From this city the Great Khan derives all the sugar that is consumed in his court, which is certainly enough to cost a pretty penny. But you must know that in these parts before they came under the rule of the Great Khan the natives did not know how to make and refine sugar as well as it is done in Egypt. They did not know how to solidify it in moulds, but merely boiled and skimmed it so that it remained in the form of a black paste. But certain Egyptians who were at the Khan's court came here and taught them how to refine it with the ashes of certain trees. As there is nothing else worth mentioning, we shall now pass on.

Fifteen miles from Unken lies the splendid city of Fu-chau, which is the capital of the kingdom. So I will tell you what I can about it.

You must know that this city of Fu-chau is the capital of the kingdom named Choncha, which is one of the nine divisions of the province of Manzi. It is an important commercial centre, inhabited by many merchants and craftsmen. The people are idolaters and subject to the Great Khan. It is garrisoned by a large force of soldiers. For you must understand that several armies of the Great Khan are stationed here, since this district is one in which there are frequent rebellions of cities and towns. This is because, as I have said before, the natives hold life very cheap, believing that they will enjoy an honoured existence in the next world and also because their dwellings are in fastnesses among the mountains. So, when they are intoxicated with the spirit of revolt, they kill their rulers, and troops have to be called in to take their strongholds and crush them. That is why several armies of the Great Khan are stationed in this city.

Through the midst of the city flows a great river, fully a mile in width. It is crossed by a very fine bridge resting on huge pontoons which are held in place by strong anchors and overlaid with planks of great size and solidity.

This neighbourhood is infested with lions, which are trapped by the following stratagem. In suitable places two deep pits are dug, one beside the other. Between them is left a strip of earth a fathom or so in breadth. Along either side of the pits is built a high fence, but the ends are left clear. At night the owner of the pits will tie up a whelp on the earth-strip between the pits and leave him there. The dog, thus tied up and abandoned by his master, will set up a ceaseless howling (incidentally, he is always a white dog). Then the lion, however far away he may be, when he hears the howls of the dog, will make a dead set for him in a raging fury. On catching sight of him as a white object, he will make a headling spring to seize him and so fall into the pit. In the morning the owner will come and kill the lion in the pit. Then the flesh will be eaten and the skin sold—and it will fetch a good price. If he prefers to take him alive, he will hoist him out of the pit with the aid of special tackle.

There are also found in this country certain animals called *papiones*, which resemble foxes. These do a great deal of damage by gnawing the sugar canes. When merchants passing through the country with caravans pitch camp in some spot for a night's rest and sleep, these *papiones* come sneaking up and make off with anything they can steal, causing great loss. So they have devised this means of catching them. They have large gourds, which they pierce on the bulge at the top, making the entrance just wide enough, so far as they can judge, for one of these creatures to thrust in its head with a vigorous push. In case the mouth of the gourd should be broken in the process, they make little holes all round it and thread a cord through them. This done, they put a little fat into the gourd near the bottom. Then they distribute a number of these gourds at various places round the caravan a little way off. When the *papiones* draw near the caravan, bent on theft, they smell the fat in the gourds and going up to them try to put in their heads, but find they cannot. Then in their greed for the food inside they push for all they are worth and thrust in their heads by main force. Being unable to withdraw them, they lift up the gourds, since these are quite light, and carry them off. But, as they cannot tell where they are going, the merchants catch them at their ease. Their flesh is very good to eat and their skins command a high price.

This same country produces geese of such a size that a single one weighs 24 lb. They have a big swelling under the throat and a sort of protuberance on top of the bill next to the nostrils, like that found on a swan only much bigger.

The country also produces sugar, in quantities past all reckoning. The city is an important centre of commerce in pearls and other precious stones, because it is much frequented by ships from India bringing merchants who traffic in the Indies. Moreover it is not far from the port of Zaiton on the ocean, a great resort of ships and merchandise from India; and from Zaiton ships come up by the big river of which I have spoken as far as the city of Fu-chau. By this means many precious wares are imported from India. There is no lack here of anything that the human body requires to sustain life. There are gardens of great beauty and charm, full of excellent fruit. In short it is such a good city and so well provided with every amenity that it is a veritable marvel.

In illustration of this we shall tell you something about it which is reported by Messer Marco and is well worthy of narration. When

Messer Maffeo, Marco's uncle, and Messer Marco himself were in this city of Fu-chau, there was in their company a certain learned Saracen, who spoke to them as follows: 'In such-and-such a place there is a community whose religion nobody knows. It is evidently not idolatrous, since they keep no idols. They do not worship fire. They do not profess Mahomet. And they do not appear to observe the Christian order. I suggest that we should go and have a talk with them. Perhaps you will recognize something of their usages.' So they went to the place and began to talk to the people and interrogate them, and ask about their usage and their creed. They seemed to be afraid that they were being interrogated with the object of depriving them of their religion. Realizing this, Messer Maffeo and Messer Marco sought to allay their fears with words of encouragement: 'Do not be alarmed. We have not come here to do you any harm, but only for your good and the improvement of your condition.' For they were afraid that their visitors had been sent by the Great Khan to make this investigation in order to get them into trouble. But Maffeo and Marco attended the place so regularly day after day, familiarizing themselves with these people and inquiring about their affairs, that they discovered that they did indeed hold the Christian faith. For they possessed books. And Maffeo and Marco, poring over them, began to interpret the writing and translate it word by word from one language to another, till they found that they were the words of the psalter. Then they inquired from what source they had received their faith and their rule; and their informants replied: 'From our forefathers.' It came out that they had in a certain temple of theirs three pictures representing three apostles of the seventy who went through the world preaching. And they declared that it was these three who had instructed their ancestors in this faith long ago, and that it had been preserved among them for 700 years; but for a long time they had been without teaching, so that they were ignorant of the cardinal doctrines. 'But to this we hold fast, which we have received from our forefathers; we worship in accordance with our books and do reverence to these three apostles!' To this Maffeo and Marco replied: 'You are Christians, and we also are Christians. We advise you to send to the Great Khan and explain to him how you stand, so that he may grant you recognition and you may be able to keep your faith and your rule freely.' For because of the idolaters they did not altogether dare to proclaim or practise their religion openly. So they sent two of their number to the Great Khan. Acting

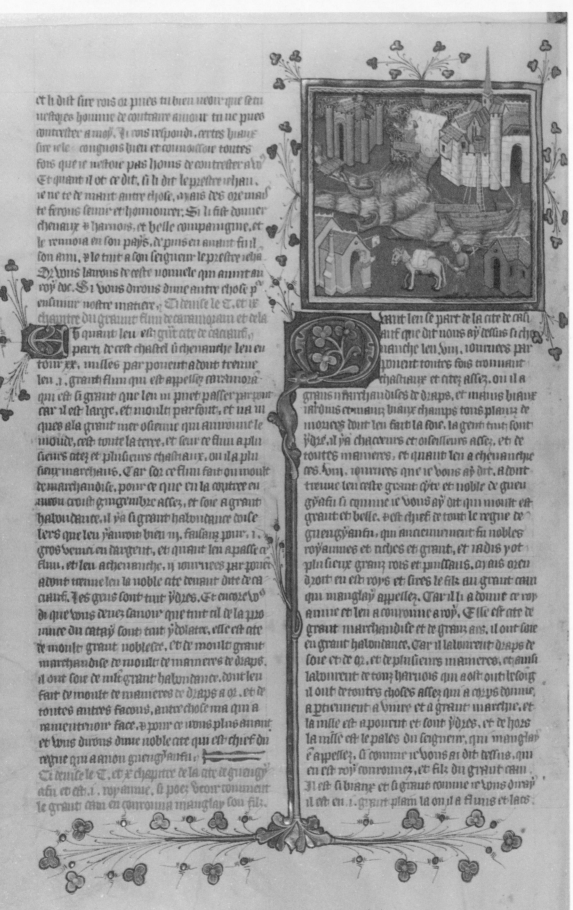

et li dist sire rois or pues tu bien veoir que se tu
veistoies houme de contraire amour tu ne pues
contrester a moy. Je vois respondi, certes biaus
sire je le conuois bien et connoistoie toutes
fois que je n'estoie pas hons de contrester a lo
Et quant il ot ce dit, si li dist le prestre jehan.
Je ne te demant autre chose, mais des ore mais
te ferons seruir et honnourer. Si li fist donner
cheuaux et harnois, et belle compaignie, et
le renuoia en son pays, depuis en auant fu
son ami, et tout a son seigneur le prestre jeha
Or vous lairons de ceste nouuele qui auint au
roy de. Si vous dirons dune autre chose p
ensuiuir nostre matiere. Ci deuise le T. et le
chapitre du grant flun de caramoran et de la

Et quant len est a ceste cite de cascatui,
len part de cest chastel u cheuanche len en
tour xx. milles par ponent adont treuue
len .i. grant flun qui est appellez caramora
qui est si grant que len ni puet passer par pont
car il est large, et moult parfont, et ua iu
ques a la grant mer osiene qui auiroune le
mode, c'est toute la terre, et seur ce flun a plu
sieurs citez et plusieurs chastiaux, ou il a plu
sieur marchans. Car sur ce flun fait on moult
de marchandise, pour ce que en la contree en
auiroit croist gengibre assez, et soie a grant
habondance, il y a si grant habondance d'oise
lers que len fauroit bien iij. faisans pour .i.
gros venut en dargent, et quant len a passe ce
flun, et len acheuanche, ij. iournees par ponent
adont treuue len la noble cite deuant dite de ca
catui. Les gens sont tout ydoles. Et encore vo
di que vous deuez sauoir que tout cil de la pro
uince du catay sont tout ydolatre, elle est cite
de moult grant noblece. Et de moult grant
marchandise de moult de manieres de draps,
il ont soie de nule grant habondance, dont len
fait de moult de manieres de draps a or, et de
toutes autres facons, autre chose na qui a
rementeuoir face, et pour ce vous plus auant
et vous dirons dune noble cite qui est chief du
regne qui a anon guenguianfu. ⸙
Ci deuise le T. et x. chapitre de la cite de guengu
afu, et est .i. royaume, si poez veoir conment
le grant chan en couronna manglay son filz.

uant len se part de la cite de casca
tui que dit uous ay testus si che
uanche len viij. iournees par
ponent toutes fois trouuant
chasteaux et citez assez, ou il a
grans marchandises de draps, et mains bias
iardins communz, biaux champs tous plains de
moures dont len fait la soie, la gent tuit sont
ydies, il y a chacceurs et oiseleurs assez, et de
toutes manieres, et quant len a cheuanche
ces viij. iournees que je uous ay dit. Adont
treuue len ceste grant cite et noble de gueu
gyafu si comme je vous ay dit qui moult est
grant et belle, c'est chief de tout le regne de
guengyanfu, qui anciennement fu nobles
royaumes et riches et grant, et iadis y ot
plusieurs grans rois et puissans, mais ore au
droit en est rois et sires le filz au grant chan
qui manglay appellez. Car il li a donne ce roy
aume et len a couronne a roy. Elle est cite de
grant marchandise et de granz ars, il ont soie
en grant habondance, car il labourent draps de
soie et de or, et de plusieurs manieres, et ainsi
labourent de touz harnois qui a ost ont lesoing
il ont de toutes choses assez qui a chaps conuie,
a ptienment a uiure et a grant marchie, et
la uille est apourue et sont ydies, et de hors
la uille est le pales du seigneur, qui manglay
e appellez, si comme je vous ai dit testus, qui
en est rois couronnez, et filz du grant chan
Il est si bians et si grant comme je vous diray
il est en .i. grant plain la ou il a fluns et lacs

on the instructions of Messer Maffeo and Messer Marco, these emissaries first presented themselves to a certain person who was head of the Christians at the Great Khan's court, so that he might broach their business in his master's presence. What more shall I say? There in the Khan's presence was this man who was head of the Christians, asserting that they were Christians and ought to be approved as such in his empire. And he who was head of the idol-worshippers, being apprised of the matter, put in a counter-plea, claiming that this ought not to be, because the aforesaid persons were and always had been idolaters and as such they were accounted. So there was great disputation about the matter in the Khan's presence. At last he grew angry and dismissing everyone summoned the two emissaries before him and asked them whether they wished to be Christians or idolaters. They answered that, if it pleased him and was not inimical to his sovereignty, they wished to be Christians as their forebears had been. Then the Great Khan ordered that they should be granted privileges whereby they should be acknowledged as Christians, and the status accorded to Christians should be applicable to all who professed their rule. And it was found that throughout the province of Manzi, here and there, there were more than 700,000 households who adhered to this rule.

To turn now to other matters, you must know that when the traveller leaves Fu-chau he crosses the river and proceeds south-eastwards for five days through a country full of well-built cities and towns and homesteads and rich in natural resources. Mountains and valleys alternate with plains. There are wide stretches of woodland, in which are many of the trees that produce camphor. There is game in plenty, both beast and bird. The people live by merchandise and industry and are subject to the Great Khan, being under the government of Fu-chau which is a part of his empire. At the end of the five days' journey lies the splendid city of Zaiton, at which is the port for all the ships that arrive from India laden with costly wares and precious stones of great price and big pearls of fine quality. It is also a port for the merchants of Manzi, that is, of all the surrounding territory, so that the total amount of traffic in gems and other merchandise entering and leaving this port is a marvel to behold. From this city and its port goods are exported to the whole province of Manzi. And I assure you that for one spice ship that goes to Alexandria or elsewhere to pick up pepper for export to Christendom, Zaiton is visited by a hundred. For you must know that it is one of the two ports in the world with the biggest flow of merchandise.

I can tell you further that the revenue accruing to the Great Khan from this city and port is something colossal, because I would have you know that all the ships coming from India pay a 10 per cent duty on all their wares, including gems and pearls, that is to say a tithe of everything. Payment for the hire of ships, that is for freight, is reckoned at the rate of 30 per cent on small wares, 44 per cent on pepper, and 40 per cent on aloes and sandalwood and all bulky wares. So that, what with freight and the imperial tithe, the merchants pay half the value of what they import. And yet from the half that falls to their share they make such a profit that they ask nothing better than to return with another cargo. So you may readily believe that this city's contribution to the Great Khan's treasury is no small one.

The river that enters the port of Zaiton is very large and wide and flows with a very strong current.* The swift flow of the river causes it to scoop out many channels, so that it splits up into several different branches at several points. It is crossed by five fine bridges, of which the biggest is fully three miles long, corresponding to the different branches into which the river divides. The piers of these bridges are built of big stones laid one on another and so shaped that they are broad in the middle and taper towards either end, both the end facing upstream and that facing the sea, which has also to meet a strong current when the tide is setting in.

The people here are idolaters and subject to the Great Khan. It is a delightful place, amply supplied with all that the human body requires; and the inhabitants are peaceable folk, fond of leisure and easy living. Many people come here from Upper India to have figures pricked out on their bodies with needles, as described above.

Let me tell you further that in this province, in a city called Tinju, they make bowls of porcelain, large and small, of incomparable beauty. They are made nowhere else except in this city, and from here they are exported all over the world. In the city itself they are so plentiful and cheap that for a Venetian groat you might buy three bowls of such beauty that nothing lovelier could be imagined. These dishes are made of a crumbly earth or clay which is dug as though from a mine and stacked in huge mounds and then left for thirty or

---

* R states, apparently through some confusion, that it is an effluent of the river that flows through Kinsai, and where it branches off from the main stream stands the city of Tinju.

forty years exposed to wind, rain, and sun. By this time the earth is so refined that dishes made of it are of an azure tint with a very brilliant sheen. You must understand that when a man makes a mound of this earth he does so for his children; the time of maturing is so long that he cannot hope to draw any profit from it himself or to put it to use, but the son who succeeds him will reap the fruit.*

The inhabitants of this city have their own distinctive speech. You must understand, however, that throughout the province of Manzi one language and one form of writing is current; but there are local differences in speech, as there are among laymen between Lombards, Provençals, Frenchmen, etc., but such that in Manzi the people of every district can understand the others' idiom.†

So much for the kingdom of Fu-chau which is one of the nine divisions. Let me add only that the Great Khan derives from it no less duty and revenue, if not more, than he does from the kingdom of Kinsai.‡

We have not told you of the nine kingdoms of Manzi, but of three only, that is Yang-chau, Kinsai, and Fu-chau. Of them, you have heard much. Of the other six also there is much that we could tell; but, because the tale would be wearisome in the telling, we will say no more. Concerning these three we have told you in order, because through them Messer Marco travelled in person. For this was the way his journey led. Concerning the others he learnt much; but, since he did not actually traverse them, he could not have described them in so much detail.

Such, then, is our account of Manzi and of Cathay and of many a province besides—of the peoples that inhabit them, of beasts and of birds, of gold and silver, gems and pearls and merchandise and many other things, as you have now heard. But our book is not yet complete with all that we wish to include. It is lacking still in all that concerns the Indians, which is something well worth making known to those who do not know it; for it offers many marvels unlike anything to be found in the rest of the world. Since therefore it is fitting and

* The three preceding sentences are based mainly on Z. R states that the vessels are painted the desired colours and then baked in the oven.
† So Z. R's version runs: 'as one might say Genoese, Milanese, Florentines, and Apulians, who, although they speak differently, can nevertheless understand one another'. Z's reference to 'laymen' is evidently intended to imply vernaculars, as distinct from the common Latin of the clergy.
‡ Z: 'more than from any of the others except Kinsai, and that simply on account of the revenue of the port of Zaiton'.

desirable to record it in our book, the master will set it down there in plain language, precisely as Messer Marco describes and relates it. Let me tell you then for a fact that Messer Marco stayed so long in India, and is so well acquainted with Indian affairs and customs and commerce, that there has scarcely ever been a man better qualified to give a true account of the country. Much that he has to say is so extraordinary that men will certainly marvel to hear it. But we shall set it down, item by item, as Messer Marco reported it in sober truth. And we shall make a start here and now, as you will be able to hear in the book that follows.*

* R adds that Marco acquired his knowledge partly when he was in India on the Great Khan's business, partly on his return trip with the bride for Arghun, and that he derived some of it from first-hand observation, some from reliable testimony, and some from mariners' charts. The rubric to the next section starts with the words: 'Here begins the book of India'.

from china to india

SINCE WHAT YOU HAVE ALREADY HEARD HAS COVERED SO many regions of the earth, we shall now pass on and make our way into India to tell you of all its marvels. To begin with, we shall tell you first of the ships in which merchants trading with India make their voyages.

This, then, I would have you know, is how they are made. They are built of the wood called spruce and of fir. They have one deck; and above this deck, in most ships, are at least sixty cabins, each of which can comfortably accommodate one merchant. They have one steering-oar and four masts. Often they add another two masts, which are hoisted and lowered at pleasure. The entire hull is of double thickness: that is to say, one plank is fastened over the top of another, and this double planking extends all the way round. It is caulked outside and in, and the fastening is done with iron nails.

Some of the ships, that is the bigger ones, have also thirteen bulkheads or partitions made of stout planks dovetailed into one another. This is useful in case the ship's hull should chance to be damaged in some place by striking on a reef or being rammed by a whale in search of food—a not infrequent occurrence, for if a whale happens to pass near the ship while she is sailing at night and churning the water to foam, he may infer from the white gleam in the water that there is food for him there and so charge full tilt against the ship and ram her, often breaching the hull at some point. In that event the water coming through the breach will run into the bilge, which is never permanently occupied. The sailors promptly find out where the breach is. Cargo is shifted from the damaged compartment into the neighbouring ones; for the bulkheads are so stoutly built that the compartments are watertight. The damage is then repaired and the cargo shifted back.

The ships are not coated with pitch, because they have no pitch. Instead they use another substance which they judge to be better than pitch. They take lime and hemp chopped up very fine and pound it together with the oil of a tree. When this mixture has been thoroughly pounded, I assure you that it sticks like glue. With this they daub their ships, and it is every bit as good as pitch.

The crew needed to man a ship ranges from 150 to 300 according to her size. They carry a much bigger cargo than ours. One ship will take as much as five or six thousand baskets of pepper. At one time their ships were even larger than those now in use; but in many places islands have been so washed away by the force of the sea that there is no longer a sufficient depth of water in the harbours to take the larger ships, so they are built with a smaller draught. They are propelled by sweeps, that is to say oars, each manned by four seamen. These ships are tended by two or three smaller craft, some manned by sixty seamen, some by eighty, some by a hundred; which also carry substantial cargoes—some of them fully 1,000 baskets of pepper. These are propelled by oars and often serve to tow the bigger vessels with ropes or hawsers, not only when they are being rowed but also when they are under sail, so long, that is, as the wind is more or less abeam, because then the smaller craft precede the larger and help it along by means of tow-ropes. When they are running before the wind, however, this would not work, as the larger craft would take the wind from the sails of the smaller and so overhaul them. The big ships also take with them as many as ten small boats lashed to their sides outboard for use in anchoring and catching fish and supplying their other needs. The tender ships also carry boats.

When a ship is in need of refitment, that is, of repair, after she has seen a year's service, they refit her as follows. They nail on another layer of planks all round, over the top of the original two, so that now there are three layers. Then they caulk her afresh. This process is repeated yearly till there are as many as six layers, after which the vessel is rejected as no longer seaworthy.

We shall tell you next of the experiment that is made, before embarking on a voyage, to find out whether the venture will fare well or badly. The seamen will take a hurdle—that is, a frame of wickerwork—and to every corner and side of it they will attach a rope, so that there are eight ropes in all, and fasten all the ropes together at the other end to a long cable. Next they will find some fool or someone who is drunk—for no one in his right sense would expose himself to so much risk—and lash him to the hurdle. This they do when it is blowing a gale. Then they set the hurdle upright in the teeth of the wind and the wind lifts it and carries it aloft, while the men hold it by hanging on to the cable. If the hurdle should tilt over while it is up in the air facing the wind, they give a slight tug to the cable and the hurdle returns to an upright position. Then they pay out more cable, and the hurdle climbs higher. And so they continue, alternately tugging and paying out as the hurdle tilts and straightens, till it would have climbed completely out of sight if only the cable were long enough. The point of the experiment is this. If the hurdle climbs straight up aloft, then it is said that the ship on whose behalf the experiment is being conducted will make a speedy and profitable voyage, and all the merchants flock to her to pay freight and passage money. If the hurdle fails to rise, no merchant will enter this particular ship, because they say that she could not complete her voyage and all sorts of disasters would overtake her. So this ship stays in port for that year.

Now that I have described the ships in which merchants voyage to and from India, let us change the subject and pass on to India itself. But first I will tell you of many islands that lie towards the east in this Ocean at which we have now arrived. We shall begin with an island that is called Japan.

Japan is an island far out at sea to the eastward, some 1,500 miles from the mainland. It is a very big island. The people are fair-complexioned, good-looking, and well-mannered. They are idolaters, wholly independent and exercising no authority over any nation but themselves.

They have gold in great abundance, because it is found there in measureless quantities. And I assure you that no one exports it from the island, because no trader, nor indeed anyone else, goes there from the mainland. That is how they come to possess so much of it—so much indeed that I can report to you in sober truth a veritable marvel concerning a certain palace of the ruler of the island. You may take it for a fact that he has a very large palace entirely roofed with fine gold. Just as we roof our houses or churches with lead, so this palace is roofed with fine gold. And the value of it is almost beyond computation. Moreover all the chambers, of which there are many, are likewise paved with fine gold to a depth of more than two fingers' breadth. And the halls and the windows and every other part of the palace are likewise adorned with gold. All in all I can tell you that the palace is of such incalculable richness that any attempt to estimate its value would pass the bounds of the marvellous.

They have pearls in abundance, red in colour, very beautiful, large and round. They are worth as much as the white ones, and indeed more. In this island the dead are sometimes buried, sometimes cremated; but everyone who is buried has one of these pearls put in his mouth. Such is the custom that prevails among them. They also have many other precious stones in abundance. It is a very rich island, so that no one could count its riches.

When tidings of its riches were brought to the Great Khan—that is, the same Kubilai who now reigns—he declared his resolve to conquer the island. Thereupon he sent two of his barons with a great fleet of ships carrying cavalry and infantry. One of these barons was named Abakan, the other Vonsamchin. Both were men of ability and courage. Now mark what happened. They set sail from Zaiton and Kinsai and put out to sea and sailed to the island. They landed and occupied some open country and a number of villages, but they had not yet captured a single city or fortified town when the following disaster overtook them. You must understand that there was great jealousy between the two commanders and neither would do anything to help the other. Now it happened one day that such a gale was blowing from the north that the troops declared that, if they did not get away, all their ships would be wrecked. So they all embarked and left the island and put out to sea. And let me tell you that, when they had sailed about four miles, the gale began to freshen and there was such a crowd of ships that many of them were smashed by colliding with one another. Those that were not jammed together with others but had enough sea-room escaped shipwreck. Not far away was another island of no great size. Those that succeeded in clearing this island made good their escape. The others who failed to get clear were driven aground by the gale. When the violence of the storm had abated and the sea grew calmer, the two barons returned to the island with those ships—and there were a great many of them—that had escaped shipwreck by keeping to the open sea. There they picked up such of the survivors as were officers, that is, captains of hundreds and thousands and ten-thousands. The others were so numerous that there was no room for them on board. Then the ships left the island and set sail for home. The troops stranded on the island, who numbered about 30,000, gave themselves up for lost men, not seeing how they were ever to get away and reach a haven of refuge. For they saw the surviving ships heading for home and leaving them in the lurch. These ships in fact completed their voyage and arrived back in their own country. So let us leave them and return to the men stranded on the island, who had given themselves up for dead.

You must understand that these 30,000, who had taken refuge on the island, thought themselves worse off than if they were dead, since they could see no possible means of escape. They were filled with bitterness and despair and did not know what to do. Such then was their plight on the island. When the ruler and people of the main island saw the invading host so routed and shattered and learnt of the survivors on the little island, they were overjoyed and exultant. As soon as the storm was over and the sea calm, they embarked on a fleet which they had for their own use and headed straight for the island and promptly landed there to capture the occupants. When the 30,000 saw that all their enemies had come ashore and that no one was left on board the ships to keep guard, then like prudent men, while the enemy were advancing to seize them, they withdrew to the far end of the island, which lay on the other side of a high ridge. Then making a hasty detour they came upon the enemy fleet from another quarter and immediately boarded it. This they contrived to do quite easily, since they found it undefended, the entire force having joined in the pursuit across the island.

What more shall I say? Once on board, they set sail from the island and crossed over to the enemy country. There they disembarked and, hoisting the banners and standards of the ruler of the island, they marched towards his capital. The residents, seeing their banners, mistook them for their own people and allowed them to enter. The invaders, finding no one there except old men and women, seized the city and drove out everyone except certain good-looking women whom they kept for their own use. In this way the city fell into the hands of the Great Khan's men.

When the ruler of the island and his followers saw that they had lost their city and that the affair had turned out so badly for them, they were ready to die with mortification. They returned to their own island in other ships and laid siege to the city on every side, so that no one could go in or come out without their leave. For seven months and more the Great Khan's men held the city, racking their brains day and night to find some means of sending word of their plight to the Great Khan. But all to no purpose. Realizing at length that they could not accomplish this, they made terms with the besiegers and surrendered on condition that their persons were spared and they stayed there for life. And this happened in the year of our Lord 1268.

Such then was the outcome of this enterprise. When the Great

Khan learnt how badly the two barons who commanded the expedition had acquitted themselves, he had one of them beheaded and sent the other to a desolate island named Zorza, which he uses as a place of execution for those who have committed grave offences. This is how the execution is carried out. When a victim is sent to this island under sentence of death, his hands are wrapped in freshly flayed buffalo hide and securely sewn up. As the skin dries, it shrinks so tight round the hands that it cannot possibly be removed. So he is left to die a painful death: he can do nothing to help himself, he has nothing to eat and if he wants to eat grass he must needs crawl on the ground. Such was the fate of the second baron.

Let me tell you next of a great marvel that occurred when these two barons took several prisoners in a castle on the island. As they had refused to surrender, it was ordered that they should all be beheaded. The order was duly carried out. All the prisoners were beheaded except eight men only, whose heads could not be cut off. This happened by virtue of certain stones that they carried on their persons. For each one of them had a stone embedded in his arm, between the flesh and skin, so that it was not visible on the surface. This stone possessed a magic property whereby anyone who had it on his person was proof against steel. When the barons were informed of the reason why these men could not be killed by the sword, they ordered them to be beaten to death with clubs, whereupon they died instantly. Afterwards these stones were extracted from their arms, and they were very highly prized.

Now that you have heard the story of this discomfiture of the Great Khan's men, we shall leave this subject and resume the thread of our narrative.

You must know that the idols of these islands are of the same type as those of Cathay and Manzi. I assure you that the islanders, and the other idolaters as well, have idols with the heads of cattle and of pigs, of dogs and sheep, and of many other sorts. There are some with heads of four faces and some with three heads, one in the right place and one on either shoulder. Some have four hands, some ten, and some a thousand. But these are the best and the ones that command the greatest reverence. When Christians ask them why they make their idols in such a diversity of shapes, they answer: 'It is in these shapes that our forefathers left them to us, and so we shall leave them to our sons and to those who come after us.' The works of these idols are so manifold and of such devilish contrivance that it

o

is not proper to speak of them in our book, since they are no fit hearing for Christians. So we shall say no more of them, but turn to other matters. I will content myself with saying that the idolaters of these islands, when they capture some man who is not one of their friends, hold him to ransom for money. If this is not forthcoming, they send out invitations to their relatives and friends, saying: 'I should like you to come and dine with me at my house.' Then they kill their captive and make a meal of him with their kinsfolk. You must understand that they first cook him; and this human flesh they consider the choicest of all foods.

To return to the matter in hand, you must know that the sea in which this island lies is called the China Sea—that is, the sea adjoining Manzi, because in the language of the islanders 'China' means Manzi. It lies towards the east and according to the testimony of experienced pilots and seamen who sail upon it and are well acquainted with the truth it contains 7,448 islands, most of them inhabited. And I assure you that in all these islands there is no tree that does not give off a powerful and agreeable fragrance and serve some useful purpose—quite as much as aloe wood, if not more so. There are, in addition, many precious spices of various sorts. The islands also produce pepper as white as snow and in great abundance, besides black pepper. Marvellous indeed is the value of the gold and other rarities to be found in these islands. But they are so far away that the voyage thither is fraught with difficulty. When ships from Zaiton or Kinsai come to these islands, they reap a great profit and a rich return. I must tell you that it takes a full year to complete the voyage, setting out in winter and returning in summer. For only two winds blow in these seas, one that wafts them out and one that brings them back; and the former blows in winter, the latter in summer. You must understand that it is a long, long voyage from this country to India. And, when I say that this sea is called the China Sea, I should explain that it is really the Ocean. But, as we say 'the sea of England' or 'the sea of Rochelle',★ so in these parts they speak of 'the China Sea' or 'the Indian Sea' and so forth. But all these names really apply to the Ocean.

From now on I will tell you no more of this country or of these islands, because they are so out-of-the-way and because we have never been there. Let me add only that the Great Khan has no

★ Z: 'the Aegean Sea'.

authority over them and they render no tribute or other acknowledgement. So let us return to Zaiton and recommence our book
from that point.*

When the traveller leaves Zaiton on a course somewhat south of
west he sails for 1,500 miles across a wide gulf called the Gulf of
Cheynam, which extends for two months' sail towards the north,
washing the shores of Manzi on the south-east and of Aniu and
Toloman besides many other provinces on the other side. Within
the gulf itself are innumerable islands, almost all of them populous.
In these are found quantities of gold dust, which is recovered from
sea water, and also of copper or brass and other things. They trade
among themselves, exchanging the products of one island for those
of another. They also trade with the mainland, selling gold, brass
and the like and buying in return what they themselves require.
Most of them produce good crops of corn. This gulf is so large and so
many peoples live in it that it seems to be a world in itself. Now let
us return to our starting-point.

After leaving Zaiton and completing the voyage of 1,500 miles
across the mouth of this gulf, the traveller reaches a country called
Chamba, a very rich country of wide extent. They have a king of
their own, speak their own language and are idolaters. They render
the Great Khan a yearly tribute of elephants and aloe wood but
nothing else. Let me tell you how this comes about. The fact is that
in the year of our Lord 1278 the Great Khan sent one of his barons
named Sogatu with a large force of cavalry and infantry against this
king† of Chamba and launched a great invasion of his kingdom.
The king was a man of great age and had not an army to match that
of the Great Khan in a pitched battle; but he maintained a stout defence of cities and fortified towns without fear of any foe. The open
country, however, and the villages were all ravaged and laid waste.
When the king saw the havoc that was being wrought in his kingdom, he was deeply distressed. He promptly summoned his emissaries and sent them to the Great Khan with a message such as you

* The following paragraph, found only in Z and R, describes a largely imaginary
gulf between China and Indo-China. The name 'Cheynam' is possibly derived from
the island of Hai-nan.
† R gives his name as 'Accambala', which has been claimed as a corruption of the
name 'Indravarman' actually borne by the king of Chamba (Southern Vietnam) at
this date, but is more probably derived by some confusion from the word 'Chamba'
itself.

will hear. The emissaries travelled post haste till they came to the Great Khan and delivered their message as follows: 'Sire, the king of Chamba salutes you as his liege lord. He sends you word that he is a man of great age and has long ruled his kingdom in peace. He is willing to be your liege man and to render you a yearly tribute of elephants, and aloe wood. He begs you courteously, imploring your mercy, to recall from his country your baron and your forces who are ravaging his kingdom.' With these words the speaker concluded his message and said no more. When the Great Khan had heard the old king's words, he took pity on him. He immediately ordered the baron and his forces to leave this kingdom and seek further conquests elsewhere. They obeyed their lord's command and promptly withdrew and went elsewhere. So this king renders the Great Khan every year a quantity of aloe wood and twenty elephants, the biggest and handsomest that can be found in his country. That is how he came to be the Great Khan's liege man and to pay him this tribute. We shall now go on to tell you more of him and of his kingdom.

You must know that in this kingdom no pretty girl can marry without first being presented to the king for his inspection. If he is pleased with her, he takes her to wife. If not, he gives her a sum of money appropriate to her station so that she may take another husband. I assure you that in the year 1285* I, Marco Polo, was in this country and that at that time this king had 326 children, male and female, including more than 150 men of an age to bear arms.

This kingdom produces great quantities of elephants and of aloe wood. There are also many groves of the wood called ebony, which is very black and is used for making chess-men and pen-cases. As there is nothing else worth noting in our book, we shall go on our way.

From Chamba a traveller who sails south-south-east for 1,500 miles comes to a very large island called Java. According to the testimony of good seamen who know it well, this is the biggest island in the world, having a circumference of more than 3,000 miles. The people are idolaters ruled by a powerful monarch and paying no tribute to anyone on earth. It is a very rich island, producing pepper, nutmegs, spikenard, galingale, cubebs, and cloves, and all the precious spices that can be found in the world. It is visited by great numbers of ships and merchants who buy a great range of merchandise, reaping hand-

* The MSS give various dates from 1275 to 1288.

some profits and rich returns. The quantity of treasure in the island is beyond all computation. And I assure you that the Great Khan has never been able to conquer it, because of the long and hazardous voyage that must be made in order to get there. It is from this island that the merchants of Zaiton and of Manzi in general have derived and continue to derive a great part of their wealth, and this is the source of most of the spice that comes into the world's markets.

On leaving Chamba* and sailing south-south-west for 700 miles, the traveller reaches two islands, one big and the other smaller, called Sondur and Condur. As these are uninhabited, let us leave them. Another 500 miles towards the south-east brings us to a large and wealthy province of the mainland whose name is Lokak. The people are idolaters, ruled by a powerful monarch and speaking a language of their own. They pay no tribute to anyone, because their country is so situated that no one can go there to work mischief. If it were accessible, the Great Khan would soon subject it to his empire. This province produces cultivated brazil wood in great abundance.† Gold is so plentiful that no one who did not see it could believe it. There are elephants and wild game in profusion. From this kingdom come all the cowrie shells that are spent in all the provinces of which I have told you. There is nothing else worth mentioning, except that it is such a savage place that few people ever go there. The king himself does not want anyone to go there or to spy out his treasure or the state of his realm. Accordingly we shall pass on and speak of other things.‡

On leaving Lokak and sailing southwards for 500 miles, the traveller reaches the island of Bintan, which is a very savage place. The forests are all of sweet-smelling wood of great utility.§ From here the route runs for sixty miles through a strait between two islands. In many places the water is not more than four paces deep, so that big ships passing through must raise their steering-oar, for

* The MSS read 'Java'; but it is clear that Java lay off the course of Polo's itinerary. His account does not suggest that he ever visited it.

† The word *berzi* (brazil) puzzled the early translators. R speaks of 'fruit called *berci* which are domesticated and as big as lemons and are very good to eat'. In one version the *berci* have become 'bears (*ursi*) as big as lions', in another 'domesticated animals resembling men', while others transmute them into 'gold' or 'Turks'!

‡ 'Lokak' is Siam or Malaya. 'Lesser Java' is Sumatra, whose modern name is derived from the city of Sumatra. The meaning of the following paragraph is doubtful, and there is probably an omission in all the versions.

§ Or 'hardness'.

they have a draught of about four paces. After this a voyage of thirty miles south-eastwards leads to an island kingdom called Malayur, which has a king and a language of its own. There is a large and splendid city here, also called Malayur, which plies a flourishing trade especially in spices, of which there is great abundance. As there is nothing else worthy of note, we shall continue on our way.

About 100 miles south-east of Bintan lies the island of Lesser Java. You may understand that it is not so little but what it extends to more than 2,000 miles in circumference. Of this island we will now give you a full and truthful account. There are eight kingdoms on the island, and eight crowned kings. The people are all idolaters and speak languages of their own—that is, each of the eight kingdoms has its own language. The island abounds in treasure and in costly products, including aloe wood, brazil, ebony, spikenard, and many sorts of spice that never reach our country because of the length and perils of the way but are exported to Manzi and Cathay. Before I tell you about these various nations separately, let me first tell you a fact about the island that will surprise everyone: the truth is that it lies so far to the south that the Pole Star is not visible there, either much or little. And now I will begin with the kingdom of Ferlec.

You must know that the people of Ferlec used all to be idolaters, but owing to contact with Saracen merchants, who continually resort here in their ships, they have all been converted to the law of Mahomet. This applies only to the inhabitants of the city. The people of the mountains live like beasts. For I assure you that they eat human flesh and every other sort of flesh, clean or unclean. They worship many different things; for whatever they see first when they wake in the morning, that they worship.

On leaving Ferlec the traveller enters Basman, which is a separate kingdom with a language of its own. The people of Basman are without a law, except such as prevails among brute beasts. They profess allegiance to the Great Khan but render him no tribute, because they are so remote that the Khan's men cannot go to them. Indeed all the peoples of the island profess him allegiance and sometimes avail themselves of passing travellers to send him objects of beauty or curiosity by way of gift, in particular a sort of black goshawk. They have wild elephants and plenty of unicorns, which are scarcely smaller than elephants. They have the hair of a buffalo and feet like an elephant's. They have a single large, black horn in the middle of the forehead. They do not attack with their horn, but only with their tongue and their knees; for their tongues are furnished with long, sharp spines, so that when they want to do any harm to anyone they first crush him by kneeling upon him and then lacerate him with their tongues. They have a head like a wild boar's and always carry it stooped towards the ground. They spend their time by preference wallowing in mud and slime. They are very ugly brutes to look at. They are not at all such as we describe them when we relate that they let themselves be captured by virgins, but clean contrary to our notions. There are a great many monkeys here of many different sorts. There are also the goshawks, black as crows, of great size and very apt at fowling.

I would have you know that those who profess to have brought pygmy men from the Indies are involved in great falsehood and deception. For I assure you that these so-called pygmies are manu-factured in this island; and I will tell you how. The truth is that there is a sort of monkey here which is very tiny and has a face very like a man's. So men take some of these monkeys, and remove all their hair, with a kind of ointment. Then they attach some long hairs to the chin in place of a beard, threading them through holes in the skin so that when the skin shrivels the holes shrink and the hairs seem to have grown there naturally. The feet and hands and other limbs which are not in conformity with the human figure are stretched and strained and remoulded by hand to the likeness of a man. Then the bodies are dried and treated with camphor and other drugs, so that they appear to be human. This is all a piece of trickery, as you have heard. For nowhere in all the Indies or in wilder regions still was there ever seen any man so tiny as these seem to be.*

So much for Basman. The next kingdom, situated in the same island, is called Sumatra. In this kingdom I myself, Marco Polo, spent five months, waiting for weather that would permit us to continue our voyage. Here again the Pole Star is never visible nor yet the stars of the Plough, either much or little. The people are idolaters and savages. They have a wealthy and powerful king and also profess allegiance to the Great Khan.

This is how we spent our five months. We† disembarked from our ships and for fear of these nasty and brutish folk who kill men

* The foregoing paragraph is based on Z. F has a briefer version, in which it is said that the monkeys' natural hair is left on the chin and chest.
† Z says: 'Marco Polo with about 2,000 people who were in his company'.

for food we dug a big trench round our encampment, extending down to the shore of the harbour at either end. On the embankment of the trench we built five wooden towers or forts; and within these fortifications we lived for five months. There was no lack of timber. But the islanders used to trade with us for victuals and the like; for there was a compact between us.

The fish here are the best in the world. The people have no wheat, but live on rice. They have no wine, except such as I will describe to you. You must know that they have a sort of tree, of which they lop off the branches. Then they set a good-sized pot beside the raw stump left on the tree, and in a day and a night it is filled. The wine thus produced is very good to drink and is a sovereign remedy for dropsy, consumption, and the spleen. The trees are like little date-palms and bear four branches; they need only to be lopped in order to produce this amount of excellent wine. And let me tell you something more. When wine ceases to ooze from the stumps, they pour water round the foot of the trees, as much as they judge to be needful, leading it through channels from the rivers. Then, when they have been watered for an hour, they begin to emit the fluid as before. There is a white wine and a bright red one. They have abundance of fine, large coconuts. They eat all sorts of flesh, clean and un-clean.

Let us now leave here and pass on to a kingdom called Dagroian. Dagroian is a separate kingdom on its own, with a king and a language of its own, but forming part of the same island. The people, who profess allegiance to the Great Khan, are out-and-out savages. They are idolaters; and I will tell you of one custom they have which is particularly bad. You must know that, when one of them, male or female, falls sick, the kinsfolk send for the magicians to find out whether the patient is due to recover. And these magicians claim by means of their enchantments and their idols and diabolic art to know whether he is destined to recover or to die. You must not suppose, because I speak of 'diabolic art', that that is their account of the matter: they attribute their knowledge to the power of the gods working through the medium of their art. If they say that he is due to die, then the kinsfolk send for certain men who are specially appointed to put such persons to death. These men come and seize the patient and put something over his mouth so as to suffocate him. When he is dead, they cook him. Then all his kinsfolk assemble and eat him whole. I assure you that they even devour all the marrow in his bones. This they do because they do not want one scrap of his substance to remain. For they say that if any scrap remained then this substance would generate worms, which would thereupon die for want of food. And by the death of these worms they declare that the dead man's soul would incur great sin and torment, because so many souls generated by his substance met their deaths. That is why they eat him whole. After they have eaten him, they take his bones and put them in a handsome casket. Then they carry this and hang it in a huge cavern in the mountains, in some place where no beast or other evil thing can touch it. I assure you further that, if they can get hold of some stranger who is not of their country, they seize him and, if he cannot ransom himself, they kill him and devour him on the spot. This then is a very bad and detestable custom.

Let me tell you next of the kingdom of Lambri, which also has a king of its own but professes allegiance to the Great Khan. The people are idolaters. The country produces abundance of brazil, besides camphor, and other precious spices in profusion. In cultivating brazil they first sow the seed; then, when small shoots have sprung up, they dig them up and replant them elsewhere; they then leave them for three years and then dig them up, roots and all.* I may tell you that we brought some of this seed back to Venice and sowed it in the earth there; but nothing came up. This was due to the cold climate.

Now here is something really remarkable. I give you my word that in this kingdom there are men who have tails fully a palm in length. They are not at all hairy. This is true of most of the men—that is, of those who live outside in the mountains, not of those in the city. Their tails are as thick as a dog's. There are also many unicorns and a profusion of wild game, both beast and bird.

Lastly, let us turn to the kingdom of Fansur, which is also part of the island of which we have been speaking. The people are idolaters with a king of their own but professing allegiance to the Great Khan. This kingdom produces the best camphor in the world, which is called *Fansuri* and is worth more than any other kind. For I assure you that it is sold for its weight in gold. They have no wheat or other corn, but live on rice and milk. They make palm-wine, such as I described above in speaking of Sumatra. And here is something else they have, which is well worthy of note as a marvel. You must know that in this province they have a flour made from trees; and I will tell

* R adds: 'and use them for dyeing'.

you how they make it.* There are certain trees here of great height and a girth that two men could just embrace. After stripping off a thin bark, you reach a layer of wood, perhaps three fingers thick, and inside this is a pith consisting entirely of flour. This flour is put in troughs full of water and stirred with a stick, so that the husks and impurities float to the surface and the pure flour settles on the bottom. This done, the water is poured off and the refined flour left at the bottom of the container. It is then seasoned and made into cakes and various paste dishes, which are exceedingly good. We ourselves proved the truth of this; for we often ate them. The wood of these trees is as heavy as iron, and when thrown into water it sinks like iron. This wood can be split in a straight line from top to bottom, like a cane. As I have said, when the tree is emptied of flour, the wood is about three fingers thick. The natives use it for making short lances— not long ones, because if they were long no one would be able to carry them, let alone wield them, owing to the heaviness of the wood. They sharpen the lances at the head and afterwards slightly scorch the point at the fire. Lances so treated will surpass any steel-tipped lance in piercing any sort of armour.

We have now told you of the kingdoms that exist in this part of the island. Of those in the other part we shall say nothing, because we were never there. So we will leave it at this point and tell you of a very little island called Gauenispola.†

When the traveller leaves Lesser Java and the kingdom of Lambri and sails northwards for about 150 miles, he reaches two islands, one of which is called Nicobar. In this island there is no king, and the people live like beasts. I assure you that they go stark naked, men and women alike, without any covering of any sort. They are idolaters. They have very beautiful cloths or sashes some three fathoms in length, made of silk of every colour. They buy them from passing traders and keep them hung over rails in their houses as a token of wealth and magnificence, just as we keep pearls and precious stones and vessels of gold and silver. They make no use of them whatsoever, but keep them only for show. And whoever has most of them, and of the greatest beauty, is esteemed as the greatest and most honour-

---

* R adds that the flour tastes like barley meal and that Marco brought back a sample of it to Venice.
† Unless the text is corrupt, a section dealing with this island (presumably one of those to the north of Sumatra) has apparently dropped out.

able. All the forests in this island are of noble trees of great worth: these are red sandal, coconuts (which among us are called Pharaoh's nuts), apples of paradise, cloves, brazil, and many other good trees. As there is nothing else worth mentioning, we shall pass on and tell you of the other island, whose name is Andaman.

Andaman is a very big island. The people have no king. They are idolaters and live like wild beasts. Now let me tell you of a race of men well worth describing in our book. You may take it for a fact that all the men of this island have heads like dogs, and teeth and eyes like dogs; for I assure you that the whole aspect of their faces is that of big mastiffs. They are a very cruel race: whenever they can get hold of a man who is not one of their kind, they devour him. They have abundance of spices of every kind. Their food is rice and milk, and every sort of flesh. They also have coconuts, apples of paradise, and many other fruit different from ours. The island lies in a sea so turbulent and so deep that ships cannot anchor there or sail away from it, because it sweeps them into a gulf from which they can never escape. This is because the sea there is so tempestuous that it is continually eating away the land, scooping out trees at the root and toppling them over and afterwards sweeping them into this gulf. It is truly marvellous how many trees are driven into the gulf without ever coming out again. Hence it happens that ships that enter the gulf are jammed in such a mass of these trees that they cannot move from the spot and so are stuck there for good.

On leaving the island of Andaman and sailing for 1,000 miles a little south of west, the traveller reaches Ceylon, which is undoubtedly the finest island of its size in all the world. Let me explain how. It has a circumference of some 2,400 miles. And I assure you that it used to be bigger than this. For it was once as much as 3,500 miles, as appears in the mariners' charts of this sea. But the north wind blows so strongly in these parts that it has submerged a great part of this island under the sea. That is why it is no longer as big as it used to be.

Now I will tell you something about the island. It is ruled by a king called Sendernam. The people are idolaters. They pay no tribute to anyone. They go quite naked, except that they cover their private parts. They have no grain other than rice. They have sesame, from which they make oil. They live on milk, flesh, and rice, and have wine made from trees such as I have described above. They have abundance of brazil, the best in the world. Let me add that they have also the most precious thing to be found anywhere in the world; for in this island, and nowhere else in the world, are produced superb and authentic rubies. The island also produces sapphires, topazes, amethysts, garnets, and many other precious stones. And I assure you that the king of this province possesses the finest ruby that exists in all the world—the finest certainly, that was ever seen or is ever likely to be seen. Let me describe it to you. It is about a palm in length and of the thickness of a man's arm. It is the most brilliant object to behold in all the world, free from any flaw and glowing red like fire. It is so precious that it could scarcely be bought for money. I tell you in all truthfulness that the Great Khan sent emissaries to this king and told him that he wished to buy this ruby and that if he would part with it he would give him the value of a city. But the king declared that he would not part with it for anything in the world, because it was an heirloom from his ancestors. For this reason the Khan could not have it at any price.

The inhabitants of Ceylon are not fighting men, but paltry and mean-spirited creatures. If they have need of the services of soldiers, they hire them from abroad, especially Saracens. Since there is nothing else here worth mentioning, we shall now pass on to India.

india

WHEN THE TRAVELLER LEAVES CEYLON AND SAILS WESTWARDS
for about sixty miles, he arrives in the great province of Maabar,
which is called Greater India.* It is indeed the best part of India. This
province forms part of the mainland. It is ruled by five kings, who
are all brothers by birth; and we will tell you of each one separately.
You may take it for a fact that it is the richest and most splendid
province in the world; and I will tell you how.

The foremost kingdom of the province is ruled by one of these
brothers, whose name is Sender Bandi Devar. In his kingdom are
found pearls of great size and beauty; for you must know that Maabar
and Ceylon between them produce most of the pearls and gems
that are to be found in the world. I will tell you how these pearls are
found and gathered.

You must understand that in this sea there is a gulf between the
island and the mainland; and in all this gulf there is no more than
eight or ten fathoms of water and in some places no more than two.
It is in this gulf that the pearls are gathered; and I tell you how. A
group of merchants will band together to form a company or partnership and will take a large ship specially adapted for the purpose,
in which each will have a handy cabin fitted for his use containing a
tub of water and other requisites. There will be a great many such
ships, because there are many merchants who devote themselves to
this sort of fishery. And all the merchants who are associated in one
ship will have several boats to tow her through the gulf. It is their
practice to hire men for a certain sum for the month of April and half
of May; for that is the fishing season in this gulf. The place where
pearls are most plentiful is called Bettala, and is on the mainland.
From there they sail out for sixty miles towards the south and there
cast anchor. Then they go out in the little boats and begin to fish in
a manner that I will describe to you. The men in the little boats, who
have been hired by the merchants, jump overboard and dive into the

* Maabar corresponds approximately to the Coromandel (Eastern) coast of India,
more specifically perhaps to the district round Tanjore. Z, here and elsewhere, speaks
of four kings, not five. Greater India, as defined below (p. 250), includes many provinces besides Maabar.

water, sometimes three fathoms down, sometimes four, sometimes as much as ten. They stay under as long as they can. When they can endure no longer, they come to the surface, rest a short while and then plunge in again; and so they continue all day. While they are at the bottom of the sea, they gather there certain shells which are called sea oysters. In these oysters are found pearls, big and small and of every variety. The shells are split open and put into the tubs of water of which I have spoken. The pearls are embedded in the flesh of the shell-fish. In the water this flesh decays and grows flabby and takes on the appearance of white of egg. In this form it floats to the surface, while the pearls divested of impurities remain at the bottom. That is how the pearls are gathered. And I assure you that the quantities obtained are beyond computation. For you must know that pearls gathered in this gulf are exported throughout the world, because most of them are round and lustrous. In the middle of May this fishing comes to a stop, because the pearl-bearing shells are no longer to be found. But it is a fact that about 300 miles away they are found in September and the earlier half of October.

I can assure you that the king of this kingdom derives an immense revenue from the duty paid on this fishery. For the merchants pay him a tithe of their takings. Over and above this they pay one pearl in twenty to men who protect the divers against predatory fish by means of incantations. These enchanters are called Brahmans. They utter their incantations by day only; at night they break off their spells, so that the fish are free to do as they please. These Brahmans are expert also in incantations against all sorts of beasts and birds and animals of every kind.

I must tell you that in all this province of Maabar there is no master tailor or dressmaker to cut or stitch cloth, because the people go stark naked all the year round. For the weather here is always temperate, that is, it is neither cold nor hot. That is why they always go naked, except that they cover their private parts with a scrap of cloth. The king wears no more than the others, apart from certain ornaments of which I will tell you. You may take it for a fact that he too goes stark naked, except for a handsome loin-cloth with a fringe all round it set with precious stones—rubies, sapphires, emeralds, and other brilliant gems—so that this scrap of cloth is worth a fortune. Slung round his neck is a cord of fine silk which hangs down a full pace in front of him, and strung on this necklace are 104 beads, consisting of large and beautiful pearls and rubies of immense value. Let me tell you why he wears this necklace. He does it because it is his task every day, morning and evening, to say 104 prayers in honour of his idols. Such is the bidding of their faith and their religion, and such was the wont of the kings who preceded him, which they left as an obligation incumbent on their successor. That is why the king wears these 104 beads round his neck. The prayer consists simply of the word 'Pacauta, Pacauta, Pacauta' and nothing more.* He also wears, in three places on his arm, bracelets of gold studded with precious stones and pearls of great size and value. In like manner he wears, in three places on his legs, three anklets adorned with costly pearls and gems. Let me tell you further that this same king wears on his toes splendid pearls and other jewels, so that it is a marvellous sight to behold. What need of more words? Suffice it that he wears in all so many gems and pearls that their price exceeds that of a fine city. Indeed no one could compute the total cost of all the jewellery he wears. And it is no wonder he wears so many, considering that all these pearls and gems are found in his own kingdom.

Let me tell you something else. No one is allowed to take out of his kingdom any large or costly gem or any pearl that weighs upwards of half a *saggio*. Several times a year throughout his reign he issues a proclamation that all who have pearls or gems of especial beauty and excellence shall bring them to his court, and he will give in return twice their value. It is the custom of the realm to pay double value for all gems of high quality. So merchants and any others who possess such stones are willing enough to take them to the court, because they are well paid. That is how it comes about that this king has such riches and so many precious stones.

Let me tell you next of some other marvels. First, you may take it for a fact that this king has fully 500 wives, that is concubines. For I assure you that, whenever he sets eye on a beautiful woman or damsel, he takes her for himself. This involved him on one occasion in an act of folly, as you shall hear. He coveted a beautiful woman who was his brother's wife and ravished her from him and kept her for himself. And his brother, who was a wise man, submitted in peace and did not quarrel with him. More than once he was on the point of making war on him, but their mother showed them her breasts, saying: 'If you fight with each other, I will cut off these breasts which gave you both suck.' And so the grievance was allowed to lapse.

* This formula is apparently based on a Tamil pronunciation of *Bhagavata*, 'Lord'.

Here is another thing at which you may well marvel. I assure you that this king has no lack of loyal henchmen of an unusual kind; for they are his henchmen in this world and the next, according to their own assertions. These henchmen attend upon the king in court; they go out riding with him; they enjoy places of great dignity in his service; wherever he goes, these barons bear him company and they exercise high authority throughout the kingdom. Then, when the king dies and his body is burning on a huge pyre, all these barons who were his henchmen, as I have told you, fling themselves into the fire and burn with the king in order to bear him company in the next world.

Here is another custom that prevails in this kingdom. When the king dies and leaves behind him a great treasure, the son who inherits would not touch it for anything in the world. For he says: 'I have all my father's kingdom and all his people; so I am well able to provide for myself as he did.' Hence the kings of this kingdom never touch their treasure, but hand it down from one to another, each accumulating his own hoard. For this reason the total accumulation is truly immense.

Let me tell you next that this country does not breed horses. Hence all the annual revenue, or the greater part of it, is spent in the purchase of horses; and I will tell you how. You may take it for a fact that the merchants of Hormuz and Kais, of Dhofar and Shihr and Aden, all of which provinces produce large numbers of battle chargers and other horses, buy up the best horses and load them on ships and export them to this king and his four brother kings. Some of them are sold for as much as 500 *saggi* of gold, which are worth more than 100 marks of silver. And I assure you that this king buys 2,000 of them and more every year, and his brothers as many. And by the end of the year not 100 of them survive. They all die through ill usage, because they have no veterinaries and do not know how to treat them. You may take it from me that the merchants who export them do not send out any veterinaries or allow any to go, because they are only too glad for many of them to die in the king's charge.

Another custom of the realm is this. When a man is guilty of a capital offence and the king has decreed his death, the offender declares that he wishes to kill himself out of respect and devotion to some particular idol. The king expresses his approval. Then all the offender's kinsfolk and friends take him and set him on a chair and give him fully a dozen swords and carry him through the city, proclaiming aloud: 'This brave man is going to kill himself for love of such-and-such an idol.' In this way they carry him through the whole city. When they have reached the place where justice is done, then the offender takes a knife and cries in a loud voice: 'I kill myself for love of such-and-such an idol.' Having spoken these words, he takes two swords and thrusts them into his thighs at one stroke. Then, he thrusts two into his arms, two into his belly, two into his chest. And so he thrusts them all in, crying aloud at each stroke: 'I kill myself for love of such-and-such an idol.' When they are all thrust in, then grasping a two-handled knife like those used for shaping hoops, he sets it against his nape, gives it a mighty pull and severs his own neck, because the knife is exceedingly sharp. After he has killed himself, his kinsfolk cremate the body amid great rejoicing.

Another custom is this. When a man is dead and his body is being cremated, his wife flings herself into the same fire and lets herself be burnt with her husband. The ladies who do this are highly praised by all. And I assure you that there are many who do as I have told you.

The people of this kingdom worship idols. Most of them worship the ox, because they say that it is a very good thing. No one would eat beef for anything in the world, and no one would kill an ox on any account. There is one race of men here called *gavi*, who eat beef. They do not indeed venture to slaughter cattle; but when an ox dies naturally or by some other mode of death, then these *gavi* eat it. Let me tell you further that they daub all their houses with cow-dung.

Here is yet another of their customs. The king and his barons and everyone else all sit on the earth. If you ask them why they do not seat themselves more honourably, they reply that to sit on the earth is honourable enough, because we were made from the earth and to the earth we must return, so that no one could honour the earth too highly and no one should slight it.

Let me tell you further that these *gavi*—that is, all the race of those that eat cattle when they die a natural death—are the same who in the old days slew Messer St Thomas the Apostle. And let me add that of all this tribe called *gavi* no one may enter the place where the body of Messer St Thomas lies. For you must know that ten men would not avail to hold one of these *gavi* in the place, nor could twenty or more bring one of them where the body lies; for the place will not receive them, by virtue of the holy body.

This kingdom produces no grain excepting only rice. And here is a greater matter, well worth recounting: in this country if a stallion

P

of noble breed covers a mare of the like mettle, the offspring is a stunted colt with its feet awry. Horses so bred are worthless and cannot be ridden.

The people here go into battle with lance and shield and they go stark naked. They are not men of any valour or spirit, but paltry creatures and mean-spirited. They kill no beasts or any living thing. When they have a mind to eat the flesh of a sheep or of any beast or bird, they employ a Saracen or some other who is not of their religion or rule to kill it for them. Another of their customs is that all of them, male and female, wash their whole body in cold water twice a day—that is, morning and evening. One who did not wash twice a day would be thought an ascetic, as we think of the Patarins.

And you must know that in eating they use only the right hand; they would never touch food with their left. Whatever is clean and fair they do and touch with the right hand, believing that the function of the left hand is confined to such needful tasks as are unclean and foul, such as wiping the nose or the breach and suchlike. Likewise they drink only out of flasks, each one from his own; for no one would drink out of another's flask. When they are drinking, they do not set the flask to their lips, but hold it above and pour the fluid into their mouth. They would not on any account touch the flask with their lips nor pass it to a stranger to drink out of. If a stranger wants to drink and has not got his own flask with him, they will pour the wine or other fluid into his hands and he will drink out of them, so that his own hands will serve him for a cup.

I assure you that in this kingdom justice is very strictly administered to those who commit homicide or theft or any other crime. Concerning debts the following rule and enactment is observed among them. If a debtor after many demands from his creditor for repayment of a debt continues day after day to put him off with promises, and if the creditor can get at him in such a way as to draw a circle round him, the debtor must not move out of the circle without first satisfying the creditor or giving firm and adequate surety for full repayment on the same day. Otherwise, if he should venture to leave the circle without payment or surety given, he would incur the penalty of death as an offender against the right and justice established by the ruler. And Messer Marco saw this done in the case of the king himself. For it happened that the king was indebted to a certain foreign merchant for some goods that he had had of him, and after many requests from the merchant repeatedly postponed repayment to save himself trouble. Then the merchant, because this delay seriously hampered him in his business, went up to the king one day when he was riding in the country and having made due preparation drew a circle round him, horse and all, on the earth. When the king saw this, he reined in his horse and did not move from the spot till the merchant had been satisfied in full. At sight of this the people standing round about exclaimed in admiration: 'See how the king has obeyed the rule of justice!' And the king replied: 'Shall I, who have established this rule, break it merely because it tells against me? Surely it is incumbent on me before all others to observe it.'

Most of the people here abstain from drinking wine. They will not admit as a witness or a guarantor either a wine-drinker or one who sails on the sea. For they say that a man who goes to sea must be a man in despair. On the other hand you should know that they do not regard any form of sexual indulgence as a sin.

The climate is amazingly hot, which explains why they go naked. There is no rain except in the months of June, July, and August.* If it were not for the rain in these three months, which freshens the air, the heat would be so oppressive that no one could stand it. But thanks to this rain the heat is tempered.

Among these people there are many experts in the art called physiognomy, that is, the recognition of the characters of men and women, whether they be good or bad. This is done merely by looking at the man or woman. They are expert too in the significance of encounters with birds or beasts, and they pay more attention to augury than any other people in the world and are more skilled in distinguishing good omens from bad. I assure you that, when a man is setting out on a journey and happens to hear someone else sneeze, he promptly sits down by the way and goes no farther; if the other sneezes a second time, he gets up and goes ahead; if not, he turns back from the journey on which he has started and goes home.†

Likewise they say that for every day in the week there is one unlucky hour, which they call *choiach*. Thus on Monday it is the hour after seven in the morning, on Tuesday after nine, on Wednesday the first hour after noon, and so forth throughout the year. All these they

---

* Actually this applies to the Malabar, not the Coromandel, Coast.

† The two following paragraphs are found only in Z (partly reproduced in R). The passage can scarcely be a mere misplaced variant of the very similar one printed below (p. 236) from F, since Z at that point gives a faithful translation of F; so it would seem that this is another case in which Polo more or less repeats himself (cf. pp. 132 and 189, or 223 and 243).

have written down and defined in their books. They tell the hour by measuring the height of a man's shadow in feet. Thus on such-and-such a day, when a man's shadow is seven feet long opposite the sun, then will be the hour of *choiach*. When it has passed this length either in increase or decrease—for as the sun rises the shadow shortens, as the sun drops it lengthens—then it is no longer *choiach*. On another day, when the shadow is twelve feet long, then will be *choiach*; and when this measure is passed, then *choiach* will be over. All this they have in writing. And you must know that in these hours they fight shy of making a bargain or doing any sort of business. While two men are in the act of bargaining together, some one will stand up in the sunlight and measure the shadow; and if it is within the limits of the forbidden hours, according to which day it may be, then he will immediately say to them: 'It is *choiach*. Do nothing.' And they will give over. Then he will measure a second time and finding that the hour is past will say to them: '*Choiach* is over. Do what you will.' And they have this sort of computation at their finger tips. For they say that, if anyone strikes a bargain in these hours, he will make no profit by it, but it will turn out badly for him.

Again, their houses are infested with certain animals called tarantulas, which run up the walls like lizards. They have a poisonous bite and do serious harm to a man if they bite him. They have an utterance as if they were saying '*chis!*' and this is the noise they make. These tarantulas are taken as an omen in the following way: when men are bargaining together in a house infested with these creatures and a tarantula utters its cry above them, they take note from which side of the bargainer, either purchaser or vendor, the cry emanates—whether left or right, before or behind or directly overhead—and according to the direction they know whether its significance is good or bad. If it is good, the bargain is struck; if bad, it is called off. Sometimes it is good for the vendor and bad for the purchaser or conversely, or for both or neither; and they guide their conduct accordingly. This lore is based on experience.

In this kingdom as soon as a child is born, whether boy or girl, the father and mother have a record made in writing of his nativity, that is, the day of his birth, the month, the lunar cycle and the hour. This they do because they guide all their actions by the counsel of astrologers and diviners who are skilled in enchantment and magic and geomancy.

Again, a man who has sons here turns them out of the house as soon as they reach the age of thirteen, denying them meals in the household. For he says that they are now of an age to earn their living and to trade at a profit as he did. He gives them some twenty or twenty-four groats apiece or the equivalent, to bargain with and make their profit. This he does so that they may gain experience and readiness in deals of all kinds and get accustomed to business. This is what the boys do. All day long they never stop running to and fro, buying this and that and then selling it. When the pearl fishery is in full swing, they hurry to the ports and buy five or six pearls from the fishers, according to the numbers they have to offer. Then they take them to the dealers, who stay indoors for fear of the sun, and say: 'Do you want these? I declare that they cost me so much. Allow me such profit as you think fit.' And the dealers give them something above the cost price. Then back they go; or else they say to the dealers: 'Would you like me to go and buy something?' In this way they become very clever and astute traders. They may take foodstuffs home for their mothers to cook and dress for them, but not so that they eat at their fathers' expense.

You must know that in this kingdom, and indeed throughout India, the beasts and birds are very different from ours—all except one bird, and that is the quail. The quails here are certainly like ours, but all the rest are very different. I assure you for a fact that there are bats here—that is, the birds that fly by night and have no feathers—which are as big as goshawks. There are goshawks as black as crows, a good deal bigger than ours and good fliers and hawkers. And let me add something else that is worth recounting: they feed their horses on flesh cooked with rice and many other cooked foods.

Let me tell you further that they have many idols in their monasteries, both male and female, and to these idols many maidens are offered in the following manner. Their mother and father offer them to certain idols, whichever they please. Once they have been offered, then whenever the monks of these idol monasteries require them to come to the monasteries to entertain the idols, they come as they are bidden; and sing and afford a lively entertainment. And there are great numbers of these maidens, because they form large bevies. Several times a week in every month they bring food to the idols to which they are dedicated; and I will explain how they bring it and how they say that the idol has eaten. Some of these maidens of whom I have spoken prepare tasty dishes of meat and other food and bring them to their idols in the monasteries. Then they lay the table before them, setting out the meal they have brought, and leave it for some time. Meanwhile they all sing and dance and afford the merriest sport in the world. And when they have disported themselves for as long a time as a great lord might spend in eating a meal, then they say that the spirit of the idols has eaten the substance of the food. Whereupon they take the food and eat together with great mirth and jollity. Finally they return—each to her own home. This they do until they take husbands. Such maidens are to be found in profusion throughout this kingdom, doing all the things of which I have told you. And the reason why they are called on to amuse the idols is this. The priests of the idols very often declare: 'The god is estranged from the goddess. One will not cohabit with the other, nor will they hold speech together. Since they are thus estranged and angry with each other, unless they are reconciled and make their peace, all our affairs will miscarry and go from bad to worse, because they will not bestow their blessing and their favour.' So these maidens go to the monastery as I have said. And there, completely naked, except that they cover their private parts, they sing before the god and goddess. The god stands by himself on an altar under a canopy, the goddess by herself on another altar under another canopy. And the people say that he often dallies with her, and they have intercourse together; but when they are estranged they refrain from intercourse, and then these maidens come to placate them. When they are there, they devote themselves to singing, dancing, leaping, tumbling, and every sort of exercise calculated to amuse the god and goddess and to reconcile them. And while they are thus entertaining them, they cry: 'O Lord, wherefore art thou wroth with thy Lady? Wherefore art thou grown cold towards her, and wherefore is thy spirit estranged? Is she not comely? Is she not pleasant? Assuredly, yea. May it please thee, therefore, to be reconciled with her and take thy delight with her; for assuredly she is exceedingly pleasant.' And then the maiden who has spoken these words will lift her leg higher than her neck and perform a pirouette for the delectation of the god and goddess. When they have had enough of this entertainment, they go home. In the morning the idol-priest will announce with great joy that he has seen the god consort with the goddess and that harmony is restored between them. And then everyone rejoices and gives thanks. The flesh of these maidens, so long as they remain maidens, is so hard that no one could grasp or pinch them in any place: for a penny they will allow a man to pinch them as hard as he can. After they are married their flesh remains hard, but not so hard as before. On account of this hardness, their breasts do not hang down, but remain upstanding and erect.

Men have their beds very lightly constructed of canes, so designed that after they have got in, when they wish to sleep, they can hoist themselves with ropes up to the ceiling and make themselves fast there. This they do in order to avoid the tarantulas of which I have spoken, whose bite is noxious, besides fleas and other vermin; and also to catch the breeze and combat the heat. They do not all do this, but only the nobles and heads of houses. The others sleep on the highways. It is a proof of the excellent justice kept by the king that when a nocturnal traveller wishes to sleep and has with him a sack of pearls or other valuables—for men travel by night rather than by day, because it is cooler—he will put the sack under his head and sleep where he is; and no one ever loses anything by theft or otherwise. If he should lose it, he receives prompt satisfaction—so long, that is, as he has been sleeping on the highway; but not if he has been sleeping away from it. In that case the presumption is against him. For the authorities will inquire: 'Why were you sleeping away from the highway, if not because you had some dishonest intention?' Accordingly he is punished, and his loss will not be made good.

I have now told you a great deal about the manners and customs of this kingdom and the behaviour of its people. We will now leave it and go on to tell you of another kingdom, whose name is Motupalli.

Motupalli is a kingdom that is reached by travelling northwards from Maabar for about 1,000 miles.* It is ruled by a queen, who is a very wise woman. For I assure you that it is fully forty years since the king her husband died. As she was deeply devoted to him, she said that God would not wish her to take another husband, since he whom she loved more than her own life was dead. That was why she declined to marry again. I can tell you that throughout her forty years' reign she has governed her kingdom well with a high standard of justice and equity, as her husband did before. And I assure you that never was lady or lord so well beloved as she is by her subjects.

* R says '500 miles', which is nearer the mark. The queen has been identified as Rudrama Devi, who abdicated c. 1295. The diamond mines, famous in Arab legend, are at Golconda and elsewhere in Hyderabad.

The people here are idolaters and tributary to none. They live on rice, flesh, milk, fish, and fruit.

This kingdom produces diamonds. Let me tell you how they are got. You must know that in the kingdom there are many mountains in which the diamonds are found, as you will hear. When it rains the water rushes down through these mountains, scouring its way through mighty gorges and caverns. When the rain has stopped and the water has drained away, then men go in search of diamonds through these gorges from which the water has come, and they find plenty. In summer, when there is not a drop of water to be found, then diamonds can be found in plenty among these mountains. But the heat is so great that it is almost intolerable. Moreover the mountains are so infested with serpents of immense size and girth that men cannot go there without grave danger. But all the same they go there as best they can and find big stones of fine quality. Let me tell you further that these serpents are exceedingly venomous and noxious, so that men dare not venture into the caves where the serpents live. So they get the diamonds by other means. You must know that there is a big deep valley so walled in by precipitous cliffs that no one can enter it. But I will tell you what men do. They take many lumps of flesh imbrued in blood and fling them down into the depths of the valley. And the lumps thus flung down pick up great numbers of diamonds, which become embedded in the flesh. Now it so happens that these mountains are inhabited by a great many white eagles, which prey on the serpents. When these eagles spy the flesh lying at the bottom of the valley, down they swoop and seize the lumps and carry them off. The men observe attentively where the eagles go, and as soon as they see that a bird has alighted and is swallowing the flesh, they rush to the spot as fast as they can. Scared by their sudden approach, the eagles fly away, leaving the flesh behind. And when they get hold of it, they find diamonds in plenty embedded in it. Another means by which they get the diamonds is this. When the eagles eat the flesh, they also eat—that is, they swallow—the diamonds. Then at night, when the eagle comes back, it deposits the diamonds it has swallowed with its droppings. So men come and collect these droppings, and there too they find diamonds in plenty. Now you have heard three ways in which diamonds are gathered. And there are many others. You must know that in all the world diamonds are found nowhere else except in this kingdom alone. But there they are both abundant and of good quality. You must not suppose that diamonds of the first water come to our countries of Christendom. Actually they are exported to the Great Khan and to the kings and noblemen of these various regions and realms. For it is they who have the wealth to buy all the costliest stones.

Let us turn now to other matters. You should know that in this kingdom are made all the best buckrams in the world—those of the finest texture and the highest value. For I assure you that they resemble cloths of Rheims linen. There is no king or queen in the world who would not gladly wear a fabric of such delicacy and beauty. The country is well stocked with beasts, including the biggest sheep in the world, and with great abundance and variety of foodstuffs. As there is nothing else worth mentioning, we will leave this kingdom and tell you of the burial-place of Messer St Thomas the Apostle.

The body of St Thomas lies in the province of Maabar in a little town. There are few inhabitants, and merchants do not visit the place; for there is nothing in the way of merchandise that could be got from it, and it is a very out-of-the-way spot. But it is a great place of pilgrimage both for Christians and for Saracens. For I assure you that the Saracens of this country have great faith in him and declare that he was a Saracen and a great prophet and call him *avariun*, that is to say 'holy man'.

The Christians who guard the church have many palm-trees that yield wine and also such as bear coconuts. One of these nuts is a meal for a man, both meat and drink. Their outer husk is matted with fibres, which are employed in various ways and serve many useful purposes. Under this husk is a food that provides a square meal for a man. It is very tasty, as sweet as sugar and as white as milk, and is in the form of a cup like the surrounding husk. Inside this food is enough juice to fill a phial. The juice is clear and cool and admirably flavoured. When a man has eaten the kernel, he drinks the juice. And so from one nut a man can have his fill of meat and drink. For each of these trees the Christians pay one groat a month to one of the brothers who are kings in Maabar.

Let me tell you a marvellous thing about this burial-place. You must know that the Christians who go there on pilgrimage take some of the earth from the place where the saintly body died and carry it back to their own country. Then, when anyone falls sick of a quartan or tertian ague or some such fever, they give him a little of this earth to drink. And no sooner has he drunk than he is cured.

adoncques si treune len la cite de ty guy qui nest pas trop grant. mais elle est moult plenteureuse de tix toutes choses et sont ydres. et ont mon noie de chartres. et sont au grant eau. Et li uent dars et de plusieurs marchandises. Car il li vieut moult de marchandise. et si ont vname assez du dit grant fluu. Et sachiez que a la se nestre partie deuers le naut lonig de ci. iij. iour nees. est la mer occiaine uisques a la cite de tou tes pars. se fait sel en moult grant quantite. Car il ya moult de bounes salines. et si ya vne cite qui aguou ty guy qui a moult est grant et riche. et noble. et en ceste cite se fait tout le sel. si que toute la puince en a assez. et si vous dirai nentte que le grant eau. eu a si grant reute. et si uueilleusement est grande. que a grant pain ne le porroit on croure qui ne le verroit. et ont mounoie de chartres. Dr nous partiuus de ci. et retouruerous a tyguy. dout nous v auous con te a dessus. si vous dirous diune cite qui est appel le laguy. Ci parole le vij. chapitre de la cite saut leu se part de laguy.

de tyguy et leu a chenauche vme iournee par seloc coutrees et chasteaux trou uaut assez. si treune leu la cite de laguy qui moult est grant et noble. et sachiez que il a so la seignourie. xxvij. citez moult grauz. et nile nobles et de moult graus marchandises qui sont moult bonnes. si que laguy est moult puissate cite. Et si diez eu ceste cite. i. des xij. barus du gut eau. Car elle est esleue pour i. des xij. sieges. Il sont ydres et ont mounoie de chartres. Et si vous di que le dit uyestir marc pol celu meimes de qui nostre liure parle. seiourna eu ceste cite de laugu. iij. aus a couuphs par le dounua dement du grant haau. Il viueut de marchau dises. et dars. Car ou y fait harnois de chena liers et bounes dannes eu grant quantite. Car en ceste cite. et enuiron des appurtenances teneure grar dannes assez que le seigneur y fait seiourner. autre chose uya qui a rauteuniour face. pour ce bo couterous nous auant. et vo dirous de ij. graus puinces qui meimes sont de mangy qui sont vers pouent et bien ya a couter. si vous couteras puurauent de la p uince de ay augtuu. Ci dit le vij. et iij.

anglin si est vme puince vers pouent et est du mangy meismes qui est vme moult noble puince et moult riche. il sout ydres et ont mounoie de chartres. et sout au grant eau et viueut dars et de marchandise il ya graut habondance de soie. Car il eu sout draps dor et de soie de toutes mauieres et de moult biaux. et si ont gut marchie de touz bles. et de toutes choses de viure Car moult est plenteureux puince. et si ont ve nois assez. de toutes bestes. et oisiaux. Et si ya graux marchans et riches dout le seigueur a mi graut pourfit de euls du droit de la marchandise. que il achateut et veudeut. Dr nous partiuus de ci que il ma chose qui face a raueuteruour. ce vo conterons de la tres noble cite de sauanfu qui bieu fait a couter eu nostre liure. Car trop est e gut fait a couter de son affaire. Ci dit le vij. et v chapitre de la tres noble cite de sauanfu. la quelle fu conquestee du grant eau. et de ses geus. chas auaut il fureut il sout teup deuaut. et si puise par euguigs es quels leu gute pierres et mango maux. y les fureut geter dedeuz la cite par quoy ceulx qui estoieut et qui gardoieut la dite cite se reudireut au grant eau. et tout ce eu par mes sire micholas pol. y uestire mafe sou frere. et uestire marc pol fiz au dit uestire micholas pol. et par ij. cittelies qu il auoieut auec eulx de leur meisuee. les qlz coseillereut au gut eau q elle ne seroit pouut puise. se ce nestout par le sus euguigs

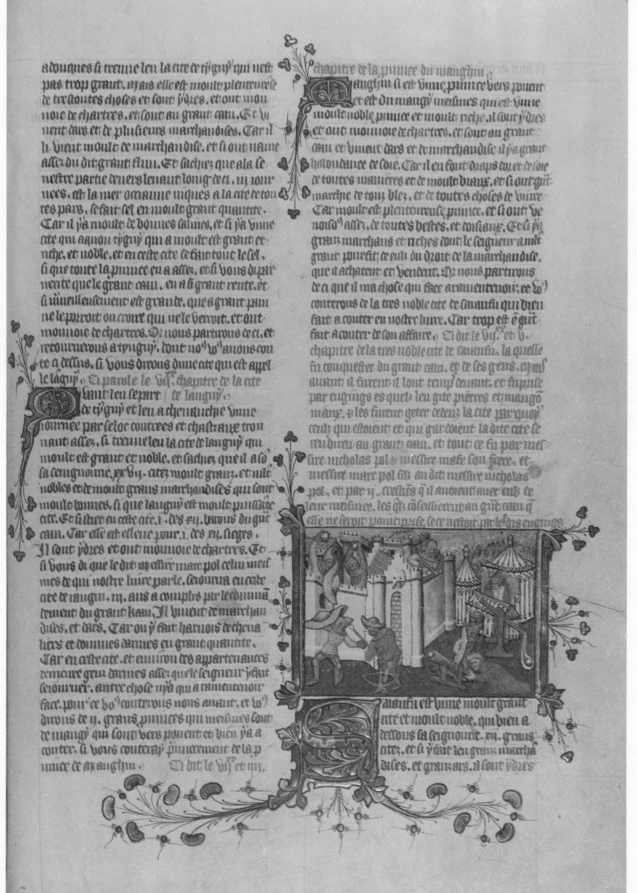

aiuchi est vme moult graut cite et moult noble. qui bieu a dessous sa seignourie. xij. graus citez. et si y fait leu grauz marcha dises. et grauz ars. il sout ydres

The remedy never fails.* And you should know that the earth is of a red colour.

Let me tell you further of a fine miracle that happened about the year of our Lord 1288. It so happened that a baron of this country† had a great quantity of a certain grain called rice. And with this he filled all the houses round about the church. When the Christians who guard the church and the saintly body saw that this idolatrous lord was filling the houses in this way, so that pilgrims had nowhere to lodge, they took it very much to heart and begged him earnestly to desist. But he, being a ruthless and haughty man, paid no heed to their prayers, but continued to fill all the houses at his own pleasure without regard to the wishes of the Christians. It was then, when he had filled all the saint's houses and provoked the indignation of the brethren, that the great miracle happened, as I will tell you. On the night after he had filled them Messer St Thomas the Apostle appeared to him with a fork in his hand and held it to the baron's throat, saying: 'Either you will empty my houses forthwith, or if you do not you must needs die an evil death.' So saying, he pressed his throat hard, so that it seemed to the baron that he was in great pain and on the point of death. When he had done this, the saint departed. Next morning the baron arose early and ordered all the houses to be emptied. And he related all that the saint had done to him, which was accounted a great miracle. At this the Christians were filled with gladness and joy and rendered great thanks and great honour to Messer St Thomas and blessed his name exceedingly. And I assure you that many other miracles happen here all the year round, which would be reckoned great marvels by any who heard them, notably the curing of Christians whose bodies are disabled or crippled.

Now that we have told you of this, we should like to tell you how the saint met his death, as it is reported by the people of these parts. The truth is that Messer St Thomas was outside his hermitage in the wood, praying to the Lord his God. And round him were many peacocks—for you must know that they are more plentiful here than anywhere in the world. And while he was thus saying his prayers, an idolater of the race and lineage of the *gavi* let fly an arrow from his

---

* Z adds that Marco took some of the earth with him to Venice and effected several cures with it.

† Z says 'the above-named king' and states that the church itself as well as the adjoining houses was filled. In this version the king is told to stop levying tribute from the saint's servants and duly obeys.

bow, intending to kill one of these peacocks who were round the saint. And he never saw the saint himself. But the shot intended for the peacock hit the saint on his right side. And when he had received the blow he worshipped his creator most fervently, and of that blow he died. But it is a fact that before he came to the place where he died he made many converts in Nubia—just how this happened we shall tell you in due order at the appropriate time and place.

To turn now to other matters, it is a fact that in this country when a child is born they anoint him once a week with oil of sesame, and this makes him grow much darker than when he was born. For I assure you that the darkest man is here the most highly esteemed and considered better than the others who are not so dark. Let me add that in very truth these people portray and depict their gods and their idols black and their devils white as snow. For they say that God and all the saints are black and the devils are all white. That is why they portray them as I have described. And similarly they make the images of their idols all black.

You must know that the men of this country have such faith in the ox and such a high regard for its sanctity that when they are going to war they take some of the hair of the wild ox of which I have told you; and those who are horsemen set some of this ox-hair on their horse's mane, while foot-soldiers fasten it to their shields. Some also bind it into their own hair. This they do because they believe that by virtue of the ox-hair they will be more surely saved and rescued from all mishap. Such is the custom among all who go to war. For this reason the hair of the wild ox is highly prized here; for no one thinks himself safe without it.

Let me tell you next of a province called Lar,* which lies to westward of the place where St Thomas the Apostle is buried. From this province are sprung all the Brahmans in the world, and it is from here that they originate. I assure you that these Brahmans are among the best traders in the world and the most reliable. They would not tell a lie for anything in the world and do not utter a word that is not true. You must know that when a foreign trader comes to this province, knowing nothing of the manners and customs of the country, he will find one of these Brahman merchants and entrust his wealth

* This name should refer to Gujarat; but it seems here to be located rather in the region of Mysore. There may also be some confusion between *Brahmans* and *Banians*.

and his wares to his keeping, requesting him to conduct his business on his behalf, lest he should be deceived through ignorance of local customs. Then the Brahman merchant will promptly take charge of the foreign merchant's wares and deal with them no less faithfully in buying and selling and look after the interests of the foreigner with no less care, indeed with more, than if they were his own. For this service he will ask no payment, unless the foreigner wishes to make him a present as an act of generosity. They eat no meat and drink no wine. They live very virtuous lives according to their own usage. They have no sexual intercourse except with their own wives. They take nothing that belongs to another. They would never kill a living creature or do any act that they believe to be sinful. And you must know that all the Brahmans in the world are known by an emblem which they wear. For they all carry a cord of cotton on their shoulder and fasten it across the chest, under the other arm, and back behind them. By this emblem they are known wherever they go. And I assure you that they have a rich king well endowed with treasures. This king is very anxious to buy pearls and other precious stones. So he has made a compact with all the merchants of his country that for all the pearls they bring from the kingdom of Maabar that they call Chola, which is the best province and the most refined in all India and the one in which the best pearls are found, he will pay them double the cost price. The Brahmans accordingly go to the kingdom of Maabar and buy all the good pearls they can get and take them to their king. They tell him truly how much they cost, and the king promptly pays them twice the amount. Thus they are never losers by the transaction. For this reason they have brought him a vast quantity of them of great size and excellent quality.

These Brahmans are idolaters and set more store by augury and the behaviour of beasts and birds than any other men in the world. Let me tell you a bit of what they do. First, the following custom prevails among them. On every day of the week they have a distinctive mark, as I will tell you. If it happens that they are bargaining about some piece of merchandise, the intending purchaser stands up and looks at his shadow in the sunlight. Then he asks: 'What day is it today?' 'It is such-and-such a day.' Then he has his shadow measured. If it is the right length for the day, he clinches the bargain; if not, he cries off and waits till the shadow reaches the point laid down in their rule. Just as I have described it to you for this day, so they have laid down for every day of the week how long the shadow ought to be. Till the shadow reaches the proper length, they will strike no bargain and do no business. But when the length is just what it ought to be, then is the hour for bargain or business.

Here is something still more noteworthy. When they are conducting a bargain, whether indoors or out, and they see a tarantula approaching—these creatures being very plentiful—if the purchaser sees that it is coming from the quarter that seems to him propitious, he buys the goods there and then; if it is coming from a quarter that seems unpropitious, he calls off the bargain and does not purchase.

Again, when they are leaving their house and hear someone sneeze, if it does not seem propitious, they stop short and go no farther. And when these Brahmans are going on their way and see a swallow flying towards them, either from in front or from left or right, if it seems according to their tradition to come from an auspicious quarter, they go ahead; if not, they go no farther but turn back.

These Brahmans live longer than anyone else in the world. This is due to their light feeding and great abstinence. They have very good teeth, thanks to a herb they are accustomed to eat, which is a great aid to digestion and is very salutary to the human body. And you must know that these Brahmans do not practise phlebotomy or any other form of blood-letting.

Among them are certain men living under a rule who are called *Yogis*. They live even longer than the others, as much as 150 or 200 years. And their bodies remain so active that they can still come and go as they will and perform all the services required by their monastery and their idols and serve them just as well as if they were younger. This comes of their great abstinence and of eating very little food and only what is wholesome. For it is their practice to eat chiefly rice and milk. Let me tell you also of a special food they eat, which I am sure will strike you as remarkable. For I assure you that they take quicksilver and sulphur and mix them together and make a drink of them, which they then drink. They declare that this prolongs life, and so they live all the longer. They drink this mixture twice a month, and make a practice of it from childhood in order to live longer. And certainly those who live to such a great age are habituated to this drink of sulphur and quicksilver.

There is a regular religious order in this kingdom of Maabar, of those who are called by this name of *Yogi*, who carry abstinence to the extremes of which I will tell you and lead a harsh and austere life.

You may take it for a fact that they go stark naked, wearing not a stitch of clothing nor even covering their private parts or any bodily member. They worship the ox, and most of them carry a little ox made of gilt copper or bronze in the middle of the forehead. You must understand that they wear it tied on. Let me tell you further that they burn cowdung and make a powder of it. With this they anoint various parts of their body with great reverence, no less than Christians display in the use of holy water. If anyone does reverence to them while they are passing in the street, they anoint him with this powder on the forehead in token of blessing. They do not eat out of platters or on trenchers; but they take their food on the leaves of apples of paradise or other big leaves—not green leaves, but dried ones; for they say that the green leaves have souls, so that this would be a sin. For in their dealings with all living creatures they are at pains to do nothing that they believe to be a sin. Indeed they would sooner die than do anything that they deemed to be sinful. When other men ask them why they go naked and are not ashamed to show their sexual member, they say: 'We go naked because we want nothing of this world. For we came into the world naked and unclothed. The reason why we are not ashamed to show our member is that we commit no sin with it, so we are not more ashamed to show it than you are when you show your hand or face or any other member which you do not employ in sinful lechery. It is because you employ this member in sin and lechery that you cover it and are ashamed of it. But we are no more ashamed of it than of our fingers, because we commit no sin with it.' Such is the justification they offer to those who ask them why they are not ashamed of their nakedness. I assure you further that they would not kill any creature or any living thing in the world, neither fly nor flea nor louse nor any other vermin, because they say that they have souls. For the same reason they refuse to eat living things because of the sin they would incur. I assure you that they do not eat anything fresh, either herb or root, until it is dried; because they declare that while they are fresh they have souls. When they wish to relieve their bowels, they go to the beach or the sea-shore and there void their excrement in the sand by the water. Then, after cleansing themselves in the water, they take a stick or rod, with which they spread out their excrement and so crumble it into the sand that nothing is visible. When asked why they do this, they reply: 'This would breed worms. And the worms thus created, when their food was consumed by the sun, would starve to death. And since that substance issues from our bodies—for without food we cannot live—we should incur grievous sin by the death of so many souls created of our substance. Therefore we annihilate this substance, so that no worms may be created from it merely to die of starvation by our guilt and default.' Let me tell you further that they sleep naked on the ground with nothing under them and nothing over them. It is truly marvellous that they do not die and that they live as long as I have told you. They also practise great abstinence in eating; for they fast all the year round and never drink anything but water.

Here is something else worth relating. They have their monks who live in monasteries to serve the idols. And this is the probation they must undergo before appointment to the office, when one has died and another is to be chosen in his place. The maidens who are offered to the idols are brought in and made to touch the probationers. They touch them on various parts of the body and embrace and fondle them and instil into them the uttermost of earthly bliss. If the man thus caressed lies completely motionless without any reaction to the maidens' touch, he passes muster and is admitted to their order. If on the other hand his member reacts to the touch, they will not keep him, but expel him forthwith, declaring that there is no place among them for a man of wantonness. So strict are these idolaters and so stubborn in their misbelief.

The reason they give for burning their dead is that if a body were not burnt it would breed worms; and when the worms had eaten it, they would inevitably die. And they say that by their death the souls of the deceased would incur great sin. That is their justification for cremating the dead. And they firmly maintain that worms have souls.

Now that we have told you of the customs of these idolaters, let us turn to a delightful story that I forgot to tell when we were dealing with Ceylon.* You shall hear it for yourselves and I am sure it will impress you.

Ceylon, as I told you earlier in this book, is a large island. Now it is a fact that in this island there is a very high mountain, so ringed by sheer cliffs that no one can climb it except by one way, of which I will tell you. For many iron chains have been hung on the side of the

* R adds that Marco heard this story when on his way home. The Mongol title *Burkhan* ('Divinity') is here used as equivalent to the Sanskrit *Buddha* ('Enlightened').

mountain, so arranged that by their means a man can climb to the top. It is said that on the top of this mountain is the monument of Adam, our first parent. The Saracens say that it is Adam's grave, but the idolaters call it the monument of Sakyamuni Burkhan. This Sakyamuni was the first man in whose name idols were made. According to their traditions he was the best man who ever lived among them, and the first whom they revered as a saint and in whose name they made idols. He was the son of a rich and powerful king. He was a man of such virtuous life that he would pay no heed to earthly things and did not wish to be king. When his father saw that he had no wish to be king or to care for any of the things of this world, he was deeply grieved. He made him a very generous offer: he promised to crown him king of the realm, so that he should rule it at his own pleasure—for he himself was willing to resign the crown and all his authority, so that his son should be sole ruler. His son replied that he would have none of it. When his father saw that he would not accept the kingship for anything in the world, his grief was so bitter that he came near to dying. And no wonder, because he had no other son and no one else to whom he might leave his kingdom. Then the king had recourse to the following scheme. For he resolved to find means of inducing his son to give his mind willingly to earthly things and accept the crown and the kingdom. So he housed him in a very luxurious palace and provided 30,000 maidens of the utmost beauty and charm to minister to him. For no male was admitted, but only these maidens; maidens waited on him at bed and board and kept him company all day long. They sang and danced before him and did all they could to delight him as the king had bidden them. But I assure you that all these maidens could not tempt the king's son to any wantonness, but he lived more strictly and more chastely than before. So he continued to lead a life of great virtue according to their usage. He was such a delicately nurtured youth that he had never been out of the palace and had never seen a dead man nor one who was not in full bodily health. For the king let no old or disabled man enter his presence. Now it happened that this youth was out riding one day along the road when he saw a dead man. He paused aghast, as one who had never seen the like, and immediately asked those who were with him what this was. They told him that it was a dead man. 'How, then?' cried the king's son. 'Do all men die?' 'Yes, truly,' said they. Then the youth said nothing but rode on his way deep in thought. He had not ridden far when he found a very old man who could not walk and had not a tooth in his head but had lost them all through old age. When the king's son saw this greybeard, he asked what was this and why could he not walk. And his companions told him that it was through old age that he had lost the power to walk and his teeth. When the king's son had learnt the truth about the dead man and the old one, he returned to his palace and resolved that he would stay no longer in this evil world, but would set out in search of him who never dies and who has created him.* So he left the palace and his father and took his way into the high and desolate mountains; and there he spent the rest of his days most virtuously and chastely and in great austerity. For assuredly, had he been a Christian, he would have been a great saint with our Lord Jesus Christ.

When this prince died, he was brought to the king his father. And when the king saw that the son whom he loved more than himself was dead, there is no need to ask if he was stricken with grief and bitterness. First he ordered a solemn mourning. Then he had an image made in his likeness, all of gold and precious stones, and caused it to be honoured by all the people of the country and worshipped as a god. And they said that he had died eighty-four times. For they say that when he died the first time he became an ox; then he died a second time and became a horse. And in this manner they say that he died eighty-four times, and that every time he became an animal—a dog or some other creature. But the eighty-fourth time he died and became a god. And he is deemed by the idolaters to be the best and greatest god they have. And you must know that this was the first idol ever made by the idolaters and hence come all the idols in the world. And this happened in the island of Ceylon in India.

Now you have heard how idols first originated. Let me tell you next that idolaters from very distant parts come here on pilgrimage, just as Christians go to the shrine of Messer St James.† And the idolaters say that the monument on this mountain is that of the king's son of whom you have just heard, and that the teeth and the hair and the bowl that are here also belonged to this prince, whose name was Sakyamuni Burkhan, that is to say, Sakyamuni the Saint. And the Saracens, who also come here in great numbers on pilgrimage, say that it is the monument of Adam our first parent and

* Or possibly 'it' (the world).
† One MS adds that this story is very like the life of St Josaphat (which is, in fact, a Christianized version of the Buddha legend.)

Q

that the teeth and hair and bowl were his also. So now you have heard how the idolaters say that he is that king's son who was their first idol and their first god, while the Saracens say that he is Adam our first parent. But God alone knows who he is or what he was. For we do not believe that Adam is in this place, since our Scripture of Holy Church declares that he is in another part of the world.

Now it happened that the Great Khan heard that on this mountain was the monument of Adam and likewise his teeth and his hair and the bowl from which he used to eat. He made up his mind that he must have these relics. So he sent here a great embassy in the year of our Lord 1284. What more shall I say? You may take it for a fact that the Great Khan's envoys with a great retinue set out on their way and journeyed so far by sea and land that they came to the island of Ceylon. They went to the king and so far succeeded in their mission that they acquired the two maxillary teeth, which were very large and thick, and some of the hair and the bowl, which was made of a very lovely green porphyry. With these acquisitions, they went their way and returned to their lord. And when they approached the great city of Khan-balik where the Great Khan was, they sent him word that they were coming and were bringing what they had been sent to fetch. Then the Great Khan ordered that all the people, both monks and others, should go out to meet these relics, which they were given to understand belonged to Adam. Why make a long story of it? Suffice it that all the people of Khan-balik went out to meet these relics and the monks received them and brought them to the Great Khan, who welcomed them with great joy and great ceremony and great reverence. And I assure you that they found in their scriptures a passage declaring that the bowl possessed this property that if anyone set in it food for one man he would have enough for five. And the Great Khan announced that he had had this put to the proof and that it was quite true.

That is how the Great Khan came by these relics of which you have heard; and what they cost him in treasure amounted to no small sum.

Now that we have told you the truth of this story in due order, let us turn to other matters.

First of all, let me tell you of the great and splendid city of Kayal. It belongs to Ashar, the eldest of the royal brothers. And you may take it that this is the port of call for all ships trading with the west—

that is with Hormuz and Kais and Aden and all Arabia—for horses and other goods. The merchants use it as a port because it is conveniently situated and affords a good market for their wares. And merchants congregate here from many parts to buy horses and various merchandise. This king is very rich in treasure; he decks his person with many gems of great price and goes about in right royal state. He governs his country well and maintains strict justice, especially in his dealings with merchants who resort thither—that is, the foreign merchants. He maintains their interests with great rectitude. So merchants are very glad to come here because of this good king who safeguards them so well. And it is a fact that they make great profits here and their trade prospers.

Further, I would have you know that this king has fully 300 wives and more; for here a man is more highly esteemed in proportion as he supports more wives. When a quarrel breaks out between these five kings, who are brothers german, sprung from one father and one mother, and they have a mind to fight with one another, then their mother, who is still alive, intervenes between them and will not let them fight. Often it happens, when her sons will not be restrained by her prayers but persist in their determination to fight, that their mother seizes a knife and cries: 'If you do not stop quarrelling and make peace together, I will kill myself here and now. And first I will cut off the breasts from my bosom with which I gave you milk.' When the sons see how deeply their mother is grieved and how tenderly she pleads with them, and reflect that it is for their own good, then they come to terms and make peace. This has happened several times. But I assure you that after their mother's death a violent quarrel will infallibly break out among them and they will destroy one another.

You should know that these people, and indeed all the peoples of India, are addicted to the habit, which affords them some satisfaction, of carrying almost continually in their mouths a certain leaf called *tambur*. They go about chewing this leaf and spitting out the resulting spittle. This habit prevails especially among the nobles and magnates and kings. They mix the leaves with camphor and other spices and also with lime, and go about continually chewing them. And this habit is very beneficial to their health. If anyone is offended with somebody and wishes to insult and affront him then when he meets him in the street he collects this mixture in his mouth and spits it in the other's face, saying: 'You are not worth this,' that is to say, what he has spat out. The other, regarding this as a deadly insult and outrage, promptly complains to the king that he has been slighted and dishonoured and craves leave to avenge himself. If the insult was directed against him and his clan, he will beg leave to match his person and his clan against the challenger's person and clan and prove whether or not he is worth no more than this; if it is a purely personal affront, then he will beg leave to settle it man to man. Then the king grants leave to both parties. If the contest is between clan and clan, each leader prepares for battle with his own following; and the only cuirass they don and wear for their protection is the skin their mother gave them at birth. When they are on the field, they strike, wound, and slay; for their swords strike home easily and a ready entry lies open to each of them. The king will be present in person and a multitude of spectators to watch the proceedings. When the king sees that many have been slain on either side and that one party appear to be gaining the upper hand and downing their adversaries, he will put between his teeth one end of a cloth that he has wrapped round him and hold out the other end at arm's length. Then the combatants cease forthwith from combat, and not another blow is struck. This is a frequent outcome. If the combat is between man and man, it will go like this. Both duellists will be naked, as they normally are, and each will have a knife.* They are adept at defending themselves with these knives; for with these they parry a blow as nimbly as they inflict one. This, then, is the procedure. As you have learnt, they are dark-skinned people. So one of them will draw a circle in white on the other's flesh, wherever he may choose, and say to him: 'Know that I will strike you within that circle and nowhere else. Guard yourself as best you can.' And the other will do as much to him. Then well for the better man, and for the worse, worse! For assuredly the blow that is first to reach its target does not go unfelt.

Now that we have said so much about this king, let us go on to speak of the realm of Quilon, which lies about 500 miles southwest of Maabar. The people are idolaters, though there are some Christians and Jews among them. They speak a language of their own. The king is tributary to none. Now I will tell you what is found in this kingdom and what are its products.

You must know that this country produces Quilon brazil which

* R says 'a sword and shield provided by the king' and adds that it is forbidden to use the point.

is very good, and also pepper in great abundance in all the fields and woods. Pepper is gathered in the months of May, June, and July. And I can tell you that the pepper trees are planted and watered and grow in cultivation. There is also plenty of good indigo, which is produced from a herb: they take this herb without the roots and put it in a big tub and add water and leave it till the herb is all rotted. Then they leave it in the sun, which is very hot and makes it evaporate and coagulate into a paste. Then it is chopped up into small pieces, as you have seen it. The heat here is so intense and the sun so powerful that it is scarcely tolerable. For I assure you that if you put an egg into one of the rivers you would not have long to wait before it boiled. Let me inform you further that merchants come here from Manzi and Arabia and the Levant and ply a thriving trade; for they bring various products from their own countries by sea and export others in return.

The country produces a diversity of beasts different from those of all the rest of the world. There are black lions with no other visible colour or mark. There are parrots of many kinds. Some are entirely white—as white as snow—with feet and beaks of scarlet. Others are scarlet and blue—there is no lovelier sight than these in the world. And there are some very tiny ones, which are also objects of great beauty. Then there are peacocks of another sort than ours and much bigger and handsomer, and hens too that are unlike ours. What more need I say? Everything there is different from what it is with us and excels both in size and beauty. They have no fruit the same as ours, no beast, no bird. This is a consequence of the extreme heat. They have no grain excepting only rice. They make wine out of sugar,* and a very good drink it is, and makes a man drunk sooner than grape wine. All that the human body needs for its living is to be had in profusion and very cheap with the one exception of grain other than rice. They have no lack of skilled astrologers. They have physicians who are adept at preserving the human body in health. They are all blackskinned and go stark naked, both males and females, except for gay loin-cloths. They regard no form of lechery or sensual indulgence as sin. Their marriage customs are such that a man may wed his cousin german or his father's widow or his brother's. And these customs prevail throughout the Indies. Now that I have told you something of this kingdom—all that is worth recounting—let us move on to Comorin.

* Z: 'dates'.

Comorin is a country of India proper in which it first becomes possible to see the pole star, which we have not seen all the way here since we left Java.* From this place you can go out thirty miles into the sea and catch a glimpse of the pole star rising out of the water for about one cubit. This is not a highly civilized place, but decidedly savage. There are beasts of various sorts, notably monkeys, some of them of such distinctive appearance that you might take them for men. There are also the apes called 'Paul cats', so peculiar that they are a real marvel. Lions, leopards, and lynxes abound. As there is nothing else worth noting, we will pass on to Ely.

Ely is a kingdom about 300 miles west of Comorin. The people are idolaters, ruled by their own king, paying tribute to none and speaking a language of their own. I will tell you plainly of the customs and products of this country; and you will be able to understand them better, because we are now approaching more civilized places.† In this province or kingdom there is no port, except that there is a big river with a very fine estuary. Pepper grows here in great abundance, and ginger too, besides plenty of other spices. The king is very rich in treasure, but not strong in man-power. However, the entrance to his kingdom is so easily defensible that no hostile army could force an entry; so he has no fear of anyone.

Let me tell you something else. Should it happen that a ship enters the estuary and goes upstream, if it is not a ship that is bound for this place they seize it and appropriate the whole cargo. They say: 'You were bound elsewhere and God has sent you to me, so that I may take all you have.' Thereupon they seize all the goods in the ship and keep them for their own and do not consider that they have done anything wrong. This practice prevails throughout all these provinces of India. If any ship is driven by stress of weather to put in at any place other than its proper destination, it is seized the moment it comes ashore and robbed of everything on board. For the inhabitants will say: 'You meant to go somewhere else; but my good luck and merit have brought you here, so that I should have all your possessions.'

You should know that ships from Manzi and elsewhere come here

---

* This suggests that some point near Cape Comorin was Marco's first point of call on one of his visits to India, probably the later one.

† *Plus domesces leus*; perhaps 'more familiar', or simply 'nearer home'. Cf. Introduction, p. 13.

in summer, load in four to eight days, and leave as soon as they can, because there is no port and it is very hazardous to linger here, because there are merely sandy beaches without any port. It is true, however, that ships of Manzi are not so much afraid to beach on sand as others are, because they are fitted with such powerful wooden anchors that they hold firm in every stress.

There are lions here and other beasts of prey, besides game in plenty.

We shall tell you next of the great kingdom of Malabar, which lies farther west and has a king and a language of its own. The people here are idolaters, tributary to none. Here the pole star is more clearly visible, seeming to rise about two cubits above the water. You must know that from Malabar, and from a neighbouring province called Gujarat, more than 100 ships cruise out every year as corsairs, seizing other ships and robbing the merchants. For they are pirates on a big scale. I assure you that they bring their wives and little children with them. They spend the whole summer on a cruise and work havoc among the merchants. Most of these villainous corsairs scatter here and there, scouring the sea in quest of merchant ships. But sometimes their evil-doing is more concerted. For they cruise in line, that is to say at distances of about five miles apart. In this way twenty ships cover 100 miles of sea. And as soon as they catch sight of a merchant ship, one signals to another by means of beacons, so that not a ship can pass through this sea undetected. But the merchants, who are quite familiar with the habits of these villainous corsairs and know that they are sure to encounter them, go so well armed and equipped that they are not afraid to face them after they have been detected. They defend themselves stoutly and inflict great damage on their attackers. But of course it is inevitable that one should be captured now and then. When the corsairs do capture a merchant ship, they help themselves to the ship and the cargo; but they do not hurt the men. They say to them: 'Go and fetch another cargo. Then, with luck, you may give us some more.'

In this kingdom there is great abundance of pepper and also of ginger, besides cinnamon in plenty and other spices, turbit and coconuts. Buckrams are made here of the loveliest and most delicate texture in the world. Many other articles of merchandise are exported. In return, when merchants come here from overseas they load their ships with brass, which they use as ballast, cloth of gold and silk, sendal, gold, silver, cloves, spikenard, and other such spices that are not produced here. You must know that ships come here from very many parts, notably from the great province of Manzi, and goods are exported to many parts. Those that go to Aden are carried thence to Alexandria.

Now that we have told you of Malabar, we shall go on to speak of Gujarat. You must understand that we do not enumerate all the cities of these kingdoms, since the list would be far too long. For every kingdom has cities and towns in plenty.

Gujarat likewise is a great kingdom. The people are idolaters and have a king and a language of their own and pay tribute to none. The country lies towards the west. Here the pole star is still more clearly visible, with an apparent altitude of six cubits. In this kingdom are the most arrant corsairs in the world. Let me tell you one of their nasty tricks. You must know that, when they capture merchants, they make them drink tamarind and sea-water, so that they pass or vomit up all the contents of their stomachs. Then the corsairs collect all that they have cast up and rummage through it to see if it contains any pearls or precious stones. For the corsairs say that when the merchants are captured they swallow their pearls and other gems to prevent their discovery. That is why they do not scruple to treat them to this drink.

There is pepper here in profusion and also ginger and indigo. There is also plenty of cotton, for the cotton trees grow here to a great height—as much as six paces after twenty years' growth. But when they reach this age they no longer produce cotton fit for spinning, but only for use in wadding or padded quilts. The growth of these trees is such that up to twelve years they produce cotton for spinning, but from twelve to twenty an inferior fibre only.

The manufactures of this kingdom include great quantities of leather goods, that is, the tanned hides of goat and buffalo, wild ox and unicorn and many other beasts. Enough is manufactured to load several ships a year. They are exported to Arabia and many other countries. For this kingdom supplies many other kingdoms and provinces. They also manufacture handsome mats of scarlet leather, embossed with birds and beasts and stitched with gold and silver of very find workmanship. They are so exquisite that they are a marvel to behold. You must understand that these leather mats of which I speak are such as the Saracens sleep on, and very good they are for the purpose. They also make cushions stitched with gold, so splendid that they are worth fully six marks of silver. And some of the mats are of such a quality that they are worth ten marks of silver. What more need I say? Suffice it that in this kingdom are produced leather goods of more consummate workmanship than anywhere in the world and of higher value.

Now that we have told you the facts about this kingdom in due order, we shall go on our way and tell you next of a kingdom called Thana.

Thana is a large and splendid kingdom lying towards the west.* It is ruled by a king and tributary to none. The people are idolaters and speak a language of their own. Pepper is not produced there in quantities, nor any other spice, as in the other kingdoms of which we have been speaking. There is no lack of incense, but it is not white but tinged with brown. This is a busy centre of commerce and a great resort of merchant shipping, exporting leather goods worked in various styles of excellent quality and design. It also exports plenty of good buckram and cotton as well. And merchants import in their ships gold and silver and brass and many other goods which the kingdom requires in exchange for such wares as they hope to sell profitably elsewhere.

Here is another item which is not creditable. I must tell you that this kingdom is the base for many corsairs who sally out to sea and take a heavy toll of merchant shipping. And, what is more, they act with the connivance of the king. For he has struck a bargain with the corsairs that they shall give him all the horses they may capture. And these form a considerable part of their booty, because, as I have mentioned earlier, there is a lively export trade in horses to all parts of India and few ships go thither without taking horses. That is why the king has made this bargain with the corsairs, by which they give him all the horses they take, while all the rest of the merchandise—gold, silver, and precious stones—they keep for themselves. Now this is a shameful compact and unworthy of a king.

Let us now pass on and talk of Cambay, a great kingdom lying towards the west. It has a king and a language of its own and is

---

* Z explains that 'west' must be understood in a purely relative sense, because Messer Marco was coming from the east 'and this account is given in accordance with his movements and routes'.

tributary to none. The people are idolaters. From this kingdom the pole star is seen more clearly; for the further you go towards the west,* the better view you get of the pole star. This kingdom is the centre of an active commerce. Indigo is plentiful here and of good quality. Buckram and cotton are produced in abundance for export to many provinces and kingdoms. There is also a brisk trade in leather goods of various style and manufacture, and this is on a big scale because the standard of workmanship is as high here as anywhere. There is also a wide range of other goods of which I will make no mention, as it would be tedious to enumerate them. Many merchant ships call here with various imports, especially gold, silver, and brass.† They bring in the products of their own countries and take out such local products as they hope to sell at a profit. You must know that in this kingdom there are no corsairs; the people live by trade and industry and are honest folk. There is nothing else worth mentioning.

Leaving Cambay, we come to the great kingdom of Somnath, which lies towards the west. The people are idolaters with a king and language of their own and tributary to none. They are not corsairs but live by trade and industry, as honest folk ought to do. For you may take it for a fact that this is a kingdom in which commerce thrives, a resort of merchants from many lands bringing in their wares and exporting others in return. Yet I must add that the people are harsh and stubborn in their idolatry. As there is nothing else worthy of note, we shall go on to speak of Kech-Makran.

This is a great kingdom with a king and language of its own. Some of the people are idolaters, but most are Saracens. They live by trade and industry. They have rice and wheat in profusion. The staple foods are rice, meat, and milk. Merchants come here in great numbers by sea and by land with a variety of merchandise and export the products of the kingdom. There is nothing else worthy of note.

I must tell you that this kingdom is the last province of India, in the quarter between west and north-west. All that lies between Maabar and this province—that is, all the kingdoms and provinces I have described from Maabar to here—constitute Greater India, the best

* Z: 'the north-west'.
† Z: 'and tutty'.

part of all the Indies. You must know that of this Greater India I have described only those provinces and cities that lie on the sea-coast. Of the inland regions I have told you nothing; for the tale would be too long in the telling. So we shall now leave this province and I will tell you of certain islands which also form part of the Indies.

the arabian sea

LET US BEGIN WITH TWO ISLANDS CALLED MALE ISLAND AND Female Island. Male Island lies in the sea some 500 miles south of Kech-Makran. The inhabitants are baptized Christians, observing the rule and customs of the Old Testament. For when a man's wife is pregnant he does not touch her again till she has given birth. After this he continues to abstain for another forty days. Then he touches her again as he will. But I assure you that in this island the men do not live with their wives or with any other women; but all the women live on the other island, which is called Female Island. You must know that the men of Male Island go over to Female Island and stay there for three months, that is March, April, and May. For these three months the men stay in the other island with their wives and take their pleasure with them. After this they return to their own island and get on with their business. I must tell you that in Male Island is found ambergris of fine quality. The inhabitants live on rice, milk, and meat. They are very good fishermen and catch so many good fish that they dry great quantities of them, so that they have plenty to eat all the year round and also sell them to others. They have no lord except a bishop, who in turn is subject to the archbishop of Socotra. They speak a language of their own. Male Island is about thirty miles distant from Female Island. According to their own account, their reason for not staying all the year round with their wives is that if they did so they could not live. The sons who are born are nursed by their mothers in Female Island till they are fourteen*years old, when they are sent to join their fathers in Male Island. When the men come to Female Island they sow the corn, which the women till and reap. The women also gather fruits, which grow there in great profusion. Otherwise they have nothing to do except to rear the children. Such then are the customs of these two islands. As there is nothing else worth mentioning, we shall go on to tell of Socotra.

The island of Socotra lies about 500 miles south of these two. The inhabitants are baptized Christians and have an archbishop. Amber-

* Z: 'twelve'.

gris is found here in great quantities. It is produced in the belly of the whale and the cachalot, which are the two biggest fish that exist in the sea. We shall tell you how whales are caught in these parts. The whale fishers have a lot of tunny fish, which they catch only for this purpose. These fish, which are very fat, they chop up small and put in big jars or pots, to which they add salt, making a plentiful supply of pickle. This done, a dozen or so of the fishers will take a small ship and loading her with these fish, and with all the pickle or briny fish-broth, will put out to sea. Then they will take certain remnants of rags or other refuse and tying them together in a bundle dip them in the pickle, which is very greasy. Having cast the bundle into the sea attached by a line to the ship, they will hoist sail and spend that day cruising to and fro on the high sea. Wherever they go, the grease in the pickle leaves a sort of trail over the water, recognizable by its oiliness. If it happens to pass by a place where a whale is, or the whale catches wind of the tunny fat lingering in the wake of the ship, he follows the trail by the scent of the tunny even for a hundred miles, if the vessel has sailed so far—so greedy is he to get at the tunny. When he has come so near the vessel that those on board catch sight of him, they throw him two or three morsels of tunny. When he has eaten he becomes intoxicated, as a man is with wine. Then some of them climb on his back, carrying an iron harpoon so barbed that once driven in it cannot be pulled out. One of them will stand this harpoon on the whale's head, while another hits it with a wooden mallet and immediately drives it home to its full length. For the whale in his drunken stupor scarcely feels the men on his back, so that they can do what they like. To the butt end of the harpoon is fastened a stout rope fully 300 paces long. At every fifty paces along the rope is fastened a cask and a plank. To the top of the cask is attached a flag, and at the bottom end is a counterpoise, so that the cask does not roll over but the flag stands upright. The last lap of the rope is made fast to a boat which they have with them. This boat will be manned by a few of the whalers, so that when the whale feeling himself wounded turns to flight, those who climbed on him to drive in the harpoon and are now left in the water may swim to the boat and scramble aboard. Then one of the casks is thrown into the water with the flag, thus allowing fifty paces of rope. When the whale dives and makes off, the boat to which the rope is fastened is towed along after him. If the whale seems to be pulling downwards too strongly, another cask with another flag is thrown overboard. And so, as he cannot pull down the casks under water, he becomes exhausted with towing them and finally succumbs to his wound and dies. The ship follows after, guided by the sight of the flags. When the whale is dead, the ship takes him in tow. Afterwards they bring him ashore on their island or a neighbouring one, where they sell him. And on a single whale they may clear a net profit of 1,000 *livres*.* This, then, is how they catch them.

The islanders produce fine cotton cloths and other merchandise in plenty, notably great quantities of salt fish—big fish of excellent quality. They live on rice, meat, and milk; for they have no other grain. They go stark naked, after the fashion of the other Indians who are idolaters. Many merchant ships visit this island with all sorts of goods for sale and export the local products at a good profit. You must know that all the merchant ships bound for Aden call in at this island.

I should explain that the archbishop of Socotra has nothing to do with the Pope at Rome, but is subject to an archbishop who lives at Baghdad. The archbishop of Baghdad sends out the archbishop of this island;† and he also sends out many others to different parts of the world, just as the Pope does. And these clergy and prelates owe obedience not to the church of Rome but to this great prelate of Baghdad whom they have as their Pope. Let me tell you further that many corsairs put in at this island at the end of a cruise and pitch camp here and sell their booty. And I assure you that they find a ready market, because the Christians of the island know that all these goods have been stolen from idolaters and Saracens, not from Christians, so they have no compunction in buying them. You should know also that, if the archbishop of Socotra dies, his successor must be sent from Baghdad; otherwise there could never be an archbishop here.

I give you my word that the Christians of this island are the most expert enchanters in the world. It is true that the archbishop does not approve of these enchantments and castigates and rebukes them for the practice. But this has no effect, because they say that their forefathers did these things of old and they are resolved to go on doing them. And the archbishop cannot override their resolve; but what he cannot cure he must needs endure. So the Christians of the

---

* R adds that they get ambergris from the belly and oil from the head.

† Z adds: 'or else the islanders elect him, and the Catholicus [cf. p. 37] confirms the election'.

island go on with their enchantments at their own sweet will. Let me tell you something about them. You may take it for a fact that these enchanters perform feats of many kinds and in no small measure bring about what they desire. If a pirate ship has done some damage to the islanders, she cannot sail from the island without first making amends for the damage done. She may set sail before a favouring breeze and make some headway on her course; but they will conjure up a headwind and force her to turn back. They can make the wind blow from whatever quarter they may wish. They can calm the sea at will, or raise a raging storm and a howling gale. They are masters of many other marvellous enchantments; but I think it better not to speak of these in this book, because these enchantments produce effects which, were men to hear of them, might set them marvelling overmuch. So let us leave it at that and say no more.

As there is nothing else worth mentioning in the island, we shall pass on to Madagascar.★

Madagascar is an island lying about 1,000 miles south of Socotra. The people are Saracens who worship Mahomet. They have four *sheikhs*—that is to say, four elders—who exercise authority over the whole island. You must know that this island is one of the biggest and best in the whole world. It is said to measure about 4,000 miles in circumference. The people live by trade and industry. More elephants are bred here than in any other province; and I assure you that not so many elephant tusks are sold in all the rest of the world put together as in this island and that of Zanzibar. The meat eaten here is only† camel-flesh. The number of camels slaughtered every day is so great that no one who had not seen it for himself could credit the report of it. They say that camel-flesh is better and more wholesome than any other;‡ that is why they eat it all the year round. The island produces scarlet sandalwood trees as big as the trees of our country. These trees would fetch a high price anywhere else; but here they have whole woods of them, as we have of other wild trees. They have plenty of ambergris, because whales abound in these seas,

★ This name is variously spelt in the MSS. Some variants, notably the form *Mogdaxo* found in Z, suggest a connexion with Mogadishu in Somalia, and there may well be some confusion here between the island and a region of the African mainland, as there seems to be below under Zanzibar, which in Marco's day may have denoted a large area in East Africa (Zenj). It seems clear that Marco did not visit either island.
† Z: 'for the most part'.
‡ Z adds: 'in this region'.

and also cachalots. And since they catch great numbers of both, they are never short of ambergris; for you know it is the whale that produces ambergris. They have leopards and lynxes and lions also in great numbers. Other beasts, such as harts, stags, and roebuck and such-like game animals, are also abundant, besides game-birds of many kinds. There are also many ostriches of huge size. The great diversity of birds, quite different from ours, is truly marvellous. Many marketable commodities are produced here. And many ships come here laden with cloth of gold and various silken fabrics, and much else besides that I will not attempt to specify, and exchange them for local products. They arrive and depart with full cargoes and the merchants make a handsome profit on the transaction.

I should add that ships cannot sail to the other islands that lie farther south, beyond Madagascar and Zanzibar, because the current sets so strongly towards the south that they would have little chance of returning. Therefore they do not venture to go. You may note that ships coming from Maabar to this island make the voyage in twenty days, whereas the return trip takes them all of three months; and this is due to the continual southward set of the current. It flows in the same direction all the time—southward, ever southward. These more southerly islands, which men do not willingly visit because of this southward drift, are very numerous, and it is said that they are inhabited by gryphon birds, which make their appearance here at certain seasons of the year. But you must know that they are by no means such as men in our country suppose, or as we portray them —half bird and half lion. According to the report of those who have seen them, it is not true that they are a blend of bird and lion; but I assure you that these men, the actual eyewitnesses, report that in build they are just like eagles but of the most colossal size. Let me tell you first what these eye-witnesses report and then what I have seen myself. They report that they are so huge and bulky that one of them can pounce on an elephant and carry it up to a great height in the air. Then it lets go, so that the elephant drops to earth and is smashed to pulp, whereupon the gryphon bird perches on the carcase and feeds at its ease. They add that they have a wing-span of thirty paces and their wing-feathers are twelve paces long and of a thickness proportionate to their length.* What I have seen myself I will tell you elsewhere, since that fits in better with the plan of the book.

* Z and R make the wing-span sixteen paces and the feathers eight.

Now that I have given you this second-hand account of the gryphon bird, let me add that the Great Khan sent special emissaries here to learn about these islands, and again to treat for the release of a previous emissary who had been detained as a captive. And these later emissaries, and the other who had been held captive, had much to tell him of the marvels of these strange islands. I assure you that they brought back with them the tusks of a wild boar of monstrous size. He had one of them weighed and found that its weight was 14 lb. You may infer for yourselves what must have been the size of the boar that had such tusks as this.* Indeed they declare that some of these boars are as big as buffaloes. There are also giraffes in plenty, and wild asses too. Altogether their beasts and birds are so different from ours that it is a marvel to hear tell of them and a greater marvel to behold them. To return for a moment to the gryphon birds, I should explain that the islanders call them *rukhs* and know them by no other name and have no idea what a gryphon is. But I feel sure from the monstrous size they attribute to the birds that they cannot be anything but gryphons.

Now that we have told you everything worth mentioning about this island and its specialities, we shall go on to tell of Zanzibar.

Zanzibar is a large and splendid island some 2,000 miles in circumference. The people are all idolaters. They have a king and a language of their own and pay tribute to none. They are a big-built race, and though their height is not proportionate to their girth they are so stout and so large-limbed that they have the appearance of giants. I can assure you that they are also abnormally strong, for one of them can carry a load big enough for four normal men. And no wonder, when I tell you that they eat food enough for five. They are quite black and go entirely naked except that they cover their private parts. Their hair is so curly that it can scarcely be straightened out with the aid of water. They have big mouths and their noses are so flattened and their lips and eyes so big that they are horrible to look at. Anyone who saw them in another country would say that they were devils.

They have elephants in plenty and drive a brisk trade in their tusks.

* R adds that the envoys also brought back a gryphon feather, which Marco himself measured and found to be eighty of his spans in length, while the girth of the quill was two of his palms. This passage is of doubtful authority; but something like it is perhaps implied by Marco's promise (not otherwise fulfilled) to tell what he had seen himself. The gigantic boars are presumably hippopotami.

R

They also have lions of a different sort from those found elsewhere, besides lynxes and leopards. What need of more words? They have all their animals different from those of the rest of the world. I can assure you that all their sheep are of one sort and one colour, that is, they are all white with black heads; in all the island you will not find ram or ewe that is not of this pattern. There are also many giraffes, which are very beautiful creatures to look at. Let me describe their appearance. You must know that the giraffe is short in the body and slopes down towards the rear, because its hind legs are short; but the front legs and neck are so long that the head is fully three paces above the ground. It has a small head and does no harm to anyone. Its colour is dappled red and white. And a very pretty sight it is. About elephants, let me add one fact that I forgot to mention: when the male wishes to cover the female, he makes a hollow in the ground and lays her in a supine position and mounts her in human fashion, because her genital organs are situated very near to the belly.

The women of this island are very ugly to look at. They have huge mouths, huge eyes, and huge noses, and their breasts are four times as big as those of other women. Altogether, their appearance is quite repulsive.

The staple diet here is rice, meat, milk, and dates. They have no grape wine; but they make a wine of rice and sugar and spices, and a very good drink it is. A brisk trade is plied here; for many merchant ships call at the island with a great variety of goods, all of which they dispose of before taking in a return cargo—chiefly of elephant tusks, which are very abundant here. There is also no lack of ambergris, since whales are caught in great numbers.

You should know that the men of the island are good fighters and acquit themselves very manfully in battle; for they are very brave and almost without fear of death. They have no horses, but fight on camels and elephants. They erect castles on the elephants' backs and cover them well and then climb up—from sixteen to twenty men together—armed with lances, swords, and stones. And this fighting on elephant-back is a formidable business. They have no arms but leather shields, lances, and swords, and the slaughter on both sides is heavy. Here is another point: when they are about to drive their elephants into the fray, they let them drink freely of their wine— that is, their own drink. This they do because, when an elephant has drunk this wine, he grows more ferocious and mettlesome and acquits himself proportionately better in battle.

Now we have told you a great part of what there is to tell about this island, its people, its fauna, and its products. As there is nothing else worth mentioning, we shall go on to speak of the great province of Abyssinia. But first we shall tell you one more thing about the Indies. You may take it for a fact that we have spoken only of the most distinguished provinces and kingdoms and islands, because there is no man in all the world who could tell the truth about all the islands of the Indies. But I have told you of the best and the flower of them all. For you must understand that a considerable proportion of the other islands of which I have made no mention are subject to those I have described. And you may know that in the Indian Ocean there are 12,700 islands, inhabited and uninhabited, as shown by the maps and writings of the practised seamen who ply in these waters. Now we have done with Greater India, which extends from Maabar to Kech-Makran and comprises thirteen major kingdoms of which we have described ten. Lesser India runs from Chamba to Motupalli and comprises eight major kingdoms. And be it always understood that I am here speaking only of kingdoms on the mainland and not counting the islands, which make up a vast number of kingdoms.

And now let us turn to the great province of Abyssinia, which is Middle India. You must know that the chief king of all this province is a Christian. And the other kings of the province, who are subject to him, number six, of whom three are Christians and three Saracens. The Christians of this province are distinguished by three marks on their faces, one from the forehead to the middle of the nose and one on either cheek. These marks are made by branding with a hot iron. And this is their baptism; for after they have been baptized in water, they are branded with this sign, which is a token of rank and a completion of the baptism. This is done when they are small; and they regard the custom not only as a badge of dignity but as an aid to health. There are also Jews in this country; and they have two marks, one on either cheek. And the Saracens have one mark only, that is, from the forehead to the middle of the nose. The Great King lives in the centre of the province, the Saracens over in the direction of Aden. In this province Messer St Thomas the Apostle preached. And after making some converts here he went to Maabar, where he met his death and where his body lies, as we have told you earlier in the book.*

* Z makes no mention of St Thomas here, but says that the Abyssinians were converted by apostles unknown.

And you must know that this great province of Abyssinia has many doughty men at arms and accomplished horsemen and no lack of horses. And there is great need of them. For they are at war with the Sultan of Aden and the Nubians and many others.* Let me tell you a notable episode that took place in the year of our Lord 1288.

The truth is that this sovereign lord of the province of Abyssinia, who is a Christian, expressed his wish to go on pilgrimage to worship at the sepulchre of Christ in Jerusalem. The barons declared that it would be too hazardous for him to go in person and recommended him instead to send a bishop or some other great prelate. The king acceded to their recommendation. He sent for a bishop who was a man of very saintly life and told him that he wished him to go in his place as far as Jerusalem to worship at the sepulchre of our Lord Jesus Christ. The bishop promised to do his bidding, as that of his liege lord. The king bade him make ready and set out with all possible speed.

What more shall I say? The bishop took leave of the king and made ready and started on his way in the guise of a pilgrim, very honourably arrayed. He journeyed so far by sea and land that he came to Jerusalem. He went straight to the sepulchre and worshipped there and did to it such reverence and honour as a Christian ought to do to such a holy and venerable thing as is this sepulchre. And he made a great offering there on behalf of the king who had sent him. When the bishop had done all that he came to do well and wisely, like the wise man that he was, then he set out on the homeward journey with all his company. He continued on his way till he came to Aden. Now you must know that in this country Christians are bitterly hated; the natives will not tolerate one of them, but look upon them as their mortal foes. So, when the sultan of Aden learnt that this bishop was a Christian and an emissary of the great king of Abyssinia, he had him arrested there and then and demanded to know whether he was a Christian. The bishop replied that he was so in very truth. The sultan told him that if he would not profess the faith of Mahomet, he would be put to utter shame and disgrace. The bishop answered that he would sooner be killed than renounce his faith. When the sultan heard this answer, he abused him shamefully and ordered that he should be circumcised. So a band of his men laid hands on him and circumcised him in the fashion of the Saracens. This done, the sultan avowed that this affront had been put upon him in scorn and con-

* R adds that, from continuous military exercise, they are reputed the best fighting men in all the provinces of India.

tempt of the king his master. And with those words he let him go. The bishop was grieved to the heart at the shame he had suffered; but he comforted himself with the thought that he had suffered it for the sake of the Christian faith, and therefore the Lord God would requite his soul in the next world.

Not to make too long a tale of it, you may take it that, when the bishop was healed and able to ride, he went on his way with his company. He travelled by sea and land till he came to Abyssinia to his lord the king. The king was overjoyed to see him and made him heartily welcome, and then asked for tidings of the sepulchre. The bishop told him the whole truth about it, and the king accounted it a holy matter and reposed great faith in it. Next he reported how the sultan of Aden had had him circumcised as a mark of scorn and contempt for his master. When the king heard how his bishop had been put to shame in contempt of himself, he was so angry that he came near to dying. In a voice that all those about him could plainly hear he vowed that he would neither wear his crown nor rule his realm if he did not wreak such vengeance that all the world would speak of it. Be well assured, therefore, that he mustered a great force of horsemen and footmen and elephants bearing stoutly fortified castles manned by fully a score of men apiece.* When all his force was arrayed, he set out on his way and came to the kingdom of Aden.† And the kings of that province marched out with a great host of Saracens, both horse and foot, to repel the invasion and took up a strong position in a pass. When the Abyssinians reached this pass and found it defended in force, a bloody battle began. But the upshot was that the kings of the Saracens, who were three in number, could not withstand the onslaught of the king of Abyssinia, whose troops were not deficient either in numbers or in prowess. For Christians are far more valiant than Saracens. The Saracens were forced to retreat, and the Christian monarch with his men entered the kingdom of Aden. Be well assured that in this pass a great multitude of Saracens met their death. What more need I say? Suffice it that at three or four strong positions the Saracens opposed the advance of the

* Z says twelve or fourteen men, explaining that at other times they carried as many as twenty, but in war they found it more convenient to limit themselves to a dozen. Despite this show of precision, the figures are impossibly high. Probably the whole attribution of war elephants to the Abyssinians is pure fantasy, as it almost certainly was in the case of Zanzibar (above p. 258).

† Polo seems to conceive this kingdom, perhaps rightly, as including territory on the western shore of the Red Sea.

Abyssinians into the kingdom of Aden; but all their efforts went for nothing, and vast quantities of them were killed. When the king of the Christians had spent about a month in the territory of his enemies, causing great havoc and destruction and killing great numbers of Saracens, he declared that now the insult to his bishop was well avenged and they could return with honour to their own country. Besides, he could do no further damage to the enemy, because he would have to traverse passes of great strength in which a few defenders could inflict heavy losses. So the Christians withdrew from the kingdom of Aden and did not stop till they had reached their own land of Abyssinia. And now you have heard how well and amply the bishop was avenged on these Saracen dogs. For the numbers killed were almost past counting, not to speak of all the lands that were ravaged and laid waste. And no wonder; for it is not fitting that Saracen dogs should lord it over Christians.

Now let us pass on and tell you more about the province of Abyssinia itself. You may take it for a fact that this province is bountifully supplied with all the means of life. The people live on rice, wheat, meat, milk, and sesame. They have elephants; but these are not native to the country but imported from the islands of the other Indies. But giraffes are native and plentiful. Lions, leopards, and lynxes abound, and a multitude of other beasts different from those of our countries. There are also wild asses in plenty and birds of many sorts unlike those found elsewhere. They have the prettiest hens to be seen anywhere, and enormous ostriches scarcely smaller than a donkey. In short the diversity of animals is such that it would be tedious to enumerate them. But you may be well assured that they have no lack of game, whether beast or bird. They have gaily coloured parrots and monkeys of many sorts, including 'Paul cats' and 'Maimon cats' of such distinctive appearance that some of them can almost be said to have the faces of men.*

Finally, let me add that Abyssinia has many cities and towns and the population includes a class of merchants living by trade. Good cotton and buckram cloths are woven here. There is much else that might be told, but it cannot claim a place in our book. So we shall go on now to speak of Aden.

In Aden there is a lord who goes by the title of sultan. The people are all Saracens who worship Mahomet and bear no good will to-

* R adds that this province is very rich in gold.

269

wards Christians. There are many cities and towns. Aden itself is the port to which all the ships from India come with their merchandise. It is a great resort of merchants. In this port they transfer their goods to other small ships, which sail for seven days along a river. At the end of this time they unload the goods and pack them on camels and carry them thus for about thirty days, after which they reach the river of Alexandria; and down this river they are easily transported to Alexandria itself. This is the route from Aden by which the Saracens of Alexandria receive pepper and spices and precious wares; and there is no other route as easy and as short as this.

Aden is also the starting point for many merchant ships sailing to the Indies. From it they export to India many fine Arab chargers, on which they make a handsome profit. For I would have you know that they sell a good horse in India for 100 marks of silver and more. And I assure you that the sultan of Aden derives a very large revenue from the heavy duties he levies from the merchants coming and going in his country. Indeed, thanks to these, he is one of the richest rulers in the world.

Let me tell you of one thing this sultan did that inflicted a heavy blow on the Christians. For you must know that, when the sultan of Egypt marched against the town of Acre and captured it, to the great loss of the Christians, this sultan of Aden contributed to his forces fully 30,000 horsemen and 40,000 camels, much to the advantage of the Saracens and the detriment of the Christians. And this he did more from ill will to the Christians than from any good will to the sultan of Egypt or from any love he bears him.

We would have you know that the ships of Aden, Hormuz, Kais, and elsewhere that sail on the Indian Ocean are often wrecked because of their frailty. If the sea there were as rough and boisterous as in our parts and as often racked by storms, not a vessel would ever complete her voyage without suffering shipwreck. But what do you think the merchants do, and the seamen who man these craft? They carry with them a number of air-tight skin bags. When tempest threatens and the seas run high, they load these bags with pearls and precious stones, if they have any, and with their clothes and a supply of essential foodstuffs and then they lash them all together to form a raft or float, so that if the ship founders in the storm they are left on the bags. And then after drifting this way or that before the gale for days on end they are at length driven to shore, no matter how far out they may be—even as much as 200 miles. When they are at sea on these rafts, every time they want to eat or drink they take supplies from the bags, which they afterwards inflate by blowing. In this way they escape. But the ships with the bulky merchandise are lost.

Let us go on now to tell of a large city which forms part of the province of Aden but has a petty ruler of its own. This city, which lies about 400 miles north-west of the port of Aden, is called Shihr. It is ruled by a count, who maintains strict justice in his domain. He has several cities and towns under his sway but is himself subject to the sultan of Aden. The people are Saracens and worship Mahomet. The city has a very good port; for I assure you that many merchant-ships come here well loaded with goods from India, and from here they export many goods to India. In particular they export innumerable fine chargers and sturdy pack-horses of great worth and price, on which the merchants make a handsome profit.

This province produces great quantities of excellent white incense, and also dates in great abundance. No grain is grown here except rice, and not much of that; but it is imported from abroad at a big profit. Fish is plentiful, notably tunnies of large size, which are so abundant that two of them can be bought for a Venetian groat. The staple diet consists of rice, meat, and fish. They have no grape wine, but make a wine of sugar, rice, and dates. And let me tell you something else. They have sheep here that have no ears, nor even ear-holes; but in the place where ears ought to be they have little horns. They are small creatures and very pretty. And here is something else that may strike you as marvellous: their domestic animals—sheep, oxen, camels, and little ponies—are fed on fish. They are reduced to this diet because in all this country and in all the surrounding regions there is no grass; but it is the driest place in the world. The fish on which these animals feed are very small and are caught in March, April, and May in quantities that are truly amazing. They are then dried and stored in the houses and given to the animals as food throughout the year. I can tell you further that the animals also eat them alive, as soon as they are drawn out of the water. There are also big fish here—and good ones too—in great profusion and very cheap. They even make biscuit out of fish. They chop a pound or so of fish into little morsels and dry it in the sun and then store it in their houses and eat it all the year round like biscuit. As for the incense of which I have spoken, which grows here in such profusion, the lord buys it for 10 gold bezants a *cantar* and then sells it to foreign merchants and others for 40 bezants a *cantar*. The lord of Shihr does this on behalf of the sultan of the province of Aden. For the sultan of Aden has incense bought up throughout his dominions at the price of 10 bezants and afterwards sold at 40, from which he derives an immense profit. As there is nothing else here worth mentioning, we shall go on to speak of Dhofar.

Dhofar is a fine city of great size and splendour lying about 500 miles north-west of Shihr. Here again the people are Saracens and worship Mahomet, and are subject to a count who is likewise subject to the sultan of Aden. You must understand that this city is still within the province of Aden. The city stands on the sea and has a very good port, frequented by many merchant ships that import and export great quantities of merchandise. Many good Arab steeds, and horses from other lands as well, are brought here, and the merchants make a handsome profit on them. The city has many other cities and towns under its sway. Here again good incense grows in profusion—I will tell you how. It is produced by trees of no great size, like little fir trees. They are gashed with knives in various places, and out of these gashes oozes the incense. Some of it even oozes from the tree itself without any gashing, in consequence of the great heat that prevails. As for the Arab steeds that are brought here, the merchants afterwards export them to India, making a good profit on the deal. As there is nothing else worth mentioning, we shall go on to tell of the gulf of Kalhat.

Kalhat is a large city lying inside the gulf which is also called Kalhat. It is a fine city on the sea-coast 600 miles north-west of Dhofar. The people are Saracens who worship Mahomet. They are subject to Hormuz; and whenever the *malik* of Hormuz is at war with neighbours more powerful than himself, he comes to this city, because it is strongly built and situated, so that here he is afraid of no one. No corn is grown here, but it is imported by sea from other places. This city has a very good port, much frequented by merchant ships from India. They find a ready market here for their wares, since it is a centre from which spices and other goods are carried to various inland cities and towns. Many fine war horses are exported from here to India, to the great gain of the merchants. The total number of horses shipped to India from this port and the others I have mentioned is past all reckoning.

The city stands at the mouth or entrance of the gulf of Kalhat, so that no ship can enter or leave the gulf except by leave of its rulers. The *malik* of this city thus has a powerful hold over the sultan of Kerman, to whom he is subject. For sometimes the sultan imposes some due on the *malik* of Hormuz or one of his brethren, and they refuse to pay it, and the sultan sends an army to enforce payment. At such times they leave Hormuz and take ship and cross over to Kalhat and stay there and do not let a single ship pass. This means a great loss to the sultan, who is accordingly obliged to make peace with the *malik* and moderate his demands for money. I should add that the *malik* of Hormuz has a castle that is even stronger than this city and commands the gulf and the sea even more effectively.

You may take it for a fact that the people of this country live on dates and salt fish, of which they enjoy abundant supplies. But admittedly there are some among them, men of wealth and consequence, who eat foods of better quality.

Now that we have told you all about the city of Kalhat and the gulf, we shall go on to tell you of Hormuz.

Hormuz lies about 300 miles north-north-west of Kalhat. A journey of about 500 miles west-north-west of Kalhat brings the traveller to Kais; but let us leave Kais and speak of Hormuz.

Hormuz is a great and splendid city on the sea, governed by a *malik* and with several cities and towns in subjection to it. The people are Saracens who worship Mahomet. The climate is excessively hot —so hot that the houses are fitted with ventilators to catch the wind. The ventilators are set to face the quarter from which the wind blows and let it blow into the house. This they do because they cannot endure the overpowering heat. But no more of this now, because we told you earlier in the book about Hormuz and Kais and Kerman. Since we went out by another route, it is fitting that we should return to this point. But as I have just remarked, since we gave you an account of this country earlier, we will not loiter here now, but will go on to talk of Turkestan, as you will plainly hear.

northern regions
& tartar wars*

IN TURKESTAN THERE IS A KING CALLED KAIDU, WHO IS nephew to the Great Khan. For he was son of the son of Chaghatai, who was the Great Khan's brother german. He has many cities and towns under his sway and is a very great lord. He is a Tartar and so are his people. They are good fighting men. And no wonder; for they are all inured to war. I assure you that Kaidu is never at peace with the Great Khan, but maintains constant warfare against him. You must understand that Turkestan lies north-west of this route from Hormuz of which we have been speaking. It lies beyond the river Gihon and extends towards the north as far as the dominions of the Great Khan.

I can tell you that Kaidu has already fought many battles with the Great Khan's men. Let me explain how the quarrel arose between them. You may take it for a fact that Kaidu was continually asking the Great Khan for his share of the conquests they had made, in particular a part of the provinces of Cathay and Manzi. And the Great Khan used to answer that he would willingly give him his share, as he did to his other sons, on condition that, like them, he would come to his court and his council whenever he was summoned. Furthermore he wished Kaidu to be obedient to him, as were his other sons and his barons. On these terms he was willing to give him a share of their conquests. Kaidu, who did not trust his uncle, declined to go. He professed himself ready to be obedient where he was; but he would not go to the Great Khan's court for anything in the world, because he feared for his life. This was the beginning of the quarrel between the two. And from it sprang a great war and many a fierce-fought battle. All the year long the Great Khan kept his armies all round Kaidu's dominions, so that neither Kaidu nor his men should do any harm to his land or his subjects. But King

* This chapter consists largely of stereotyped speeches and descriptions of battles whose interminably repeated formulae have no claim to historical accuracy and certainly do less than justice to Tartar eloquence, strategy, and tactics (see Introduction, p. 12). I have felt justified in pruning to some slight extent the verbosity of the original.

Kaidu, for all the Great Khan's armies, has not ceased from incursions into his territory and has fought several engagements with forces that attacked him. I can tell you that, if he exerted all his strength, Kaidu could put fully 100,000 horsemen in the field, all seasoned warriors inured to warfare and battle. Moreover he has with him several barons of the imperial lineage—that is, of the lineage of Chinghiz Khan; for since Chinghiz was the founder of the Empire, the first to hold lordship and to conquer half the world, they speak of his stock as the imperial lineage. And now let me tell you something of the battles that Kaidu fought with the armies of the Great Khan.

First, I will describe their method of fighting. Every soldier is ordered to carry into battle sixty arrows, thirty smaller ones for piercing and thirty larger with broad heads for discharging at close quarters. With these latter they wound one another in the face or arms and cut through bow-strings and inflict heavy losses. When they have shot away all their arrows, they lay hold of sword or club and deal mighty blows. After this explanation, let us return to the matter in hand.

The fact is that in the year of our Lord 1266, King Kaidu with his cousins, one of whom was named Yesudar, assembled a great host and attacked two of the Great Khan's barons, who were also cousins of Kaidu but held land of the Great Khan. Their names were Chibai and Chiban, and they were sons of Chaghatai, who was a baptized Christian and brother german to the Great Khan Kubilai. What shall I tell you? Kaidu with his men joined battle with these two, who also had large forces at their command, so that the total numbers engaged, counting both sides together, amounted to some 100,000 horsemen. The battle was fiercely contested, and many fell on either side. At length the victory fell to Kaidu, who inflicted heavy losses on his opponents. But the two brothers, his cousins, escaped unscathed; for they had good horses, which bore them speedily from the field.

After this victory Kaidu increased in arrogance and pride. Returning victorious to his own country he remained at peace for two years, and in all this time the Great Khan made no move against him. At the end of the two years he assembled another host, an immense multitude of horsemen. He knew that at Karakorum was a son of the Great Khan, whose name was Numughan, and with him was George, the grandson of Prester John. These two barons also had a huge force of cavalry. Kaidu set out from his kingdom with all his host and they rode on their way, without encountering any adventure worthy of note, till they drew near to Karakorum. When the two barons got word of his approach, they showed no sign of dismay but gave proof of hardihood and valour. They mustered all their forces, which amounted to more than 60,000 horsemen, and marched out against the invaders till they had come within ten miles of King Kaidu, and then they pitched their camp in good order. And Kaidu with all his host was encamped in that very plain. So both parties rested and prepared themselves as best they could for combat. Not to make too long a tale of it, you must know that on the third day after the Great Khan's son and Prester John's grandson had arrived, both parties armed and arrayed themselves at an early hour. Neither side had any great advantage over the other; for each comprised some 60,000 horsemen, well armed with bows and arrows, swords and clubs and shields. Each was drawn up in six squadrons under able commanders. Soon both armies were drawn up in battle array and only waiting for the sound of the kettle-drums. For the Tartars do not dare to start a battle till their lord's drums begin to beat; and while they are waiting it is their custom to sing and to play very sweetly on their two-stringed* instruments and to make very merry in expectation of battle. Accordingly, both armies, while they waited for the sound of the kettle-drums, sang and played so well that it was a marvel to hear. Then at last the drums began to beat, and the soldiers made no more delay, but both sides alike charged against the foe. They set their hands to their bows and the arrows to the string. Then you might have seen the air filled with arrows as though with rain and many a man and many a horse mortally stricken. Then you might have heard such a clamour and a tumult that the thunder of heaven would have gone unheard. Then none could have doubted that they were mortal enemies. So long as their arrows lasted, those who were fit and able did not cease to shoot—for you may well imagine that many of them were dead or wounded to death, so that it was in an ill hour for both armies that that day's fighting began. When all the arrows were spent, they put their bows in their bow-cases, set hand to sword or club and fell upon one another, dealing lusty blows. Then you might have seen hands and arms hacked off and man after man biting the dust. For be well assured that it was not long after the conflict that all the ground was piled with dead and dying. Without a doubt King Kaidu displayed great prowess. But for his presence, his army would more than once have fled the field.

* Z: 'four-stringed'.

But he fired them with such ardour that they held their ground stubbornly. And on the other side also the two leaders acquitted themselves manfully. All in all, this was one of the bloodiest battles ever fought between Tartar armies. The clash of swords and the battering of clubs drowned the thunder of heaven. Both armies spent the last ounce of their strength in unstinted efforts to inflict defeat. But all to no purpose. The fighting lasted till evening, but neither army had availed to drive the other from the field. It was a piteous sight to see how many lay slain on either side. In an ill hour indeed had that day's strife begun. How many wives were widowed! How many children orphaned! How many mothers and sweethearts driven to lamentation and weeping! When the sun went down upon the battlefield, the issue was still undecided. Both armies withdrew to their camps, so wearied and far spent that there was not a man of them but had more mind to rest than to fight. Glad they were to rest that night after the deadly work of the day. When morning broke, Kaidu the king, who had received tidings that the Great Khan was sending a mighty host to attack him, made up his mind that he would do ill to loiter. So, in the first light of dawn, he and his troops donned their armour and mounted their steeds and set out on their homeward journey. When the Great Khan's son and Prester John's grandson saw them depart, they were too worn and weary for pursuit, but let them go in peace. And Kaidu and his men rode on their way and did not stop till they had come to their own kingdom, to Samarkand in Turkestan. And there they stayed without further warfare.

The Great Khan was bitterly angry with Kaidu for the continual damage he did to his people and his land. He thought to himself that, if he were not his nephew, he would never escape the ill death he had earned. But the ties of blood restrained him from robbing his kinsman of life or lands. And so Kaidu escaped death at the hands of the Great Khan.

Now you must know that Kaidu had a daughter called Aiyaruk, a Tartar name which signifies 'Bright Moon'. This damsel was so strong that in all the kingdom there was no squire or gallant who could vanquish her. But I assure you that she used to vanquish them all. The king her father wished to give her a husband. But she steadfastly refused, declaring that she would never take a husband till she found some nobleman who could get the better of her in a trial of strength. And the king her father had given her the privilege of marrying whom she would. Now you must first understand that it is a custom commonly observed among the Tartars that, if any king, prince, or other noble wishes to take a wife, he does not look for a woman of rank or a social equal; but, if she is beautiful and fair to look upon, he takes her to wife even though she is not of noble birth. For they say that no family or stock takes its name from the woman but from the man only, as a man is never called 'son of Bertha' or 'son of Mary', but 'son of Peter', or 'son of Martin'. That is why in choosing a wife they pay no regard to the nobility of her birth but only to her charm and beauty.

When the king's daughter heard that her father had granted her the privilege of marrying whom she would, she was overjoyed. She made it known in many parts of the world that any youth of gentle birth might come and try his strength with her and if he could vanquish her she would take him as her husband. When word of this offer got abroad in many lands and kingdoms, I assure you that many gentlemen from many parts came to make trial with her. And this is how the trial was made. The king with a great throng of men and women was in the great hall of the palace. Then his daughter entered the hall, wearing a tunic of sendal richly adorned, and the youth entered also wearing a tunic of sendal.★ This was the bargain: if the youth could so far vanquish her as to force her to the ground, he should have her to wife; if she vanquished him, he must forfeit a hundred horses to her. In this way she had gained more than 10,000 horses. For never a squire nor a gallant could she find who was a match for her. And no wonder; for she was so well formed in every limb, so big-built, and so strapping, that she was little short of a giantess.

Now it happened in the year of Our Lord 1280 that there came the son of a rich king who was very handsome and youthful. He came attended by a very fine company and leading a thousand very fine horses to try his strength with the damsel. King Kaidu was delighted; for it was his wish that he should have his daughter to wife, since he knew that he was a son of the king of Pumar.† And he urged her privately to let herself be vanquished. But she declared that she would not do so for anything in the world. On the appointed day the king and queen and a great gathering of men and women

★ In Z's version the trial takes place in a tent and both contestants wear garments of deer-skin.
† This name appears in one MS only.

were assembled in the great hall. Then in came the king's daughter and the king's son, both so handsome and so winsome that they were a marvel to look upon. And I assure you that this youth was so sturdy and stalwart that he found no one who could match him in strength. The bargain was duly struck and the youth pledged himself, if he was vanquished, to forfeit the thousand horses he had brought especially for this contest. Then the pair came to grips. And all those who were present said among themselves that they wished the youth might win, so that he might wed the king's daughter. And the king and queen shared their wish. But why make a long tale of it? Suffice it that, when the two had come to grips, one pulled this way and the other that. But the upshot was that the king's daughter vanquished her opponent and threw him on the pavement of the palace.* And so the prince lost his thousand horses. And such was his grief and shame that, as soon as he had risen to his feet, he lost no time in departing with all his company and returning to his father, bitterly mortified and ashamed that after finding no man who could stand against him he should be worsted by a woman. And I assure you that there was no one in the hall who did not share his grief.

King Kaidu took this same daughter of his into many battles. And in every affray there was never a knight more doughty than she. For many a time it happened that she plunged in among the enemy and seized a knight by force and carried him off into her own ranks.

Now that I have told you the story of this damsel, let me tell you next of a great battle between King Kaidu and Arghun, son of Abaka, khan of the Levant. You must know that Abaka, the lord of the Levant, ruled over many provinces and territories, and his lands bordered on those of King Kaidu in the neighbourhood of the Solitary Tree, which in the Book of Alexander is called 'the Dry Tree'. In order to protect his people and territories from attack by Kaidu and his men, he sent his son Arghun with a large force of cavalry to the region of the Dry Tree as far as the river Gihon. And Arghun stayed there, in the plain of the Dry Tree, and kept careful guard over the many cities and towns of the region.

Now it happened that Kaidu got together a great force of cavalry under the command of his brother, a brave and able soldier named Barak, and told Barak that he wished him to march against Arghun. Barak promised to do his bidding and exert all his power against

* Z: 'on the ground'.

Arghun and his men. He set out accordingly with all his host, a formidable array, and rode for many days without encountering any adventure worthy of record till they reached the river Gihon within ten miles of Arghun's position.* Meanwhile, what of Arghun? When he knew that Barak had come with a large force, he arrayed all his troops. And not more than three days passed before the two armies were both in camp, fully arrayed and armed. When the opposing hosts were drawn up and the kettle-drums began to beat, they lost no time in charging into the fray. Then you might have seen such volleys of arrows loosed on either side that they filled the air like rain. When both armies had shot away their arrows and many a man and many a steed lay slain, then they set hand to sword or club and laid about them in brutal and unsparing conflict, hewing off hands and arms, slaughtering steeds, and dealing cruel wounds. So loud was the tumult and the uproar that the thunder of heaven would have gone unheard. It was not long till the ground was strewn with dead and dying. What need of many words? Suffice it that Barak and his men could not withstand the onslaught of Arghun. He retired with his men and returned across the river. And Arghun and his men pursued them with great slaughter.

It was not long after this victory that news came to Arghun that Abaka his father was dead. Deeply grieved, he set out with his army to return to his father's court and claim the succession. But he had a journey of forty days to go before he reached it. Meanwhile, it so happened that a brother of Abaka named Ahmad Sultan, who had turned Saracen, had no sooner heard of his brother's death than he decided that he might become lord in his place, since Arghun was so far away. So he mustered a large force, went straight to Abaka's court and seized the lordship for himself. At the same time he found such a quantity of treasure that the sum is almost past belief and lavished it so freely on his barons and knights that it was truly marvellous. And the recipients fell to saying that Ahmad Sultan was a good lord and they would have no other. And indeed he exercised his lordship well and to the general satisfaction. But he was guilty of one discreditable act, for which he was blamed by many; for he took all Abaka's wives and kept them for himself.

Now you may be sure that he had not been lord for long when he had news that Arghun was approaching with a large army. He wasted no time and showed no dismay, but resolutely summoned

* This battle took place in 1269 in the region north of Herat.

s

281

his barons and his followers. Within a week he had got together a great quantity of horsemen, who were eager to march against Arghun and declared among themselves that they asked nothing better than to kill him or to seize him and put him to great torment. When he had mustered fully 60,000 cavalry, he set out to meet Arghun, and after riding for ten days he learnt that Arghun was only five days' march away and was advancing with a force fully equal to his own. Thereupon he pitched camp in a good wide plain, well suited for a battlefield, and there awaited his coming. When the army was duly encamped, he summoned all his men to an assembly and addressed them thus:

'Good sirs, you know well that I have a right to be liege lord of all that belonged to my brother Abaka, because I was son of the same father and it fell to me to conquer all the lands and provinces that we now hold. It is true that Arghun was my brother's son and some might say that the lordship should be his. But, with all due respect to such as would say this, they do not reason well. Since my brother held the lordship for so long, that is a good cause why I should have it after his death. During his life I was fully entitled to a half of it; but in my magnanimity I left it all to him. I beg of you therefore, since the matter stands as I have told you, let us defend our right against Arghun and let the kingdom and the lordship remain to us all. For I give you my word that I ask for myself only the honour and renown. Yours shall be the profit and the substance and lordships throughout our lands and provinces. Now I will say no more; for I know that you are wise men who love the right and will act in accordance with our general honour and advantage.'

With these words he ended his speech. And the barons and knights and the others who were present and heard what he had to say replied with one voice that they would not fail him so long as they had breath in their bodies and would stand by him against all the world and against Arghun in particular. They told him to have no fear but that they would deliver Arghun into his hands. So Ahmad was assured of the good will of his followers. And they had no more to say till battle was joined.

To turn now to Arghun, you may be well assured that, when he learnt that Ahmad was waiting for him with such a multitude at his command, he did not remain unmoved. But he told himself that to give way to melancholy and show that he was afraid of his enemies would do great harm to his cause, because his men would be disheartened. So he resolved to put a brave face on it. He sent for all his barons and counsellors, and having assembled a large company in his pavilion—for he had chosen a favourable site to pitch camp—he addressed them thus:

'Brothers and friends, you know how dearly my father loved you. While he lived, he looked on you as brothers and sons. And you know in how many great battles you took part with him and how you helped him to conquer all the lands he held. You know too that I was the son of the man who loved you so well. And I myself love you as I love my own life. Therefore, since this is truth that I have told you, both right and reason demand that you should help me against one who defies both reason and right and wishes to do us no less a wrong than to disinherit us of our lands. Remember too that he is not of our faith but a renegade—a Saracen who worships Mahomet. Think what a worthy thing it would be that Saracens should lord it over Tartars! Is it not fitting then, brothers and friends, that heart and will should grow strong within you to do what must be done to ensure that this shall not be? I ask every man of you to play a man's part and to strive with might and main to fight so bravely that we shall win this battle and the lordship will remain with us, not pass to the Saracens. Assuredly every man may be confident of victory, since we are fighting for the right and our foes for the wrong. I will say no more, but to ask every man to resolve to do his best.'

With this he made an end. And when the barons and knights there present heard these words so well and wisely spoken, each one said to himself that he would sooner die than do less than his utmost to win the battle. While the rest stood silent and speechless, one great baron rose to his feet and spoke as follows:

'My lord Arghun, we all know without a shadow of doubt that what you have spoken is the truth. So I will answer for all your men who are here to fight by your side that we will pledge our word not to fail while we have breath in our bodies. We would rather die one and all than be robbed of victory in this battle. Our assurance of victory does indeed rest in the great right that is on our side and the great wrong on theirs. Therefore I advise and urge that we prepare with all possible speed to go and seek out our enemy. And I adjure all my comrades to give such an account of themselves in this battle that men will speak of us throughout the world.'

The veteran said no more, and no one else wished to add a word;

for all were of one mind with him and asked no better than to join battle with the foe. And when the next day dawned, Arghun and his men were early afoot, all agog to be at the enemy. They rode till they came to the plain where Ahmad was encamped, and pitched their camp in due order about ten miles from his. Then Arghun picked two men in whom he reposed great faith and sent them to his uncle charged with a message. The two envoys, who were men of ripe years and discretion, took leave of their lord, mounted their horses, and were off without more ado. They rode straight to the camp and dismounted at Ahmad's pavilion, where they found him with a great company of barons. They knew him well, and he them. They greeted him courteously, and Ahmad with a cheerful mien made them welcome and seated them in front of him in the pavilion. After a brief wait one of the two envoys rose to his feet and spoke thus:

'Lord Ahmad, your nephew Arghun marvels greatly at what you have done—that you have robbed him of his lordship and come to join with him in mortal combat. Assuredly it is not well done and you have not acted as a good uncle ought towards his nephew. Therefore he sends this message by us: that he begs you in all friendliness, as one who looks upon you not only as his uncle but as his father, to desist from this conduct and let there be no battle or enmity between you. He declares that he is willing to treat you with the respect due to an elder and a father and to make you lord over all his land. That is the message and the request that your nephew sends you by our mouths.'

That was all he said. And this was Ahmad's reply: 'Good sirs, what my nephew says is beside the point. The land is mine, not his; for I conquered it no less than his father did. Tell him therefore that, if he so desires, I will make him a great lord and give him land enough, and he will rank with my sons and the greatest barons in my service. If this does not content him, let him be well assured that I will do my utmost to put him to death. This is my fixed resolve, and you will never have another offer or other terms from me.'

When the messengers heard these words of the sultan, they asked again: 'Is this the only answer you will give us?'

'That it is,' said Ahmad. 'You will get no other so long as I live.'

At these words the messengers made no longer stay, but set out at once and rode back to their lord's camp. They dismounted at Arghun's pavilion and told him what they had learnt of Ahmad. At this he was moved to such a pitch of anger that he cried aloud, so that all around could hear him: 'Since my uncle has done me such a wrong, I will not live or rule if I do not wreak a revenge of which the whole world will speak.' Then, addressing himself to his barons and his knights, he added: 'Now nothing remains but to deal out the speediest possible death to these false traitors. Tomorrow let us attack them and do what in us lies to crush them.'

So throughout that night they made all needful preparation for a pitched battle. And Ahmad Sultan, who had learnt from his spies that Arghun was planning to attack on the morrow, made his preparations likewise and urged his men to acquit themselves bravely.

When morning came, Arghun and his men armed themselves for the fray. He disposed his troops skilfully in battle array, warmly exhorted them to do their best, and advanced upon the enemy. And Ahmad, who had done likewise, did not await his coming, but advanced to meet him. When the two armies met face to face, they were so eager to come to blows that they charged straight into murderous combat. Then you might have seen showers of arrows pouring from the sky like rain and heard a loud and lamentable out-cry of riders falling to the ground stricken with mortal wounds. When the arrows were spent, they laid about them lustily with sword and club, hewing off hands and arms and heads, and drowning with their uproar the thunder of heaven. How many a lusty warrior was robbed of life by that day's work! How many a woman doomed to life-long weeping and lamentation! But why make a long tale of it? Enough that Arghun fought valiantly that day and set his men an example of true prowess. But all in vain. Ill-chance and fortune went against him and worked his discomfiture. When his men could endure no longer, they turned heel and fled as best they could. And Ahmad and his men pursued them with great slaughter. And I must tell you that in that pursuit Arghun himself was captured, and with his capture the victors abandoned the pursuit and returned to their tents rejoicing. And Ahmad had his nephew bound with fetters and vigilantly guarded.

After his victory Ahmad, who was a man much given to lechery, elected to return to his court to take his pleasure with all the fair ladies whom he had at his disposal. He left one of his chief *maliks* in command of all his army, charging him to guard Arghun as he valued his life and to bring the troops home by easy stages so as to spare their strength. The *malik* promised to obey his command.

Ahmad with a large retinue set out on his return journey. And Arghun was left a prisoner in fetters, so sorrowful that he longed to die.

Now it so happened that a great Tartar baron, a man of ripe years, took pity on Arghun and reflected that they were guilty of great wickedness and disloyalty in keeping their lord a prisoner. So he resolved to do his utmost to have him set free. Without a moment's delay he went to a number of other great barons and pointed out to them what a wicked deed it was to hold their lord a prisoner, and what a good deed it would be to set him free and make him their lord, as by right he ought to be. When the others had heard what he had laid before them, and reflected that he was one of the wisest of men and acknowledged that what he said was no more than the truth, they were all of one mind and told him that they would do this gladly. Thereupon Boga, the man who had put forward this proposal, and his confederates, whose names were Elchidai, Togan, Tegana, Togachar, Ulatai, and Samagar, went to the pavilion where Arghun was imprisoned, and Boga, as the ringleader in this conspiracy, addressed him thus:

'Lord Arghun, we are well aware that we did wrong to take you prisoner. So we are now resolved to make amends by setting you free and accepting you for our liege lord, as you ought rightfully to be.'

When Arghun heard these words, he believed they were spoken in mockery and answered in bitter anger: 'Good Sirs, you do great wrong to mock me. Is it not enough that, when duty bids you acknowledge me as your lord, you hold me confined in fetters? No doubt you *are* well aware that you are doing a great wrong and a great outrage. Therefore I beg you to go your ways and not make a mock of me.'

'Lord Arghun,' said Boga, 'be well assured that I do not speak in mockery but in all seriousness. By the law we reverence, I swear it.' Then all the barons swore to accept him as their lord; and Arghun swore that he would bear them no grudge for taking him prisoner, but would look upon them with as much favour as Abaka his father had done. When these oaths had been solemnly sworn, Arghun's fetters were struck off and he was acknowledged as lord. Thereupon he ordered them to shoot a volley of arrows at the tent of the commander, the *malik* who had been holding him prisoner; and without delay they loosed such a shower of arrows into the pavilion that the *malik* was killed. This done, Arghun assumed the lordship and issued his orders as lord and was obeyed by all. I might add that the man we have referred to as the *malik* was called Sultan and was first in authority under Ahmad.

As soon as Arghun found himself in command, he lost no time in setting out to return to court. So it came about one day, while Ahmad was at court in his chief palace and holding high revel, that there came to him a messenger, who said: 'Sire, I bring you news— not such as I should wish to bring, but very bad news indeed. Know that the barons have set Arghun free and accepted him as lord, and have killed our dear friend Sultan. And I bring you word that they are coming here post haste to seize and kill you. So you must do what you think best.'

When Ahmad had received this message and assured himself of the good faith of the messenger, he was so terror-stricken that he did not know what to do. Nonetheless, like the brave man he was, he told the messenger that he must not dare to breathe a word of the matter to a living soul and, having received a promise of obedience, he promptly set out with his most trusted followers to ride to the sultan of Egypt, with whom he hoped to find refuge. And no one knew where he was going except those who were with him. When he had ridden for six days, he came to a pass where there was only one way by which he could go. At this pass the captain of the guard recognized him and saw that he was a fugitive. So he decided to seize him, which he could easily do, since Ahmad had only a handful of followers; and he lost no time in acting on the decision. Ahmad begged for mercy and offered him a great treasure if he would let him go. But the captain, who was devoted to Arghun, swore that all the treasure in the world would not stop him from seizing the traitor and putting him in the hands of his rightful lord. What need of more words? The captain of the guard, having seized Ahmad, set out immediately for court with a well-equipped company, taking his captive with him and guarding him so strictly that he could not escape. They rode without stopping till they reached the court; and there they found Arghun, who had arrived only three days before and was furious to learn that Ahmad had fled. When the captain arrived bringing Ahmad, Arghun was so overjoyed that nothing could have pleased him better. He told his uncle that he was no welcome guest and would be dealt with according to the dictates of reason. He ordered him to be led away and then without taking counsel with anyone, directed that he should be put to death and his body destroyed. The attendant to whom he gave this order took Ahmad and led him to some place where he was never seen again. And no wonder; for he had him put to death and his body flung into some place where no one ever found it.

When Arghun was thus established in the chief palace in full enjoyment of his lordship, all the barons from every part who had been subject to Abaka his father came to do homage to him as to their lord and obeyed him as they ought to do. And Arghun sent Ghazan his son with some 30,000 horsemen to the Dry Tree—that is, to that district—for the protection of his land and people. And you must understand that this recovery of the lordship by Arghun occurred in the year of our Lord 1286. Ahmad Sultan held the lordship for two years, and Arghun reigned for six years. At the end of this time he died of an illness, though rumour has it that he was poisoned.

After Arghun's death an uncle of his named Kaikhatu, who was brother german to his father Abaka, seized the lordship.* This he could do well enough, because Ghazan was far away at the Dry Tree. When word of these events came to Ghazan, he was grieved to learn of his father's death and still more grieved to learn of Kaikhatu's usurpation. He could not leave his post for fear of his enemies; but he declared that, when time and place served, he would march against Kaikhatu to such purpose that he would be avenged on him as his father had been on Ahmad. Meanwhile Kaikhatu held the lordship, and all were obedient to him except those who were with Ghazan. He took the wife of Arghun his nephew and kept her for himself. He used to take great pleasure in female society, being a man much addicted to lechery. Then, after holding the lordship for two years, he died; and you must know that he was poisoned.

After his death his uncle Baidu, who was a Christian, seized the lordship in the year 1294. He was accepted as lord by everyone except Ghazan and his army. Ghazan was grieved to learn of Kaikhatu's death, because it robbed him of his vengeance; but he vowed to wreak such revenge on Baidu that all the world would speak of it. And this time he made up his mind to delay no longer, but to march straight against Baidu and put him to death. So he mustered all his men and started on his way. Baidu on his side got together a large

* Kaikhatu was actually Arghun's brother, as correctly stated in the Prologue (p. 30). Arghun's death occurred in March 1291, and his 'court' was probably at Tabriz.

force and went ten days' journey to meet him. Then he pitched his camp and waited for Ghazan and his troops to join battle with him, urgently exhorting his own men to do their best. To cut a long story short, he had not waited two days before Ghazan and his host arrived. And on the very day of their arrival they joined in deadly combat. But Baidu could not long withstand Ghazan's attack, especially as it happened after the battle had begun that many of his followers turned against him and went over to Ghazan. In this battle Baidu was not only defeated but killed, and the victorious Ghazan returned to court and took the lordship. All the barons did homage to him and obeyed him as their liege lord. So Ghazan began to reign in the year 1294.

So now you have heard the history of this affair from Abaka to Ghazan. And you must know that it all began with Hulagu, the conqueror of Baghdad and brother of the Great Khan Kubilai. For Hulagu was father to Abaka, Abaka to Arghun, and Arghun to Ghazan, who now reigns.

Since I have told you about these Tartars of the Levant, let us now leave them and turn to Turkestan, so that you may hear all about it. But as a matter of fact we have already told you about Turkestan and how it is ruled by Kaidu, so we have no more to tell. We shall accordingly pass on and tell you of the provinces and people who live towards the north.

You must know that in the north there is a king called Kaunchi. He is a Tartar and all his people are Tartars. They observe the Tartar law, which is very brutish. But they observe it after the old fashion of Chinghiz Khan and the other genuine Tartars. So I will tell you something about it.

You must understand that they make one of their gods of felt and call him Natigai. They also provide him with a wife. And they say that these two gods, Natigai and his wife, are the gods of earth and watch over their flocks and crops and all their earthly goods. They worship them. And when they have good food to eat, they smear their god's mouth with it. Altogether they live like brute beasts.

Kaunchi is subject to no one. It is a fact that he is of the stock of Chinghiz Khan—the imperial lineage—and a near kinsman of the Great Khan. He has neither city nor town in his dominion; but his

people spend their lives among vast plains and high mountains. They
live on the flesh and milk of their herds, without any grain. He has a
great many subjects; but he does not lead them into war or battle
against anyone, but rules them in great peace. They have enormous
herds of camels, horses, cattle, sheep, and other beasts. In his country
there are big bears, pure white and more than twenty palms in
length, big black foxes, wild asses, plenty of sables—the same that
produce the costly furs of which I have told you, which are worth
more than 1,000 bezants for one man's fur—vair in abundance and
great multitudes of Pharaoh's rats, on which they live all the summer,
since they are creatures of some size. Altogether they have no lack
of wild game, since the country they inhabit is wild and inaccessible.

You must know too that there is a stretch of this country where
no horses can go, because it is a land of many lakes and marshes and
so covered with ice and mud and mire that no horse can go there.
This bad tract extends for thirteen days' journey. At the end of each
day's journey there is a posting station, where messengers crossing
the country can find lodging. At each of these stations are kept fully
forty huge dogs, scarcely smaller than donkeys. These dogs transport
the messengers from one station to the next, that is, for a day's
journey. Let me tell you how. As I have said, this is a stretch of
country where no horse can go, because of the ice and mud. This
tract of thirteen days' journey lies in an immense valley between two
mountains; that is why it is so icy and so muddy that it is impassable
for horses. For the same reason it would not bear wheeled vehicles.
Accordingly they have made sledges without wheels, so constructed
as to glide over ice or mud or mire without getting too deeply embedded. Sledges of this sort are common in our country; for they
are such as are used for carrying hay and straw in winter, when rain-
fall is heavy and roads are miry. On these sledges they lay a bear-
skin, and one of these messengers takes his seat on top. The sledge is
then pulled by a team of six dogs—the huge ones of which I have
spoken. The dogs have no one to lead them, but they run straight to
the next post; and they drag the sledge very well through ice and
mud. So they go from one station to another. And you must understand that the keeper of the station also mounts on a sledge and is
pulled by a team of dogs, and guides them by the best and shortest
route. When they have come to the next post, they find sledges and
teams ready to take them on their way. And those that have brought

Quant len se part de lysle de Seilan et len va par poment xl. milles, atot
treuue len la grant puince de ma
abar, qui est apelee lynde greigne
qui soit et si est de terre ferme, et la
chiez que en ceste puince a. v. roys qui sont freres
charnez, et si vous dirai de chascun par soi, elle
est la plus noble puince et la plus riche qui soit
el monde. Du chief de ce regne est roys .i. des v.
freres et est roys couronnez, et auon sauder lun
di demar en son regne se treuuent les peerlz pl
grosses v moult belles. Et vous dirai comment
il se treuuent. Or sachiez que il a en ceste mer un
grouk entre lysle de Seilan et la terre ferme et
en tour ce glouk y a une baue que de .x. ou de xij.
pas et en tel lieu une pas ij. et ceulx qui les vont
prendre les perles si ont leurs nez et vontt en
ce glouk du mois dauril iusqua demi mai et
vontt en .i. lieu qui sapelle botelai. Et vontt
en mer bien xl. milles en ce glouk et illec getent
leur antres et entrent de leur grant nez en leur
petitis, mais sachiez que il serontt plusieurs mir
cheans les quelx ferontt compaignie ensaluble,
et leur conuuent trouuer plusieurs hommes
qui nage, si que il les panoient dauril iusques en
mi mai, et si conuent auanti au roy le disieme
de ce que il prennent et si leur conuent auch doun
ner aus hommes qui vont coniurane pour trou
uer les perles, le vintisme de quanque il pren
nent auch, et ce est de xx. luue v nomment les
gens ceux qui enchantent les poissons a bulia
naar v leur enchantement dure celui iour

tant seulement que il les auront enchantez, car la
uiut est cessant leu chaucemeut. Et si sachiez auch
que ces abamanins seuent enchanter les bestes v les
oisaus et tous les autres animal. Et qui uent li ho
me sout especiees uarges, si se getent aus lyenue et
nour sour lysme mises au fons qui en a te uij. milzs
aux pas dyane, et tant demeurent sour yane com
me il pueent et tant y demeurent que il treuuent
auxl les coquilles ou sout les perles si sout ces co
quilles si tartes comme les ostagues voles le capt
de lamer, En ces coquilles se treuuent les pelles
grosses v menues et de toutes facons, car il sout
les pelles a la char tichues de ces quo quilles et
en ceste mainier se pechent les perles en grant
quantite, Quar de ci illent les perles qui selpau
dent par tout le monde, Et sachez que le roy de
ce lieu en a moult grant droit de ces perles et mult
grant tresor, et sachez que passe demi may il
ne treuuent plus de coquilles, on len treuue les
perles bien est vours que loing de ci a CCC.
milles se treuuent auch, mais ce est de septembre
iusques a demi octobre. Sachitz que en ceste pro
uince de manalur ua maistre tailleur pour
conure ne pour tailler robe pour ce que il y ount
tour iouz tous nus saux ce que il cueuruent leur
nature de .i. pou de drap. Et auch les hommes
comme les femmes et les riches comme les pou
res, Et auch les roys, saux ce que il portent cel
le chose comme ie vous dirai, il a entour le col .i.
fil d'au le quel est tres tout plain de pierres preci
ses, Ce sout rubiz, saphirs esmeraudes si que cest
grant ualue de rubier et uauti .i. grant tresor et
si auch tout tout le pis du col iusques aul uubue
cst .i. pas .i. fil soutil gros de soie, si ya iiij. grosses
pelles et si ya auch rubiz plusieurs, pour quoi si
come il dient il portent ce cordon de perles grosses
et rubiz C. v iiij. si est porce que il li couuient
chascun ior dire C. v iiij. oroisons de ses ydres.
Quar auch est leur loy et leur mainere, Quar
auch le firent tuit li autir roy leur auucstre v
auch et auch le laissecrent quil le deuuent fai
re. Encore porte le dit roy par ses bras en iij.
lieus besaux dor tous plains de pierres et de pri
les grosses et de grant uaillance et aus iaubes
v aus doi des piez, si que ie vous di ce que ie
si porter sus lui dor v de pierres v de perles si

them so far turn back. So they traverse the whole of this tract, pulled all the time by the dogs.*

I assure you that the people who live in the valleys and mountains of this tract are great trappers. They catch quantities of small animals that fetch a very high price and bring them a handsome profit, such as sable, ermine, vair, *ercolin*, black foxes, and many other precious animals, from which they make costly furs. They set traps from which nothing can escape. The climate here is so cold that the inhabitants build underground houses and live all the time underground.

As there is nothing else here worth mentioning, we shall go on to tell you of a region where there is perpetual darkness.

A long way beyond this kingdom, still farther to the north, is a province which is called the Land of Darkness, because perpetual darkness reigns there,† unlit by sun or moon or star—such darkness as there is in our countries in the early evening. The people here have no ruler; but they live like brute beasts in subjection to none. Sometimes, however, the Tartars enter their country in the following manner. They enter riding on mares that have foals. And they leave the foals at the entrance to the country, so that the mares may return to their young, finding their way back where men would be lost. Having entered thus mounted on mares, the Tartars rob the natives of all they can find and then give free rein to the mares to return to their foals; and the mares find their way without difficulty.

These people have great quantities of costly furs—sable, whose immense value I have already noted, ermine, *ercolin*, vair, and black fox, and many others. They are all trappers, who acquire such numbers of these furs that it is truly marvellous. And all these they sell to neighbouring tribes within the bounds of daylight; for they take them into the lands of daylight and sell them there. And the traders who buy them make a huge profit. And I assure you that these dwellers in the Darkness are tall and well-formed in all their limbs, but very pale and colourless.

This province adjoins one end of Great Russia. So, as there is no more to tell of it worth mentioning, we shall pass on and tell you next of the province of Russia.

* Two MSS give a different account of this dog-team service, and speak of it as used by traders, not by official messengers.
† R adds: 'for most of the winter months'; but this is probably a later rationalization.

Russia is a very large province lying towards the north. The people are Christians and observe the Greek rite. They have several kings and speak a language of their own. They are very simple folk, but they are very good-looking, both men and women; for they are fair-skinned and blond. Their country is strongly defended by defiles and passes. They are tributary to none, except that from time to time they pay tribute to a Tartar king of the West, whose name is Toktai, but not a heavy one. It is not a country of much commercial wealth. It is true, however, that it produces precious furs—sable, ermine, vair, *ercolin*, and foxes in abundance, the best and most beautiful in the world. There are also many silver mines, yielding no small amount of silver. But there is nothing else worth mentioning; so we shall leave Russia and speak of the Black Sea, working round it, province by province and nation by nation, so that you may receive a clear account. And we shall begin with Constantinople. But before doing so I will tell you of a province lying between north and north-west whose name is Lac. It borders on Russia, has a king of its own and is peopled by Christians and Saracens. It produces good furs in plenty, which are exported far and wide by traders. The people live by commerce and industry. But there is nothing else worth mentioning. But, before going on, I must tell one thing more about Russia which I had omitted to mention.

You must know that in Russia the cold is more intense than anywhere else in the world—so intense that men can scarcely survive it. Indeed, were it not for the many stove-houses that exist there, the inhabitants could not avoid dying of cold. There are great numbers of these stove-houses, built by the piety of noblemen and magnates, as hospitals are built in our country. To these all classes of people continually resort as the need arises. Sometimes such fierce cold prevails that men who are going about the country either on their way home or from place to place on business are very nearly frozen after leaving one stove-house and before reaching the next, although they are so close together that the distance from one to another is only about sixty paces. Even so, when a man departs warmed through from one stove-house, he is frozen before he gets to the next. Then he goes in to get warm, and when he is warmed through he goes on to the next; and so on till he reaches his home or other destination. They always go at a run, so that they may pass quickly from one stove-house to the next without freezing too hard on the way. It often happens, if a man is too thinly clad or too old to hurry or of a

293

weaker constitution and nature than others, or because his home is too far away, that he is overcome by cold before he can get from one stove-house to the next and drops to the ground. And there he would die; but other passers-by immediately pick him up and bring him to a stove-house and strip him there, and exposure to the warmth restores natural vitality. This is how the stove-houses are made. They are square buildings made of large beams laid one on top of another and so close-fitting that nothing can be seen through the chinks. The chinks are then well stopped up with lime and other materials, so that neither wind nor cold can penetrate from outside. At the top of the building in the roof is a vent-hole from which the smoke issues when a fire is lit to heat it. They are supplied with big stocks of logs, with which men heap up a blazing fire. While the logs are giving off smoke, the vent-hole is opened and the smoke escapes; when no more smoke is given off, the vent-hole is closed with a thick shutter of felt, and there remains a mass of glowing embers which keeps the building very warm. Lower down, in the side of the building, is a window with a very thick and solid shutter of felt, which they open if they want to let in the light and there is no wind. On windy days, if they want to let in the light, they open the vent-hole in the roof. The door leading into the building is also of felt. That is how the stove-houses are built. Every gentleman of rank and wealth has a stove-house of his own.

Let me tell you of one of their customs. They make an excellent wine out of honey and panic, which is called mead; and with this they hold great drinking-bouts in the following fashion. They form numerous clubs of men and women, especially nobles and magnates, ranging from thirty to fifty persons—husbands and wives and children. Each club elects its own king or captain and makes its own statutes, so that anyone who makes an unseemly remark or does something contrary to statute is punished by the imposition of a fine. There are men equivalent to tavern-keepers who have stocks of this mead for sale. The clubs resort to these taverns and spend a whole day in drinking. They call these drinking bouts *stravitza*. In the evening the tavern-keepers make a reckoning of the mead they have drawn, and everyone pays the share allotted to him, and to his wife and children if they are present. While they are engaged in these *stravitza*, they borrow money on the security of their children from merchants who come from Khazaria, Sudak, and other neighbouring countries, and then spend it on drink, and so they sell their own children. During these all-day bouts the ladies do not withdraw to relieve themselves, but their handmaids contrive to give them relief unobserved, when need arises, with the aid of large sponges. Let me tell you something that happened on one occasion. A man and his wife were going home in the evening after one of these bouts, when the wife paused to relieve herself. The cold was so fierce that the hairs of her thighs froze on to the grass, so that she could not move for the pain and cried aloud. Her husband, reeling drunk and distressed at her plight, stooped down and began to breathe over her, hoping to melt the ice by the warmth of his breath. But, while he breathed, the moisture of his breath congealed and so the hairs of of his beard froze together with his wife's and he too was stuck there unable to move for pain. Before they could budge from the spot, other helpers had to come and break the ice.

The money current among these people consists of gold rods about half a foot in length and worth perhaps 5 *gros sous* apiece. For small change they reckon in heads of martens.

Russia is such a huge province that it extends as far as the Ocean. In this Ocean there are islands that breed many gerfalcons and peregrines, which are exported to several parts of the world. From Russia it is no great distance to Norway, and were it not for the cold it would be a quick journey. But the great cold makes it difficult.

Now let us leave these regions to turn to the Black Sea, as I promised above. It is true that there are many merchants and others who know it well; but still there are a great many more who do not know it. So for their sake it is worth while to set down the facts in writing. Let us begin, then, with the mouth of the Black Sea, the strait of Constantinople. At the entrance to the sea, on the western side, stands a mountain called the Faro. But, now that we have embarked on this topic, we have had second thoughts about setting it down in writing; for after all it is very well known to many people. So let us drop the subject and start on another one. I will tell you instead about those Tartars who are Lords of the West.

The first Tartar Lord of the West was Sain, who was a very great and powerful king. He it was who conquered Russia, Comania, Alania, Lac, Menjar, Circassia, Gothia, and Khazaria. Before he conquered them, they were all subject to the Comanians; but they did not all hold together or form a unity. For that reason they lost their lands and were driven out and scattered all over the world. Those who were not driven out, but are still there, were reduced to servitude by this king Sain. Sain's successors were Batu, Barka, Mongu-temur, Tuda-mongu, and Toktai, who now reigns.

Let me tell you now of a great battle that was fought between Barka, Lord of the West, and Hulagu, Lord of the Levant. In the year 1261 a great dispute arose between these two concerning a province at the boundary of their territories, which each of them claimed as his by right and neither would surrender. When war had been declared between them, each of them summoned all his followers and together they mustered one of the greatest armaments ever seen. For neither spared any effort to gain the mastery. During the six months that elapsed after the declaration, each of them assembled fully 300,000 horsemen, well equipped with all that was needed for battle according to their usage. When all was in readiness, Hulagu set out with all his men; and they rode for many days without meeting any adventure worthy of note till they came to a great plain which lies between the Iron Gates and the Sea of Sarai.* Here he pitched his camp in due order. And I assure you that with all its costly pavilions and tents it was manifestly the camp of a man of great riches. Here, then, on the boundary of their two domains, he waited to see if Barka and his troops would appear.

To turn now to Barka, when he learnt that Hulagu was on the march, he lost no time in setting out with his own troops and riding to the same great plain, where he pitched camp in due order about ten miles from the enemy. His camp was no less splendid than Hulagu's; for anyone who saw the pavilions of cloth of gold and the costly tents would wonder if a richer or more brilliant camp had ever been seen. And he had a far greater force than his adversary; it would be no lie to say that they numbered 350,000 horsemen. And after encamping they rested for two days. On the third day he summoned an assembly of his men and addressed them thus:

'Good sirs, you know that since I came to rule this realm I have loved you as brothers and sons, and that many of you have already taken part with me in many great battles and have helped me to conquer a large part of the land we now hold. You know too that all that I have is as much yours as mine. Since this is so, it behoves every man of you to do his best to uphold our honour. Up till now, we

---

* I.e., the Caucasus and the Caspian. Actually this war, which is mentioned in the Prologue (p. 22), did not go very well for Hulagu.

have not failed in this. Now the mighty and powerful Hulagu wishes to do battle with us in a wrongful cause. Since it is true that wrong is on his side and right on ours, you may be assured of victory. Furthermore, he has only 300,000 horsemen, while we have 350,000, as good as his or better. On all scores, therefore, we can count on victory. Since we have come so far for no other purpose than to fight this battle, it is my wish that we should fight it in three days from now, and to such effect that our affairs may go from good to better. I urge you, therefore, with all my heart, to act as brave men and so that all the world may fear us. And now I will say no more, except to ask each man of you to be ready on the appointed day and to remember to play his part like a man.'

To turn now to Hulagu, the story goes that when he heard that Barka had come against him with such a mighty host, he likewise assembled a great company of trusty men and addressed them thus:

'Dear brothers, sons, and friends, you know that all my life long you have stood by me and helped me. Down to this day you have fought by my side in many battles, and none that we did not win. Now we are matched with the mighty Barka, and I know well that he has as many men as we or more, but not so good. Were they twice as many as they are, I am confident that with such men as ours we should put them to rout. Since we know by our spies that they propose to attack us in three days' time—and I am glad of it—I ask every man of you to be ready on that day and to act as he is accustomed to act. There is one thing only of which I wish to remind you: it is better to die on the field for honour's sake, if so it must be, than to admit defeat. Let every man, then, so acquit himself that our honour may be saved and our foes vanquished and slain.'

After both the leaders had spoken to this effect, they waited till the appointed day, preparing meanwhile all that they knew would be required.

When the day came, Hulagu rose early and arrayed his men to the best of his knowledge, well and wisely, like the wise man he was. He marshalled them in thirty battalions, each containing 10,000 horsemen and led by a capable commander; and then bade them advance against the enemy. So they advanced till they had covered half the space between the two camps; and there they halted. Meanwhile Barka on his side marshalled his troops no less wisely in thirty-five battalions, and they advanced to within half a mile of the enemy. There they too halted for a breathing-space. Then they continued their advance. When they were two crossbow-shots apart, they paused once more and set all their ranks in orderly array. The plain where they were drawn up was the finest and the widest that was known, near or far, and the one best suited to the manoeuvres of the greatest number of cavalry. And indeed it had to be; for seldom, if ever, were so many horsemen engaged in a single action. And both their leaders were among the most powerful men in the world. They were also near kinsmen, both being of the imperial lineage of Chinghiz Khan.

So both armies paused a short while, eagerly awaiting the sound of the kettle-drums. No sooner had the drums begun to beat than the two armies charged full tilt, letting fly such a cloud of arrows that the very sky was hidden from sight. Many indeed were the men and horses that fell lifeless to the ground, as must needs be when so many arrows are let fly at once. When not another arrow was left in its quiver, they set hand to sword and club and laid about them lustily, till the earth was stained scarlet with the blood of the fallen. Seldom, if ever, did so many meet their death on a single battlefield; for it is long indeed since a battle was fought in the world of such a magnitude as this. In an ill hour did this day's fighting begin for both armies alike; and clearly did they show that they bore one another no goodwill but were mortal enemies. King Hulagu acquitted himself so manfully that it was plain he was a fit man to rule a realm and wear a crown. He fought bravely in his own person and brought great encouragement to his men. All who beheld him, friends and foes alike, were struck with awe; for he seemed not a man but a thunderbolt and a storm-wind. Barka for his part bore himself most bravely, in a fashion to win the praise of the world. But his prowess availed him nothing on that day; for so many of his men were mown down that they could endure no longer. When the fight had lasted till evening, they broke and fled the field with the best speed to which they could spur their horses. When Hulagu and his men saw that they were routed, they gave chase, smiting and slaying and work-ing such havoc that it was pitiful to see. After a while they desisted and returned to their pavilions. There they disarmed, and those who had suffered hurt had their wounds washed and bound. They were so weary and battle-worn that there was not one but had more mind for repose than for combat. After they had had a night's rest, Hulagu ordered that the bodies of all the fallen, friend and foe alike, should be burnt. And so it was done. And after all was finished,

T

King Hulagu returned to his own country with as many of his men as had survived the battle; for be well assured that, victors though they were, they had suffered heavy loss. But his enemies' losses were heavier by far—so great, indeed, that no one who heard the number could readily believe it. With that, let us take our leave of the victorious Hulagu, and we will tell you of a battle that was fought among themselves by the Tartars of the West.

It happened after the death of a certain Lord of the Western Tartars, whose name was Mongu-temur, that the lordship passed to Tula-bugha, who was only a young lad. And this Tulabugha was put to death by one Tuda-mongu, a man of great power and authority, with the aid of another king of the Tartars, who was called Noghai. After a brief reign, Tuda-mongu died and was succeeded by Toktai, a vigorous and capable ruler. Meanwhile two sons of Tulabugha had grown to man's estate and were well able to bear arms. These two brothers, who also were not lacking in vigour and ability, assembled a goodly company and went to Toktai's court. When they were admitted to his presence, they saluted him courteously on bended knee. Toktai welcomed them warmly and bade them stand up. Then the elder of the two addressed him thus:

'Lord Toktai, I will tell you as well as I can why it is that we have come to you. The truth is, as you know, that we were sons of Tulabugha, who was killed by Tuda-mongu and Noghai. Concerning Tuda-mongu there is nothing I can say, since he is dead. The subject of our appeal is Noghai. We beg you, as the righteous ruler you are, to summon him to your presence and do justice upon him for our father's death. That is why we have come here, and that is our suit to you.'

Toktai, who well knew that the youth had spoken truly, answered with these words: 'My good friend, I will willingly do as you ask. I will summon Noghai to my presence and will deal with him as justice may demand.'

Then he sent two envoys to Noghai to bid him come to his court and answer the charge brought against him by Tulabugha's sons concerning their father's death. But Noghai merely laughed at the envoys' words and refused to obey the summons. When the messengers brought back this answer to Toktai's court, he took it very much amiss, and cried aloud, so that all around could hear him: 'So help me God! Either Noghai will come to my presence to answer this charge or I will march against him with all my forces to destroy him.'

Without a moment's delay he entrusted two other envoys with a message for Noghai. They rode to his court and, being admitted to his presence, saluted him courteously. After Noghai had made them welcome, one of them spoke thus: 'Sire, Toktai sends word that, if you will not come to his court to answer this charge, he will march against you with all his forces and do all the harm he can both to your possessions and to your person. Consider therefore what you will do in this matter and send back word by us.' Noghai took these words very much amiss, and answered thus: 'Sirs, go back now to your lord and tell him on my account that I have little fear of any force he can bring against me. Tell him too that, if he attacks me, I will not wait for him to invade my territory, but will meet him halfway. That is my answer.' Such then was the message that the envoys took back to Toktai.

When Toktai saw that he was left with no choice but to fight, he immediately sent out couriers in many directions to bid all those who owed him allegiance take up arms for a war against Noghai. What more need I say? He mustered the greatest array imaginable. And Noghai, when he knew for a fact that Toktai was planning to attack him in such force, likewise mustered a huge array—not as great as Toktai's, because he had not so many men at his command, but a mighty array for all that. When Toktai had completed his preparations, he set out with fully 200,000 horsemen and came to the good, wide plain of Nerghi* and there encamped to await Noghai's coming. For he knew that he was coming as fast as he could to do battle. And be well assured that the two sons of Tulabugha were there also with a goodly company of horsemen to avenge their father's death. Meanwhile Noghai on his side, when he learnt that Toktai had moved against him, set out with fully 150,000 horsemen—tried and valiant warriors and better men-at-arms than Toktai's. It was not two days after Toktai had reached this plain that he too arrived there and pitched camp in due order some ten miles away. With all its gay pavilions of cloth of gold and its splendid tents, it seemed indeed the camp of a rich king. And as for Toktai's camp, being not less splendid or less rich, but even more so, it was a marvel to behold. Here then in the plain of Nerghi the two armies rested, so as to be fresh on the day of battle.

* Probably near the river Don. Noghai's lordship was in the Ukraine.

300

Here Toktai called an assembly of his men and addressed them thus: 'Sirs, we have come here to fight against King Noghai and his men, and with good reason. For you know that all this hatred and bitterness has arisen because Noghai will not come to answer the charge brought by the sons of Tulabugha. And assuredly, since he thus flies in the face of reason, it is right and proper that we should be victors in this battle, and it should bring about his death or undoing. Therefore you may all hearten yourselves with a good hope of victory. Nonetheless, I beg of you, as earnestly and devoutly as I can, to strain every nerve to ensure that our enemies are indeed brought to destruction and death.'

Meanwhile, Noghai on his side addressed his men as follows: 'Brothers and friends, you know that we have won many great battles and fierce encounters and have matched ourselves successfully against many better men than these. Let this knowledge strengthen your assurance of victory, together with the fact that right is on our side. For you know that it was no lord of mine who summoned me to his court to answer a charge brought by others. Now I will say no more, except to urge every man of you to do his best, that we may so acquit ourselves in this battle that all the world will speak of us and that we and our heirs shall be dreaded for the rest of our days.'

On the morrow of the speeches the two leaders arrayed their troops for battle with great skill. King Toktai formed twenty battalions, each under a capable commander, while king Noghai formed fifteen; for each battalion consisted of 10,000 horsemen. Then both armies advanced till they were within a crossbow-shot of each other. There they both halted. But they had not long to wait before the kettle-drums began to beat. Then they both charged and let fly their arrows in such numbers that many a steed and many a rider fell to earth dead or wounded to death. When they had no more arrows to shoot, they set hand to sword and club and laid about them lustily. The shouting of men and the clash of swords drowned the thunder of heaven. So great was the number of the slain that seldom was it surpassed in any battle. But without doubt it was greater on Toktai's side than on Noghai's; for Noghai's were the better men. The sons of Tulabugha performed great feats of arms, putting forth all their strength to avenge their father's death. But all in vain; for it was beyond their power to inflict death upon King Noghai. In an ill hour was that grievous fight begun; for to many men who rose that morning hale and hearty it spelt death, and to many a woman widowhood. And small wonder that such a battle bore such fruit. Toktai strove with all his might to uphold his forces and his honour and performed mighty exploits, so as to earn the praise of all the world. He plunged into the midst of the foe as though he cared nothing for death. He laid about him to right and left. He scattered serried ranks asunder. He brought heavy loss that day on friends as well as enemies—on his enemies by the deaths he dealt with his own hand; on his friends by the incitement he gave to many to rush upon the foe and dauntlessly expose themselves to death. And of Noghai I may say no less. He achieved such feats in his own person that no one on either side was his peer. And assuredly he earned the highest mead of praise in all that day's battle. He ventured as fearlessly among his foes as a lion among wild beasts. Smiting and slaying, he charged in wherever the press was thickest, and scattered warriors this way and that as if they were small game. And his followers, fired by his example, nerved themselves to heroic efforts and to their adversaries brought dire calamity.

But why make a long tale of it? Suffice it that all that Toktai's men had done to uphold their honour availed them nothing. They had to do with men who were more than their match. The point came when they saw plainly that if they made a longer stay they would all be dead men. So, when they saw that they could hold out no longer, they fled the field as best they could. And Noghai and his men gave chase, slaughtering without mercy. So Noghai won the day. And those who were killed in this battle numbered not less than 60,000. But king Toktai escaped, and so did the sons of Tulabugha.*

But you must know that for this action king Toktai had not assembled all his available forces; for he firmly believed that those he had were enough to ensure victory, since Noghai was taking the field with fewer troops by a quarter than his. But, as you have heard, he was defeated by the superior quality of Noghai's men. So afterwards, having assembled his entire force, he rose manfully against Noghai and defeated and killed him together with four of his sons, all doughty and valiant men. And so vengeance was done for the death of Tulabugha.

* The following paragraph, which occurs only in Z, apparently refers to events of autumn 1299, after Marco's release from captivity.

epilogue*

YOU HAVE HEARD ALL THE FACTS ABOUT TARTARS AND
Saracens as far as they can be told, and about their customs, and
about the other countries of the world as far as they can be explored
and known, except that we have not spoken to you of the Black Sea
or the provinces that lie around it, although we ourselves have
explored it thoroughly. I refrain from telling you this, because it
seems to me that it would be tedious to recount what is neither
needful nor useful and what is daily recounted by others. For there
are so many who explore these waters and sail upon them every day
—Venetians, Genoese, Pisans, and many others who are constantly
making this voyage—that everybody knows what is to be found
there. Therefore I say nothing on this topic. For our part, as to how
we took leave of the Great Khan, you have heard in the prologue to
this book, in the chapter that tells of the troubles encountered by
Messer Maffeo and Messer Niccolò and Messer Marco in getting his
leave to depart and of the happy chance that led to our departure.
And you must know that, but for this chance, we might never have
got away for all our pains, so that there is little likelihood that we
should ever have returned to our own country. But I believe it was
God's will that we should return, so that men might know the things
that are in the world, since, as we have said in the first chapter of this
book, there was never man yet, Christian or Saracen, Tartar or
Pagan, who explored so much of the world as Messer Marco, son of
Messer Niccolò Polo, great and noble citizen of the city of Venice.

THANKS BE TO GOD

AMEN AMEN

* This Epilogue (apart from the final 'Deo gratias. Amen') is found only in a Tuscan
version dating from the early fourteenth century. It is unlikely that it formed part of
the original book; but it is included here on it own merits, as the work of a near
contemporary who felt the need to round off Polo's abrupt conclusion with a more
artistic tail-piece.

genealogical table

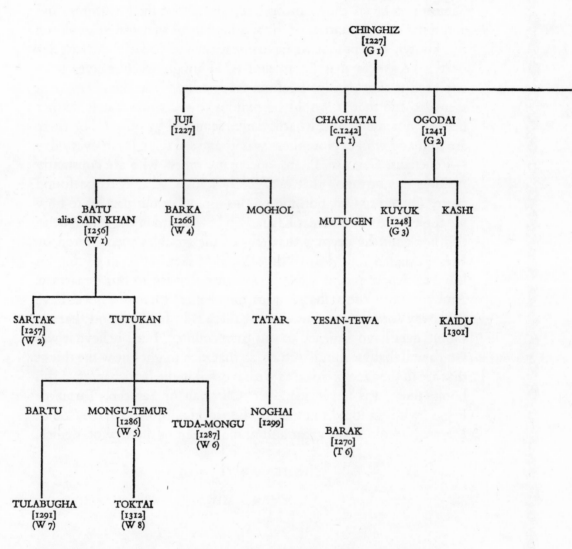

G = Great Khan. L = Khan of the Levant. T = Khan of Turkestan. W = Khan of the West (the 'Golden Horde'). Numbers denote order of succession. Figures in square brackets are dates of death. The table includes only persons mentioned by Polo or necessary in order to show the relationships of those mentioned.

304

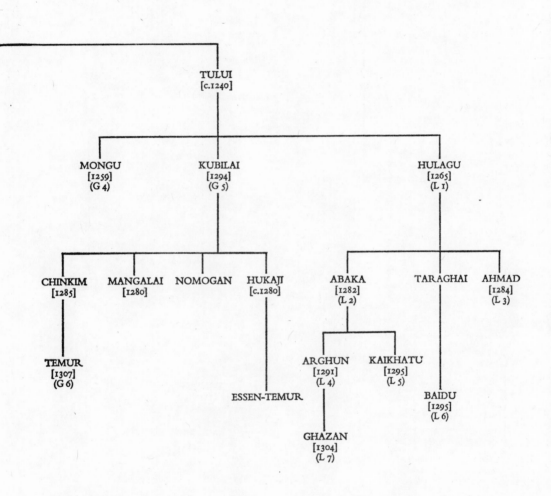

index

Square brackets are used to indicate explanatory matter additional to the text. After a person's name, a single date in square brackets, unless otherwise indicated, is the date of his death. r = reigned. After a place-name, a form added in square brackets represents the standard modern form (or a conjectural identification) of a place that is differently spelt in the text. A form added in round brackets represents approximately the original MS spelling. See Introduction, p. 17.

Abaka, Khan of Levant [r. 1265–82], 26, 272–4, 281

Abyssinia (Abasce, Middle India), [Ethiopia], 15, 259–62

Acre [Christian stronghold in Palestine]: captured by Saracens [1291], 263; Polos at, 24–6

Adam's Peak and Grave, in Ceylon, 240–2

Aden (Adan), in Arabia, 224, 243, 248, 254, 260–5

Afghanistan, places in, 58–63, 273 n.

ague [malaria], cures for, 61, 233–4

Ahmad, khan of Levant [r. 1282–4], 273–80

Ahmad (Acmat), governor of Peking [1282], 108–12

Ai-yaruk daughter of Kaidu, 270–2

Ak-balik ['White City', Turkish name of Ch'êng-ting in Ho-peh], 137

Ak-balik Manzi [(?) in the Han valley, Shen-hsi], 141

Alamut, see Mulehet

Alania [N.E. of Caucasus], Alans, 175 n., 178, 286

Alaodin [Ala ud-Din, ob. 1255], head of the Assassins, 54–7

Alexander the Great, king of Macedonia [323 B.C.]: legends of, 11, 14, 35, 54, 58, 60, 272; styled Zulkarnein ['Lord of the Horns'], 60

Alexandria, in Egypt, 200, 248, 263

almanacks, calendars, 132–3, 227–8

aloes, 90, 201, 210–12, 214

Altai mountain (Mongolia), burial-place of Khans, 78, 83

Altou Khan [see note], 78

ambergris, 252–4, 255, 256, 258

Amoy, see Zaiton

ancestor worship, 152

Andaman (Angaman) Islands [in Bay of Bengal], 219

animals: abstention from killing, 62, 73, 225, 236, 238; exotic, 229, 245, 257, 258, 262; idols with heads of, 209; incantations against, 222

Aniu [(?) in S.E. Yün-nan or Indo-China], 157 n., 160–1, 211

An-king-fu, see Ngan-king

Apostles, the Seventy, 199; see also James; Thomas

apples of paradise [(?) bananas or oranges], 49, 219, 238

Arabia, Arabs, 36, 243, 245, 248, 263–6

Araxes, river, see Euphrates

archers, archery, 35, 47, 61, 80, 82, 95–6, 103, 151, 156, 268, etc.

Arctic Ocean, 84, 286

Arctic regions, 283

Arghun, Khan of Levant [r. 1284–91], 10, 28, 84, 203 n., 272, 280–1

Armenia, Greater, 33, 34, 50

Armenia, Lesser [Cilicia, S.E. Asia Minor, settled by Armenians about A.D. 1080], 14, 26, 33

Armenians, 33–4, 36, 43

armies, organizations and tactics of, 38, 80–2, 95, 99–100, 124, 155–6, 188, 196

armour, etc.: manufacture of, 47–8, 87, 117, 140, 173; leathern, 80, 95, 103, 151

arms, 80, 96, 103, 218, 226, 244, 258, etc.

asbestos, see salamander

ascetics, 62, 73, 90–2, 226, 236–9

Ashar, king of Kayal, 242–4

Asidin Sultan [Ghiyās ud-Din, sultan of Delhi, ob. 1286], 50

Assassins ['Hashish-eaters'], Moslem sect, 55–7

asses, 46, 49; wild, 47, 53, 75, 118, 257, 262, 282

astrologers, astronomers, 37, 69, 77, 89–90, 95, 102, 106, 108, 116, 121, 130, 132–3, 145, 170–1, 182, 189, 228, 245

augury and omens, 113–14, 129, 205–6, 227–8, 236–7

avariun [Arabic Hawāri, plural Hawāriyūn, 'Apostle of Christ'], 233

Ayas (Laias) in Lesser Armenia, 24–6, 33

Badakhshan (Balascian) [in Afghanistan], 50, 60–2

Index

Baghdad, 9, 37–43, 254, 281; patriarch of, 37 n., 254

Baidu, Khan of Levant [r. 1295], said to be a Christian, 280, 281

Baku [in the Caucasus], 34 n., 36

balass rubies, 60

Baldwin I, Emperor of Constantinople [r. 1204–6], 8

Baldwin II [last Latin Emperor of Constantinople, r. 1237–61], 21

Balkh [in Afghanistan], 58

bangles, 160, 223

Banians [merchants], 235 n.

Barak [or Boraq, great-grandson of Chaghatai], Khan of Turkestan [1270], 22, 272, 273

Bargu [in Siberia], 83

Barka [Berke], Khan of the West [r. 1257–66], 22, 287–90

barley, huskless, 61

Barsamo, St [Barsauma of Samosata, ob. 458], monastery of, 44

Bǝrskol [(?) in Manchuria], 97

Basman [(?) Pasai in N. Sumatra], 214–15

Basra (Bascra) [in Iraq], 37

baths: cold, 34, 165, 181–2, 187, 226; hot, 53, 130, 165, 182, 187

bats, giant, 229

Batu alias Sain Khan, first khan of the West [r. 1224–57], 78, 287

Bayan Ching-siang, 'Hundred Eyes', Tartar general [1295], 170–1, 178–9, 192

Bayburt (Paipurth), in Armenia, 34

beacons: at sea, 247; signals sent by, 110

beads, for telling prayers, 145 n., 222–3

beards, wearing of, 110

bears, 117–18, 141, 142, 147, 150, 282; white, 282

beasts, men living like, 73, 214, 218, 281, 284

beds, suspended, 231

bells, 108, 127, 158

Belor [Kafiristan], 63

Bengal (Bangala) [(?) confused with Pegu], 154, 159–60

Bettala [(?) Patlam in Ceylon], 221

Bintan (Pentan) island [near Singapore], 214

birds: caught during moult, 84; descriptions of, 14, 48, 49, 84, 85, 87–8, 245; exotic, 229, 245, 256, 257, 262; not found at great altitude, 63

birth, customs connected with, 152, 189, 228, 235

birthdays, celebration of, 114–15

birthmark, 35

Black Sea ('Great Sea'), 10, 13, 22, 36, 284, 286, 294

blood, drunk by Tartars, 81

blood-letting, 237

bloodshed, objection to, 97, 108

Bolgara [on Volga], Polos at, 22

Brahmans, 222–3, 235–7

branding: as a mark of religion, 259; of cattle, 83; of criminals, 134

brazil wood, 213–14, 217, 219, 244

bridges, described, 136, 142, 179, 180, 196, 197, 201

Brius [Kin-sha-kiang], river, 148

Bucephalus, breed of, 60

'buckram' [(?) muslin], 34, 37, 145, 233, 247–50, 262

Buddha (Sakyamuni) [c. 483 B.C.], 14, 98, 240–2

Buddhists, see idolaters

buffaloes, 80, 149, 151, 160, 209, 248

Bukhara [in Turkestan], said to be in Persia, Polos at, 22

Bulagan (Bolgana), Queen, wife of Arghun [1286], 28–9

Bundukdar (Bondocdaire), Baibars, Mamluk sultan of Egypt [r. 1259–76], 26

Burma, see Mien

cachalots [sperm-whales], 253, 256

Cachar Modun [(?) east of Peking], 120–2

Caichu, castle [(?) in Shan-hsi], 138–9

calendars, see almanacks

Caliph, 37–43

Cambay (Canbaet) [in Gujarat], W. India, 250

camels, 35, 46, 50, 73, 79, 83, 88, 113, 115, 189, 255, 258, 263, 264, 282

camlets, 86, 145

camphor, 69, 200, 215, 217, 243

canals, 177, 180

canes [bamboos]: used in building, etc., 88–9, 140, 177, 194; fires of, to scare wild beasts, 143

cannibalism, 90, 196, 210, 214, 217, 219

carpets, 33, 135

carriages, 138, 184, 187

Caspian Sea (Sea of Baku, Ghelukelan, or Sarai), 36, 287

Cathay [N. China], 7, 37, 38, 66, 136–42, 163–9, 214, 267; customs of, 126–7, 133–5, 154, 165–7; Tartar rule resented in, 94, 108, 109–10, 164–5

Catholicus (Nestorian patriarch or Jacobite metropolitan), 37, 254 n.

cattle, oxen, etc.: branding of, 83; carts drawn by, 79; dung of, 225, 238; fed on fish, 264; humped, 49, 159; images of, as amulets, 238; killed by plague, 129; wild yaks, etc., 84, 117, 118, 145, 159, 248; hair of, worn as charm, 235; worship of, 225, 235, 238

cave-dwellers, 59

Index

Ceylon, 219–21, 239–42

Chagan-Nor, 'White Pool', [(?) in Chahar], 87

Chaghatai [son of Chinghiz, Khan of Turkestan, ob. 1242], 50, 267–8; said to be a Christian, 64, 268

Chamba (Cianba) [or Champa, in S. Vietnam], 211–13, 259

Changan (Ciangan) [(?) in Kiang-su or Che-kiang], 179

Chang-chau (Cangiu, Cinghin-giu) [in Kiang-su], 178

Changli [(?) T'si-nan-fu in Shan-tung], 164

Changlu (Cianglu) [T'sang-chau in Ho-peh], 163–4

Chanshan (Ciansian) [(?) in Che-kiang], 195

Chao-hien, Sung emperor of S. China [1278], 170

characters: national, 33, 35, 43, 46, 59, 61, 63, 64, 70, 76–81, 134, 144, 160–2, 178, 185, 195–6, 201, 206, 218–19, 220, 235, 259–60, 267, 283; due to soil, 48–9

Charchan, in Turkestan, 66

charcoal, 176, 193

charity and poor-relief, 129–32, 171–2, 186, 193

charts, used by Polo, 203 n., 219, 259

Ch'êng-ting, see Ak-balik

Ch'eng-tu-fu (Sindufu) [capital of Sze-ch'wan], 141–3, 161–2

chess-men, 212

Cheynam [(?) Hai-nan], gulf of, 211

Chibai and Chiban, said to be sons of Chaghatai, 268

children: exposure and adoption of, 171–2; male, turned out of home at thirteen, 228–9; posthumously married, 83; sale of, 192, 285–6

China, sea of, 210; see also Cathay; Manzi

Chinghiz or Jenghiz Khan [r. 1206–27], founder of Mongol empire, 7, 8, 15, 76–9, 89, 94, 102, 104–5, 268, 281, 289

Chinju (Cingiu) [(?) Hsien-nu-miao in Kiang-su], 173

Chin-kiang-fu (Cinghianfu) [in Kiang-su], 177–8

Chinkim (Chinghiz), son of Kubilai [1285], 102, 104–5, 110–11, 112

Cho-chau (Giogiu) [in Ho-peh], 136, 163–4

Chola (Soli) [district south of Madras], 236

Choncha, see Fu-chau

Chorcha [in Manchuria], 75, 97

Christ: legend of, 72; napkin of, 72; venerated by Tartars, 98; visited by Magi, 44–5

Christian religion, Tartar converts to, 64, 96, 268, 280

Christians: in Abyssinia, 259–62; in Central Asia and China, see Nestorians; in India, 233–5, 244; in service of Great Khan, 77, 97, 110, 177–8, head of, 200; in Socotra, 252–5

Christians: 'imperfect', 14, 36–7; inter-marrying with idolaters, 71; mutual estrangement of sects, 43; observing customs of Old Testament, 252; Saracens hostile to, 14, 40, 43, 64, 97, 254, 260–3; supposed sect [(?) Manichees], investigated by Polos, 199–200; see also Greek church; Latin Church; Jacobites; Nestorians; Prester John

Chüan-chau, see Zaiton

church: at Samarkand, miraculous column in, 64; of St Thomas in India, 234

churches in China, etc., see Nestorians

cinnamon, 145, 148, 247

Circassia (Zic) [in the Caucasus], 286

Clement IV, Pope [1265–8], 24

climate: cold, 34, 48, 60, 63, 71, 84, 88, 282–6; dry, 227, 264; enervating, 33; hot, 46, 49, 51–2, 61, 227, 231, 245, 265–6; pestilent, 152; salubrious, 61, 72, 180; temperate, 54, 62, 222

clock, 186

cloves, 148, 212, 219, 248

coal ('black stones'), 130

coconuts (Pharaoh's nuts), 51, 216, 219, 233, 247

Columbus, Christopher [1506], influenced by Polo, 16

Comania, Comanians [Turkish tribe, N.W. of Caucasus], 35, 286

Comorin (Comari), S. India, 245, 246

Condur and Sondur [Condore Is., off Cochin China], 213

Constantinople, 8, 284, 286; emperor of, see Baldwin; Polos at, 8, 21–2, 31

coral, 62, 145

Coromandel Coast, see Maabar

costume: absence of, 14 n., 218, 238, 244; bark-cloth, 161; belts, 44, 117; footwear, 59, 117, 135; headwear, 59, 165; ladies', 61; liveries, 118; loin cloths only, 219, 222, 230, 245, 254, 257; ornate, 80, 114–17, 190, 222, 271; sack-cloth, 91; skin, 59, 61, 63, 145, 271 n.

cotton, 37, 47, 61, 64–5, 159, 196, 236, 249–50, 254, 262; trees, 248

Cowries, used as currency, 148, 152, 160, 213

cramoisy (crimson cloth), 37

Crimea, 8, 22, 286–7

crocodiles, 149–50

Crusade, Fourth, 8

curfew, 108, 186

currency, 145, 147, 148, 152, 160, 161, 163, 286; paper, 122–4, 161, etc.

Index

Dagroian [in N. Sumatra], 216–17

Damascus [in Syria], 57

dancing, 70

dancing girls, 229–30

Darius [Codomannus], king of Persia [330 B.C.], 54; daughter (legendary) of, 58, 60

darkness: produced by magic, 49–50, 62; region of, 283

date wine, 51, 245 n., 264

dates, date palms, 37, 47, 49, 51–3, 258, 264, 266

David, styled Malik [king], king of Georgia, 35

debt, recovery of, 226–7

deer: musk, 85, 104, 141, 145, 147; rein, 83; roe, etc., 88, 104, 118, 122, 141, 147, 159, 181, 191, 256

desert: haunted, 67, 84; used as refuge, 66

Desert: of Lop [Gobi], 66–7, 70; of Mongolia, 73; of Persia, 46, 53–4, 58; of Turkestan, 66

devils: Africans look like, 257; white, 235

Dhofar (Dufar), in Arabia, 224, 265

diamonds, how obtained, 231 n., 232–3

diet: ascetic, 90–1, 237–9; peculiarities of, 49, 51, 61–2, 80–2, 126, 148–9, 152, 181, 185, 195–6, 214, 216, 217, 219, 226, 232, 236–7, 250, 252, 254, 258, 264, 266, etc.

Dilivar [(?) Lahore], in India, 50

divers, for pearls, 221–3

dogs (hounds), as decoys, 197; body thrown to, 111; dung of, as emetic, 151; eaten, 79, 185; for hunting, 59, 117–18, 145, 161–2; men with faces like, 219; necklaces for, 148; sledges pulled by, 282–3

drinking parties, Russian, 285–6

drums, 96, 185–6, 269, 273, 289, 292

duels, 244

eagles, birth-mark of, 35; preying on serpents, 232; trained, 118

ear-rings, 61

earth, sitting on, 225; sleeping on, 231, 239

Easter, observed by Kubilai, 98

ebony, 212, 214

Egrigaia [(?) Ning-hsia in Kan-su], 86

Egypt, 24, 26, 118, 196, 197, 263, 279

elephants, 51, 95, 105, 115, 120, 154–9, 211–13, 255–6, 257–8, 262

Ely [north of Cananore] on Malabar Coast, 246–7

embroidery, needlework, 48, 101, 115, 117

emetics, 151, 248

England, Sea of, 210

Ercis (Arzizi), in Armenia, 34

Ercolin (fur-bearing animal), 283–4

Erguiul [(?) Liang-chau in Kan-su], 84–6

ermine, 80, 120, 121, 283–4

erosion of land, 205, 219, 232

Erzerum (Arziron), in Armenia, 34

Erzincan (Arzingan), in Armenia, 34

Essen-temur, son of [Hukaji son of] Kubilai, 148, 154

Etzina [(?) Kara-khoto, in Mongolia], 73

eunuchs, 100, 159

Euphrates, river [(?) Araxes], said to flow into the Caspian, 36

eye salve, 54

excrement, disposal of, 238

Facfur, king of Manzi, 164 n., 170–2, 190–2

falcons, falconers, 14, 48, 79, 87, 88, 94, 116, 117–22, 137, 152; gerfalcons, 84, 87, 88, 119, 120, 286, sign of, 30, 128; goshawks, 35, 119, 214–15, 229; lanner, 61, 73, 145; peregrine, 84, 119, 286; saker, 60, 73, 119, 145

Fansur [Barus, W. coast of Sumatra], 217–18

Faro, near Constantinople, 286

Ferlec [Periak in N. Sumatra], 214

fevers, 61, 233

fire: affected by altitude, 63; precautions against, 185; worship of, 44, 91, 199

fish: as food for cattle, etc., 264; gigantic, 192; miraculous behaviour of, 35–6; predatory [sharks], charms against, 222

foxes, 80, 118, 282–4

France, king of, 29

francolins, 49, 51, 181

frankincense, see incense

French, 'Franks', 12, 107, 151 n.; language, 11, 16, 202

Friars, 26, 44, 62, 90 n.

Fu-chau (Fugiu), 194 n., 197–200; kingdom of, alias Choncha [approx. Fu-kien province], 194 n., 195–200

funeral customs, 52, 68–9, 78–9, 107, 160, 189–90, 206–7, 216–17, 224, 239, 241, etc.

furs, kinds of, 80, 282–3

fur-trappers and fur-traders, 283–4

gambling, prohibited, 134

gardens, 51, 54–5, 164, 182, 184, 187, 191, 194, 198

Gauenispola, islet N. of Sumatra, 218

gavi [(?) pariahs], 225, 234

Genoa [in Italy], 11, 21, 33, 36, 202 n., 294

geomancy, 37, 228

George, Nestorian ruler, identified with Prester John, 15, 86, 268–70

Georgia, 34–6

Germans, 9, 107, 175

Ghazan, Khan of the Levant [r. 1295–1304], 30–1, 145, 280–1

Ghinghintalas [(?) Barkol in Turkestan], 71–2

Ghiuju (Ghiugiu, etc.) [(?) in Che-kiang], 194

Gihon, river, 36 n.; *see also* Oxus

ginger, 140-1, 148, 159, 179, 195-6, 246-8

giraffes, 257-8, 262

girdles, blessed, worn to relieve pain, 44

glove-making, 101

Gobi, *see* Lop

Gog and Magog, 87

Golconda, in Hyderabad, 231 n.

gold: abundant, 206, 213, 262 n.; buildings covered with, 88, 103-4, 158, 190, 206; exchange values of, 123-4, 147, 149, 152, 157; idols covered with, 72, 241; nuggets of, 149; ornaments of, 61, 160; rods of, as currency, 286; teeth covered with, 151; trade in, 159, 160, 210, 248-50; treasure of, 37, 104; vessels of, 104, 113

gold, cloth of, 13, 35, 37, 43, 47, 51, 87, 107, 114, 120, 123, 248, 256, etc.

gold-dust, 145, 148-9, 211

Golden King (Roi Dor), 138-9

Gospels, 40, 98

Gothia [S. Crimea], 286

Greek church, 35, 284

Greeks, in Turkey, 33

Gregory X, Pope [1271-6], Tedaldo Visconti, 24-6

gryphon birds, rukhs, 256-7

guilds, 131, 183, 193

Gujarat (Gozurat), in W. India [should include Thana, Cambay and Somnath], 235 n., 247-9

hair-styles, 35, 62, 91, 196

half-breeds, 49, 86

Han-chung (Cuncun) [in S. Shen-hsi], 141

Hang-chau, *see* Kinsai

Hawah (Ava), in Persia, 45

hawks, hawking, *see* falcons

Herat, in Afghanistan, 273 n.

hermits, 62

hippopotami, 257 n.

Ho-chau (Caagiu) [in Sze-ch'wan], 78

Ho-chung-fu alias P'u-chau-fu (Cacianfu) [in Shan-hsi, east, not west, of Hwang-ho], 140

Ho-kien-fu (Cacianfu) [in Ho-peh], 163

honey, drink made of, 285

Horiat, Tartar tribe, 89

Hormuz, Old, Persian port, 43, 46, 50-3, 224, 243, 263, 265-7

horses: eaten, 79; exported to India, 46, 51, 150, 160, 224, 243, 249, 263-5; food of, 229, 264; good, 33, 60, 148, 150, 260, 264; horned, descended from Bucephalus, 60; killed at royal funeral, 79; little, 264; mares guided by foals, 283; method of riding, 150-1; not bred in India, 46, 224-6;

post, 125-9; scared by elephants, 156; Tartar, 34, 36, 79; white, reserved for Khan's family, 89, 115

hospitality, 70-1, 185

hospitals, 186, 284

houses: in Kinsai, 185; Tartar, 79; underground, 59, 283

Hukaji (Cogachin) [*c.* 1280], son of Kubilai, 149

Hulagu (Alau), brother of Kubilai, Khan o the Levant [1265], 22, 38, 57, 281, 287-90; miscalled Great Khan, 38, 78 n.

hunting, 33, 59, 61, 79, 88, 117-22, 137, 140-1, 152, etc.; *see also* dogs; trapping

Hwai-ngan-chau (Coigangiu) [in Kiang-su], 169-72

Hwang-Ho, river, *see* Kara-moran

Hyderabad, in India, 231 n.

I-ching, *see* Sinju

idolaters [Buddhists and Hindus], 14, 61, 62, 63, 144, 250, 257, etc.; customs of, 68-71, 72-3, 82, 89-92, 133-4, 146, 152-4, 159, 189-90, 209-10, 214, 216-17, 218-19, 236-9; head of, at Khan's court, 200; inculcate charity, 8-9, 14, 132-3

idols, 24, 68, 72-3, 80, 90-2, 165, 166-7, 209, 235, etc.; maidens dedicated to, 229-31, 239; origin of, 62, 98, 240-2; suicide in honour of, 224-5

incense, frankincense, 44, 45, 90-1, 115, 116, 134, 154, 166, 249; white, cultivation of, 264-5

India, 7, 37, 62, 149, 221-51; export of horses to, 46, 51, 150, 160, 224, 242-3, 249, 263-5; Greater, 221, 250, 251, 259; Lesser [Indo-China], 259; Marco Polo in, 9, 29, 203, 246 n.; merchants and trade of, 43, 50, 107, 159, 181, 187, 198, 200, 204-6, 263-5; Middle, Abyssinia, 259; Upper [(?) = Greater], 201

Indian Sea or Ocean, 30, 37, 46, 51, 62, 210, 263-6; islands in, 218-20, 251-9

Indies, 210-11, 251, 259

indigo, 245, 248, 250

inns, hostelries, 106-7, 136, 141, 184, 192, 285

insect pests, 79, 129, 231, 238

Iraq, 43

Iron Gates [Pass of Derbend, between Caucasus and Caspian], 35, 287

Isfahan, in Persia, 46, 48

Ishkasham (Scasem) [on the Panja river in Afghanistan], 59

Italy, dialects of, 202, 202 n.

Jacobite Christians, 14, 36, 37, 43; patriarch [metropolitan] of, 36-7

Index

James, St, the Apostle, shrine of [Santiago di Compostella in Spain], 241

Japan (Cipangu), 206–10

Java, 15, 212; Lesser, *see* Sumatra

Jenghiz Khan, *see* Chinghiz

Jerusalem: holy oil from, 24–7; pilgrimage to, 260–1

Jesus, *see* Christ

jewels, gems, precious stones: double price paid for, 223, 236; sources of, 47, 60, 65–6, 86, 146, 206, 220, 232; trade in, 13, 22, 43, 51, 107, 181, 198, 200–1, 236, 248–9, 263; restrictions on, 60, 146, 223; treasure of, 37–8, 104; wearing of, 61, 114, 183, 190, 223, 243; world's largest ruby, 220

Jews, 14, 36, 97, 98, 244, 259

John the Baptist, St, church of, 64

Josaphat, St, 241 n.

jugglers, 114; conquer Burma, 158

jujubes (fruit) made into bread, 168

justice, administration of, 62, 82, 108, 125, 134, 171, 182, 186, 226, 231, 243, 264; *see also* punishment

Kaidu [grandson of Ogodai, not Chaghatai; ob. 1301], 64 n., 93, 94, 98, 267–72, 281; Ai-yaruk, daughter of, 270–2

Kaiju (Caigiu) [(?) in Kiang-su], 169

Kaikhatu son of Abaka, Khan of the Levant [r. 1291–5], 30–1, 280

Kain, in E. Persia, 46, 54

Kaindu (Gaindu) [(?) Ning-yuen in Sze-ch'wan], 146, 148

Kais (Chisi) [island in Persian Gulf], 37, 46, 224, 243, 263, 266

Kaisarieh [alias Caesarea] (Casserie) in Turkey, 33, 34

Kala Atashparastan, in Persia, 44

Kalachan (Calacian) [(?) Ting-yuan-ying in Kan-su], 86

Kalhat [or Kelat] (Calatu), in Arabia, 265–6; gulf of [Persian Gulf], 265–6

Kamadin [near Jiruft] (Camandi), in Persia, 49

Kamasal (Canosalmi), in Persia, 50

Kamul [alias Hami, north of Gobi Desert], 70

Kan-chau (Canpiciu) [in Kan-su], 72–3, 84

Kan-p'u (Ganfu), port of Hang-chau, 187

Kan-su [province in N.W. China named from Kan-chau & Su-chau], *see* Tangut

Kao-yu (Caiu) [in Kiang-su], 172, 173

Kara-jang: province [Yun-nan in W. China], 27, 148–54; city [Ta-li-fu], 149

Kara-Khoja (Carachoco) [in Uighuristan], 71

Kara-khoto, in Mongolia, *see* Etzina

Karakorum, capital of the Mongols, 7, 9, 75, 83, 268–9

Karaman [in Turkey], 33

Kara-moran [Turkish for 'Black River', i.e. Hwang-Ho], 139, 169, 172

Karaunas, 49–50

Kashan, in Persia, 45

Kashgar, in Turkestan, 14, 63–4

Kashmir (Kesimur), Kashmiris, 50, 62, 90

Kasvin, in Persia, 46

Kaugigu [(?) Laos or Tonking], 157 n., 159–61

Kauli [(?) N. Korea], 97

Kaunchi (Conci), a Tartar ruler of the Far North, 281–2

Kayal (Cail) [near Tinnevelly, Madras prov.], 242–4

Kech-Makran (Kesmacoran) [Makran coast, with Kech in Baluchistan], 250–2, 259

Kemenfu, *see* Shang-tu

Kerman, in Persia, 47–8, 52, 53, 266

Khan-balik (Cambalu) [Peking], 8, 10, 98, 102–12, 122, 124–5, 131–2, 136, 163, 177, 242

Khazaria (Gazarie) [N. of Crimea], 285–6

Khotan, in Turkestan, 65

Kiang-sui (Quiansui), river, *see* Yang-tze-kiang

Kien-ning-fu (Quenlifu) [in Fu-kien], 194 n., 196

kings: mythical origin of, 71; obedient to own laws, 227; people without, 36, 76 n., 218

Kinsai [Hang-chau, in Che-kiang], 10, 171, 179–95, 207, 210

kite, man-lifting, 205–6

Kokachin, Tartar princess, bride for Arghun, 29, 30–1, 203 n.

Konya [or Iconium], in Turkey, 34

koumiss, Tartar drink, 80

Kubilai, fifth Great Khan [r. 1257–94]: allegiance to, without tribute, 214–17; appearance of, 100; banquets of, 90–1, 112–17; campaigns of, 93–100, 154–9, 164, 169–72, 207–9, 211–12, 268–70; character of, 8, 10, 23–4, 28, 87, 93, 102, 129, 158; death of, 31 n.; enactments of, 111, 127, 134, 146, 151, 183; family and household of, 100–2, 111–12, 140, 267–9; history of, 78, 93; missions of, 23–4, 203 n., 220, 242, 257; opposition to, in Cathay and Manzi, 110, 164, 185, 197; palaces of, 87–9, 102–5; Polos at court of, 22–9, 159; religious attitude of, 8, 23, 97–9, 111, 200, 242

Kuh-banan (Cobinan), in Persia, 53–4

Kuiju (Cuigiu or Ciugiu) [(?) Kwei-chau province; city unidentified], 157 n., 161–2

Kuju (Cugiu) [(?) in Che-kiang], 195

Kungurat (Ungrac), Tartar tribe, 101

Kurdistan, in Persia, Kurds, 37, 46, 57

Index

Kuyuk, third Great Khan [r. 1246–8], 78
Kwa-chau (Caigiu) [in Kian-su], 177

Lac [(?) Lezghia in the Caucasus], 284, 286
Lahore, see Dilivar
Lambri [near Kota Raja, N.W. Sumatra], 217
languages, barbarous, 33; different dialects of, 202; difficult, 148; Polo's knowledge of, 17 n., 23, 27, 199
lapis lazuli, azure, 60, 86, 105
Lar [(?) Gujarat], in India, 235
Latin: church, 23; emperor, see Baldwin; merchants, 23, 29, 43
leather: boiled, 103; fine, 117; mats, cushions, etc., made of, 248–9
Leonard, St, monastery of, in Georgia, 35–6
leopards, 246, 256, 258, 262; [cheetahs], used for hunting, 88, 118
Levant, Khanate of, 8, 22, 26, 30, 33–58, 82, 84, 272–81, 286–90; merchants of, 245
Linju (Lingiu or Lingin) [(?) Su-chau-fu in Shang-tung], 167 n., 168
lions [including tigers], 58, 117, 120, 141, 142, 147, 150, 174, 195–7, 245–7, 256, 258, 262; sign of, 30, 100; trapping of, 161–2, 197
Litan Sangon, rebellion of, 164–5
locusts, 129
Lokak [(?) Siam or Malaya], 213–14
longevity, 62, 237, 239
Lop [(?) Charklik in Turkestan], 66; [Gobi], desert of, 13, 66–8
lost property, 119; found by idols, 166–7
Luristan (Lor), in Persia, 46
lynxes (or ounces), 118, 141, 147, 246, 256, 258, 262

Maabar [Coromandel Coast], India, 221–36, 250, 256, 259
Madagascar [or Mogadishu, in Somalia] (Mogdaxo, etc.), 8, 255–7; islands south of, 256–7
Magi, 12, 44–5
magicians, 49, 61, 89–90, 98–9, 108, 145, 152–4, 179 n., 189, 228, 255; animals charmed by, 222; cures effected or predicted by, 216–17
Mahomet, prophet [632]: banner of, 38; law of, 37, 47; regarded as messenger of God, 43; teaching of, about Paradise, 55; 'worshippers' of, 14, 33, 36, 47, 62, 63, 98, 255, 262–6, etc.; see also Saracens
Maimon cats [(?) baboons], 262
Malabar (Melibar), in S.W. India [should include Quilon & Ely], 50 n., 227 n., 247–8
Malaya, see Lokak
Malayur [(?) Malayu in S.E. Sumatra], 214
U

Male and Female Islands [(?) fabulous], 252
malik [Arab ruler subject to a sultan], 265–6, 277–9; cf. 35
Manchuria, see Chorcha
'Mandeville, Sir John', book attributed to [written c. 1366], 16
Mangalai, third son of Kubilai [1280], 140
mangonels, 174–5
Manzi (Mangi) [S. China], 94, 137, 154, 168, 169, 172–211, 186–9, 214, 267; king of, 169–72, 190–2; merchants of, 213, 245–8; princess of, 31; national character of, 178, 185; queen of, 170 n., 171–2; Tartar conquest of, 169–72
marble, 88, 103, 136, 140, 142, 196
Mardin, in Iraq, 37
markets, 59, 157, 180–3
marriage: between dead children, 83; customs and marital relations, 65, 70–1, 91, 144, 146–7, 149, 159, 165–6, 189, 225, 231, 236, 245, 252, 270–2, 273; polygamous, 73, 79–80, 85–6, 126–7, 138, 191, 212, 223, 243
mats, 91, 248–9
mead, Russian, 285
Mediterranean Sea, 13, 33
Mekrit (Siberian nomads), 83–4
Menjar [unidentified; probably not Hungary], 286
merchants or traders, 8–10, 12–13, 33, 37, 64, 107, 123, 140, 142, 161, 174, 176–8, 183, 191, 200–1, 211, 213, 226–7, 245–50, 254–5, 258, 262, 283 n., 284, 286, etc.; goods of, confiscated at death, 51; protection of, 46–7, 243; reliable, 185, 235; skilful, 179, 229
Mien [Burma], 9, 154, 157–8; conquered by Kubilai, 158; city of [(?) Tagaung in Burma], 157–8
milk: camels', 113; dried, 81–2; mares', 79–80, 89, 113
Ming dynasty in China [1368–1643], 10
miracles, 35–6, 40–3, 44–6, 64–5, 99, 234
mirrors, steel, 54
Mogadishu, in Somalia, see Madagascar
monasteries: Buddhist or Hindu, 62, 68, 72, 91, 136, 176–7, 183, 229–30, 237, 242; tests for probationers, 239; Christian, 35, 44
Mongols, Mungul, 7–10; identified with Magog, 87; see also Tartars
Mongu, fourth Great Khan [r. 1252–9], 10, 38, 70–1, 78, 143
Mongu-temur, Khan of the West [r. 1267–80], 287, 290
monkeys, 215, 246, 262; called 'Paul cats', 246, 262; 'Maimon cats' [(?) baboons], 262; embalmed, sold as pygmies, 215
Monte Corvino, Giovanni di, archbishop of Peking [1328], 10

313

Moses, 'God of the Jews', 98

Mosul, in Iraq, 34, 36, 43

Motupalli [Mutifili], [in Guntur, Madras prov.], 231-3, 259

mountains: air of, fatal to foreigners, 152; fastnesses and fortresses in, 58-9, 61, 62, 152, 157, 160, 197; healthy, 61; highest in the world, 63; moved by miracle, 40-3

mulberry: bark, paper made from, 122; leaves, silkworms fed on, 122, 137, 140

Mulehet [(?) Alamut, near Tehran], in Persia, stronghold of the Assassins, 12, 54-7

Mungul, see Mongols

Mus, in Iraq, 37

music, 69, 70, 96, 114, 190, 269

musk, origin of, 85, 144-5, 147

muslin, 37 n.

nakh and nasich (kinds of brocade), 37, 87

Nasr-uddin (Nescradin), Tartar general, 155-7

Natigai, Tartar god, 80, 133, 281

Nayan [great-great-grandson of a brother of Chinghiz], called uncle of Kubilai, 93-8

necromancy, study of, 37, 90

Negropont [Euboea, in Greece], Polos at, 25, 31

Negroes, 14 n., 257

Nerghi, plain of [in Russia], 291

Nestorian Christians, 14, 15, 37, 43, 65; churches of, 64, 72, 86, 163 n., 177, 192; in Polos' retinue, 175; patriarch of, 37, 254

New Year, celebration of, 115

Ngan-king alias An-king-fu (Namghi) [in An-hwei], 174

Nicobar (Necuveran) island [in Bay of Bengal], 218

Nigudar (Nogodar) [(?) grandson or great-grandson of Chaghatai], king of the Karaunas, 50

Nile river, 263

Noah's Ark, in Armenia, 34

Noghai [Tartar emir in Ukraine; ob. 1299], 290-3

nomads, 22, 33, 48, 79, 83, 281-2

Norway, 286

Nubia [south of Egypt], 235, 260

Numughan (Nomogan), son of Kubilai [after 1275], 268

Ocean [Arctic], 84, 286; Indian, 30, 37, 46, 51, 62, 210, 219-20, 251-66; [Pacific], 120, 136, 139, 142, 148, 169, 173, 180, 187, 206-10; islands of, 171-2; variously named, 210

Odoric of Pordenone, Franciscan missionary [1331], 10

Ogodai, second Great Khan [1227-41], 78 n.

oil: from Holy Sepulchre, 24-7; [petroleum], springs of, 34-5

ondanique [high-grade Indian (Hundwaniy) steel], 47, 54, 71

ostriches, 256, 262

Oxus (Gihon), river, 267, 272-3

palaces, descriptions of, 88-9, 102-7, 137-8, 140-1, 190-1, 206

Palestine, Promised Land, 33

palm, see dates; wine

Pamir, 'Roof of the World', 13, 63

panic-grass, 47, 87, 126, 139-40, 285

Pao-ying (Pauchin [in Kiang-su]), 172

paper money, see currency

papiones [(?) jackals], 198

Paradise: counterfeit, 55-7; apples of, see apples; rivers of, 36 n.

parks, 88, 104-5, 140

parrots, 51, 245, 262

partridges, 47-8, 53, 87-8, 181

Pashai [in Kafiristan], 50, 61-2

pasturage, rich, 34, 50-1, 58, 63, 75, 79, 104, 160

Patarins [Albigensians or similar heretics], 91, 226

'Paul cats', 246, 262

pavilions, description of, 120-1

peacocks, 234-5, 245

pearls, 37, 51, 61, 104, 107, 114, 115, 123, 181, 198, 200, 201, 206-7, 223, 231, 236, 248, 263; fishing for, 146, 221-3, 229

Pegolotti, Francesco Balducci [c. 1343], 10, 12

Pei-chau, see Piju

Peking, see Khan-balik

Pem [(?) Keriya], in Turkestan, 65

pepper, consumption of, 183; cultivation of, 245, 246-9; trade in, 200, 205, 210, 212, 263

Persia, 44-58; national character, 48-9; Tartar conquest of, 36, 44, 47, 49; see also Levant

Pharaoh's nuts, see coconuts

Pharaoh's rats [name applied to jerboas and (?) marmots], 79, 282

philosophers, 179

physicians, 116, 121, 152-4, 179, 182, 245

physiognomy, 37, 227

pictures, 88, 103-4, 138, 140, 190, 199

Piju (Pingiu, etc.) [(?) Pei-chau in Kiang-su], 167 n., 168-9

pilgrimage, 233-4, 241, 260-1

P'ing-yang-fu (Pianfu) [in Shan-hsi], 137

pirates or corsairs, 247-9, 255

Pisa [in Tuscany], 11, 21, 294

pitch, substitutes for, 52, 204

ploughing, by yaks, 85

poison, 72, 151, 280

Index

Pole Star, 214-15, 246-50; regions north of, 15, 84

Po-Lo, Chinese official, 9

Polo, family, help in siege of Siang-yang-fu, 9, 174-5

Polo, Maffeo [c. 1310], brother of Niccolò, 8-10, 21-31, 73, 98, 199-200, 294

Polo, Marco [c. 1253-1324]: as linguist, 17 n., 27, 199; as reporter, etc., 12-16, 27-8, 202-3; called 'Messer', 28; called 'Il Milione', 12; document used by, 180; informants of, 21, 44-5, 54, 71, 138, 182-3, 203 n., 234, 256-7; manuscripts of, 16-17; movements of, 9-11, 25-31, 44, 73, 136, 159, 169, 192, 202, 212, 215-16, 239 n., 246 n., 249 n., 255 n., 294; notes made by, 11; objects brought to Venice by, 85 n., 217, 218 n., 234 n.; personal experiences of, 27, 50, 61, 167, 173, 193, 199-200; personal observations of, 21, 71, 180, 192, 203 n., 217-18, 227

Polo, Marco, the elder [c. 1280], brother of Niccolò, 8

Polo, Niccolò [before 1300], father of Marco, 8-10, 21-31, 73, 98, 294

Ponte, Messer, Venetian Podestà in Constantinople, 21

Pope, 23, 29, 72, 98-9, 254; see also Clement; Gregory

population, records of, 192

porcelain, manufacture of, 201

porcupines, 59

post: imperial, 125-6; carried by dog-sleighs, 282-3

poultry: pretty [(?) guinea-fowl], 262; with hair (silkies), 196

Prester John, 15, 75-8, 86-7, 138-9, 169, 268-70

prostitutes, 107, 182

psalms, 77, 199

Pulisanghin river [Hun-ho, alias Sang-Kan], 136

Pumar (?), prince of, 271-2

punishment, modes of, 82, 97, 107 n., 108, 111, 113, 151, 209; see also justice

pygmies, faked, 215

queen, kingdom ruled by, 231

quicksilver and sulphur, as drug, 237-8

Quilon (Coilum) in India, 244-5

quilts, 248

Ramusio, Giambattista, Polo's editor and biographer [1557], 10, 11, 17

Red Sea, 261 n.; called a river, 263

reindeer, 83

Rheims [in France], linen of, 233

rhinoceros, see unicorn

rhubarb, 72, 179

rice, 61-2, 126, 131, 141, 159, 177, 216, 219, 225, 234, 245, 250, 262, 264, etc.; see also wine

rivers, underground, 53

roads: marked by trees and cairns, 63, 129-30; paved (causeways), 172, 177, 187; sleeping on, 231

robbers, 37, 46-7, 50, 58, 144, 283; see also pirates

Rochelle [in France], Sea of, 210

Rome, church of, 23, 36, 72

Roof of the World (Pamir), 13, 63

rubies, 60, 220, 222

Rudbar (Reobar), in Persia, plain of, 49-52

Rudrama Devi, queen of Telingana [c. 1300], 231 n.

Ruemedan Ahmad [Rukn ud-Din Mahmud], emir of Hormuz, 51, 53

rukhs, see gryphons

Russia, 8, 284-7

Rustichello of Pisa, Polo's collaborator, 11-12, 14, 15, 16, 17, 21; (?) called 'the master', 203

sable (fur), 80, 120, 121, 282-4

Sa-chau [alias Tun-huang in Kan-su], 68

sacrifices and libations, 68, 78-9, 80, 89-91, 153, 224-5, 229-30

sago, preparation of, 217-18

Sain Khan, see Batu

Sakyamuni, see Buddha

salamander [asbestos], origin and treatment of, 71-2

salt: desert of [Nemek-sar in Persia], 53; sources, 59, 147, 148-9, 163, 176, 193; tax on, 149, 163, 172-3, 193; used as currency, 145, 147

Samarkand, in Turkestan, 9, 64-5, 270

sandalwood, 201, 219, 255

Saracen, learned, friend of Polos, 199

Saracens [Moslems], 36, 250, 284, etc.; beliefs of, 43, 55, 98, 111, 233, 240, 241-2; converts to faith of, 43-4, 82, 214, 273; customs of, 47, 49, 82, 111, 126, 248-9, 259, 294; employment of, 62, 110, 220, 226; hostile to Christians, 14, 40, 64, 97, 254, 260-3; priest of, 43; see also Mahomet

Sarai [(?) Old Sarai near mouth of Volga], Polos at, 22; Sea of, see Caspian

savages, 63, 213-18, 281, 283

Saveh, in Persia, burial-place of Magi, 44, 45

sendal [costly fabric], 136, 143, 163, 179, 248, 271

Sender Bandi [Sundara Pandya], devar [king] of Maabar, 221

Sendernam [(?) Chandra Banu], called king of Ceylon, 219

Index

Sergius, Mar, Nestorian official, 178

serpents, with legs [crocodiles], 149–50; venomous, 232

sesame, 61, 219, 262; oil of, children anointed with, 235

sexual indulgence: abstinence from, 73, 91, 236–41; not regarded as sin, 73, 227, 245

Shabankara (Soncara), in Persia, 46

Shang-tu (Chandu, 'Xanadu') alias Kai-ping-fu (Kemen-fu), [in Chahar], 26–7, 88–9, 110, 127

sharks, 222

sheep: not found in Manzi, 195 (but cf. 181); Barbary, 258; earless, 264; fat-tailed, 49; fed on fish, 264; horns of, made into bowls and cairns, 63; horns of, second pair, 264; large, 83, 233; sacrificed to idols, 68, 153; wild [Polo's sheep], 61, 63

Sheikh ('Old Man') of the Mountain, head of the Assassins, 54–7

sheikhs (esceque), 255

Shibarghan (Sapurgan) [in Afghanistan], 58

Shihr [alias Esh Shehr] (Scier, Escier), in Arabia, 224, 264–5

ships: Chinese, 29, 168–9, 175–7, 204–6, 213–14, 246–7; freight of, 200; on Indian Ocean, defects of, 51–2, 263–4; off course, seizure of, 246; pearl-fishers', 221–2; pleasure-boats, 184; struck by lightning, 129; trapped in gulf, 219; whalers', 253–4; wrecked, 204, 207, 263

Shiraz (Serazi), in Persia, 46

Shulistan, in Persia, 46

Siam, see Lokak

Siang-yang-fu (Saianfu) [in Hu-peh], 9, 174–5

Sie-chi, dowager empress, 170 n., 180

Sighinan, mountain in Badakh-shan, 60

Siju (Singiu, etc.) [Su-t'sien alias Si-chau in Kiang-su], 167 n., 169

Sikin-tinju, [(?) Kien-chau in Manchuria], 97

silk: embroidered, 48; ghilan, 36; tax on, 131, 193; trade in, 13, 51, 107, 162, 164, 248, 256; weaving of, 34, 35–7, 43, 47, 87, 107, 185, etc.; yazdi, 47

silkworms, fed on mulberry leaves, 122, 137, 140

silver: buildings covered with, 103–4, 158; exchange value of, 123–4, 148, 152, 157; mines of, 34, 60, 87, 152, 284; ornaments of, 61, 160; thread of, 117; trade in, 248–50; treasure of, 37–8, 104, 113

Si-ngan-fu (Quengianfu) [in Shen-hsi], 140

Sindachu [(?) Hsüan-hwa, formerly Hsüan-te-chau, in Chahar], 87

Sinju (Singiu) [(?) Si-ning-fu in Kan-su], 84

Sinju (Singiu) [(?) I-ching alias Chen-chau in Kiang-su], 175–6

Sinju Matu (Singiumatu) [(?) T'si-ning-chau in Shan-tung], 167–8

Sivas (Sevasto), in Turkey, 33, 34

skins: costume of, 59, 61, 63, 145, 271 n.; inflated, used as floats, 263

slaves, 73, 152, 192; children sold as, 192, 285–6; effigies of, 68–9, 83, 189; trade in, 159

sledges, pulled by dogs, 282–3

sneeze, as omen, 227, 237

Socotra (Scotra) island in Arabian Sea, 252–5

Somnath (Semenat) [in Gujarat], W. India, 250

Sondur, see Condur

Spain, king of, 29

spices, 13, 33, 37, 51, 130, 159, 181, 193, 200, 214, 219, 248, 263, 265; main source of, 210, 212; unknown to the West, 140, 145, 148, 214

spicewood, 120

spikenard, 140, 159, 212, 214, 248

spirits: deserts haunted by, 67, 84; propitiation of, 153

spittoons, 135

spodium [metallic residue], 54

springs, hot, 53

steel, 47, 54, 71; see also ondanique

stones: combustible [coal], 130; magic, protecting wearer against steel, 209; precious, see jewels

stove-houses, Russian, 284–5

Strabo, Greek geographer [c. A.D. 21], 16

sturgeon, 36

Su-chau (Suggiu), [in Kan-su], 72

Su-chau (Sugiu) [in Kiang-su], 178–9

Sudak (Soldaia) [in the Crimea], 8, 22, 285

sugar: canes, 198; refining of, 196; wine made of, 245, 264

suicide, 190, 224–5

sulphur, 61; and quicksilver, as drug, 237

Sultan, malik subordinate to Ahmad Khan, 278–9

Sumatra, island (Lesser Java), 30, 214–18, 246; city (Samara, Saundra, etc.) [near Pasai in N. Sumatra], 213 n., 215–16

Su-t'sien, see Siju

swallows, augury by, 237

tablets, gold and silver, granted to the Khan's emissaries, 24, 29–30, 99–100, 124–5, 128

Tabriz (Toris), in Iraq [now in N.W. Persia], 34, 40, 43–4, 280 n.

Tagaung, see Mien

Tai-chau (Tigiu) [in Kiang-su], 173

Taidu [Ta-tu, N.E. of Old Peking], 105–7, 111

tails, men with, 217

T'ai-yuan-fu (Taiuanfu) [in Shan-hsi], 137

Talikhan (Taican, Dolgana) [now in Afghanistan], 58–9

tallies, 152

tambur (betel-leaf), chewing and spitting of, 243–4

Tandinfu [(?) Yen-chau in Shan-tung], 164–5, 167

Tangut [Kan-su, in N.W. China], 68–73, 84–6

Tanjore, S.E. India, 221 n.

Tanpiju (Tanpigiu, etc.) [(?) in Che-kiang], 194

'tarantulas' [(?) geckoes], 231; augury by, 228, 237

Tartars [Mongols]: adopt foreign customs, 29, 131–2; ambitions of, 7, 38, 76; appoint subordinate rulers at pleasure, 34, 47, 140, 188; civil wars of, 12, 22, 29, 93–8, 267–81, 287–93; converted to Christianity, 64, 96, 268, 280; converted to law of Mahomet, 43–4, 82, 273; customs of, 27, 78–83, 114–15, 131–2, 151, 166–7, 281, 294; devastation caused by, 44, 49, 58, 66, 143; languages of, 17, 23, 27; nomadic, 22, 79, 281–2; none in the time of Alexander, 35; protecting merchants, 46–7; refugees from, 36; religious beliefs of, 80, 281; rise of, 14, 38, 75–8, 268; warfare and military organization of, 38, 80–2, 94–5, 99–100, 124, 175, 267 n., 267–8

tattooing, 151–2, 159–60, 201

taxes and customs, 131, 142, 149, 163, 173–4, 176, 182–3, 193, 201, 202, 222, 263–6; exemption from, 129

teachers, 182

Tedaldo [Visconti] of Piacenza, Papal legate, see Gregory X

teeth: covered with gold, 151; herb beneficial to, 237

templars, Grand Master of, 26

Temur [1307] grandson and successor of Kubilai, 102, 105

Tenduk [(?) in Mongolia], 86; battle of, 77–8

Thana [near Bombay] in India, 249

Thomas, St, the Apostle, 225, 234, 259; shrine of [at Mailapur, near Madras], 233–5

Tibet (Tebet) [including parts of Sze-ch'wan, Yün-nan, etc.], Tibetans, 90, 143–8

Tiflis, in Georgia, 36

tigers, see lions

Tigris, river, at Baghdad, 37; see also Volga

Tinju (Tingiu, etc.) [(?) Chuan-chau in Fu-kien, perhaps confused with Jao-chau in Kiang-si, near a famous porcelain centre], 201 n.

Toktai, son of Mongu-temur, Khan of the West [r. 1291–1312], 284, 287, 290–3

Toloman [(?) in Yün-nan or Kwei-chau], 157 n., 160–1, 211

tomaun (unit of 10,000), 81, 192–3

tombs, described, 44, 158

transmigration of souls, 134, 241

trapping, methods of, 149–50, 197–8, 283

Trebizond [on S. shore of Black Sea], 31, 34

Tree, Dry or Solitary [a (?) plane growing in desert, in Khorassan], 30, 46, 54, 272, 280

trees: box, 35; fragrant, 210, 213; kings generated from sap of, 71; pine, 75; planted by highways, 129–30; transplanted full-grown, 105

Tripoli, William of, Dominican friar, 26

T'sang-chau, see Changlu

T'si-nan-fu, see Changli

T'si-ning-chau, see Sinju Matu

Tuda-mongu, khan of the West [r. 1280–7], 287, 290

Tulabugha, khan of the West [r. 1287–91], 290–3

Tun [now Firdaus], in E. Persia, 46, 54

Turcomans, 33–4

Turkestan (Great Turkey), 8, 15, 63–6, 266–73, 281; see also Khans

Turkey (Turcomanie), 33–4

Turks, language of, 17 n., 24, 33

turquoises, 47–8, 146

turtle doves, 49

Tu-tsong, Sung Emperor of S. China [1274], 170 n.

tutty [zinc oxide], 39, 250 n.

Ucaca [alias Ukek, on the Volga], Polos at, 22

Uighuristan (lcoguristam) [round Turfan, in Turkestan], 71

umbrellas, ceremonial, 100

Ung, Mongol tribe, identified with Gog, 87

Ung, Khan, 'Prester John', 15, 75, 138

unicorn [rhinoceros], 157, 214–15, 217, 248

Unken (Unquen or Vuguen) [(?) in Fu-kien], 196

vegetables, souls of, 238

Venice [in Italy]: Doge of, 21; merchants of, 8, 33, 294; Polos at, 21–2, 25, 31, 217

ventilators or wind-fans, 266

veterinaries, banned from going to India, 224

Vicenza, Nicholas of, Dominican friar, 26

vines, vineyards, 59, 64, 65, 136–7, 146

visions, 41, 234

Vochan (Vocian) [(?) Yung-ch'ang in Yün-nan], 151–7

Volga ('Tigris'), river, 22 n., 36 n.

Vughin [(?) in Kiang-su], 179

Index

Vuju (Vugiu, etc.) [(?) in Che-kiang], 194
Vuju [(?) in Kiang-su], 179

wagons, 79, 168
Wakhan (Vocan) [in Afghanistan], 63
warlike spirit, 33, 35, 55–6, 62, 80–1, 160–2, 168, 196, 258, 267; lack of, 33, 170, 179, 185, 201, 220, 226
water: bitter, 53–4, 66–7; brackish, 53, 67; holy, 238; natural hot, 53; scarce, 58
weather, changed by magic, 62, 89–90, 98–9, 145, 255
Western Khanate [Kipchak], 7–8, 22, 47, 284, 286–93
whales, 204, 253–4, 255–6, 258
wheat: unwholesome in bread, 148; wine made of, 147–8
widows, suicide of, 225
winds, seasonal, 52, 210
wine, 71, 90, 98, 113, 136–7, 181; abstinence from, 227, 236; date, 51, 245 n., 264; drunk by Saracens when boiled, 47, 59; palm, 216, 217, 219, 233; rice, 130, 147–8, 152, 159, 161, 181, 193, 258, 264; sugar, 245, 264; wheat, 147
women: beauty of, 54, 62, 85–6, 100–1, 146, 183, 185, 196, 258, 284; dedicated to idols, 229–31, 239; status of, 79, 152, 165–6, 185
wood: for ship-building, 204; hard, 51 n., 54, 218

workshops, 183
worms, souls of, 217, 238–9
wrestling match, 271–2
writing, 70, 182, 202

Xanadu, see Shang-tu

Yachi (Iaci) [Yün-nan-fu alias Kun-ming in Yün-nan], 148–9
yaks, 85 n.
Yang-chau (Yangiu) [in Kiang-su], governed by Marco Polo, 9, 173, 175; province, 173
Yang-tze-kiang (Kiang-sui, Brius), 142, 148, 176–7
Yarkand, in Turkestan, 65
Yazd, in Persia, 47
Ydifu [(?) in Chahar], 87
Yen-chau, see Tandinfu
Yesudar, cousin of Kaidu, 268
Yogis [Ciugui], 14 n., 237–9
Yün-nan, see Kara-jang; Tibet

Zaiton [Amoy region, esp. Chuan-chau, in Fu-kien], 194 n., 198, 200–1, 207, 210–11, 213
Zanzibar [or 'Zenj' in E. Africa], 255 n., 257–9
Zar-dandan [Persian for 'Gold-teeth', a people of Yün-nan], 151, 157
Zorza, island used as place of execution, 209
Zurficar, Turkish companion of Marco, 71